M000097321

Contents

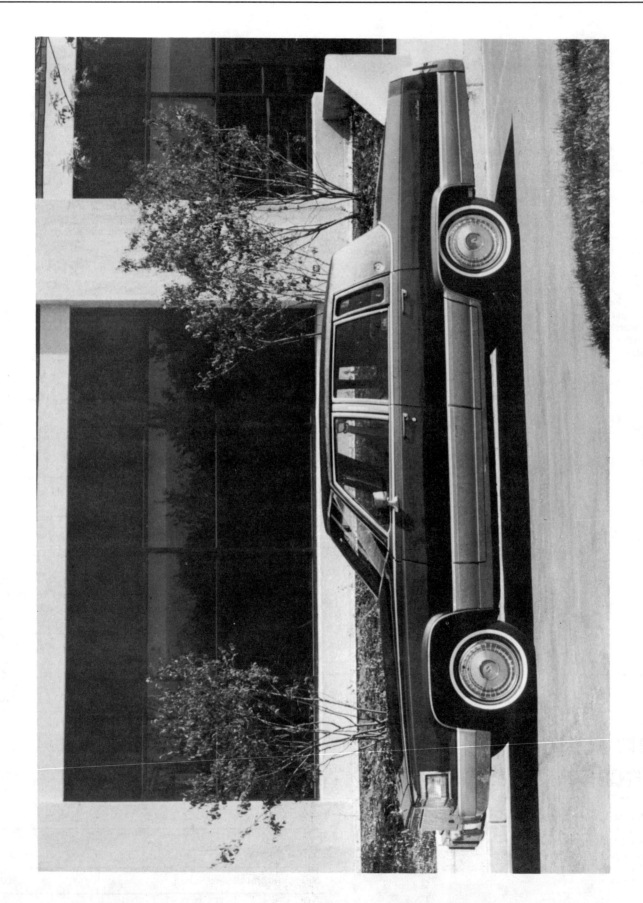

1990 Cadillac Brougham

About this manual

Its purpose

The purpose of this manual is to help you get the best value from your vehicle. It can do so in several ways. It can help you decide what work must be done, even if you choose to have it done by a dealer service department or a repair shop; it provides information and procedures for routine maintenance and servicing; and it offers diagnostic and repair procedures to follow when trouble occurs.

We hope you use the manual to tackle the work yourself. For many simpler jobs, doing it yourself may be quicker than arranging an appointment to get the vehicle into a shop and making the trips to leave it and pick it up. More importantly, a lot of money can be saved by avoiding the expense the shop must pass on to you to cover its labor and overhead costs. An added benefit is the sense of satisfaction and accomplishment that you feel after doing the job yourself.

Using the manual

The manual is divided into Chapters. Each Chapter is divided into numbered Sections, which are headed in bold type between horizontal lines. Each Section consists of consecutively numbered paragraphs.

At the beginning of each numbered section you will be referred to any illustrations which apply to the procedures in that section. The reference numbers used in illustration captions pinpoint the pertinent Section and the Step within that section. That is, illustration 3.2 means the illustration refers to Section 3 and Step (or paragraph) 2 within that Section.

Procedures, once described in the text, are not normally repeated. When it's necessary to refer to another Chapter, the reference will be given as Chapter and Section number. Cross references given without use of the word "Chapter" apply to Sections and/or paragraphs in the same Chapter. For example, "see Section 8" means in the same Chapter.

References to the left or right side of the vehicle assume you are sitting in the driver's seat, facing forward.

Even though we have prepared this manual with extreme care, neither the publisher nor the author can accept responsibility for any errors in, or omissions from, the information given.

NOTE

A **Note** provides information necessary to properly complete a procedure or information which will make the procedure easier to understand.

CAUTION

A **Caution** provides a special procedure or special steps which must be taken while completing the procedure where the **Caution** is found. Not heeding a **Caution** can result in damage to the assembly being worked on.

WARNING

A **Warning** provides a special procedure or special steps which must be taken while completing the procedure where the **Warning** is found. Not heeding a **Warning** can result in personal injury.

Introduction to the Cadillac rear-wheel drive models

The Cadillac models covered in this manual have the conventional front engine/rear-wheel drive layout.

Both V6 and V8 engines have been used over the long life of these models. Carburetors are used on earlier models and fuel injection is used on later models.

The engine drives the rear wheels through an automatic transmission via a driveshaft and solid rear axle.

The front suspension is independent, using coil springs. Leaf springs or coil springs with trailing arms are used in the rear suspension, depending on the model.

The steering box is mounted to the left of the engine and is connected to the steering arms through a series of rods. Power assist is standard on all models.

The brakes on earlier models are disc-type at the front and drum-type at the rear. Later models have disc-type brakes at all four wheels. Power assist is standard on all models.

Vehicle identification numbers

Modifications are a continuing and unpublicized process in vehicle manufacturing. Since spare parts manuals and lists are compiled on a numerical basis, the individual vehicle numbers are essential to correctly identify the component required.

Vehicle Identification Number (VIN)

This very important identification number is located on a plate attached to the left side cowling just inside the windshield (see illustration). The VIN also appears on the Vehicle Certificate of Title and Registration. It contains information such as where and when the vehicle was manufactured, the model year and the body style.

Body identification plate

The body identification plate is normally located in the engine compartment either on the upper surface of the radiator support or on the left upper surface of the firewall (see illustration). Like the VIN it contains valuable information about the manufacture of the vehicle, as well as information on the options with which it is equipped. This plate is especially useful for matching the color and type of paint for repair work.

Engine identification number

The engine identification number can be found in a variety of locations, depending on engine type. On V6 and 368 cubic inch V8 engines, the number is located on a pad at the left rear of the engine block, behind the intake manifold (see illustration). On 307 and 350 cubic inch V8 engines, the number is at the left front of the block, below the cylinder head (see illustration). On HT 4100 engines, the number is on a plate at the left rear of the block (see illustration). On 425, 472 and 500 cubic inch V8 engines, the number is at the rear of the engine, either beneath the rear of the left cylinder head or on a pad behind the intake manifold.

The Vehicle Identification Number (VIN) is visible from outside the vehicle, through the driver's side of the windshield

The body identification plate is normally found on the radiator support or upper surface of the engine compartment firewall

On V6 and 368 cubic inch V8 engines, the ID number is stamped into a pad at the left rear of the engine block, behind the intake manifold

On 307 and 350 cubic inch V8 engines, the ID number is at the left front of the block

On HT 4100 engines, the ID number is stamped into a plate at the left rear of the block

Location of the transmission ID plate
on THM 200 transmissions

On THM 350 and 400 transmissions,
the ID number is usually stamped into
the right side of the housing

Location of the transmission ID number
on THM 700 transmissions

Automatic transmission identification number

On THM 200 transmissions, the transmission number is on a plate affixed to the right side of the transmission **(see illustration)**. On THM 350, 400 and 700 transmissions, the number is usually stamped into the right side of the housing **(see illustrations)**.

Vehicle Emissions Control Information (VECI) label

On models so equipped, the emissions control information label is found under the hood, normally on the radiator shroud or support. This label contains information on the emissions control equipment installed on the vehicle, as well as tune-up specifications.

Buying parts

Replacement parts are available from many sources, which generally fall into one of two categories – authorized dealer parts departments and independent retail auto parts stores. Our advice concerning these parts is as follows:

Retail auto parts stores: Good auto parts stores will stock frequently needed components which wear out relatively fast, such as clutch components, exhaust systems, brake parts, tune-up parts, etc. These stores often supply new or reconditioned parts on an exchange basis, which can save a considerable amount of money. Discount auto parts stores are often very good places to buy materials and parts needed for general vehicle maintenance such as oil, grease, filters, spark plugs, belts, touch-up paint, bulbs, etc. They also usually sell tools and general accessories, have convenient hours, charge lower prices and can often be found not far from home.

Authorized dealer parts department: This is the best source for parts which are unique to the vehicle and not generally available elsewhere (such as major engine parts, transmission parts, trim pieces, etc.).

Warranty information: If the vehicle is still covered under warranty, be sure that any replacement parts purchased – regardless of the source – do not invalidate the warranty!

To be sure of obtaining the correct parts, have engine and chassis numbers available and, if possible, take the old parts along for positive identification.

Maintenance techniques, tools and working facilities

Maintenance techniques

There are a number of techniques involved in maintenance and repair that will be referred to throughout this manual. Application of these techniques will enable the home mechanic to be more efficient, better organized and capable of performing the various tasks properly, which will ensure that the repair job is thorough and complete.

Fasteners

Fasteners are nuts, bolts, studs and screws used to hold two or more parts together. There are a few things to keep in mind when working with fasteners. Almost all of them use a locking device of some type, either a lockwasher, locknut, locking tab or thread adhesive. All threaded fasteners should be clean and straight, with undamaged threads and undamaged corners on the hex head where the wrench fits. Develop the habit of replacing all damaged nuts and bolts with new ones. Special locknuts with nylon or fiber inserts can only be used once. If they are removed, they lose their locking ability and must be replaced with new ones.

Rusted nuts and bolts should be treated with a penetrating fluid to ease removal and prevent breakage. Some mechanics use turpentine in a spout-type oil can, which works quite well. After applying the rust penetrant, let it work for a few minutes before trying to loosen the nut or bolt. Badly rusted fasteners may have to be chiseled or sawed off or removed with a special nut breaker, available at tool stores.

If a bolt or stud breaks off in an assembly, it can be drilled and removed with a special tool commonly available for this purpose. Most automotive machine shops can perform this task, as well as other repair procedures, such as the repair of threaded holes that have been stripped out.

Flat washers and lockwashers, when removed from an assembly, should always be replaced exactly as removed. Replace any damaged washers with new ones. Never use a lockwasher on any soft metal surface (such as aluminum), thin sheet metal or plastic.

Fastener sizes

For a number of reasons, automobile manufacturers are making wider and wider use of metric fasteners. Therefore, it is important to be able to tell the difference between standard (sometimes called U.S. or SAE) and metric hardware, since they cannot be interchanged.

All bolts, whether standard or metric, are sized according to diameter, thread pitch and length. For example, a standard 1/2 – 13 x 1 bolt is 1/2 inch in diameter, has 13 threads per inch and is 1 inch long. An M12 – 1.75 x 25 metric bolt is 12 mm in diameter, has a thread pitch of 1.75 mm (the distance between threads) and is 25 mm long. The two bolts are nearly identical, and easily confused, but they are not interchangeable.

In addition to the differences in diameter, thread pitch and length, metric and standard bolts can also be distinguished by examining the bolt heads. To begin with, the distance across the flats on a standard bolt head is measured in inches, while the same dimension on a metric bolt is sized in millimeters (the same is true for nuts). As a result, a standard wrench should not be used on a metric bolt and a metric wrench should not be used on a standard bolt. Also, most standard bolts have slashes radiating out from the center of the head to denote the grade or strength of the bolt, which is an indication of the amount of torque that can be applied to it. The greater the number of slashes, the greater the strength of the bolt. Grades 0 through 5 are commonly used on automobiles. Metric bolts have a property class (grade) number, rather than a slash, molded into their heads to indicate bolt strength. In this case, the higher the number, the stronger the bolt. Property class numbers 8.8, 9.8 and 10.9 are commonly used on automobiles.

Strength markings can also be used to distinguish standard hex nuts from metric hex nuts. Many standard nuts have dots stamped into one side, while metric nuts are marked with a number. The greater the number of dots, or the higher the number, the greater the strength of the nut.

Metric studs are also marked on their ends according to property class (grade). Larger studs are numbered (the same as metric bolts), while smaller studs carry a geometric code to denote grade.

Grade 1 or 2   Grade 5   Grade 8

Bolt strength markings (top — standard/SAE/USS; bottom — metric)

Grade	Identification
Hex Nut Grade 5	3 Dots
Hex Nut Grade 8	6 Dots

Class	Identification
Hex Nut Property Class 9	Arabic 9
Hex Nut Property Class 10	Arabic 10

Standard hex nut strength markings

Metric hex nut strength markings

CLASS 10.9   CLASS 9.8   CLASS 8.8

Metric stud strength markings

It should be noted that many fasteners, especially Grades 0 through 2, have no distinguishing marks on them. When such is the case, the only way to determine whether it is standard or metric is to measure the thread pitch or compare it to a known fastener of the same size.

Standard fasteners are often referred to as SAE, as opposed to metric. However, it should be noted that SAE technically refers to a non-metric *fine thread* fastener only. Coarse thread non-metric fasteners are referred to as USS sizes.

Since fasteners of the same size (both standard and metric) may have different strength ratings, be sure to reinstall any bolts, studs or nuts removed from your vehicle in their original locations. Also, when replacing a fastener with a new one, make sure that the new one has a strength rating equal to or greater than the original.

Tightening sequences and procedures

Most threaded fasteners should be tightened to a specific torque value (torque is the twisting force applied to a threaded component such as a nut or bolt). Overtightening the fastener can weaken it and cause it to break, while undertightening can cause it to eventually come loose. Bolts, screws and studs, depending on the material they are made of and their thread diameters, have specific torque values, many of which are noted in the Specifications at the beginning of each Chapter. Be sure to follow the torque recommendations closely. For fasteners not assigned a specific torque, a general torque value chart is presented here as a guide. These torque values are for dry (unlubricated) fasteners threaded into steel or cast iron (not aluminum). As was previously mentioned, the size and grade of a fastener determine the amount of torque that can safely be

Metric thread sizes	Ft-lbs	Nm
M-6	6 to 9	9 to 12
M-8	14 to 21	19 to 28
M-10	28 to 40	38 to 54
M-12	50 to 71	68 to 96
M-14	80 to 140	109 to 154

Pipe thread sizes		
1/8	5 to 8	7 to 10
1/4	12 to 18	17 to 24
3/8	22 to 33	30 to 44
1/2	25 to 35	34 to 47

U.S. thread sizes		
1/4 – 20	6 to 9	9 to 12
5/16 – 18	12 to 18	17 to 24
5/16 – 24	14 to 20	19 to 27
3/8 – 16	22 to 32	30 to 43
3/8 – 24	27 to 38	37 to 51
7/16 – 14	40 to 55	55 to 74
7/16 – 20	40 to 60	55 to 81
1/2 – 13	55 to 80	75 to 108

Standard (SAE and USS) bolt dimensions/grade marks

G   Grade marks (bolt length)
L   Length (in inches)
T   Thread pitch (number of threads per inch)
D   Nominal diameter (in inches)

Metric bolt dimensions/grade marks

P   Property class (bolt strength)
L   Length (in millimeters)
T   Thread pitch (distance between threads in millimeters)
D   Diameter

applied to it. The figures listed here are approximate for Grade 2 and Grade 3 fasteners. Higher grades can tolerate higher torque values.

Fasteners laid out in a pattern, such as cylinder head bolts, oil pan bolts, differential cover bolts, etc., must be loosened or tightened in sequence to avoid warping the component. This sequence will normally be shown in the appropriate Chapter. If a specific pattern is not given, the following procedures can be used to prevent warping.

Initially, the bolts or nuts should be assembled finger-tight only. Next, they should be tightened one full turn each, in a criss-cross or diagonal pattern. After each one has been tightened one full turn, return to the first one and tighten them all one-half turn, following the same pattern. Finally, tighten each of them one-quarter turn at a time until each fastener has been tightened to the proper torque. To loosen and remove the fasteners, the procedure would be reversed.

Component disassembly

Component disassembly should be done with care and purpose to help ensure that the parts go back together properly. Always keep track of the sequence in which parts are removed. Make note of special characteristics or marks on parts that can be installed more than one way, such as a grooved thrust washer on a shaft. It is a good idea to lay the disassembled parts out on a clean surface in the order that they were removed. It may also be helpful to make sketches or take instant photos of components before removal.

When removing fasteners from a component, keep track of their locations. Sometimes threading a bolt back in a part, or putting the washers and nut back on a stud, can prevent mix-ups later. If nuts and bolts cannot be returned to their original locations, they should be kept in a compartmented box or a series of small boxes. A cupcake or muffin tin is ideal for this purpose, since each cavity can hold the bolts and nuts from a particular area (i.e. oil pan bolts, valve cover bolts, engine mount bolts, etc.). A pan of this type is especially helpful when working on assemblies with very small parts, such as the carburetor, alternator, valve train or interior dash and trim pieces. The cavities can be marked with paint or tape to identify the contents.

Whenever wiring looms, harnesses or connectors are separated, it is a good idea to identify the two halves with numbered pieces of masking tape so they can be easily reconnected.

Gasket sealing surfaces

Throughout any vehicle, gaskets are used to seal the mating surfaces between two parts and keep lubricants, fluids, vacuum or pressure contained in an assembly.

Many times these gaskets are coated with a liquid or paste-type gasket sealing compound before assembly. Age, heat and pressure can sometimes cause the two parts to stick together so tightly that they are very difficult to separate. Often, the assembly can be loosened by striking it with a soft-face hammer near the mating surfaces. A regular hammer can be used if a block of wood is placed between the hammer and the part. Do not hammer on cast parts or parts that could be easily damaged. With any particularly stubborn part, always recheck to make sure that every fastener has been removed.

Avoid using a screwdriver or bar to pry apart an assembly, as they can easily mar the gasket sealing surfaces of the parts, which must remain smooth. If prying is absolutely necessary, use an old broom handle, but keep in mind that extra clean up will be necessary if the wood splinters.

After the parts are separated, the old gasket must be carefully scraped off and the gasket surfaces cleaned. Stubborn gasket material can be soaked with rust penetrant or treated with a special chemical to soften it so it can be easily scraped off. A scraper can be fashioned from a piece of copper tubing by flattening and sharpening one end. Copper is recommended because it is usually softer than the surfaces to be scraped, which reduces the chance of gouging the part. Some gaskets can be removed with a wire brush, but regardless of the method used, the mating surfaces must be left clean and smooth. If for some reason the gasket surface is gouged, then a gasket sealer thick enough to fill scratches will have to be used during reassembly of the components. For most applications, a nondrying (or semi-drying) gasket sealer should be used.

Hose removal tips

Warning: *If the vehicle is equipped with air conditioning, do not disconnect any of the A/C hoses without first having the system depressurized by a dealer service department or a service station.*

Hose removal precautions closely parallel gasket removal precautions. Avoid scratching or gouging the surface that the hose mates against or the connection may leak. This is especially true for radiator hoses. Because of various chemical reactions, the rubber in hoses can bond itself to the metal spigot that the hose fits over. To remove a hose, first loosen the hose clamps that secure it to the spigot. Then, with slip-joint pliers, grab the hose at the clamp and rotate it around the spigot. Work it back and forth until it is completely free, then pull it off. Silicone or other lubricants will ease removal if they can be applied between the hose and the outside of the spigot. Apply the same lubricant to the inside of the hose and the outside of the spigot to simplify installation.

As a last resort (and if the hose is to be replaced with a new one anyway), the rubber can be slit with a knife and the hose peeled from the spigot. If this must be done, be careful that the metal connection is not damaged.

If a hose clamp is broken or damaged, do not reuse it. Wire-type clamps usually weaken with age, so it is a good idea to replace them with screw-type clamps whenever a hose is removed.

Tools

A selection of good tools is a basic requirement for anyone who plans to maintain and repair his or her own vehicle. For the owner who has few tools, the initial investment might seem high, but when compared to the spiraling costs of professional auto maintenance and repair, it is a wise one.

Micrometer set

Dial indicator set

Dial caliper

Hand-operated vacuum pump

Timing light

Compression gauge with spark plug
hole adapter

Damper/steering wheel puller

General purpose puller

Hydraulic lifter removal tool

Valve spring compressor

Valve spring compressor

Ridge reamer

Piston ring groove cleaning tool

Ring removal/installation tool

Ring compressor

Cylinder hone

Brake hold-down spring tool

Brake cylinder hone

Clutch plate alignment tool

Tap and die set

To help the owner decide which tools are needed to perform the tasks detailed in this manual, the following tool lists are offered: *Maintenance and minor repair, Repair/overhaul* and *Special.*

The newcomer to practical mechanics should start off with the maintenance and minor repair tool kit, which is adequate for the simpler jobs performed on a vehicle. Then, as confidence and experience grow, the owner can tackle more difficult tasks, buying additional tools as they are needed. Eventually the basic kit will be expanded into the repair and overhaul tool set. Over a period of time, the experienced do-it-yourselfer will assemble a tool set complete enough for most repair and overhaul procedures and will add tools from the special category when it is felt that the expense is justified by the frequency of use.

Maintenance and minor repair tool kit

The tools in this list should be considered the minimum required for performance of routine maintenance, servicing and minor repair work. We recommend the purchase of combination wrenches (box-end and open-end combined in one wrench). While more expensive than open end wrenches, they offer the advantages of both types of wrench.

Combination wrench set (1/4-inch to 1 inch or 6 mm to 19 mm)
Adjustable wrench, 8 inch
Spark plug wrench with rubber insert
Spark plug gap adjusting tool
Feeler gauge set
Brake bleeder wrench
Standard screwdriver (5/16-inch x 6 inch)
Phillips screwdriver (No. 2 x 6 inch)
Combination pliers – 6 inch
Hacksaw and assortment of blades
Tire pressure gauge
Grease gun
Oil can
Fine emery cloth
Wire brush

Battery post and cable cleaning tool
Oil filter wrench
Funnel (medium size)
Safety goggles
Jackstands(2)
Drain pan

Note: *If basic tune-ups are going to be part of routine maintenance, it will be necessary to purchase a good quality stroboscopic timing light and combination tachometer/dwell meter. Although they are included in the list of special tools, it is mentioned here because they are absolutely necessary for tuning most vehicles properly.*

Repair and overhaul tool set

These tools are essential for anyone who plans to perform major repairs and are in addition to those in the maintenance and minor repair tool kit. Included is a comprehensive set of sockets which, though expensive, are invaluable because of their versatility, especially when various extensions and drives are available. We recommend the 1/2-inch drive over the 3/8-inch drive. Although the larger drive is bulky and more expensive, it has the capacity of accepting a very wide range of large sockets. Ideally, however, the mechanic should have a 3/8-inch drive set and a 1/2-inch drive set.

Socket set(s)
Reversible ratchet
Extension – 10 inch
Universal joint
Torque wrench (same size drive as sockets)
Ball peen hammer – 8 ounce
Soft-face hammer (plastic/rubber)
Standard screwdriver (1/4-inch x 6 inch)
Standard screwdriver (stubby – 5/16-inch)
Phillips screwdriver (No. 3 x 8 inch)
Phillips screwdriver (stubby – No. 2)

Pliers – vise grip
Pliers – lineman's
Pliers – needle nose
Pliers – snap-ring (internal and external)
Cold chisel – 1/2-inch
Scribe
Scraper (made from flattened copper tubing)
Centerpunch
Pin punches (1/16, 1/8, 3/16-inch)
Steel rule/straightedge – 12 inch
Allen wrench set (1/8 to 3/8-inch or 4 mm to 10 mm)
A selection of files
Wire brush (large)
Jackstands (second set)
Jack (scissor or hydraulic type)

Note: *Another tool which is often useful is an electric drill with a chuck capacity of 3/8-inch and a set of good quality drill bits.*

Special tools

The tools in this list include those which are not used regularly, are expensive to buy, or which need to be used in accordance with their manufacturer's instructions. Unless these tools will be used frequently, it is not very economical to purchase many of them. A consideration would be to split the cost and use between yourself and a friend or friends. In addition, most of these tools can be obtained from a tool rental shop on a temporary basis.

This list primarily contains only those tools and instruments widely available to the public, and not those special tools produced by the vehicle manufacturer for distribution to dealer service departments. Occasionally, references to the manufacturer's special tools are included in the text of this manual. Generally, an alternative method of doing the job without the special tool is offered. However, sometimes there is no alternative to their use. Where this is the case, and the tool cannot be purchased or borrowed, the work should be turned over to the dealer service department or an automotive repair shop.

Valve spring compressor
Piston ring groove cleaning tool
Piston ring compressor
Piston ring installation tool
Cylinder compression gauge
Cylinder ridge reamer
Cylinder surfacing hone
Cylinder bore gauge
Micrometers and/or dial calipers
Hydraulic lifter removal tool
Balljoint separator
Universal-type puller
Impact screwdriver
Dial indicator set
Stroboscopic timing light (inductive pick-up)
Hand operated vacuum/pressure pump
Tachometer/dwell meter
Universal electrical multimeter
Cable hoist
Brake spring removal and installation tools
Floor jack

Buying tools

For the do-it-yourselfer who is just starting to get involved in vehicle maintenance and repair, there are a number of options available when purchasing tools. If maintenance and minor repair is the extent of the work to be done, the purchase of individual tools is satisfactory. If, on the other hand, extensive work is planned, it would be a good idea to purchase a modest tool set from one of the large retail chain stores. A set can usually be bought at a substantial savings over the individual tool prices, and they often come with a tool box. As additional tools are needed, add–on sets, individual tools and a larger tool box can be purchased to expand the tool selection. Building a tool set gradually allows the cost of the tools to be spread over a longer period of time and gives the mechanic the freedom to choose only those tools that will actually be used.

Tool stores will often be the only source of some of the special tools that are needed, but regardless of where tools are bought, try to avoid cheap ones, especially when buying screwdrivers and sockets, because they won't last very long. The expense involved in replacing cheap tools will eventually be greater than the initial cost of quality tools.

Care and maintenance of tools

Good tools are expensive, so it makes sense to treat them with respect. Keep them clean and in usable condition and store them properly when not in use. Always wipe off any dirt, grease or metal chips before putting them away. Never leave tools lying around in the work area. Upon completion of a job, always check closely under the hood for tools that may have been left there so they won't get lost during a test drive.

Some tools, such as screwdrivers, pliers, wrenches and sockets, can be hung on a panel mounted on the garage or workshop wall, while others should be kept in a tool box or tray. Measuring instruments, gauges, meters, etc. must be carefully stored where they cannot be damaged by weather or impact from other tools.

When tools are used with care and stored properly, they will last a very long time. Even with the best of care, though, tools will wear out if used frequently. When a tool is damaged or worn out, replace it. Subsequent jobs will be safer and more enjoyable if you do.

Working facilities

Not to be overlooked when discussing tools is the workshop. If anything more than routine maintenance is to be carried out, some sort of suitable work area is essential.

It is understood, and appreciated, that many home mechanics do not have a good workshop or garage available, and end up removing an engine or doing major repairs outside. It is recommended, however, that the overhaul or repair be completed under the cover of a roof.

A clean, flat workbench or table of comfortable working height is an absolute necessity. The workbench should be equipped with a vise that has a jaw opening of at least four inches.

As mentioned previously, some clean, dry storage space is also required for tools, as well as the lubricants, fluids, cleaning solvents, etc. which soon become necessary.

Sometimes waste oil and fluids, drained from the engine or cooling system during normal maintenance or repairs, present a disposal problem. To avoid pouring them on the ground or into a sewage system, pour the used fluids into large containers, seal them with caps and take them to an authorized disposal site or recycling center. Plastic jugs, such as old antifreeze containers, are ideal for this purpose.

Always keep a supply of old newspapers and clean rags available. Old towels are excellent for mopping up spills. Many mechanics use rolls of paper towels for most work because they are readily available and disposable. To help keep the area under the vehicle clean, a large cardboard box can be cut open and flattened to protect the garage or shop floor.

Whenever working over a painted surface, such as when leaning over a fender to service something under the hood, always cover it with an old blanket or bedspread to protect the finish. Vinyl covered pads, made especially for this purpose, are available at auto parts stores.

Booster battery (jump) starting

Observe these precautions when using a booster battery to start a vehicle:

a) Before connecting the booster battery, make sure the ignition switch is in the Off position.
b) Turn off the lights, heater and other electrical loads.
c) Your eyes should be shielded. Safety goggles are a good idea.
d) Make sure the booster battery is the same voltage as the dead one in the vehicle.
e) The two vehicles MUST NOT TOUCH each other!
f) Make sure the transmission is in Neutral (manual) or Park (automatic).
g) If the booster battery is not a maintenance-free type, remove the vent caps and lay a cloth over the vent holes.

Connect the red jumper cable to the positive (+) terminals of each battery.

Connect one end of the black jumper cable to the negative (−) terminal of the booster battery. The other end of this cable should be connected to a good ground on the vehicle to be started, such as a bolt or bracket on the engine block (see illustration). Make sure the cable will not come into contact with the fan, drivebelts or other moving parts of the engine.

Start the engine using the booster battery, then, with the engine running at idle speed, disconnect the jumper cables in the reverse order of connection.

Make the booster battery cable connections in the numerical order shown (note that the negative cable of the booster battery is NOT attached to the negative terminal of the dead battery)

Jacking and towing

Jacking

The jack supplied with the vehicle should only be used for raising the vehicle when changing a tire or placing jackstands under the frame. **Warning:** *Never work under the vehicle or start the engine while this jack is being used as the only means of support.*

The vehicle should be on level ground with the wheels blocked and the transmission in Park. If a tire is being changed, loosen the lug nuts one-half turn and leave them in place until the wheel is raised off the ground. Make sure no one is in the vehicle as it's being raised off the ground.

Place the jack under the vehicle in the indicated position **(see illustrations)**. Operate the jack with a slow, smooth motion until the wheel is raised off the ground. Remove the lug nuts, pull off the wheel, install the spare and thread the lug nuts back on with the bevelled sides facing in. Tighten them snugly, but wait until the vehicle is lowered to tighten them completely.

Lower the vehicle, remove the jack and tighten the lug nuts (if loosened or removed) in a criss-cross pattern. If possible, tighten them with a torque wrench (see Chapter 1 for the torque figures). If you don't have access to a torque wrench, have the nuts checked by a service station or repair shop as soon as possible.

Towing

Vehicles can be towed with all four wheels on the ground, provided speeds do not exceed 35 mph and the distance is not over 50 miles, otherwise transmission damage can result.

Equipment specifically designed for towing should be used and must be attached to the main structural members of the vehicle, not the bumper or brackets.

Safety is a major consideration when towing and all applicable state and local laws must be obeyed. A safety chain system must be used at all times.

While towing, the parking brake must be released and the transmission must be in Neutral. The steering must be unlocked (ignition switch in the OFF position). Remember that power steering and power brakes will not work with the engine off.

On earlier models, a bumper jack is used to raise the vehicle – it either fits into a slot in the bumper, as shown here, or hooks onto the lower edge of the bumper at a specific location (see the owner's manual for the location)

Later model jacking details

Automotive chemicals and lubricants

A number of automotive chemicals and lubricants are available for use during vehicle maintenance and repair. They include a wide variety of products ranging from cleaning solvents and degreasers to lubricants and protective sprays for rubber, plastic and vinyl.

Cleaners

Carburetor cleaner and choke cleaner is a strong solvent for gum, varnish and carbon. Most carburetor cleaners leave a dry-type lubricant film which will not harden or gum up. Because of this film it is not recommended for use on electrical components.

Brake system cleaner is used to remove grease and brake fluid from the brake system, where clean surfaces are absolutely necessary. It leaves no residue and often eliminates brake squeal caused by contaminants.

Electrical cleaner removes oxidation, corrosion and carbon deposits from electrical contacts, restoring full current flow. It can also be used to clean spark plugs, carburetor jets, voltage regulators and other parts where an oil-free surface is desired.

Demoisturants remove water and moisture from electrical components such as alternators, voltage regulators, electrical connectors and fuse blocks. They are non-conductive, non-corrosive and non-flammable.

Degreasers are heavy-duty solvents used to remove grease from the outside of the engine and from chassis components. They can be sprayed or brushed on and, depending on the type, are rinsed off either with water or solvent.

Lubricants

Motor oil is the lubricant formulated for use in engines. It normally contains a wide variety of additives to prevent corrosion and reduce foaming and wear. Motor oil comes in various weights (viscosity ratings) from 5 to 80. The recommended weight of the oil depends on the season, temperature and the demands on the engine. Light oil is used in cold climates and under light load conditions. Heavy oil is used in hot climates and where high loads are encountered. Multi-viscosity oils are designed to have characteristics of both light and heavy oils and are available in a number of weights from 5W-20 to 20W-50.

Gear oil is designed to be used in differentials, manual transmissions and other areas where high-temperature lubrication is required.

Chassis and wheel bearing grease is a heavy grease used where increased loads and friction are encountered, such as for wheel bearings, balljoints, tie-rod ends and universal joints.

High-temperature wheel bearing grease is designed to withstand the extreme temperatures encountered by wheel bearings in disc brake equipped vehicles. It usually contains molybdenum disulfide (moly), which is a dry-type lubricant.

White grease is a heavy grease for metal-to-metal applications where water is a problem. White grease stays soft under both low and high temperatures (usually from −100 to +190-degrees F), and will not wash off or dilute in the presence of water.

Assembly lube is a special extreme pressure lubricant, usually containing moly, used to lubricate high-load parts (such as main and rod bearings and cam lobes) for initial start-up of a new engine. The assembly lube lubricates the parts without being squeezed out or washed away until the engine oiling system begins to function.

Silicone lubricants are used to protect rubber, plastic, vinyl and nylon parts.

Graphite lubricants are used where oils cannot be used due to contamination problems, such as in locks. The dry graphite will lubricate metal parts while remaining uncontaminated by dirt, water, oil or acids. It is electrically conductive and will not foul electrical contacts in locks such as the ignition switch.

Moly penetrants loosen and lubricate frozen, rusted and corroded fasteners and prevent future rusting or freezing.

Heat-sink grease is a special electrically non-conductive grease that is used for mounting electronic ignition modules where it is essential that heat is transferred away from the module.

Sealants

RTV sealant is one of the most widely used gasket compounds. Made from silicone, RTV is air curing, it seals, bonds, waterproofs, fills surface irregularities, remains flexible, doesn't shrink, is relatively easy to remove, and is used as a supplementary sealer with almost all low and medium temperature gaskets.

Anaerobic sealant is much like RTV in that it can be used either to seal gaskets or to form gaskets by itself. It remains flexible, is solvent resistant and fills surface imperfections. The difference between an anaerobic sealant and an RTV-type sealant is in the curing. RTV cures when exposed to air, while an anaerobic sealant cures only in the absence of air. This means that an anaerobic sealant cures only after the assembly of parts, sealing them together.

Thread and pipe sealant is used for sealing hydraulic and pneumatic fittings and vacuum lines. It is usually made from a teflon compound, and comes in a spray, a paint-on liquid and as a wrap-around tape.

Chemicals

Anti-seize compound prevents seizing, galling, cold welding, rust and corrosion in fasteners. High-temperature anti-seize, usually made with copper and graphite lubricants, is used for exhaust system and exhaust manifold bolts.

Anaerobic locking compounds are used to keep fasteners from vibrating or working loose and cure only after installation, in the absence of air. Medium strength locking compound is used for small nuts, bolts and screws that may be removed later. High-strength locking compound is for large nuts, bolts and studs which aren't removed on a regular basis.

Oil additives range from viscosity index improvers to chemical treatments that claim to reduce internal engine friction. It should be noted that most oil manufacturers caution against using additives with their oils.

Gas additives perform several functions, depending on their chemical makeup. They usually contain solvents that help dissolve gum and varnish that build up on carburetor, fuel injection and intake parts. They also serve to break down carbon deposits that form on the inside surfaces of the combustion chambers. Some additives contain upper cylinder lubricants for valves and piston rings, and others contain chemicals to remove condensation from the gas tank.

Miscellaneous

Brake fluid is specially formulated hydraulic fluid that can withstand the heat and pressure encountered in brake systems. Care must be taken so this fluid does not come in contact with painted surfaces or plastics. An opened container should always be resealed to prevent contamination by water or dirt.

Weatherstrip adhesive is used to bond weatherstripping around doors, windows and trunk lids. It is sometimes used to attach trim pieces.

Undercoating is a petroleum-based, tar-like substance that is designed to protect metal surfaces on the underside of the vehicle from corrosion. It also acts as a sound-deadening agent by insulating the bottom of the vehicle.

Waxes and polishes are used to help protect painted and plated surfaces from the weather. Different types of paint may require the use of different types of wax and polish. Some polishes utilize a chemical or abrasive cleaner to help remove the top layer of oxidized (dull) paint on older vehicles. In recent years many non-wax polishes that contain a wide variety of chemicals such as polymers and silicones have been introduced. These non-wax polishes are usually easier to apply and last longer than conventional waxes and polishes.

Safety first!

Regardless of how enthusiastic you may be about getting on with the job at hand, take the time to ensure that your safety is not jeopardized. A moment's lack of attention can result in an accident, as can failure to observe certain simple safety precautions. The possibility of an accident will always exist, and the following points should not be considered a comprehensive list of all dangers. Rather, they are intended to make you aware of the risks and to encourage a safety conscious approach to all work you carry out on your vehicle.

Essential DOs and DON'Ts

DON'T rely on a jack when working under the vehicle. Always use approved jackstands to support the weight of the vehicle and place them under the recommended lift or support points.

DON'T attempt to loosen extremely tight fasteners (i.e. wheel lug nuts) while the vehicle is on a jack – it may fall.

DON'T start the engine without first making sure that the transmission is in Neutral (or Park where applicable) and the parking brake is set.

DON'T remove the radiator cap from a hot cooling system – let it cool or cover it with a cloth and release the pressure gradually.

DON'T attempt to drain the engine oil until you are sure it has cooled to the point that it will not burn you.

DON'T touch any part of the engine or exhaust system until it has cooled sufficiently to avoid burns.

DON'T siphon toxic liquids such as gasoline, antifreeze and brake fluid by mouth, or allow them to remain on your skin.

DON'T inhale brake lining dust – it is potentially hazardous (see Asbestos below)

DON'T allow spilled oil or grease to remain on the floor – wipe it up before someone slips on it.

DON'T use loose fitting wrenches or other tools which may slip and cause injury.

DON'T push on wrenches when loosening or tightening nuts or bolts. Always try to pull the wrench toward you. If the situation calls for pushing the wrench away, push with an open hand to avoid scraped knuckles if the wrench should slip.

DON'T attempt to lift a heavy component alone – get someone to help you.

DON'T rush or take unsafe shortcuts to finish a job.

DON'T allow children or animals in or around the vehicle while you are working on it.

DO wear eye protection when using power tools such as a drill, sander, bench grinder, etc. and when working under a vehicle.

DO keep loose clothing and long hair well out of the way of moving parts.

DO make sure that any hoist used has a safe working load rating adequate for the job.

DO get someone to check on you periodically when working alone on a vehicle.

DO carry out work in a logical sequence and make sure that everything is correctly assembled and tightened.

DO keep chemicals and fluids tightly capped and out of the reach of children and pets.

DO remember that your vehicle's safety affects that of yourself and others. If in doubt on any point, get professional advice.

Asbestos

Certain friction, insulating, sealing, and other products – such as brake linings, brake bands, clutch linings, torque converters, gaskets, etc. – contain asbestos. *Extreme care must be taken to avoid inhalation of dust from such products since it is hazardous to health.* If in doubt, assume that they *do* contain asbestos.

Fire

Remember at all times that gasoline is highly flammable. Never smoke or have any kind of open flame around when working on a vehicle. But the risk does not end there. A spark caused by an electrical short circuit, by two metal surfaces contacting each other, or even by static electricity built up in your body under certain conditions, can ignite gasoline vapors, which in a confined space are highly explosive. Do not, under any circumstances, use gasoline for cleaning parts. Use an approved safety solvent.

Always disconnect the battery ground (–) cable *at the battery* before working on any part of the fuel system or electrical system. Never risk spilling fuel on a hot engine or exhaust component.

It is strongly recommended that a fire extinguisher suitable for use on fuel and electrical fires be kept handy in the garage or workshop at all times. Never try to extinguish a fuel or electrical fire with water.

Fumes

Certain fumes are highly toxic and can quickly cause unconsciousness and even death if inhaled to any extent. Gasoline vapor falls into this category, as do the vapors from some cleaning solvents. Any draining or pouring of such volatile fluids should be done in a well ventilated area.

When using cleaning fluids and solvents, read the instructions on the container carefully. Never use materials from unmarked containers.

Never run the engine in an enclosed space, such as a garage. Exhaust fumes contain carbon monoxide, which is extremely poisonous. If you need to run the engine, always do so in the open air, or at least have the rear of the vehicle outside the work area.

If you are fortunate enough to have the use of an inspection pit, never drain or pour gasoline and never run the engine while the vehicle is over the pit. The fumes, being heavier than air, will concentrate in the pit with possibly lethal results.

The battery

Never create a spark or allow a bare light bulb near a battery. They normally give off a certain amount of hydrogen gas, which is highly explosive.

Always disconnect the battery ground (–) cable *at the battery* before working on the fuel or electrical systems.

If possible, loosen the filler caps or cover when charging the battery from an external source (this does not apply to sealed or maintenancefree batteries). Do not charge at an excessive rate or the battery may burst.

Take care when adding water to a non maintenance–free battery and when carrying a battery. The electrolyte, even when diluted, is very corrosive and should not be allowed to contact clothing or skin.

Always wear eye protection when cleaning the battery to prevent the caustic deposits from entering your eyes.

Household current

When using an electric power tool, inspection light, etc., which operates on household current, always make sure that the tool is correctly connected to its plug and that, where necessary, it is properly grounded. Do not use such items in damp conditions and, again, do not create a spark or apply excessive heat in the vicinity of fuel or fuel vapor.

Secondary ignition system voltage

A severe electric shock can result from touching certain parts of the ignition system (such as the spark plug wires) when the engine is running or being cranked, particularly if components are damp or the insulation is defective. In the case of an electronic ignition system, the secondary system voltage is much higher and could prove fatal.

Conversion factors

Length (distance)
Inches (in)	X	25.4	= Millimetres (mm)	X 0.0394	= Inches (in)
Feet (ft)	X	0.305	= Metres (m)	X 3.281	= Feet (ft)
Miles	X	1.609	= Kilometres (km)	X 0.621	= Miles

Volume (capacity)
Cubic inches (cu in; in³)	X	16.387	= Cubic centimetres (cc; cm³)	X 0.061	= Cubic inches (cu in; in³)
Imperial pints (Imp pt)	X	0.568	= Litres (l)	X 1.76	= Imperial pints (Imp pt)
Imperial quarts (Imp qt)	X	1.137	= Litres (l)	X 0.88	= Imperial quarts (Imp qt)
Imperial quarts (Imp qt)	X	1.201	= US quarts (US qt)	X 0.833	= Imperial quarts (Imp qt)
US quarts (US qt)	X	0.946	= Litres (l)	X 1.057	= US quarts (US qt)
Imperial gallons (Imp gal)	X	4.546	= Litres (l)	X 0.22	= Imperial gallons (Imp gal)
Imperial gallons (Imp gal)	X	1.201	= US gallons (US gal)	X 0.833	= Imperial gallons (Imp gal)
US gallons (US gal)	X	3.785	= Litres (l)	X 0.264	= US gallons (US gal)

Mass (weight)
Ounces (oz)	X	28.35	= Grams (g)	X 0.035	= Ounces (oz)
Pounds (lb)	X	0.454	= Kilograms (kg)	X 2.205	= Pounds (lb)

Force
Ounces-force (ozf; oz)	X	0.278	= Newtons (N)	X 3.6	= Ounces-force (ozf; oz)
Pounds-force (lbf; lb)	X	4.448	= Newtons (N)	X 0.225	= Pounds-force (lbf; lb)
Newtons (N)	X	0.1	= Kilograms-force (kgf; kg)	X 9.81	= Newtons (N)

Pressure
Pounds-force per square inch (psi; lbf/in²; lb/in²)	X	0.070	= Kilograms-force per square centimetre (kgf/cm²; kg/cm²)	X 14.223	= Pounds-force per square inch (psi; lbf/in²; lb/in²)
Pounds-force per square inch (psi; lbf/in²; lb/in²)	X	0.068	= Atmospheres (atm)	X 14.696	= Pounds-force per square inch (psi; lbf/in²; lb/in²)
Pounds-force per square inch (psi; lbf/in²; lb/in²)	X	0.069	= Bars	X 14.5	= Pounds-force per square inch (psi; lbf/in²; lb/in²)
Pounds-force per square inch (psi; lbf/in²; lb/in²)	X	6.895	= Kilopascals (kPa)	X 0.145	= Pounds-force per square inch (psi; lbf/in²; lb/in²)
Kilopascals (kPa)	X	0.01	= Kilograms-force per square centimetre (kgf/cm²; kg/cm²)	X 98.1	= Kilopascals (kPa)
Millibar (mbar)	X	100	= Pascals (Pa)	X 0.01	= Millibar (mbar)
Millibar (mbar)	X	0.0145	= Pounds-force per square inch (psi; lbf/in²; lb/in²)	X 68.947	= Millibar (mbar)
Millibar (mbar)	X	0.75	= Millimetres of mercury (mmHg)	X 1.333	= Millibar (mbar)
Millibar (mbar)	X	0.401	= Inches of water (inH₂O)	X 2.491	= Millibar (mbar)
Millimetres of mercury (mmHg)	X	0.535	= Inches of water (inH₂O)	X 1.868	= Millimetres of mercury (mmHg)
Inches of water (inH₂O)	X	0.036	= Pounds-force per square inch (psi; lbf/in²; lb/in²)	X 27.68	= Inches of water (inH₂O)

Torque (moment of force)
Pounds-force inches (lbf in; lb in)	X	1.152	= Kilograms-force centimetre (kgf cm; kg cm)	X 0.868	= Pounds-force inches (lbf in; lb in)
Pounds-force inches (lbf in; lb in)	X	0.113	= Newton metres (Nm)	X 8.85	= Pounds-force inches (lbf in; lb in)
Pounds-force inches (lbf in; lb in)	X	0.083	= Pounds-force feet (lbf ft; lb ft)	X 12	= Pounds-force inches (lbf in; lb in)
Pounds-force feet (lbf ft; lb ft)	X	0.138	= Kilograms-force metres (kgf m; kg m)	X 7.233	= Pounds-force feet (lbf ft; lb ft)
Pounds-force feet (lbf ft; lb ft)	X	1.356	= Newton metres (Nm)	X 0.738	= Pounds-force feet (lbf ft; lb ft)
Newton metres (Nm)	X	0.102	= Kilograms-force metres (kgf m; kg m)	X 9.804	= Newton metres (Nm)

Power
Horsepower (hp)	X	745.7	= Watts (W)	X 0.0013	= Horsepower (hp)

Velocity (speed)
Miles per hour (miles/hr; mph)	X	1.609	= Kilometres per hour (km/hr; kph)	X 0.621	= Miles per hour (miles/hr; mph)

Fuel consumption*
Miles per gallon, Imperial (mpg)	X	0.354	= Kilometres per litre (km/l)	X 2.825	= Miles per gallon, Imperial (mpg)
Miles per gallon, US (mpg)	X	0.425	= Kilometres per litre (km/l)	X 2.352	= Miles per gallon, US (mpg)

Temperature

Degrees Fahrenheit = ($°C \times 1.8$) + 32   Degrees Celsius (Degrees Centigrade; °C) = ($°F - 32$) $\times$ 0.56

*It is common practice to convert from miles per gallon (mpg) to litres/100 kilometres (l/100km), where mpg (Imperial) x l/100 km = 282 and mpg (US) x l/100 km = 235

Troubleshooting

Contents

This section provides an easy reference guide to the more common problems which may occur during the operation of the vehicle. These problems and possible causes are grouped under various components or systems, such as Engine, Cooling system, etc., and also refer to the Chapter and/or Section which deals with the problem.

Remember that successful troubleshooting is not a mysterious black art practiced only by professional mechanics. It's simply the result of a bit of knowledge combined with an intelligent, systematic approach to the problem. Always work by a process of elimination, starting with the simplest solution and working through to the most complex – and never overlook the obvious. Anyone can forget to fill the gas tank or leave the lights on overnight, so don't assume you are exempt from such oversights.

Finally, always get clear in your mind why a problem has occurred and take steps to ensure that it doesn't happen again. If the electrical system fails because of a poor connection, check all other connections in the system to make sure that they don't fail as well. If a particular fuse continues to blow, find out why – don't just go on replacing fuses. Remember, failure of a small component can often be indicative of potential failure or incorrect functioning of a more important component or system.

Engine

1   Engine will not rotate when attempting to start

1   Battery terminal connections loose or corroded. Check the cable terminals at the battery. Tighten the cable or remove corrosion as necessary.
2   Battery discharged or faulty. If the cable connections are clean and tight on the battery posts, turn the key to the On position and switch on the headlights and/or windshield wipers. If they fail to function, the battery is discharged.
3   Automatic transmission not completely engaged in Park.
4   Broken, loose or disconnected wiring in the starting circuit. Inspect all wiring and connectors at the battery, starter solenoid and ignition switch.
5   Starter motor pinion jammed in flywheel ring gear. Remove the starter and inspect the pinion and flywheel at earliest convenience.
6   Starter solenoid faulty (Chapter 5).
7   Starter motor faulty (Chapter 5).
8   Ignition switch faulty (Chapter 12).

2   Engine rotates but will not start

1   Fuel tank empty.
2   Battery discharged (engine rotates slowly). Check the operation of electrical components as described in previous Section.
3   Battery terminal connections loose or corroded. See previous Section.
4   Carburetor flooded and/or fuel level in carburetor incorrect. This will usually be accompanied by a strong fuel odor from under the hood. Wait a few minutes, depress the accelerator pedal all the way to the floor and attempt to start the engine.
5   Choke control inoperative (Chapter 1).
6   Fuel not reaching carburetor or fuel injectors. With the ignition switch in the Off position, open the hood, remove the top plate of the air cleaner assembly and observe the top of the carburetor (manually move the choke plate back if necessary). Have an assistant depress the accelerator pedal and check that fuel spurts into the carburetor. If not, check the fuel filter (Chapter 1), fuel lines and fuel pump (Chapter 4).
7   Fuel injector or fuel pump faulty (fuel injected vehicles) (Chapter 4).
8   No power to fuel pump (Chapter 4).
9   Worn, faulty or incorrectly gapped spark plugs (Chapter 1).
10   Broken, loose or disconnected wiring in the starting circuit (see previous Section).

11   Distributor loose, causing ignition timing to change. Turn the distributor as necessary to start the engine, then set the ignition timing as soon as possible (Chapter 1).
12   Broken, loose or disconnected wires at the ignition coil or faulty coil (Chapter 5).

3   Starter motor operates without rotating engine

1   Starter pinion sticking. Remove the starter (Chapter 5) and inspect.
2   Starter pinion or flywheel teeth worn or broken. Remove the cover at the rear of the engine and inspect.

4   Engine hard to start when cold

1   Battery discharged or low. Check as described in Section 1.
2   Choke control inoperative or out of adjustment (Chapter 4).
3   Carburetor flooded (see Section 2).
4   Fuel supply not reaching the carburetor (see Section 2).
5   Carburetor/fuel injection system in need of overhaul (Chapter 4).
6   Distributor rotor carbon tracked and/or mechanical advance mechanism rusted (Chapter 5).
7   Fuel injection malfunction (Chapter 4).

5   Engine hard to start when hot

1   Air filter clogged (Chapter 1).
2   Fuel not reaching the injectors (see Section 2).
3   Corroded electrical leads at the battery (Chapter 1).
4   Bad engine ground (Chapter 1).
5   Starter worn (Chapter 5).
6   Corroded electrical leads at the fuel injection (Chapter 4).

6   Starter motor noisy or excessively rough in engagement

1   Pinion or flywheel gear teeth worn or broken. Remove the cover at the rear of the engine (if so equipped) and inspect.
2   Starter motor mounting bolts loose or missing.

7   Engine starts but stops immediately

1   Loose or faulty electrical connections at distributor, coil or alternator.
2   Insufficient fuel reaching the carburetor or fuel injector (Chapter 4).
3   Vacuum leak at the gasket surfaces of the carburetor or throttle body. Make sure that all mounting bolts/nuts are tightened securely and that all vacuum hoses connected to the carburetor or fuel injection unit and manifold are positioned properly and in good condition.

8   Engine lopes while idling or idles erratically

1   Vacuum leakage. Check mounting bolts/nuts at the carburetor/throttle body and intake manifold for tightness. Make sure that all vacuum hoses are connected and in good condition. Use a stethoscope or a length of fuel hose held against your ear to listen for vacuum leaks while the engine is running. A hissing sound will be heard. Check the carburetor/fuel injector and intake manifold gasket surfaces.
2   Leaking EGR valve or plugged PCV valve (see Chapters 1 and 6).
3   Air filter clogged (Chapter 1).
4   Fuel pump not delivering sufficient fuel to the carburetor/fuel injector (see Section 7).
5   Carburetor out of adjustment (Chapter 4).
6   Leaking head gasket. If this is suspected, take the vehicle to a repair shop or dealer where the engine can be pressure checked.

7   Timing chain and/or gears worn (Chapter 2).
8   Camshaft lobes worn (Chapter 2).

9   Engine misses at idle speed

1   Spark plugs worn or not gapped properly (Chapter 1).
2   Faulty spark plug wires (Chapter 1).
3   Choke not operating properly (Chapter 1).
4   Sticking or faulty emissions system components (Chapter 6).
5   Clogged fuel filter and/or foreign matter in fuel. Remove the fuel filter (Chapter 1) and inspect.
6   Vacuum leaks at the intake manifold or at hose connections. Check as described in Section 8.
7   Incorrect idle speed or idle mixture (Chapter 1).
8   Incorrect ignition timing (Chapter 1).
9   Uneven or low cylinder compression. Check compression as described in Chapter 1.

10   Engine misses throughout driving speed range

1   Fuel filter clogged and/or impurities in the fuel system (Chapter 1). Also check fuel output at the carburetor/fuel injector (see Section 7).
2   Faulty or incorrectly gapped spark plugs (Chapter 1).
3   Incorrect ignition timing (Chapter 1).
4   Cracked distributor cap, disconnected distributor wires or damaged distributor components (Chapter 1).
5   Leaking spark plug wires (Chapter 1).
6   Faulty emissions system components (Chapter 6).
7   Low or uneven cylinder compression pressures. Remove the spark plugs and test the compression with gauge (Chapter 1).
8   Weak or faulty ignition system (Chapter 5).
9   Vacuum leaks at the carburetor/throttle body or vacuum hoses (see Section 8).

11   Engine stalls

1   Idle speed incorrect (Chapter 1).
2   Fuel filter clogged and/or water and impurities in the fuel system (Chapter 1).
3   Choke improperly adjusted or sticking (Chapter 1).
4   Distributor components damp or damaged (Chapter 5).
5   Faulty emissions system components (Chapter 6).
6   Faulty or incorrectly gapped spark plugs (Chapter 1). Also check spark plug wires (Chapter 1).
7   Vacuum leak at the carburetor/throttle body or vacuum hoses. Check as described in Section 8.

12   Engine lacks power

1   Incorrect ignition timing (Chapter 1).
2   Excessive play in distributor shaft. At the same time, check for worn rotor, faulty distributor cap, wires, etc. (Chapters 1 and 5).
3   Faulty or incorrectly gapped spark plugs (Chapter 1).
4   Fuel injection unit not adjusted properly or excessively worn (Chapter 4).
5   Faulty coil (Chapter 5).
6   Brakes binding (Chapter 1).
7   Automatic transmission fluid level incorrect (Chapter 1).
8   Fuel filter clogged and/or impurities in the fuel system (Chapter 1).
9   Emissions control system not functioning properly (Chapter 6).
10   Use of substandard fuel. Fill tank with proper octane fuel.
11   Low or uneven cylinder compression pressures. Test with compres-

sion tester, which will detect leaking valves and/or blown head gasket (Chapter 2C).

13   Engine backfires

1   Emissions system not functioning properly (Chapter 6).
2   Ignition timing incorrect (Chapter 1).
3   Faulty secondary ignition system (cracked spark plug insulator, faulty plug wires, distributor cap and/or rotor) (Chapters 1 and 5).
4   Carburetor/fuel injection system in need of adjustment or worn excessively (Chapter 4).
5   Vacuum leak at the throttle body or vacuum hoses. Check as described in Section 8.
6   Valve clearances incorrectly set, and/or valves sticking in guides (Chapter 2).
7   Crossed plug wires (Chapter 1).

14   Pinging or knocking engine sounds during acceleration or uphill

1   Incorrect grade of fuel. Fill tank with fuel of the proper octane rating.
2   Ignition timing incorrect (Chapter 1).
3   Carburetor/fuel injection system in need of adjustment or overhaul (Chapter 4).
4   Improper spark plugs. Check plug type against the Vehicle Emissions Control Information label located in engine compartment. Also check plugs and wires for damage (Chapter 1).
5   Worn or damaged distributor components (Chapter 5).
6   Faulty emissions system (Chapter 6).
7   Vacuum leak. Check as described in Section 8.
8   Carbon build-up in cylinders (Chapter 2).

15   Engine diesels (continues to run) after switching off

1   Idle speed too high (Chapter 1).
2   Electrical solenoid at side of carburetor not functioning properly (not all models).
3   Ignition timing incorrectly adjusted (Chapter 1).
4   Thermo-controlled air cleaner heat valve not operating properly (Chapter 6).
5   Excessive engine operating temperature. Probable causes of this are malfunctioning thermostat, clogged radiator, faulty water pump (Chapter 3).
6   Incorrect grade of fuel. Fill tank with fuel of the proper octane rating.

Engine electrical system

16   Battery will not hold a charge

1   Alternator drivebelt defective or not adjusted properly (Chapter 1).
2   Electrolyte level low or battery discharged (Chapter 1).
3   Battery terminals loose or corroded (Chapter 1).
4   Alternator not charging properly (Chapter 5).
5   Loose, broken or faulty wiring in the charging circuit (Chapter 5).
6   Short in the vehicle wiring causing a continual drain on the battery.
7   Battery defective internally.

17   Ignition light fails to go out

1   Fault in alternator or charging circuit (Chapter 5).
2   Alternator drivebelt defective or not properly adjusted (Chapter 1).

18   Ignition light fails to come on when key is turned on

1   Warning light bulb defective (Chapter 12).
2   Alternator faulty (Chapter 5).
3   Fault in the printed circuit, dash wiring or bulb holder (Chapter 12).

19   "Check engine" light comes on

See Chapter 6

Fuel system

20   Excessive fuel consumption

1   Dirty or clogged air filter element (Chapter 1).
2   Incorrectly set ignition timing (Chapter 1).
3   Choke sticking or improperly adjusted (Chapter 1).
4   Emissions system not functioning properly (not all vehicles, see Chapter 6).
5   Carburetor idle speed and/or mixture not adjusted properly (Chapter 1).
6   Carburetor/fuel injection internal parts excessively worn or damaged (Chapter 4).
7   Low tire pressure or incorrect tire size (Chapter 1).

21   Fuel leakage and/or fuel odor

1   Leak in a fuel feed or vent line (Chapter 4).
2   Tank overfilled. Fill only to automatic shut-off.
3   Emissions system filter clogged (Chapter 1).
4   Vapor leaks from system lines (Chapter 4).
5   Carburetor/fuel injection internal parts excessively worn or out of adjustment (Chapter 4).

Cooling system

22   Overheating

1   Insufficient coolant in system (Chapter 1).
2   Water pump drivebelt defective or not adjusted properly (Chapter 1).
3   Radiator core blocked or radiator grille dirty and restricted (Chapter 3).
4   Thermostat faulty (Chapter 3).
5   Fan blades broken or cracked (Chapter 3).
6   Radiator cap not maintaining proper pressure. Have cap pressure tested by a service station or repair shop.
7   Ignition timing incorrect (Chapter 1).

23   Overcooling

1   Thermostat faulty (Chapter 3).
2   Inaccurate temperature gauge (Chapter 12)

24   External coolant leakage

1   Deteriorated or damaged hoses or loose clamps. Replace hoses and/or tighten clamps at hose connections (Chapter 1).
2   Water pump seals defective. If this is the case, water will drip from the weep hole in the water pump body (Chapter 1).
3   Leakage from radiator core or header tank. This will require the radiator to be professionally repaired (see Chapter 3 for removal procedures).
4   Engine drain plugs or water jacket core plugs leaking (see Chapter 2).

25   Internal coolant leakage

Note: *Internal coolant leaks can usually be detected by examining the oil. Check the dipstick and inside of the rocker arm cover for water deposits and milky oil.*
1   Leaking cylinder head gasket. Have the cooling system pressure tested.
2   Cracked cylinder bore or cylinder head. Dismantle engine and inspect (Chapter 2).

26   Coolant loss

1   Too much coolant in system (Chapter 1).
2   Coolant boiling away due to overheating (see Section 16).
3   Internal or external leakage (see Sections 26 and 27).
4   Faulty radiator cap. Have the cap pressure tested.

27   Poor coolant circulation

1   Inoperative water pump. A quick test is to pinch the top radiator hose closed with your hand while the engine is idling, then let it loose. You should feel the surge of coolant if the pump is working properly (Chapter 1).
2   Restriction in cooling system. Drain, flush and refill the system (Chapter 1). If necessary, remove the radiator (Chapter 3) and have it reverse flushed.
3   Water pump drivebelt defective or not adjusted properly (Chapter 1).
4   Thermostat sticking (Chapter 3).

Automatic transmission

Note: *Due to the complexity of the automatic transmission, it is difficult for the home mechanic to properly diagnose and service this component. For problems other than the following, the vehicle should be taken to a dealer service department or reputable repair shop.*

28   General shift mechanism problems

1   Chapter 7 deals with checking and adjusting the shift linkage on automatic transmissions. Common problems which may be attributed to poorly adjusted linkage are:
   Engine starting in gears other than Park or Neutral.
   Indicator on shifter pointing to a gear other than the one actually being used.
   Vehicle moves when in Park.
2   Refer to Chapter 7 to adjust the linkage.

**29   Transmission will not downshift with accelerator
        pedal pressed to the floor**

Chapter 7 deals with adjusting the TV cable to enable the transmission to downshift properly.

30   Transmission slips, shifts rough, is noisy or has no drive in forward or reverse gears

1   There are many probable causes for the above problems, but the home mechanic should be concerned with only one possibility – fluid level.
2   Before taking the vehicle to a repair shop, check the level and condition of the fluid as described in Chapter 1. Correct fluid level as necessary or change the fluid and filter if needed. If the problem persists, have a professional diagnose the probable cause.

31   Fluid leakage

1   Automatic transmission fluid is a deep red color. Fluid leaks should not be confused with engine oil, which can easily be blown by air flow to the transmission.
2   To pinpoint a leak, first remove all built-up dirt and grime from around the transmission. Degreasing agents and/or steam cleaning will achieve this. With the underside clean, drive the vehicle at low speeds so air flow will not blow the leak far from its source. Raise the vehicle and determine where the leak is coming from. Common areas of leakage are:

   a) *Pan: Tighten mounting bolts and/or replace pan gasket as necessary (see Chapters 1 and 7).*
   b) *Filler pipe: Replace the rubber seal where pipe enters transmission case.*
   c) *Transmission oil lines: Tighten connectors where lines enter transmission case and/or replace lines.*
   d) *Vent pipe: Transmission overfilled and/or water in fluid (see checking procedures, Chapter 1).*
   e) *Speedometer connector: Replace the O-ring where speedometer cable enters transmission case (Chapter 7).*

Driveshaft

32   Oil leak at front of driveshaft

Defective transmission rear oil seal. See Chapter 7 for replacement procedures. While this is done, check the splined yoke for burrs or a rough condition which may be damaging the seal. This can be removed with crocus cloth or a fine whetstone.

33   Knock or clunk when the transmission is under initial load (just after transmission is put into gear)

1   Loose or disconnected rear suspension components. Check all mounting bolts, nuts and bushings (Chapter 10).
2   Loose driveshaft bolts. Inspect all bolts and nuts and tighten them to the specified torque.
3   Splined driveshaft in need of lubrication (Chapter 1).
4   Worn or damaged universal joint bearings. Check for wear (Chapter 8).

34   Metallic grating sound consistent with vehicle speed

Pronounced wear in the universal joint bearings. Check as described in Chapter 8.

35   Vibration

Note: *Before assuming that the driveshaft is at fault, make sure the tires are perfectly balanced and perform the following test.*

1   Install a tachometer inside the vehicle to monitor engine speed as the vehicle is driven. Drive the vehicle and note the engine speed at which the vibration (roughness) is most pronounced. Now shift the transmission to a different gear and bring the engine speed to the the same point.
2   If the vibration occurs at the same engine speed (rpm) regardless of which gear the transmission is in, the driveshaft is NOT at fault since the driveshaft speed varies.
3   If the vibration decreases or is eliminated when the transmission is in a different gear at the same engine speed, refer to the following probable causes.
4   Bent or dented driveshaft. Inspect and replace as necessary (Chapter 8).
5   Undercoating or built-up dirt, etc. on the driveshaft. Clean the shaft thoroughly and recheck.
6   Worn universal joint bearings. Remove and inspect (Chapter 8).
7   Driveshaft and/or companion flange out of balance. Check for missing weights on the shaft. Remove the driveshaft (Chapter 8) and reinstall 180-degrees from original position, then retest. Have the driveshaft professionally balanced if the problem persists.

Rear axle

36   Noise

1   Road noise. No corrective procedures available.
2   Tire noise. Inspect the tires and check tire pressures (see Chapter 1).
3   Rear wheel bearings loose, worn or damaged (Chapter 10).

37   Vibration

See probable causes under Driveshaft. Proceed under the guidelines listed for the driveshaft. If the problem persists, check the rear wheel bearings by raising the rear of the vehicle and spinning the wheels by hand. Listen for evidence of rough (noisy) bearings. Remove and inspect (Chapter 8).

38   Oil leakage

1   Pinion seal damaged (Chapter 8).
2   Axleshaft oil seals damaged (Chapter 8).
3   Differential inspection cover leaking. Tighten the bolts or replace the gasket as required (Chapter 8).

Brakes

Note: *Before assuming that a brake problem exists, make sure that the tires are in good condition and inflated properly (see Chapter 1), that the front end alignment is correct and that the vehicle is not loaded with weight in an unequal manner.*

39   Vehicle pulls to one side during braking

1   Defective, damaged or oil contaminated brake pads or shoes on one side. Inspect as described in Chapter 9.
2   Excessive wear of brake shoe or pad material or drum/disc on one side. Inspect and correct as necessary.
3   Loose or disconnected front suspension components. Inspect and tighten all bolts to the specified torque (Chapter 10).

4   Defective drum brake or caliper assembly. Remove the drum or caliper and inspect for a stuck piston or other damage (Chapter 9).

40   Noise (high-pitched squeal with the brakes applied)

Disc brake pads worn out. The noise comes from the wear sensor rubbing against the disc (does not apply to all vehicles). Replace the pads with new ones immediately (Chapter 9).

41   Excessive brake pedal travel

1   Partial brake system failure. Inspect the entire system (Chapter 9) and correct as required.
2   Insufficient fluid in the master cylinder. Check (Chapter 1), add fluid and bleed the system if necessary (Chapter 9).
3   Brakes not adjusting properly. Make a series of starts and stops with the vehicle is in Reverse. If this does not correct the situation, remove the drums and inspect the self-adjusters (Chapter 9).

42   Brake pedal feels spongy when depressed

1   Air in the hydraulic lines. Bleed the brake system (Chapter 9).
2   Faulty flexible hoses. Inspect all system hoses and lines. Replace parts as necessary.
3   Master cylinder mounting bolts/nuts loose.
4   Master cylinder defective (Chapter 9).

43   Excessive effort required to stop vehicle

1   Power brake booster not operating properly (Chapter 9).
2   Excessively worn linings or pads. Inspect and replace if necessary (Chapter 9).
3   One or more caliper pistons or wheel cylinders seized or sticking. Inspect and rebuild as required (Chapter 9).
4   Brake linings or pads contaminated with oil or grease. Inspect and replace as required (Chapter 9).
5   New pads or shoes installed and not yet seated. It will take a while for the new material to seat against the drum (or disc).

44   Pedal travels to the floor with little resistance

Little or no fluid in the master cylinder reservoir caused by leaking wheel cylinder(s), leaking caliper piston(s), loose, damaged or disconnected brake lines. Inspect the entire system and correct as necessary.

45   Brake pedal pulsates during brake application

1   Wheel bearings not adjusted properly or in need of replacement (Chapter 1).
2   Caliper not sliding properly due to improper installation or obstructions. Remove and inspect (Chapter 9).
3   Rotor or drum defective. Remove the rotor or drum (Chapter 9) and check for excessive lateral runout, out of round and parallelism. Have the drum or rotor resurfaced or replace it with a new one.

Suspension and steering systems

46   Vehicle pulls to one side

1   Tire pressures uneven (Chapter 1).
2   Defective tire (Chapter 1).
3   Excessive wear in suspension or steering components (Chapter 10).
4   Front end in need of alignment.
5   Front brakes dragging. Inspect the brakes as described in Chapter 9.

47   Shimmy, shake or vibration

1   Tire or wheel out-of-balance or out-of-round. Have professionally balanced.
2   Loose, worn or out-of-adjustment wheel bearings (Chapters 1 and 8).
3   Shock absorbers and/or suspension components worn or damaged (Chapter 10).

48   Excessive pitching and/or rolling around corners or during braking

1   Defective shock absorbers. Replace as a set (Chapter 10).
2   Broken or weak springs and/or suspension components. Inspect as described in Chapter 10.

49   Excessively stiff steering

1   Lack of fluid in power steering fluid reservoir (Chapter 1).
2   Incorrect tire pressures (Chapter 1).
3   Lack of lubrication at steering joints (Chapter 1).
4   Front end out of alignment.
5   See also section titled *Lack of power assistance*.

50   Excessive play in steering

1   Loose front wheel bearings (Chapter 1).
2   Excessive wear in suspension or steering components (Chapter 10).
3   Steering gearbox out of adjustment (Chapter 10).

51   Lack of power assistance

1   Steering pump drivebelt faulty or not adjusted properly (Chapter 1).
2   Fluid level low (Chapter 1).
3   Hoses or lines restricted. Inspect and replace parts as necessary.
4   Air in power steering system. Bleed the system (Chapter 10).

52   Excessive tire wear (not specific to one area)

1   Incorrect tire pressures (Chapter 1).
2   Tires out of balance. Have professionally balanced.
3   Wheels damaged. Inspect and replace as necessary.
4   Suspension or steering components excessively worn (Chapter 10).

53   Excessive tire wear on outside edge

1   Inflation pressures incorrect (Chapter 1).
2   Excessive speed in turns.

3 Front end alignment incorrect (excessive toe-in). Have professionally aligned.
4 Suspension arm bent or twisted (Chapter 10).

---

54 Excessive tire wear on inside edge

1 Inflation pressures incorrect (Chapter 1).

2 Front end alignment incorrect (toe-out). Have professionally aligned.
3 Loose or damaged steering components (Chapter 10).

---

55 Tire tread worn in one place

1 Tires out of balance.
2 Damaged or buckled wheel. Inspect and replace if necessary.
3 Defective tire (Chapter 1).

Chapter 1   Tune-up and routine maintenance

Contents

Specifications

Recommended lubricants and fluids

Engine oil type	API grade SG or SG/CC multigrade and fuel efficient oil
Viscosity	See accompanying chart
Automatic transmission fluid type	Dexron II automatic transmission fluid
Differential lubricant type	SAE 80W or 80W-90 GL-5 gear lubricant
Limited slip or controlled differential	Add GM limited slip additive to the specified lubricant
Brake fluid type	DOT 3 brake fluid
Power steering fluid type	GM power steering fluid or equivalent

---

RECOMMENDED SAE VISCOSITY GRADE ENGINE OILS

FOR BEST FUEL ECONOMY AND COLD STARTING, SELECT THE LOWEST SAE VISCOSITY GRADE OIL FOR THE EXPECTED TEMPERATURE RANGE

LOOK FOR THIS LABEL

Ignition system

Spark plug type and gap	Refer to the tune-up decal or VECI label in the engine compartment
Ignition timing	Refer to the tune-up decal or VECI label in the engine compartment
Ignition point gap	
New	0.019 in
Used	0.016 in
Dwell angle	30-degrees

Engine firing order

V6 engine	1-6-5-4-3-2
V8 engine	
368, 425, 472 and 500 cu in	1-5-6-3-4-2-7-8
All others	1-8-4-3-6-5-7-2

Brakes

Disc brake pad lining thickness (minimum)	1/8 in
Drum brake shoe lining thickness (minimum)	1/16 in

Torque specifications

	Ft-lbs
Automatic transmission pan bolts	12
Carburetor/throttle body mounting nuts/bolts	10 to 15
Differential cover bolts	10 to 20
Spark plugs	15
Wheel lug nuts	
1970 through 1976	100 to 130
1977 on	90 to 100

Typical engine compartment component layout (viewed from the front of the vehicle)

1   Air cleaner housing
2   Brake fluid reservoir
3   Windshield washer fluid
     reservoir
4   Oil dipstick
5   Upper radiator hose

6   Air conditioner drivebelt
7   Oil filler cap
8   Alternator
9   Battery
10   Engine coolant reservoir

1

Underside view of the engine/transmission

1	Radiator drain fitting	5	Steering gear	8	Shock absorber	11	Oil filter
2	Radiator	6	Tie-rod end grease fitting	9	Shift linkage	12	Exhaust pipe
3	Drivebelt and pulleys	7	Balljoint grease fitting	10	Oil drain plug	13	Brake caliper
4	Power steering hose						location

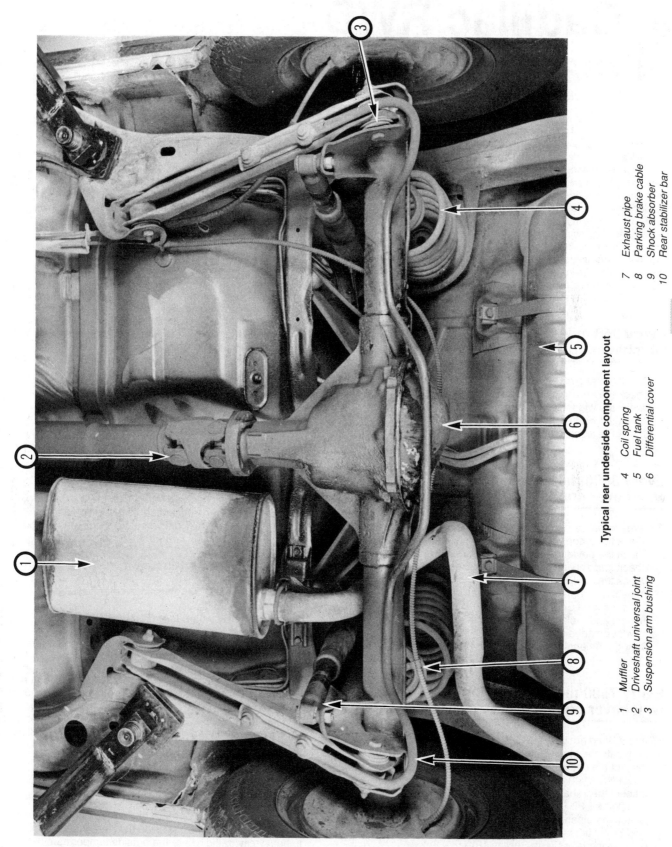

Typical rear underside component layout

1 Muffler
2 Driveshaft universal joint
3 Suspension arm bushing

4 Coil spring
5 Fuel tank
6 Differential cover

7 Exhaust pipe
8 Parking brake cable
9 Shock absorber
10 Rear stabilizer bar

1

1 Cadillac RWD maintenance schedule

The following maintenance intervals are based on the assumption that the vehicle owner will be doing the maintenance or service work, as opposed to having a dealer service department do the work. Although the time/mileage intervals are loosely based on factory recommendations, most have been shortened to ensure, for example, that such items as lubricants and fluids are checked/changed at intervals that promote maximum engine/driveline service life. Also, subject to the preference of the individual owner interested in keeping his or her vehicle in peak condition at all times, and with the vehicle's ultimate resale in mind, many of the maintenance procedures may be performed more often than recommended in the following schedule. We encourage such owner initiative.

When the vehicle is new it should be serviced initially by a factory authorized dealer service department to protect the factory warranty. In many cases the initial maintenance check is done at no cost to the owner (check with your dealer service department for more information).

Every 250 miles or weekly, whichever comes first

Check the engine oil level (see Section 4)
Check the engine coolant level (see Section 4)
Check the windshield washer fluid level (see Section 4)
Check the brake fluid level (see Section 4)
Check the tires and tire pressures (see Section 5)

Every 3000 miles or 3 months, whichever comes first

All items listed above plus:
Check the automatic transmission fluid level (see Section 6)
Check the power steering fluid level (see Section 7)
Check and service the battery (see Section 8)
Check the cooling system (see Section 9)
Inspect and replace, if necessary, all underhood hoses (see Section 10)
Inspect and replace, if necessary, the windshield wiper blades (see Section 11)
Change the engine oil and oil filter (see Section 12)

Every 7500 miles or 12 months whichever comes first

All items listed above plus:
Lubricate the chassis components (see Section 13)
Inspect the suspension and steering components (see Section 14)*
Inspect the exhaust system (see Section 15)*
Check the EFE (heat riser) system (see Section 16)*
Check the differential lubricant level (see Section 17)*
Rotate the tires (see Section 18)
Check the brakes (see Section 19)*
Inspect the fuel system (see Section 20)
Check the carburetor choke operation – if equipped (see Section 21)

Check the carburetor/throttle body mounting nut torque (see Section 22)
Check the throttle linkage (see Section 23)
Check the thermostatically-controlled air cleaner (see Section 24)
Check the engine drivebelts (see Section 25)
Check the seatbelts (see Section 26)
Check the Neutral start switch (see Section 27)

Every 12,000 miles or 15 months, whichever comes first

All items listed above plus:
Replace the ignition contact points (if equipped) an adjust the dwell angle (see Section 28)
Check and adjust, if necessary, the engine idle speed (see Section 29)
Replace the fuel filter (see Section 30)
Replace the air filter and PCV filter (see Section 31)
Check and adjust if necessary the ignition timing (see Section 32)

Every 30,000 miles or 24 months, whichever comes first

All items listed above plus:
Change the automatic transmission fluid (see Section 33)**
Change the differential lubricant (see Section 34)
Check and repack the front wheel bearings (see Section 35)
Service the cooling system (drain, flush and refill) (see Section 36)
Inspect and replace, if necessary, the PCV valve (see Section 37)
Inspect the evaporative emissions control system (see Section 38)
Check the EGR system (see Section 39)
Replace the spark plugs (see Section 40)
Inspect the spark plug wires, distributor cap and rotor (see Sections 41 and 42)

* This item is affected by "severe" operating conditions as described below. If your vehicle is operated under severe conditions, perform all maintenance indicated with an asterisk (*) at 3000-mile/3 month intervals. Severe conditions are indicated if you mainly operate the vehicle under one or more of the following:
In dusty areas
Towing a trailer
Idling for extended periods and/or low speed operation
When outside temperatures remain below freezing and when most trips are less than four miles

** If operated under one or more of the following conditions, change the automatic transmission fluid every 12,000 miles:
In heavy city traffic where the outside temperature regularly reaches 90-degrees F (32-degrees C) or higher
In hilly or mountainous terrain
Frequent trailer pulling

2 Introduction

This Chapter is designed to help the home mechanic maintain Cadillac rear wheel drive models with the goals of maximum performance, economy, safety and reliability in mind.

Included is a master maintenance schedule (page 32), followed by procedures dealing specifically with each item on the schedule. Visual checks, adjustments, component replacement and other helpful items are included. Refer to the accompanying illustrations of the engine compartment and the underside of the vehicle for the locations of various components.

Servicing your vehicle in accordance with the mileage/time maintenance schedule and the step-by-step procedures will result in a planned maintenance program that should produce a long and reliable service life. Keep in mind that it is a comprehensive plan, so maintaining some items but not others at the specified intervals will not produce the same results.

As you service your vehicle, you will discover that many of the procedures can – and should – be grouped together because of the nature of the particular procedure you're performing or because of the close proximity of two otherwise unrelated components to one another.

For example, if the vehicle is raised for chassis lubrication, you should inspect the exhaust, suspension, steering and fuel systems while you're under the vehicle. When you're rotating the tires, it makes good sense to check the brakes since the wheels are already removed. Finally, let's suppose you have to borrow or rent a torque wrench. Even if you only need it to tighten the spark plugs, you might as well check the torque of as many critical fasteners as time allows.

The first step in this maintenance program is to prepare yourself before the actual work begins. Read through all the procedures you're planning to do, then gather up all the parts and tools needed. If it looks as if you might run into problems during a particular job, seek advice from a mechanic or an experienced do-it-yourselfer.

3 Tune-up general information

The term tune-up is used in this manual to represent a combination of individual operations rather than one specific procedure.

If, from the time the vehicle is new, the routine maintenance schedule is followed closely and frequent checks are made of fluid levels and high wear items, as suggested throughout this manual, the engine will be kept in relatively good running condition and the need for additional work will be minimized.

More likely than not, however, there will be times when the engine is running poorly due to lack of regular maintenance. This is even more likely if a used vehicle, which has not received regular and frequent maintenance checks, is purchased. In such cases, an engine tune-up will be needed outside of the regular routine maintenance intervals.

The first step in any tune-up or diagnostic procedure to help correct a poor running engine is a cylinder compression check. A compression check (see Chapter 2, Part C) will help determine the condition of internal engine components and should be used as a guide for tune-up and repair procedures. If, for instance, a compression check indicates serious internal engine wear, a conventional tune-up will not improve the performance of the engine and would be a waste of time and money. Because of its importance, the compression check should be done by someone with the right equipment and the knowledge to use it properly.

The following procedures are those most often needed to bring a generally poor running engine back into a proper state of tune.

Minor tune-up

Check all engine related fluids (see Section 4)
Clean, inspect and test the battery (see Section 8)
Check and adjust the drivebelts (see Section 25)
Replace the spark plugs (see Section 40)
Inspect the distributor cap and rotor (see Section 42)
Inspect the spark plug and coil wires (see Section 41)

Check and adjust the ignition timing (see Section 32)
Check the PCV valve (see Section 37)
Check the air and PCV filters (see Section 31)
Check the cooling system (see Section 9)
Check all underhood hoses (see Section 10)

Major tune-up

All items listed under Minor tune-up plus . . .
Check the EGR system (see Section 39)
Check the ignition system (see Chapter 5)
Check the charging system (see Chapter 5)
Check the fuel system (see Section 20)
Replace the air and PCV filters (see Section 31)
Replace the distributor cap and rotor (see Section 42)
Replace the spark plug wires (see Section 41)
Replace the ignition points (see Section 28)

4 Fluid level checks

Note: *The following are fluid level checks to be done on a 250 mile or weekly basis. Additional fluid level checks can be found in specific maintenance procedures which follow. Regardless of intervals, be alert to fluid leaks under the vehicle which would indicate a fault to be corrected immediately.*

1 Fluids are an essential part of the lubrication, cooling, brake and windshield washer systems. Because the fluids gradually become depleted and/or contaminated during normal operation of the vehicle, they must be periodically replenished. See Recommended lubricants and fluids at the beginning of this Chapter before adding fluid to any of the following components. **Note:** *The vehicle must be on level ground when fluid levels are checked.*

Engine oil

Refer to illustrations 4.4a, 4.4b and 4.6

2 The engine oil level is checked with a dipstick that extends through a tube and into the oil pan at the bottom of the engine.
3 The oil level should be checked before the vehicle has been driven, or about 15 minutes after the engine has been shut off. If the oil is checked immediately after driving the vehicle, some of the oil will remain in the upper engine components, resulting in an inaccurate reading on the dipstick.
4 Pull the dipstick from the tube and wipe all the oil from the end with a clean rag or paper towel **(see illustration)**. Insert the clean dipstick all the

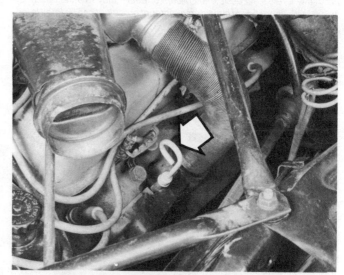

4.4a **The engine oil dipstick on most models is located on the left side of the engine, toward the front (arrow)**

OPERATING
RANGE

FULL

ADD

4.4b   The oil level must be maintained between the marks at all times – it takes one quart of oil to raise the level from the ADD mark to the FULL mark

4.6   Oil is added to the engine after removing the twist-off cap

way back into the tube, then pull it out again. Note the oil at the end of the dipstick. Add oil as necessary to keep the level between the ADD mark and the FULL mark on the dipstick **(see illustration)**.

5   Do not overfill the engine's lubricating system by adding too much oil, since this may result in oil fouled spark plugs, oil leaks or oil seal failures.

6   Oil is added to the engine after removing a twist-off cap **(see illustration)**. A funnel may help to reduce spills.

7   Checking the oil level is an important preventive maintenance step. A consistently low oil level indicates oil leakage through damaged seals, defective gaskets or past worn rings or valve guides. If the oil looks milky in color or has water droplets in it, the cylinder head gasket(s) may be blown or the head(s) or block may be cracked. The engine should be checked immediately. The condition of the oil should also be checked. Whenever you check the oil level, slide your thumb and index finger up the dipstick before wiping off the oil. If you see small dirt or metal particles clinging to the dipstick, the oil should be changed (see Section 12).

Engine coolant

Refer to illustrations 4.10a and 4.10b

Warning: *Do not allow antifreeze to come in contact with your skin or painted surfaces of the vehicle. Flush contaminated areas immediately with plenty of water. Don't store new coolant or leave old coolant lying around where it's accessible to children or pets – they're attracted by its sweet taste. Ingestion of even a small amount of coolant can be fatal! Wipe*

up garage floor and drip pan coolant spills immediately. Keep antifreeze containers covered, and repair leaks in your cooling system immediately.

8   Most vehicles covered by this manual are equipped with a pressurized coolant recovery system. A white plastic coolant reservoir located in the engine compartment is connected by a hose to the radiator filler neck. If the engine overheats, coolant escapes through a valve in the radiator cap and travels through the hose into the reservoir. As the engine cools, the coolant is automatically drawn back into the cooling system to maintain the correct level.

9   If your particular vehicle is not equipped with a coolant recovery system, the level should be checked by removing the radiator cap. However, the cap should not under any circumstances be removed while the system is hot, as escaping steam could cause serious injury. Wait until the engine has completely cooled, then wrap a thick cloth around the cap and turn it to its first stop. If any steam escapes from the cap, allow the engine to cool further. Then remove the cap and check the level in the radiator. It should be about two to three inches below the bottom of the filler neck.

10   The coolant level in the reservoir should be checked regularly. **Warning:** *Do not remove the radiator cap to check the coolant level when the engine is warm.* The level in the reservoir varies with the temperature of the engine. When the engine is hot, the coolant level should be at or near the FULL mark **(see illustration)**. If it isn't, allow the engine to cool, then remove the cap from the reservoir and add a 50/50 mixture of ethylene glycol-based antifreeze and water **(see illustration)**.

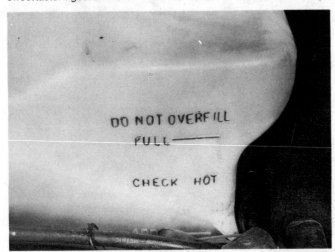

4.10a   Check the coolant level with the engine hot – it should be visible through the translucent reservoir

4.10b   To add coolant, pop the top off the reservoir

4.15   The washer fluid reservoir is normally located at the left rear of the engine compartment – to add fluid, pop off the top

4.19a   Early models have a cast iron brake master cylinder with a cover which must be removed to check the fluid level – use a screwdriver to unsnap the retainer

11   Drive the vehicle and recheck the coolant level. If only a small amount of coolant is required to bring the system up to the proper level, water can be used. However, repeated additions of water will dilute the antifreeze and water solution. In order to maintain the proper ratio of antifreeze and water, always top up the coolant level with the correct mixture. An empty plastic milk jug or bleach bottle makes an excellent container for mixing coolant. Do not use rust inhibitors or additives.

12   If the coolant level drops consistently, there may be a leak in the system. Inspect the radiator, hoses, filler cap, drain plugs and water pump (see Section 9). If no leaks are noted, have the radiator cap pressure tested by a service station.

13   If you have to remove the radiator cap, wait until the engine has cooled, then wrap a thick cloth around the cap and turn it to the first stop. If coolant or steam escapes, let the engine cool down longer, then remove the cap.

14   Check the condition of the coolant as well. It should be relatively clear. If it's brown or rust colored, the system should be drained, flushed and refilled. Even if the coolant appears to be normal, the corrosion inhibitors wear out, so it must be replaced at the specified intervals.

4.19b   On early models, keep the brake fluid level 1/4-inch below the top edge of the reservoir

Windshield washer fluid

Refer to illustration 4.15

15   Fluid for the windshield washer system is located in a plastic reservoir in the engine compartment **(see illustration)**.

16   In milder climates, plain water can be used in the reservoir, but it should be kept no more than two-thirds full to allow for expansion if the water freezes. In colder climates, use windshield washer system antifreeze, available at any auto parts store, to lower the freezing point of the fluid. Mix the antifreeze with water in accordance with the manufacturer's directions on the container. **Caution:** *Don't use cooling system antifreeze – it will damage the vehicle's paint.*

17   To help prevent icing in cold weather, warm the windshield with the defroster before using the washer.

Battery electrolyte

18   Most vehicles with which this manual is concerned are equipped with a battery which is permanently sealed (except for vent holes) and has no filler caps. Water doesn't have to be added to these batteries at any time. If a maintenance-type battery is installed, the caps on the top of the battery should be removed periodically to check for a low water level. This check is most critical during the warm summer months.

Brake fluid

Refer to illustrations 4.19a, 4.19b and 4.20

19   The brake master cylinder is mounted on the front of the power booster unit in the engine compartment. On earlier models it will be necessary to remove the reservoir cover to check the fluid level **(see illustrations)**.

20   The fluid inside on later models is readily visible. The level should be above the MIN marks on the reservoirs **(see illustration)**. If a low level is indicated, be sure to wipe the top of the reservoir cover with a clean rag to prevent contamination of the brake and/or clutch system before removing the cover.

4.20   On later models, the fluid level inside the brake reservoirs is easily checked by observing the level from outside – fluid can be added to the reservoir after the cover is removed by prying up on the tabs

5.2   A tire tread depth indicator should be used to monitor tire wear – they are available at auto parts stores and service stations and cost very little

21   When adding fluid, pour it carefully into the reservoir to avoid spilling it onto surrounding painted surfaces. Be sure the specified fluid is used, since mixing different types of brake fluid can cause damage to the system. See Recommended lubricants and fluids at the front of this Chapter or your owner's manual. **Warning:** *Brake fluid can harm your eyes and damage painted surfaces, so use extreme caution when handling or pouring it. Do not use brake fluid that has been standing open or is more than one year old. Brake fluid absorbs moisture from the air. Excess moisture can cause a dangerous loss of braking effectiveness.*

22   At this time the fluid and master cylinder can be inspected for contamination. The system should be drained and refilled if deposits, dirt particles or water droplets are seen in the fluid.

23   After filling the reservoir to the proper level, make sure the cover is on tight to prevent fluid leakage.

24   The brake fluid level in the master cylinder will drop slightly as the pads and the brake shoes at each wheel wear down during normal operation. If the master cylinder requires repeated additions to keep it at the proper level, it's an indication of leakage in the brake system, which should be corrected immediately. Check all brake lines and connections (see Section 17 for more information).

25   If, upon checking the master cylinder fluid level, you discover one or both reservoirs empty or nearly empty, the brake system should be bled (see Chapter 9).

5   Tire and tire pressure checks

Refer to illustrations 5.2, 5.3, 5.4a, 5.4b and 5.8

1   Periodic inspection of the tires may spare you the inconvenience of being stranded with a flat tire. It can also provide you with vital information regarding possible problems in the steering and suspension systems before major damage occurs.

2   The original tires on this vehicle are equipped with 1/2-inch side bands that will appear when tread depth reaches 1/16-inch, but they don't appear until the tires are worn out. Tread wear can be monitored with a simple, inexpensive device known as a tread depth indicator **(see illustration)**.

3   Note any abnormal tread wear **(see illustration)**. Tread pattern irregularities such as cupping, flat spots and more wear on one side than the other are indications of front end alignment and/or balance problems. If any of these conditions are noted, take the vehicle to a tire shop or service station to correct the problem.

Condition	Probable cause	Corrective action	Condition	Probable cause	Corrective action
Shoulder wear	• Underinflation (both sides wear) • Incorrect wheel camber (one side wear) • Hard cornering • Lack of rotation	• Measure and adjust pressure. • Repair or replace axle and suspension parts. • Reduce speed. • Rotate tires.	Feathered edge Toe wear	• Incorrect toe	• Adjust toe-in.
Center wear	• Overinflation • Lack of rotation	• Measure and adjust pressure. • Rotate tires.	Uneven wear	• Incorrect camber or caster • Malfunctioning suspension • Unbalanced wheel • Out-of-round brake drum • Lack of rotation	• Repair or replace axle and suspension parts. • Repair or replace suspension parts. • Balance or replace. • Turn or replace. • Rotate tires.

5.3   This chart will help you determine the condition of your tires, the probable cause(s) of abnormal wear and the corrective action necessary

5.4a   If a tire loses air on a steady basis, check the valve core first to make sure it's snug (special inexpensive wrenches are commonly available at auto parts stores)

5.4b   If the valve core is tight, raise the corner of the vehicle with the low tire and spray a soapy water solution onto the tread as the tire is turned slowly – slow leaks will cause small bubbles to appear

5.8   To extend the life of your tires, check the air pressure at least once a week with an accurate gauge (don't forget the spare!)

4   Look closely for cuts, punctures and embedded nails or tacks. Sometimes a tire will hold air pressure for a short time or leak down very slowly after a nail has embedded itself in the tread. If a slow leak persists, check the valve stem core to make sure it's tight **(see illustration)**. Examine the tread for an object that may have embedded itself in the tire or for a "plug" that may have begun to leak (radial tire punctures are repaired with a plug that's installed in a puncture). If a puncture is suspected, it can be easily verified by spraying a solution of soapy water onto the puncture area **(see illustration)**. The soapy solution will bubble if there's a leak. Unless the puncture is unusually large, a tire shop or service station can usually repair the tire.
5   Carefully inspect the inner sidewall of each tire for evidence of brake fluid leakage. If you see any, inspect the brakes immediately.
6   Correct air pressure adds miles to the lifespan of the tires, improves mileage and enhances overall ride quality. Tire pressure cannot be accurately estimated by looking at a tire, especially if it's a radial. A tire pressure gauge is essential. Keep an accurate gauge in the vehicle. The pressure gauges attached to the nozzles of air hoses at gas stations are often inaccurate.
7   Always check tire pressure when the tires are cold. Cold, in this case, means the vehicle has not been driven over a mile in the three hours preceding a tire pressure check. A pressure rise of four to eight pounds is not uncommon once the tires are warm.
8   Unscrew the valve cap protruding from the wheel or hubcap and push the gauge firmly onto the valve stem **(see illustration)**. Note the reading on the gauge and compare the figure to the recommended tire pressure shown on the placard on the driver's side door pillar. Be sure to reinstall the valve cap to keep dirt and moisture out of the valve stem mechanism. Check all four tires and, if necessary, add enough air to bring them up to the recommended pressure.
9   Don't forget to keep the spare tire inflated to the specified pressure (refer to your owner's manual or the tire sidewall). Note that the pressure recommended for the compact spare is higher than for the tires on the vehicle.

6   Automatic transmission fluid level check

Refer to illustrations 6.3 and 6.6
1   The automatic transmission fluid level should be carefully maintained. Low fluid level can lead to slipping or loss of drive, while overfilling can cause foaming and loss of fluid.
2   With the parking brake set, start the engine, then move the shift lever through all the gear ranges, ending in Park. The fluid level must be checked with the vehicle level and the engine running at idle. **Note:** *Incorrect fluid level readings will result if the vehicle has just been driven at high*

6.3   The automatic transmission dipstick is located at the rear of the engine compartment, usually on the right side

speeds for an extended period, in hot weather in city traffic, or if it has been pulling a trailer. If any of these conditions apply, wait until the fluid has cooled (about 30 minutes).
3   With the transmission at normal operating temperature, remove the dipstick from the filler tube **(see illustration)**. The dipstick is located at the rear of the engine compartment on the passenger's side on most models.

6.6   When checking the automatic transmission fluid level,
it is important to note the fluid temperature

7.2   The power steering fluid reservoir is located near the front of
the engine – twist the cap counterclockwise to remove it

If the fluid at the end of the dipstick is a dark reddish-brown color, or if it
smells burned, it should be changed. If you are in doubt about the condition of the fluid, purchase some new fluid and compare the two for color
and smell.

7.6   The markings on the power steering fluid dipstick
indicate the safe range

7   Power steering fluid level check

Refer to illustrations 7.2 and 7.6

1   Unlike manual steering, the power steering system relies on fluid
which may, over a period of time, require replenishing.
2   The fluid reservoir for the power steering pump is located on the pump
body at the front of the engine **(see illustration)**.
3   For the check, the front wheels should be pointed straight ahead and
the engine should be off.
4   Use a clean rag to wipe off the reservoir cap and the area around the
cap. This will help prevent any foreign matter from entering the reservoir
during the check.
5   Twist off the cap and check the temperature of the fluid at the end of
the dipstick with your finger.
6   Wipe off the fluid with a clean rag, reinsert the dipstick, then withdraw
it and read the fluid level. The level should be at the HOT mark if the fluid is
hot to the touch **(see illustration)**. It should be at the COLD mark if the
fluid is cool to the touch. Never allow the fluid level to drop below the ADD
mark.
7   If additional fluid is required, pour the specified type directly into the
reservoir, using a funnel to prevent spills.
8   If the reservoir requires frequent fluid additions, all power steering
hoses, hose connections and the power steering pump should be carefully
checked for leaks.

4   Carefully touch the fluid at the end of the dipstick to determine if it is
cool, warm or hot. Wipe the fluid from the dipstick with a clean rag and
push it back into the filler tube until the cap seats.
5   Pull the dipstick out again and note the fluid level.
6   If the fluid feels cool, the level should be about 1/8 to 3/8-inch below
the ADD mark **(see illustration)**. If it feels warm, the level should be near
the lower part of the operating range. If the fluid is hot, the level should be
near the FULL HOT mark. If additional fluid is required, add it directly into
the tube using a funnel. It takes about one pint to raise the level from the
ADD mark to the FULL HOT mark with a hot transmission, so add the fluid
a little at a time and keep checking the level until it's correct.
7   The condition of the fluid should also be checked along with the level.

8   Battery check and maintenance

Refer to illustrations 8.1, 8.4 and 8.6
Warning: *Certain precautions must be followed when checking and servicing the battery. Hydrogen gas, which is highly flammable, is always present in the battery cells, so keep lighted tobacco and all other open flames
and sparks away from the battery. The electrolyte inside the battery is actually dilute sulfuric acid, which will cause injury if splashed on your skin or
in your eyes. It will also ruin clothes and painted surfaces. When removing
the battery cables, always detach the negative cable first and hook it up
last!*

8.4   Remove the cell caps to check the water level in the battery – if the level is low, add distilled water only

1

8.1   Tools and materials required for battery maintenance

1   **Face shield/safety goggles** – When removing corrosion with a brush, the acidic particles can easily fly up into your eyes
2   **Rubber gloves** – Another safety item to consider when servicing the battery; remember that's acid inside the battery!
3   **Battery terminal cable cleaner** – This wire brush cleaning tool will remove all traces of corrosion from the battery and cable
4   **Treated felt washers** – Placing one of these on each terminal, directly under the cable end, will help prevent corrosion (be sure to get the correct type for side terminal batteries)
5   **Baking soda** – A solution of baking soda and water can be used to neutralize corrosion
6   **Petroleum jelly** – A layer of this on the battery terminal bolts will help prevent corrosion

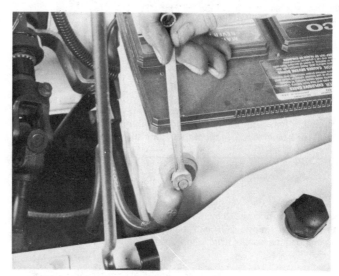

8.6   Make sure the battery terminal bolts are tight

1   Battery maintenance is an important procedure which will help ensure that you are not stranded because of a dead battery. Several tools are required for this procedure **(see illustration)**.
2   When checking/servicing the battery, always turn the engine and all accessories off.
3   A sealed (sometimes called maintenance-free), side-terminal battery is standard equipment on these vehicles. The cell caps cannot be removed, no electrolyte checks are required and water cannot be added to the cells. However, if a standard top-terminal aftermarket battery has been installed, the following maintenance procedure can be used.
4   Remove the caps and check the electrolyte level in each of the battery cells **(see illustration)**. It must be above the plates. There's usually a split-ring indicator in each cell to indicate the correct level. If the level is low, add distilled water only, then reinstall the cell caps. **Caution:** *Overfilling the cells may cause electrolyte to spill over during periods of heavy charging, causing corrosion and damage to nearby components.*

5   The external condition of the battery should be checked periodically. Look for damage such as a cracked case.
6   Check the tightness of the battery cable bolts **(see illustration)** to ensure good electrical connections. Inspect the entire length of each cable, looking for cracked or abraded insulation and frayed conductors.
7   If corrosion (visible as white, fluffy deposits) is evident, remove the cables from the terminals, clean them with a battery brush and reinstall them. Corrosion can be kept to a minimum by applying a layer of petroleum jelly or grease to the bolt threads.
8   Make sure the battery carrier is in good condition and the holddown clamp is tight. If the battery is removed (see Chapter 5 for the removal and installation procedure), make sure that no parts remain in the bottom of the carrier when it's reinstalled. When reinstalling the hold-down clamp, don't overtighten the bolt.
9   Corrosion on the carrier, battery case and surrounding areas can be removed with a solution of water and baking soda. Apply the mixture with a small brush, let it work, then rinse it off with plenty of clean water.

ALWAYS CHECK hose for chafed or burned areas that may cause an untimely and costly failure.

SOFT hose indicates inside deterioration. This deterioration can contaminate the cooling system and cause particles to clog the radiator.

HARDENED hose can fail at any time. Tightening hose clamps will not seal the connection or stop leaks.

SWOLLEN hose or oil soaked ends indicate danger and possible failure from oil or grease contamination. Squeeze the hose to locate cracks and breaks that cause leaks

9.4a   Hoses, like drivebelts, have a habit of failing at the worst possible time – to prevent the inconvenience of a blown radiator or heater hose, inspect them carefully, as shown here

9.4b   Be sure to check the underside of each hose; chafing like this, which is caused by contact with the air conditioning belt, is a common problem on the upper radiator hose – this hose should be replaced immediately

10   Any metal parts of the vehicle damaged by corrosion should be coated with a zinc-based primer, then painted.

11   Additional information on the battery, charging and jump starting can be found in the front of this manual and in Chapter 5.

9   Cooling system check

Refer to illustrations 9.4a and 9.4b

1   Many major engine failures can be attributed to a faulty cooling system. If the vehicle is equipped with an automatic transmission, the cooling system also cools the transmission fluid and thus plays an important role in prolonging transmission life.

2   The cooling system should be checked with the engine cold. Do this before the vehicle is driven for the day or after it has been shut off for at least three hours.

3   Remove the radiator cap by turning it to the left until it reaches a stop. If you hear a hissing sound (indicating there is still pressure in the system), wait until this stops. Now press down on the cap with the palm of your hand and continue turning to the left until the cap can be removed. Thoroughly clean the cap, inside and out, with clean water. Also clean the filler neck on the radiator. All traces of corrosion should be removed. The coolant inside the radiator should be relatively transparent. If it is rust colored, the system should be drained and refilled (see Section 36). If the coolant level is not up to the top, add additional antifreeze/coolant mixture (see Section 4).

4   Carefully check the large upper and lower radiator hoses along with the smaller diameter heater hoses which run from the engine to the firewall. On many models the heater return hose runs directly to the radiator. Inspect each hose along its entire length, replacing any hose which is cracked, swollen or shows signs of deterioration. Cracks may become more apparent if the hose is squeezed (**see illustrations**). Regardless of condition, it's a good idea to replace hoses with new ones every two years.

5   Make sure that all hose connections are tight. A leak in the cooling system will usually show up as white or rust colored deposits on the areas adjoining the leak. If wire-type clamps are used at the ends of the hoses, it may be a good idea to replace them with more secure screw-type clamps.

6   Use compressed air or a soft brush to remove bugs, leaves, etc. from the front of the radiator or air conditioning condenser. Be careful not to damage the delicate cooling fins or cut yourself on them.

7   Every other inspection, or at the first indication of cooling system problems, have the cap and system pressure tested. If you don't have a pressure tester, most gas stations and repair shops will do this for a minimal charge.

10   Underhood hose check and replacement

General

1   **Caution:** *Replacement of air conditioning hoses must be left to a dealer service department or air conditioning shop that has the equipment to depressurize the system safely. Never remove air conditioning components or hoses until the system has been depressurized.*

2   High temperatures in the engine compartment can cause the deterioration of the rubber and plastic hoses used for engine, accessory and emission systems operation. Periodic inspection should be made for cracks, loose clamps, material hardening and leaks. Information specific to the cooling system hoses can be found in Section 9.

3   Some, but not all, hoses are secured to the fittings with clamps. Where clamps are used, check to be sure they haven't lost their tension, allowing the hose to leak. If clamps aren't used, make sure the hose has not expanded and/or hardened where it slips over the fitting, allowing it to leak.

Vacuum hoses

4   It's quite common for vacuum hoses, especially those in the emissions system, to be color coded or identified by colored stripes molded into them. Various systems require hoses with different wall thicknesses, col-

11.6   The two types of wiper blade elements commonly used on these models

lapse resistance and temperature resistance. When replacing hoses, be sure the new ones are made of the same material.

5   Often the only effective way to check a hose is to remove it completely from the vehicle. If more than one hose is removed, be sure to label the hoses and fittings to ensure correct installation.

6   When checking vacuum hoses, be sure to include any plastic T-fittings in the check. Inspect the fittings for cracks and the hose where it fits over the fitting for distortion, which could cause leakage.

7   A small piece of vacuum hose (1/4-inch inside diameter) can be used as a stethoscope to detect vacuum leaks. Hold one end of the hose to your ear and probe around vacuum hoses and fittings, listening for the "hissing" sound characteristic of a vacuum leak. **Warning:** *When probing with the vacuum hose stethoscope, be very careful not to come into contact with moving engine components such as the drivebelt, cooling fan, etc.*

Fuel hose

Warning: *There are certain precautions which must be taken when inspecting or servicing fuel system components. Work in a well ventilated area and do not allow open flames (cigarettes, appliance pilot lights, etc.) or bare light bulbs near the work area. Mop up any spills immediately and do not store fuel soaked rags where they could ignite. On fuel-injected models, the fuel system pressure must be relieved before any fuel lines can be disconnected (see* Chapter 4).

8   Check all rubber fuel lines for deterioration and chafing. Check especially for cracks in areas where the hose bends and just before fittings, such as where a hose attaches to the fuel filter.

9   High quality fuel line, usually identified by the word Fluroelastomer printed on the hose, should be used for fuel line replacement. Never, under any circumstances, use unreinforced vacuum line, clear plastic tubing or water hose for fuel lines.

10   Spring-type clamps are commonly used on fuel lines. These clamps often lose their tension over a period of time, and can be "sprung" during removal. Replace all spring-type clamps with screw clamps whenever a hose is replaced.

Metal lines

11   Sections of metal line are often used for fuel line between the fuel pump and carburetor or fuel injection system. Check carefully to be sure the line has not been bent or crimped and that cracks have not started in the line.

12   If a section of metal fuel line must be replaced, only seamless steel tubing should be used, since copper and aluminum tubing don't have the strength necessary to withstand normal engine vibration. **Caution:** *On fuel-injected models, the fuel system pressure must be relieved before any fuel lines are disconnected (see Chapter 4).*

13   Check the metal brake lines where they enter the master cylinder and brake proportioning unit (if used) for cracks in the lines or loose fittings. Any sign of brake fluid leakage calls for an immediate thorough inspection of the brake system.

---

11   Wiper blade inspection and replacement

Refer to illustration 11.6

1   The windshield wiper and blade assembly should be inspected periodically for damage, loose components and cracked or worn blade elements.

2   Road film can build up on the wiper blades and affect their efficiency, so they should be washed regularly with a mild detergent solution.

3   The action of the wiping mechanism can loosen the bolts, nuts and fasteners, so they should be checked and tightened, as necessary, at the same time the wiper blades are checked.

4   If the wiper blade elements (sometimes called inserts) are cracked, worn or warped, they should be replaced with new ones.

5   Pull the wiper blade/arm assembly away from the glass.

6   Two methods are used to retain the rubber wiper blade element to the blade assembly **(see illustration)**. This "refill", as it is sometimes called, can be replaced without removing or disassembling the wiper mechanism.

7   One method uses a press-type button, in most cases colored red. Depress the button and then slide the rubber element off of the wiper blade. To install a new element, press the button and slide the new piece into place. Once centered on the blade, it will lock into place.

8   The other method incorporates a spring-type retainer clip at the end of the removable element. When the retainer is pinched together, the element can slide out of the blade assembly. A small pair of pliers can be used to squeeze the retainer. When installing a new element, be certain that the metal insert passes through all of the retaining tabs of the blade assembly.

9   Reinstall the blade assembly on the arm, wet the windshield and check for proper operation.

---

12   Engine oil and filter change

Refer to illustrations 12.3, 12.9, 12.14 and 12.18

1   Frequent oil changes are the most important preventive maintenance procedures that can be done by the home mechanic. As engine oil ages, it becomes diluted and contaminated, which leads to premature engine wear.

2   Although some sources recommend oil filter changes every other oil change, we feel that the minimal cost of an oil filter and the relative ease with which it is installed dictate that a new filter be installed every time the oil is changed.

12.9   The oil drain plug is located at the bottom of the oil pan and should be removed with a socket or box-end wrench – DO NOT use an open-end wrench as the corners of the bolt can be easily rounded off

12.3   These tools are required when changing the engine oil and filter

1   *Drain pan – It should be fairly shallow in depth, but wide to prevent spills*
2   *Rubber gloves – When removing the drain plug and filter, you will get oil on your hands (the gloves will prevent burns)*
3   *Breaker bar – Sometimes the oil drain plug is tight and a long breaker bar is needed to loosen it*
4   *Socket – To be used with the breaker bar or a ratchet (must be the correct size to fit the drain plug – 6-point preferred)*
5   *Filter wrench – This is a metal band-type wrench, which requires clearance around the filter to be effective*
6   *Filter wrench – This type fits on the bottom of the filter and can be turned with a ratchet or breaker bar (different size wrenches are available for different types of filters)*

3   Gather together all necessary tools and materials before beginning this procedure **(see illustration)**.
4   You should have plenty of clean rags and newspapers handy to mop up any spills. Access to the underside of the vehicle is greatly improved if the vehicle can be lifted on a hoist, driven onto ramps or supported by jackstands. **Warning:** *Do not work under a vehicle which is supported only by a bumper, hydraulic or scissors-type jack.*
5   If this is your first oil change, get under the vehicle and familiarize yourself with the locations of the oil drain plug and the oil filter. The engine and exhaust components will be warm during the actual work, so note how they are situated to avoid touching them when working under the vehicle.
6   Warm the engine to normal operating temperature. If the new oil or any tools are needed, use this warm-up time to gather everything necessary for the job. The correct type of oil for your application can be found in Recommended lubricants and fluids at the beginning of this Chapter.
7   With the engine oil warm (warm engine oil will drain better and more built-up sludge will be removed with it), raise and support the vehicle. Make sure it's safely supported!
8   Move all necessary tools, rags and newspapers under the vehicle. Set the drain pan under the drain plug. Keep in mind that the oil will initially flow from the pan with some force; position the pan accordingly.
9   Being careful not to touch any of the hot exhaust components, use a

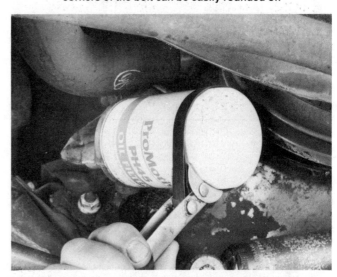

12.14   Use a strap-type oil filter wrench to loosen the filter; note that the wrench is positioned at the bottom of the filter, where the filter has the most strength. If access makes removal difficult, other types of filter wrenches are available

wrench to remove the drain plug near the bottom of the oil pan **(see illustration)**. Depending on how hot the oil is, you may want to wear gloves while unscrewing the plug the final few turns.
10   Allow the old oil to drain into the pan. It may be necessary to move the drain pan as the oil flow slows to a trickle.
11   After all the oil has drained, wipe off the drain plug with a clean rag. Small metal particles may cling to the plug and would immediately contaminate the new oil.
12   Clean the area around the drain plug opening and reinstall the plug. Tighten the plug securely with the wrench. If a torque wrench is available, use it to tighten the plug.
13   Move the drain pan into position under the oil filter.
14   Use the filter wrench to loosen the oil filter **(see illustration)**. Chain or metal band filter wrenches may distort the filter canister, but it doesn't matter since the filter will be discarded anyway.
15   Completely unscrew the old filter. Be careful; it's full of oil. Empty the oil inside the filter into the drain pan.
16   Compare the old filter with the new one to make sure they're the same type.

12.18   Lubricate the oil filter gasket with clean engine oil before installing the filter on the engine

11 LUBE
FITTINGS ○

13.2   This diagram shows where the lubrication points are located

13.1   Materials required for chassis and body lubrication

1   **Engine oil** – *Light engine oil in a can like this can be used for door and hood hinges*
2   **Graphite spray** – *Used to lubricate lock cylinders*
3   **Grease** – *Grease, in a variety of types and weights, is available for use in a grease gun. Check the Specifications for your requirements.*
4   **Grease gun** – *A common grease gun, shown here with a detachable hose and nozzle, is needed for chassis lubrication. After use, clean it thoroughly!*

low the oil to drain into the pan, then check the level on the oil dipstick (see Section 4 if necessary). If the oil level is above the ADD mark, start the engine and allow the new oil to circulate.

24   Run the engine for only about a minute and then shut it off. Immediately look under the vehicle and check for leaks at the oil pan drain plug and around the oil filter. If either is leaking, tighten with a bit more force.

25   With the new oil circulated and the filter now completely full, recheck the level on the dipstick and add more oil as necessary.

26   During the first few trips after an oil change, make it a point to check frequently for leaks and proper oil level.

27   The old oil drained from the engine cannot be reused in its present state and should be disposed of. Oil reclamation centers, auto repair shops and gas stations will normally accept the oil, which can be refined and used again. After the oil has cooled it can be drained into a suitable container (capped plastic jugs, topped bottles, milk cartons, etc.) for transport to one of these disposal sites.

13   Chassis lubrication

Refer to illustrations 13.1, 13.2 and 13.6

1   Refer to Recommended lubricants and fluids at the front of this Chapter to obtain the necessary grease, etc. You'll also need a grease gun **(see illustration)**. Occasionally plugs will be installed rather than grease fittings. If so, grease fittings will have to be purchased and installed.

2   Look under the vehicle and see if grease fittings or plugs are installed **(see illustration)**. If there are plugs, remove them and buy grease fittings,

17   Use a clean rag to remove all oil, dirt and sludge from the area where the oil filter mounts to the engine. Check the old filter to make sure the rubber gasket isn't stuck to the engine. If the gasket is stuck to the engine (use a flashlight if necessary), remove it.

18   Apply a light coat of clean oil to the rubber gasket on the new oil filter **(see illustration)**.

19   Attach the new filter to the engine, following the tightening directions printed on the filter canister or packing box. Most filter manufacturers recommend against using a filter wrench due to the possibility of overtightening and damage to the seal.

20   Remove all tools, rags, etc. from under the vehicle, being careful not to spill the oil in the drain pan, then lower the vehicle.

21   Move to the engine compartment and locate the oil filler cap.

22   If an oil can spout is used, push the spout into the top of the oil can and pour the fresh oil through the filler opening. A funnel may also be used.

23   Pour four quarts of fresh oil into the engine. Wait a few minutes to al-

13.6   After wiping the grease fitting (arrow) clean, push the nozzle firmly into place and pump the grease into the component – usually about two pumps of the gun will be sufficient

14.4   Wear indicators are built into the lower balljoints to aid in their inspection

which will thread into the component. A dealer or auto parts store will be able to supply the correct fittings. Straight, as well as angled, fittings are available.

3   For easier access under the vehicle, raise it with a jack and place jack-stands under the frame. Make sure it's safely supported by the stands. If the wheels are to be removed at this interval for tire rotation or brake inspection, loosen the lug nuts slightly while the vehicle is still on the ground.

4   Before beginning, force a little grease out of the nozzle to remove any dirt from the end of the gun. Wipe the nozzle clean with a rag.

5   With the grease gun and plenty of clean rags, crawl under the vehicle and begin lubricating the components.

6   Wipe the balljoint grease fitting nipple clean and push the nozzle firmly over it **(see illustration)**. Squeeze the trigger or handle on the grease gun to force grease into the component. The balljoints should be lubricated until the rubber seal is firm to the touch. Do not pump too much grease into the fittings as it could rupture the seal. For all other suspension and steering components, continue pumping grease into the fitting until it oozes out of the joint between the two components. If it escapes around the grease gun nozzle, the nipple is clogged or the nozzle is not completely seated on the fitting. Resecure the gun nozzle to the fitting and try again. If necessary, replace the fitting with a new one.

7   Wipe the excess grease from the components and the grease fitting. Repeat the procedure for the remaining fittings.

8   While you are under the vehicle, clean and lubricate the parking brake cable, along with the cable guides and levers. This can be done by smearing some of the chassis grease onto the cable and its related parts with your fingers.

9   Open the hood and smear a little chassis grease on the hood latch mechanism. Have an assistant pull the hood release lever from inside the vehicle as you lubricate the cable at the latch.

10   Lubricate all the hinges (door, hood, etc.) with engine oil to keep them in proper working order.

11   The key lock cylinders can be lubricated with spray graphite or silicone lubricant, which is available at auto parts stores.

12   Lubricate the door weatherstripping with silicone spray. This will reduce chafing and retard wear.

---

14   Suspension and steering check

Refer to illustration 14.4

1   Indications of a fault in these systems are excessive play in the steering wheel before the front wheels react, excessive sway around corners, body movement over rough roads or binding at some point as the steering wheel is turned.

2   Raise the front of the vehicle periodically, support it securely on jack-stands and visually check the suspension and steering components for wear.

3   Check the wheel bearings. Do this by spinning the front wheels. Listen for any abnormal noises and watch to make sure the wheel spins true (doesn't wobble). Grab the top and bottom of the tire and pull in and out on it. Notice any movement which would indicate a loose wheel bearing assembly. If the bearings are suspect, refer to Section 35 and Chapter 10 for more information.

4   From under the vehicle check for loose bolts, broken or disconnected parts and deteriorated rubber bushings on all suspension and steering components. Look for grease or fluid leaking from the steering assembly. Check the power steering hoses and connections for leaks. Check the balljoints for wear **(see illustration)**.

5   Have an assistant turn the steering wheel from side to side and check the steering components for free movement, chafing and binding. If the steering doesn't react with the movement of the steering wheel, try to determine where the slack is located.

---

15   Exhaust system check

---

1   With the engine cold (at least three hours after the vehicle has been driven), check the complete exhaust system from the manifold to the end of the tailpipe. Be careful around the catalytic converter, which may be hot even after three hours. The inspection should be done with the vehicle on a hoist to permit unrestricted access. If a hoist isn't available, raise the vehicle and support it securely on jackstands.

2   Check the exhaust pipes and connections for signs of leakage and/or corrosion indicating a potential failure. Make sure that all brackets and hangers are in good condition and tight.

3   Inspect the underside of the body for holes, corrosion, open seams, etc., which may allow exhaust gases to enter the passenger compartment. Seal all body openings with silicone sealant or body putty.

4   Rattles and other noises can often be traced to the exhaust system, especially the hangers, mounts and heat shields. Try to move the pipes, mufflers and catalytic converter. If the components can come in contact with the body or suspension parts, secure the exhaust system with new brackets and hangers.

16.2   The EFE heat riser valve used on early models is located at the connection between the exhaust manifold and the exhaust pipe

ACTUATOR AND ROD

16.5   The EFE system actuator and rod used on later models

17.2   Use a ratchet and extension to remove the differential check/fill plug

16   EFE (heat riser) system check

Refer to illustrations 16.2 and 16.5

1   The heat riser and the Early Fuel Evaporation (EFE) system both perform the same job, but each functions in a slightly different manner.
2   The heat riser is a valve inside the exhaust pipe, near the junction between the exhaust manifold and pipe. It can be identified by an external weight and spring **(see illustration)**.
3   With the engine and exhaust pipe cold, try moving the weight by hand. It should move freely.
4   Again with the engine cold, start the engine and watch the heat riser. Upon starting, the weight should move to the closed position. As the engine warms to normal operating temperature, the weight should move the valve to the open position, allowing a free flow of exhaust through the tailpipe. Since it could take several minutes for the system to heat up, you could mark the cold weight position, drive the vehicle, and then check the weight.
5   The EFE system also blocks off exhaust flow when the engine is cold. However, this system uses more precise temperature sensors and vacuum to open and close the exhaust pipe valve **(see illustration)**.
6   Locate the EFE actuator, which is bolted to a bracket on the right side of the engine. It will have an actuating rod attached to it which will lead down to the valve inside the pipe. In some cases the entire mechanism, including actuator, will be located at the exhaust pipe-to-manifold junction.
7   With the engine cold, have an assistant start the engine as you watch the actuating rod. It should immediately move to close off the valve as the engine warms. This process may take some time, so you might want to mark the position of the rod when the valve is closed, drive the vehicle to reach normal operating temperature, then open the hood and check that the rod has moved to the open position.

17   Differential lubricant level check

Refer to illustrations 17.2 and 17.3

1   The differential has a check/fill plug which must be removed to check the lubricant level. If the vehicle is raised to gain access to the plug, be sure to support it safely on jackstands – DO NOT crawl under the vehicle when it's supported only by a jack.
2   Remove the lubricant check/fill plug from the side of the differential **(see illustration)**.
3   The lubricant level should be at the bottom of the plug opening **(see illustration)**. If not, use a syringe to add the proper lubricant until it just starts to run out of the opening. On some models a tag is located in the area of the plug which gives information regarding lubricant type.
4   Install the plug and tighten it securely.

17.3   Use your little finger as a dipstick to make sure the differential lubricant level is even with the bottom of the opening

18.2   Tire rotation diagram for bias ply (left) and radial (right) tires

18   Tire rotation

Refer to illustration 18.2

1   The tires should be rotated at the specified intervals and whenever uneven wear is noticed.
2   Refer to the accompanying illustration for the preferred tire rotation pattern.
3   Refer to the information in Jacking and towing at the front of this manual for the proper procedures to follow when raising the vehicle and changing a tire. If the brakes are to be checked, do not apply the parking brake as stated. Make sure the tires are blocked to prevent the vehicle from rolling as it is raised.
4   Preferably, the entire vehicle should be raised at the same time. This can be done on a hoist or by jacking up each corner and then lowering the vehicle onto jackstands placed under the frame rails. Always use four jackstands and make sure the vehicle is safely supported.
5   After rotation, check and adjust the tire pressures as necessary and be sure to check the lug nut tightness.
6   For further information on the wheels and tires, refer to Chapter 10.

19   Brake check

Note: *For detailed photographs of the brake system, refer to Chapter 9.*
Warning: *Brake system dust may contain asbestos, which is hazardous to your health. DO NOT blow it out with compressed air and DO NOT in-* hale it. DO NOT use gasoline or solvents to remove the dust. Use brake system cleaner or denatured alcohol only.

1   In addition to the specified intervals, the brakes should be inspected every time the wheels are removed or whenever a defect is suspected.
2   To check the brakes, raise the vehicle and place it securely on jack-stands. Remove the wheels (see Jacking and towing at the front of the manual, if necessary).

Disc brakes

Refer to illustration 19.4 and 19.6

3   Disc brakes are used on the front wheels of all models as well as on the rear wheels on some later models. Extensive rotor damage can occur if the pads are not replaced when needed.
4   These models are equipped with a wear sensor attached to the inner pad. This is a small, bent piece of metal which is visible from the inboard side of the brake caliper. When the pad wears to the specified limit, the metal sensor rubs against the rotor and makes a screeching sound **(see illustration)**.
5   The disc brake calipers, which contain the pads, are visible with the wheels removed. There is an outer pad and an inner pad in each caliper. All pads should be inspected.
6   Each caliper has a "window" to inspect the pads. Check the thickness of the lining by looking into the caliper at each end and down through the inspection window at the top of the housing **(see illustration)**. If the wear sensor is very close to the rotor or the pad material has worn to about 1/8-inch or less, the pads require replacement.

19.4   The brake pad wear indicators will contact the disc and make a squealing noise when the pad is worn

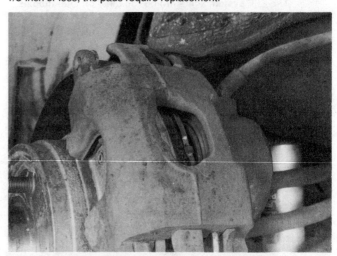

19.6   With the wheel removed, the brake pad lining can be inspected through the caliper window and at each end of the caliper

19.11   Use a hammer and chisel to remove the plug from the brake backing plate

BACKING PLATE

19.12   If necessary, use a screwdriver and adjusting tool to back off the star wheel so the brake drum can be removed

7   If you are unsure about the exact thickness of the remaining lining material, remove the pads for further inspection or replacement (refer to Chapter 9).
8   Before installing the wheels, check for leakage and/or damage (cracking, splitting, etc.) around the brake hose connections. Replace the hose or fittings as necessary, referring to Chapter 9.
9   Check the condition of the rotor. Look for scoring, gouging and burned spots. If these conditions exist, the hub/rotor assembly should be removed for servicing (see Section 35 and Chapter 9).

Drum brakes

Refer to illustrations 19.11, 19.12 and 19.14

10   Remove the drum by pulling it off the axle and brake assembly. If this proves difficult, make sure the parking brake is released, then squirt penetrating lubricant around the center hub areas. Allow the lubricant to soak in and try again to pull the drum off.
11   If the drum still cannot be pulled off, the brake shoes will have to be adjusted. This is done by first removing the plug from the drum or backing plate with a hammer and chisel **(see illustration)**.
12   With the plug removed, push the lever off the star wheel and then use a small screwdriver to turn the star wheel, which will move the linings away from the drum **(see illustration)**.
13   With the drum removed, do not touch any brake dust (see the Warning at the beginning of this Section).
14   Note the thickness of the lining material. If the material has worn away to within 1/16-inch of the recessed rivets or metal backing, the shoes should be replaced **(see illustration)**. The shoes should also be replaced if they are cracked, glazed (shiny surface) or wet with brake fluid.
15   Make sure that all the brake assembly springs are connected and in good condition.
16   Check the brake components for any signs of fluid leakage. With your finger, carefully pry back the rubber cups on the wheel cylinders located at the top of the brake shoes. Any leakage is an indication that the wheel cylinders should be overhauled immediately (see Chapter 9). Also check brake hoses and connections for signs of leakage.
17   Wipe the inside of the drum with a clean rag and brake cleaner or denatured alcohol. Again, be careful not to breath the dangerous asbestos dust.
18   Check the inside of the drum for cracks, score marks, deep scratches and hard spots, which will appear as small discolorations. If these imperfections cannot be removed with fine emery cloth, the drum must be taken to a machine shop equipped to turn the drums.
19   If after the inspection process all parts are in good working condition, reinstall the brake drum (using a metal or rubber plug if the knockout was removed).
20   Install the wheels and lower the vehicle.

19.14   The brake shoe lining thickness is measured from the outer surface of the lining to the metal shoe

Parking brake

21   The parking brake operates from a foot pedal and locks the rear brake system. The easiest method of periodically checking the operation of the parking brake assembly is to park the vehicle on a steep hill with the parking brake set and the transmission in Neutral. If the parking brake cannot prevent the vehicle from rolling, it is in need of adjustment (see Chapter 9).

---

20   Fuel system check

Warning: *Gasoline is extremely flammable, so take extra precautions when you work on any part of the fuel system. Don't smoke or allow open flames or bare light bulbs near the work area, and don't work in a garage where a natural gas-type appliance (such as a water heater or clothes dryer) with a pilot light is present. If you spill any fuel on your skin, rinse it off immediately with soap and water. When you perform any kind of work on the fuel tank, wear safety glasses and have a Class B type fire extinguisher on hand.*

1   The fuel tank is located at the rear of the vehicle.
2   The fuel system is most easily checked with the vehicle raised on a hoist so the components underneath the vehicle are readily visible and accessible.

21.3   The carburetor choke plate is visible after removing the air cleaner top plate

24.5   When the engine is cold, the damper door blocks off the snorkel passage, allowing air warmed by the exhaust to enter the carburetor

3   If the smell of gasoline is noticed while driving or after the vehicle has been in the sun, the system should be thoroughly inspected immediately.
4   Remove the gas filler cap and check for damage, corrosion and an unbroken sealing imprint on the gasket. Replace the cap with a new one if necessary.
5   With the vehicle raised, inspect the gas tank and filler neck for punctures, cracks and other damage. The connection between the filler neck and the tank is especially critical. Sometimes a rubber filler neck will leak due to loose clamps or deteriorated rubber, problems a home mechanic can usually rectify. **Warning:** *Do not, under any circumstances, try to repair a fuel tank yourself (except rubber components) unless you have had considerable experience. A welding torch or any open flame can easily cause the fuel vapors to explode if the proper precautions are not taken!*
6   Carefully check all rubber hoses and metal lines leading away from the fuel tank. Check for loose connections, deteriorated hoses, crimped lines and other damage. Follow the lines to the front of the vehicle, carefully inspecting them all the way. Repair or replace damaged sections as necessary. **Warning:** *On fuel injected models the fuel system is under pressure and no component should be disconnected without first relieving the pressure (see Chapter 4).*
7   If a fuel odor is still evident after the inspection, refer to Section 38.

21   Carburetor choke check

Refer to illustration 21.3
1   The choke operates when the engine is cold, and thus this check can only be performed before the vehicle has been started for the day.
2   Open the hood and remove the top plate of the air cleaner assembly. It is usually held in place by a wing nut at the center. If any vacuum hoses must be disconnected, make sure you tag the hoses for reinstallation in their original positions. Place the top plate and wing nut aside, out of the way of moving engine components.
3   Look at the center of the air cleaner housing. You will notice a flat plate at the carburetor opening **(see illustration)**.
4   Press the accelerator pedal to the floor. The plate should close completely. Start the engine while you watch the plate at the carburetor. Do not position your face directly over the carburetor, as the engine could backfire, causing serious burns. When the engine starts, the choke plate should open slightly.
5   Allow the engine to continue running at an idle speed. As the engine warms up to operating temperature, the plate should slowly open, allowing more cold air to enter through the top of the carburetor.
6   After a few minutes, the choke plate should be fully open to the vertical position. Blip the accelerator to make sure the fast idle cam disengages.

7   You will notice that the engine speed corresponds with the plate opening. With the plate fully closed, the engine should run at a fast idle speed. As the plate opens and the throttle is moved to disengage the fast idle cam, the engine speed will decrease.

22   Carburetor/throttle body mounting nut/bolt torque check

1   The carburetor or throttle body is attached to the top of the intake manifold by several bolts or nuts. These fasteners can sometimes work loose from vibration and temperature changes during normal engine operation and cause a vacuum leak.
2   If you suspect that a vacuum leak exists at the bottom of the carburetor or throttle body, obtain a length of hose about the diameter of fuel hose. Start the engine and place one end of the hose next to your ear as you probe around the base with the other end. You will hear a hissing sound if a leak exists (be careful of hot or moving engine components).
3   Remove the air cleaner assembly, tagging each hose to be disconnected with a piece of numbered tape to make reassembly easier.
4   Locate the mounting nuts or bolts at the base of the carburetor or throttle body. Decide what special tools or adapters will be necessary, if any, to tighten the fasteners.
5   Tighten the nuts or bolts securely and evenly. Do not overtighten them, as the threads could strip.
6   If, after the nuts or bolts are properly tightened, a vacuum leak still exists, the carburetor or throttle body must be removed and a new gasket installed. See Chapter 4 for more information.
7   After tightening the fasteners, reinstall the air cleaner and return all hoses to their original positions.

23   Throttle linkage inspection

1   Inspect the throttle linkage for damaged or missing parts and for binding and interference when the accelerator pedal is operated.
2   Lubricate the various linkage pivot points with engine oil.

24   Thermostatic air cleaner check

Refer to illustrations 24.5 and 24.6
1   Some engines are equipped with a thermostatically controlled air cleaner which draws air to the carburetor from different locations, depending upon engine temperature.
2   This is a visual check. If access is limited, a small mirror may have to be used.

24.6   As the engine warms up, the damper door moves down to close off the heat stove passage and open the snorkel passage so outside air can enter the carburetor

25.3a   Here are some of the more common problems associated with drivebelts (check the belts very carefully to prevent an untimely breakdown)

3   Open the hood and locate the damper door inside the air cleaner assembly. It is inside the long snorkel of the metal air cleaner housing.

4   If there is a flexible air duct attached to the end of the snorkel, leading to an area behind the grille, disconnect it at the snorkel. This will enable you to look through the end of the snorkel and see the damper inside.

5   The check should be done when the engine is cold. Start the engine and look through the snorkel at the damper, which should move to a closed position. With the damper closed, air cannot enter through the end of the snorkel, but instead enters the air cleaner through the flexible duct attached to the exhaust manifold and the heat stove passage (see illustration).

6   As the engine warms up to operating temperature, the damper should open to allow air through the snorkel end (see illustration). Depending on outside temperature, this may take 10 to 15 minutes. To speed up this check you can reconnect the snorkel air duct, drive the vehicle, then check to see if the damper is completely open.

25   Drivebelt check, adjustment and replacement

Check

Refer to illustrations 25.3a, 25.3b and 25.4

1   The drivebelts, or V-belts as they are sometimes called, are located at the front of the engine and play an important role in the overall operation of the vehicle and its components. Due to their function and material make-up, the belts are prone to failure after a period of time and should be inspected and adjusted periodically to prevent major engine damage. On some later models, a single serpentine belt is used which drives all of the components. A tensioner keeps this belt at the correct tension; no adjustment is necessary.

2   The number of belts used on a particular vehicle depends on the accessories installed. Drivebelts are used to turn the alternator, power steering pump, water pump and air-conditioning compressor. Depending on the pulley arrangement, more than one of these components may be driven by a single belt.

3   With the engine off, open the hood and locate the various belts at the front of the engine. Using your fingers (and a flashlight, if necessary), move along the belts checking for cracks and separation of the belt plies. Also check for fraying and glazing, which gives the belt a shiny appearance (see illustrations). Both sides of each belt should be inspected, which means you will have to twist the belt to check the underside.

4   The tension of each belt is checked by pushing on the belt at a distance halfway between the pulleys. Push firmly with your thumb and see how much the belt moves (deflects) (see illustration). A rule of thumb is that if the distance from pulley center-to-pulley center is between 7 and 11 inches, the belt should deflect 1/4-inch. If the belt travels between pulleys spaced 12 to 16 inches apart, the belt should deflect 1/2-inch.

25.3b   If the vehicle is equipped with a single serpentine belt, check it for signs of wear like these

25.4   Drivebelt tension can be checked with a straightedge and a ruler

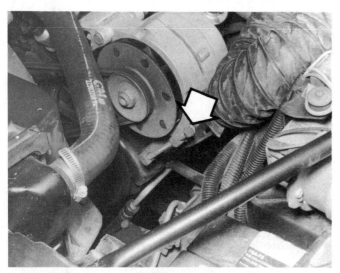

25.8   On some later models, the alternator drivebelt tension is adjusted by turning the adjustment bolt (arrow)

Adjustment

Refer to illustration 25.8

5   If it is necessary to adjust the belt tension, either to make the belt tighter or looser, it is done by moving the belt-driven accessory on the bracket.
6   For each component there will be an adjusting bolt and a pivot bolt. Both bolts must be loosened slightly to enable you to move the component.
7   After the two bolts have been loosened, move the component away from the engine to tighten the belt or toward the engine to loosen the belt. Hold the accessory in position and check the belt tension. If it is correct, tighten the two bolts until just snug, then recheck the tension. If the tension is all right, tighten the bolts.
8   To adjust the alternator drivebelt on some later models, loosen the pivot bolt and turn the adjusting bolt to tension the belt **(see illustration)**.
9   It will often be necessary to use some sort of prybar to move the accessory while the belt is adjusted. If this must be done to gain the proper leverage, be very careful not to damage the component being moved or the part being pried against.

Replacement

10   To replace a belt, follow the above procedures for drivebelt adjustment but slip the belt off the pulleys and remove it. Since belts tend to wear out more or less at the same time, it's a good idea to replace all of them at the same time. Mark each belt and the corresponding pulley grooves so the replacement belts can be installed properly.
11   Take the old belts with you when purchasing new ones in order to make a direct comparison for length, width and design.
12   Adjust the belts as described earlier in this Section.
13   When replacing a serpentine drivebelt (used on some later models) insert a 1/2-inch drive breaker bar into the tensioner and rotate it counter-clockwise to release the belt tension. Make sure the new belt is routed correctly (refer to the label in the engine compartment). Also, the belt must completely engage in the grooves in the pulleys.

---

26   Seat belt check

---

1   Check the seat belts, buckles, latch plates and guide loops for any obvious damage or signs of wear.
2   On later models, check that the seat belt reminder light comes on when the key is turned on.
3   The seat belts on later models are designed to lock up during a sudden stop or impact, yet allow free movement during normal driving. Check that the retractors return the belt against your chest while driving and rewind the belt fully when the buckle is unlatched.

28.1   Tools and materials needed for ignition point replacement and dwell angle adjustment

1   *Distributor cam lube* – *Sometimes this special lubricant comes with the new points; however, it's a good idea to buy a tube and have it on hand*
2   *Screw starter* – *This tool has special claws which hold the screw securely as it's started, which helps prevent accidental dropping of the screw*
3   *Magnetic screwdriver* – *Serves the same purpose as 2 above. If you don't have one of these special screwdrivers, you risk dropping the point mounting screws down into the distributor body.*
4   *Dwell meter* – *A dwell meter is the only accurate way to determine the point setting (gap). Connect the meter according to the instructions supplied with it.*
5   *Blade-type feeler gauges* – *These are required to set the initial point gap (space between the points when they are open)*
6   *Ignition wrenches* – *These special wrenches are made to work within the tight confines of the distributor. Specifically, they are needed to loosen the nut/bolt which secures the leads to the points.*

4   If any of the above checks reveal problems with the seat belt system, replace parts as necessary.

---

27   Neutral start switch check

Warning: *During the following checks there is a chance that the vehicle could lunge forward, possibly causing damage or injuries. Allow plenty of room around the vehicle, firmly apply the parking brake and hold down the regular brake pedal during the checks.*

1   These models are equipped with a Neutral start switch which prevents the engine from starting unless the shift lever is in Neutral or Park (automatic).
2   Try to start the vehicle in each gear. The engine should crank only in Park or Neutral.

28.2   Although it is possible to restore ignition points that are pitted, burned and corroded (as shown here), they should be replaced

28.7   Loosen the nut and disconnect the primary and condenser wires from the points – note the ignition point mounting screws (arrows)

1

3   Check that the steering column lock allows the key to go into the Lock position only when the shift lever is in Park.
4   The ignition key should come out only in the Lock position. Refer to Chapter 7 for more information on the Neutral start switch.

28   Ignition point replacement

Refer to illustrations 28.1, 28.2, 28.7, 28.9, 28.16, 28.17 and 28.29

1   The ignition points must be replaced at regular intervals on vehicles not equipped with electronic ignition. Occasionally the rubbing block will wear enough to require adjustment of the points. It's also possible to clean and dress them with a fine file, but replacement is recommended since they are relatively accessible and very inexpensive. Several special tools are required for this procedure **(see illustration)**.
2   After removing the distributor cap and rotor (see Section 42), the ignition points are plainly visible. They can be examined by gently prying them open to reveal the condition of the contact surfaces **(see illustration)**. If they're rough, pitted, covered with oil or burned, they should be replaced, along with the condenser. **Caution:** *This procedure requires the removal of small screws which can easily fall down into the distributor. To retrieve them, the distributor would have to be removed and disassembled. Use a magnetic or spring-loaded screwdriver and be extra careful.*
3   If not already done, remove the distributor cap by positioning a screwdriver in the slotted head of each latch. Press down on the latch and rotate it 1/2-turn to release the cap from the distributor body (see Section 42).
4   Position the cap (with the spark plug wires still attached) out of the way. Use a length of wire to hold it out of the way, if necessary.
5   Remove the rotor, which is held in place with two screws.
6   If equipped with a radio frequency interference shield (RFI), remove the mounting screws and the two-piece shield to gain access to the ignition points.
7   Note how they are routed, then disconnect the primary and condenser wire leads from the points **(see illustration)**. The wires may be attached with a small nut (which should be loosened, but not removed), a small screw or by a spring-loaded terminal. **Note:** *Some models are equipped with ignition points which include the condenser as an integral part of the point assembly. If your vehicle has this type, the condenser removal procedure below will not apply and there will be only one wire to detach from the points, rather than the two used with a separate condenser assembly.*
8   Loosen the two screws which secure the ignition points to the breaker

28.9   The condenser is attached to the breaker plate by a single screw

plate, but don't completely remove the screws (most ignition point sets have slots at these locations). Slide the points out of the distributor.
9   The condenser can now be removed from the breaker plate. Loosen the mounting strap screw and slide the condenser out or completely remove the condenser and strap **(see illustration)**. If you remove both the condenser and strap, be careful not to drop the mounting screw down into the distributor body.
10   Before installing the new points and condenser, clean the breaker plate and the cam on the distributor shaft to remove all dirt, dust and oil.
11   Apply a small amount of distributor cam lube (usually supplied with the new points, but also available separately) to the cam lobes.
12   Position the new condenser and tighten the mounting strap screw securely.
13   Slide the new point set under the mounting screw heads and make sure the protrusions on the breaker plate fit into the holes in the point base (to properly position the point set), then tighten the screws securely.
14   Attach the primary and condenser wires to the new points. Make sure the wires are routed so they don't interfere with breaker plate or advance weight movement.

28.16   Before adjusting the point gap, the rubbing block must be resting on one of the cam lobes (which will open the points)

28.17   With the points open, insert a 0.019-inch thick feeler gauge and turn the adjustment screw with a 1/8-inch Allen wrench

15   Although the gap between the contact points (dwell angle) will be adjusted later, make the initial adjustment now, which will allow the engine to be started.

16   Make sure that the point rubbing block is resting on one of the high points of the cam **(see illustration)**. If it isn't, turn the ignition switch to Start in short bursts to reposition the cam. You can also turn the crankshaft with a breaker bar and socket attached to the large bolt that holds the vibration damper in place.

17   With the rubbing block on a cam high point (points open), insert a 0.019-inch feeler gauge between the contact surfaces and use an Allen wrench to turn the adjustment screw until the point gap is equal to the thickness of the feeler gauge **(see illustration)**. The gap is correct when a slight amount of drag is felt as the feeler gauge is withdrawn.

18   If equipped, install the RFI shield.

19   Before installing the rotor, check it as described in Section 42.

20   Install the rotor. The rotor is indexed with a square peg underneath on one side and a round peg on the other side, so it will fit on the advance mechanism only one way. If so equipped, tighten the rotor mounting screws securely.

21   Before installing the distributor cap, inspect it as described in Section 42.

22   Install the distributor cap and lock the latches under the distributor body by depressing and turning them with a screwdriver.

23   Start the engine and check the dwell angle and ignition timing.

24   Whenever new ignition points are installed or the original points are cleaned, the dwell angle must be checked and adjusted.

25   Precise adjustment of the dwell angle requires an instrument called a dwell meter. Combination tach/dwell meters are commonly available at reasonable cost from auto parts stores. An approximate setting can be obtained if a meter isn't available.

26   If a dwell meter is available, hook it up following the manufacturer's instructions.

27   Start the engine and allow it to run at idle until normal operating temperature is reached (the engine must be warm to obtain an accurate reading). Turn off the engine.

28   Raise the metal door in the distributor cap. Hold it in the open position with tape if necessary.

29   Just inside the opening is the ignition point adjustment screw. Insert a 1/8-inch Allen wrench into the adjustment screw socket **(see illustration)**.

30   Start the engine and turn the adjustment screw as required to obtain the specified dwell reading on the meter. Dwell angle specifications can be found at the beginning of this Chapter and on the tune-up decal or VECI label in the engine compartment. If there's a discrepancy between the two, assume the VECI label or tune-up decal is correct. **Note:** *When adjusting*

28.29   With the door open, an Allen wrench can be inserted into the adjustment screw socket and turned to adjust the point dwell

the dwell, aim for the lower end of the dwell specification range. Then, as the points wear, the dwell will remain within the specified range over a longer period of time.

31   Remove the Allen wrench and close the door on the distributor. Turn off the engine and disconnect the dwell meter, then check the ignition timing (see Section 32).

32   If a dwell meter isn't available, use the following procedure to obtain an approximate dwell setting.

33   Start the engine and allow it to idle until normal operating temperature is reached.

34   Raise the metal door in the distributor cap. Hold it in the open position with tape if necessary.

35   Just inside the opening is the ignition point adjustment screw. Insert a 1/8-inch Allen wrench into the adjustment screw socket (see illustration 28.29).

36   Turn the Allen wrench clockwise until the engine begins to misfire, then turn the screw 1/2-turn counterclockwise.

37   Remove the Allen wrench and close the door. As soon as possible have the dwell angle checked and/or adjusted with a dwell meter to ensure optimum performance.

IDLE SPEED (SOLENOID) SCREW

29.4 The idle speed on earlier models can be adjusted with a screw that's usually on the left side of the carburetor – on this carburetor, the screw is part of an anti-dieseling solenoid

30.6 Two wrenches are required to loosen the carburetor fuel filter nuts

1

29 Idle speed check and adjustment

Refer to illustration 29.4

1   Engine idle speed is the speed at which the engine operates when no accelerator pedal pressure is applied. On later models this speed is governed by the ECM, while on earlier models the idle speed can be adjusted. The idle speed is critical to the performance of the engine itself, as well as many engine sub-systems.

2   A hand-held tachometer must be used when adjusting idle speed to get an accurate reading. The exact hook-up for these meters varies with the manufacturer, so follow the particular directions included with the instrument.

3   Since the manufacturer recommended many different adjustment procedures over the time period covered by this manual, it would be impractical to cover all types in this Section. Most models have a tune-up decal or Vehicle Emission Control Information (VECI) label located in the engine compartment with instructions for setting idle speed.

4   For most applications, the idle speed is set by turning an adjustment screw located on the left side of the carburetor. This screw changes the amount the throttle plate is held open by the throttle linkage. The screw may be on the linkage itself or may be part of a device such as an idle speed solenoid **(see illustration)**.

5   Once you have found the idle screw, experiment with different length screwdrivers until the adjustment can be easily made without coming into contact with hot or moving engine components.

6   Follow the instructions on the tune-up decal or Vehicle Emission Control Information label, which will probably include disconnecting certain vacuum or electrical connections. To plug a vacuum hose after disconnecting, insert a suitable size metal rod into the opening, or thoroughly wrap the open end with tape to prevent any vacuum loss through the hose.

7   If the air cleaner is removed, the vacuum hose to the snorkel should be plugged.

8   Make sure the parking brake is firmly set and the wheels blocked to prevent the vehicle from rolling. This is especially true if the transmission is to be in Drive. An assistant inside the vehicle pressing on the brake pedal is the safest method.

9   For all applications, the engine must be completely warmed up to operating temperature, which will automatically render the choke fast idle inoperative.

30 Fuel filter replacement

Warning: *Gasoline is extremely flammable, so take extra precautions when you work on any part of the fuel system. Don't smoke or allow open flames or bare light bulbs near the work area, and don't work in a garage where a natural gas-type appliance (such as a water heater or clothes dryer) with a pilot light is present. If you spill any fuel on your skin, rinse it off immediately with soap and water. When you perform any kind of work on the fuel tank, wear safety glasses and have a Class B type fire extinguisher on hand.*

Carbureted models

Carburetor-mounted filter

Refer to illustrations 30.6 and 30.8

1   On most models a fuel filter is located inside the fuel inlet nut at the carburetor. It's made of either pleated paper or porous bronze and cannot be cleaned or reused.

2   The job should be done with the engine cold (after sitting at least three hours). The necessary tools include open-end wrenches to fit the fuel line nuts. Flare nut wrenches (which wrap around the nut) should be used if available. In addition, you have to obtain the replacement filter (make sure it's for your specific vehicle and engine) and some clean rags.

3   Remove the air cleaner assembly (see Chapter 4). If vacuum hoses must be disconnected, be sure to note their positions and/or tag them to ensure that they are reinstalled correctly.

4   Follow the fuel line from the fuel pump to the point where it enters the carburetor. In most cases the fuel line will be metal all the way from the fuel pump to the carburetor.

5   Place some rags under the fuel inlet fittings to catch spilled fuel as the fittings are disconnected.

6   With the proper size wrench, hold the fuel inlet nut immediately next to the carburetor body. Now loosen the fitting at the end of the metal fuel line. Make sure the fuel inlet nut next to the carburetor is held securely while the fuel line is disconnected **(see illustration)**.

7   After the fuel line is disconnected, move it aside for better access to the inlet nut. Don't crimp the fuel line.

30.8 Carburetor fuel filter – exploded view

30.22 On 1975 through 1979 fuel injected models, the filter is located under the engine

30.27 Unscrew the canister for access to the filter element

8 Unscrew the fuel inlet nut, which was previously held steady. As this fitting is drawn away from the carburetor body, be careful not to lose the thin washer-type gasket on the nut or the spring, located behind the fuel filter. Also pay close attention to how the filter is installed (**see illustration**).
9 Compare the old filter with the new one to make sure they're the same length and design.
10 Reinstall the spring in the carburetor body.
11 Place the filter in position (a gasket is usually supplied with the new filter) and tighten the nut. Make sure it's not cross-threaded. Tighten it securely, but be careful not to overtighten it as the threads can strip easily, causing fuel leaks. Reconnect the fuel line to the fuel inlet nut, again using caution to avoid cross-threading the nut. Use a back-up wrench on the fuel inlet nut while tightening the fuel line fitting.
12 Start the engine and check carefully for leaks. If the fuel line fitting leaks, disconnect it and check for stripped or damaged threads. If the fuel line fitting has stripped threads, remove the entire line and have a repair shop install a new fitting. If the threads look all right, purchase some thread sealing tape and wrap the threads with it. Inlet nut repair kits are available at most auto parts stores to overcome leaking at the fuel inlet nut.

Fuel pump-mounted filter
13 On some early models a filter is mounted in the fuel pump.
14 Raise the front of the vehicle and support it securely on jackstands. With the engine cold, place a container, newspapers or rags under the fuel pump.
15 Clamp the fuel pump inlet hose shut during this operation, otherwise fuel will siphon from the tank when the filter is removed.
16 Disconnect the fuel pump outlet hose. Using two wrenches (flare-nut wrenches are best), hold the large nut on the fuel pump with a wrench and loosen and disconnect the fitting at the end of the metal fuel line.
17 Use the two wrenches again, one to steady the nut welded to the pump and the other one to loosen and remove the outlet fitting retaining the filter.
18 Remove the filter from the fuel pump housing. Be careful not to damage the metal gasket and make sure the spring retaining the filter does not fall out of the pump housing.
19 Place the new filter in position in the nut and screw the assembly into the pump housing finger tight. The old gasket can be reused if it is not damaged.
20 Using two wrenches, tighten the outlet nut securely. Connect the fuel line and tighten it securely, again using two wrenches.
21 Remove the clamp from the inlet hose and lower the vehicle.

30.33 Fuel filter mounting details for 1980 through 1989 fuel injected models

1	Filter	5	Clamps
2	Bracket	6	Fuel line
3	Bracket bolts	7	Fuel line
4	Hose		

FRONT OF CAR

OPEN POSITION

CLOSED POSITION

VIEW A

VIEW B

30.34   Fuel filter mounting details for 1990 fuel injected models

1	Fuel feed line	5	Filter mounting bolt
2	Fuel return line	6	Frame
3	Fuel filter	7	Label
4	Fuel line retainer		

Fuel injected models

Refer to illustration 30.22

Warning: *The fuel injection system maintains considerable pressure, even with the engine off. This pressure must be relieved before working on the fuel system. On port fuel injected models (1975 through 1979), follow the fuel system pressure relief procedure in Chapter 4. On throttle body fuel injected models (1980 on), loosen the fuel tank cap before working on the fuel system. This will allow the system self-bleeding feature to release the pressure.*

22   Fuel injected engines employ a canister or in-line fuel filter, located either near the fuel tank or under the engine **(see illustration)**.

1975 through 1979

Refer to illustration 30.27

23   On these models the filter element is located inside a removable canister.
24   Depressurize the fuel system (see Chapter 4).
25   Raise the vehicle and support it securely on jackstands.
26   Place a container under the filter to catch any spilled fuel.
27   Grasp the canister securely, unscrew it, then remove the filter element **(see illustration)**.
28   Place the new filter element in position and install the canister.

1980 on

Refer to illustrations 30.33 and 30.34

29   Two types of filters are used on these models: a canister type on earlier models and an in-line type on later models.
30   Loosen the fuel tank cap.
31   Place a container, newspapers or rags under the filter.
32   On canister-type filters, refer to Steps 27 and 28 for replacement.
33   On inline filter-equipped models through 1989, use two wrenches (one as a back-up) to disconnect each fuel line, then unbolt the filter from the frame **(see illustration)**. Use flare-nut wrenches, if available, to disconnect the lines.
34   On 1990 models, the fuel lines are attached to the filter with plastic connectors which can be detached by squeezing the plastic tabs on the male connectors and then pulling the connectors apart **(see illustration)**. Prior to installing the new filter, apply a few drops of clean engine oil to the male connector end. Push the connectors together until they click into place.

31   Air filter and PCV filter replacement

Refer to illustrations 31.2, 31.4, 31.7 and 31.9

1   At the specified intervals, the air filter and (if equipped) PCV filter should be replaced with new ones. The engine air cleaner also supplies

31.2   The first step in removing the air filter is unscrewing the wing nut on top of the housing

31.4   After setting the top plate aside, the filter element can be lifted out of the housing

31.7   The PCV filter on most models is located in the air cleaner housing

31.9   The PCV filter used on some models is located in the rocker arm cover (arrow); pull the assembly out of the cover and wash it with solvent at the specified interval

filtered air to the PCV system.

2   The filter is located on top of the carburetor or throttle body and is replaced by unscrewing the wing nut from the top of the filter housing and lifting off the cover **(see illustration)**.

3   While the top plate is off, be careful not to drop anything down into the carburetor or air cleaner assembly.

4   Lift the air filter element out of the housing **(see illustration)** and wipe out the inside of the air cleaner housing with a clean rag.

5   Place the new filter in the air cleaner housing. Make sure it seats properly in the bottom of the housing.

6   The PCV filter is also located inside the air cleaner housing on some models. Remove the top plate and air filter as previously described, then locate the PCV filter on the inside of the housing.

7   Remove the old filter **(see illustration)**.

8   Install the new PCV filter and the new air filter.

9   On some models, the PCV filter is located in the rocker arm cover **(see illustration)**. This type of filter doesn't require replacement; pull it out of the rocker cover and wash it with solvent at the specified intervals.

10   Install the top plate and any hoses which were disconnected.

32   Ignition timing check and adjustment

Refer to illustrations 32.2 and 32.6

Note: *It is imperative that the procedures included on the tune-up or Vehicle Emissions Control Information (VECI) label be followed when adjusting the ignition timing. The label will include all information concerning preliminary steps to be performed before adjusting the timing, as well as the timing specifications.*

1   At the specified intervals, whenever the ignition points have been replaced, the distributor removed or a change made in the fuel type, the ignition timing should be checked and adjusted.

2   Locate the Tune-up or VECI label under the hood and read through and perform all preliminary instructions concerning ignition timing. Some special tools will be needed for this procedure **(see illustration)**.

3   Before attempting to check the timing, make sure the ignition point dwell angle is correct (Section 28), and the idle speed is as specified (Section 29).

32.2   Tools needed to check and adjust the ignition timing

1   Vacuum plugs – Vacuum hoses will, in most cases, have to be disconnected and plugged. Molded plugs in various shapes and sizes are available for this.
2   Inductive pick-up timing light – Flashes a bright concentrated beam of light when the number one spark plug fires. Connect the leads according to the instructions supplied with the light.
3   Distributor wrench – On some models, the hold-down bolt for the distributor is difficult to reach and turn with conventional wrenches or sockets. A special wrench like this must be used.

4   If specified on the tune-up or VECI label, disconnect the vacuum hose from the distributor and plug the open end of the hose with a rubber plug, rod or bolt of the proper size.
5   Connect a timing light in accordance with the manufacturer's instructions. Generally, the light will be connected to power and ground sources and to the number one spark plug wire. The number one spark plug is the

first spark plug on the right side of the engine on 425, 472, 500 and 368 V8 engines; it's the first plug on the left (driver's side) on all other engines.
6   Locate the numbered timing tag on the front cover of the engine (**see illustration**). It's located just behind the lower crankshaft pulley. Clean it off with solvent if necessary to read the printing and small grooves.
7   Use chalk or paint to mark the groove in the crankshaft pulley.
8   Put a mark on the timing tab in accordance with the number of degrees called for on the VECI label or the tune-up label in the engine compartment. Each peak or notch on the timing tab represents two degrees. The word Before or the letter A indicates advance and the letter O indicates Top Dead Center (TDC). As an example, if your vehicle specifications call for eight degrees BTDC (Before Top Dead Center), you will make a mark on the timing tab four notches before the O.
9   Check that the wiring for the timing light is clear of all moving engine components, then start the engine and warm it up to normal operating temperature.
10   Aim the flashing timing light at the timing mark by the crankshaft pulley, again being careful not to come in contact with moving parts. The marks should appear to be stationary. If the marks are in alignment, the timing is correct.
11   If the notch is not lining up with the correct mark, loosen the distributor hold-down bolt and rotate the distributor until the notch is lined up with the correct timing mark.
12   Retighten the hold-down bolt and recheck the timing.
13   Turn off the engine and disconnect the timing light. Reconnect the vacuum advance hose, if removed, and any other components which were disconnected.

1

---

33   Automatic transmission fluid and filter change

Refer to illustrations 33.7, 33.10 and 33.11
1   At the specified time intervals, the transmission fluid should be drained and replaced. Since the fluid will remain hot long after driving, perform this procedure only after the engine has cooled down completely.
2   Before beginning work, purchase the specified transmission fluid (see Recommended lubricants and fluids at the front of this Chapter) and a new filter.
3   Other tools necessary for this job include jackstands to support the vehicle in a raised position, a drain pan capable of holding at least eight pints, newspapers and clean rags.
4   Raise the vehicle and support it securely on jackstands.
5   With a drain pan in place, remove the front and side pan mounting bolts.
6   Loosen the rear pan bolts approximately four turns.
7   Carefully pry the transmission pan loose with a screwdriver, allowing the fluid to drain (**see illustration**).

32.6   The ignition timing marks are located at the front of the engine

33.7   With the rear bolts in place but loose, pull the front of the pan down to let the fluid drain

33.10   After removing the bolts or screws, lower the filter from the transmission

33.11   Some models have an O-ring on the filter spout; if it does not come out with the filter, reach up into the opening with your finger to retrieve it

8   Remove the remaining bolts, pan and gasket. Carefully clean the gasket surface of the transmission to remove all traces of the old gasket and sealant.
9   Drain the fluid from the transmission pan, clean it with solvent and dry it with compressed air.
10   Remove the filter from the mount inside the transmission (see illustration).
11   Install a new filter and (if equipped) O-ring (see illustration).
12   Make sure the gasket surface on the transmission pan is clean, then install a new gasket. Put the pan in place against the transmission and, working around the pan, tighten each bolt a little at a time until the torque figure listed in this Chapter's Specifications is reached.
13   Lower the vehicle and add about seven pints of the transmission fluid listed in this Chapter's Specifications through the filler tube (see Section 6).
14   With the transmission in Park and the parking brake set, run the engine at a fast idle, but don't race it.
15   Move the gear selector through each range and back to Park. Check

the fluid level. You'll probably need to add some.
16   Check under the vehicle for leaks during the first few trips.

34   Differential lubricant change

Refer to illustrations 34.6a, 34.6b, 34.6c and 34.8
1   Some differentials can be drained by removing the drain plug, while on others it's necessary to remove the cover plate on the differential housing. As an alternative, a hand suction pump can be used to remove the differential lubricant through the filler hole. If there is no drain plug and a suction pump isn't available, be sure to obtain a new gasket at the same time the gear lubricant is purchased.
2   Raise the vehicle and support it securely on jackstands. Move a drain pan, rags, newspapers and wrenches under the vehicle.
3   Remove the fill plug from the differential.

34.6a   Remove the bolts from the lower edge of the cover . . .

34.6b   . . . then loosen the top bolts and let the lubricant drain

34.6c   After the oil is drained, remove the cover

**34.8   Carefully scrape the old gasket material off to ensure a
leak-free seal with the new gasket**

4   If equipped with a drain plug, remove the plug and allow the differential lubricant to drain completely. After the lubricant has drained, install the plug and tighten it securely.
5   If a suction pump is being used, insert the flexible hose. Work the hose down to the bottom of the differential housing and pump the lubricant out.
6   If the differential is being drained by removing the cover plate, remove the bolts on the lower half of the plate **(see illustration)**. Loosen the bolts on the upper half and use them to keep the cover loosely attached **(see illustration)**. Allow the lubricant to drain into the pan, then completely remove the cover **(see illustration)**.
7   Using a lint-free rag, clean the inside of the cover and the accessible areas of the differential housing. As this is done, check for chipped gears and metal particles in the lubricant, indicating that the differential should be more thoroughly inspected and/or repaired.
8   Thoroughly clean the gasket mating surfaces of the differential housing and the cover plate. Use a gasket scraper or putty knife to remove all traces of the old gasket **(see illustration)**.
9   Apply a thin layer of RTV sealant to the cover flange and then press a new gasket into position on the cover. Make sure the bolt holes align properly.
10   Place the cover on the differential housing and install the bolts. Tighten the bolts securely.
11   On all models, use a hand pump, syringe or funnel to fill the differential housing with the specified lubricant until it's level with the bottom of the plug hole.
12   Install the filler plug and tighten it securely.

**35.1   Tools and materials needed for front wheel
bearing maintenance**

1   *Hammer* – *A common hammer will do just fine*
2   *Grease* – *High-temperature grease which is formulated specially for front wheel bearings should be used*
3   *Wood block* – *If you have a scrap piece of 2x4, it can be used to drive the new seal into the hub*
4   *Needle-nose pliers* – *Used to straighten and remove the cotter pin in the spindle*
5   *Torque wrench* – *This is very important in this procedure; if the bearing is too tight, the wheel won't turn freely – if it's too loose, the wheel will "wobble" on the spindle. Either way, it could mean extensive damage.*
6   *Screwdriver* – *Used to remove the seal from the hub (a long screwdriver would be preferred)*
7   *Socket/breaker bar* – *Needed to loosen the nut on the spindle if it's extremely tight*
8   *Brush* – *Together with some clean solvent, this will be used to remove old grease from the hub and spindle*

35   Front wheel bearing check, repack and adjustment

Refer to illustrations 35.1, 35.6, 35.7, 35.8, 35.11 and 35.15
1   In most cases the front wheel bearings will not need servicing until the brake pads are changed. However, the bearings should be checked whenever the front of the vehicle is raised for any reason. Several items, including a torque wrench and special grease, are required for this procedure **(see illustration)**.
2   With the vehicle securely supported on jackstands, spin each wheel and check for noise, rolling resistance and freeplay.
3   Grasp the top of each tire with one hand and the bottom with the other. Move the wheel in and out on the spindle. If there's any noticeable movement, the bearings should be checked and then repacked with grease, or replaced if necessary.
4   Remove the wheel.
5   Fabricate a wood block (1-1/16 inches by 1/2-inch by 2-inches long) which can be slid between the brake pads to keep them separated. Remove the brake caliper (Chapter 9) and hang it out of the way on a piece of wire.

35.6   Dislodge the grease cap by working around the outer
circumference with a hammer and chisel

35.7   Use needle-nose pliers to straighten the cotter pin and
pull it out

35.8   Front wheel bearing components – exploded view

35.11   Use a screwdriver to pry the grease seal from the back
side of the hub

6   Pry the dust cap out of the hub using a screwdriver or hammer and
chisel (see illustration).

7   Straighten the bent ends of the cotter pin, then pull the cotter pin out of
the locking nut (see illustration). Discard the cotter pin and use a new one
during reassembly.
8   Remove the wheel bearing nut and washer from the end of the spindle
(see illustration).
9   Pull the hub assembly out slightly, then push it back into its original
position. This should force the outer bearing off the spindle enough so it
can be removed.
10   Pull the hub off the spindle.
11   Use a screwdriver to pry the seal out of the rear of the hub (see illustration). As this is done, note how the seal is installed.
12   Remove the inner wheel bearing from the hub.
13   Use solvent to remove all traces of the old grease from the bearings,
hub and spindle. A small brush may prove helpful; however make sure no
bristles from the brush embed themselves inside the bearing rollers. Allow
the parts to air dry.
14   Carefully inspect the bearings for cracks, heat discoloration, worn
rollers, etc. Check the bearing races inside the hub for wear and damage.
If the bearing races are defective, the hubs should be taken to a machine
shop with the facilities to remove the old races and press new ones in.
Note that the bearings and races come as matched sets and old bearings
should never be installed on new races.

35.15   Work the grease completely into the rollers

36.4   The radiator drain fitting is located at the bottom of the radiator

15   Use high-temperature front wheel bearing grease to pack the bearings. Work the grease completely into the bearings, forcing it between the rollers, cone and cage from the back side **(see illustration)**.
16   Apply a thin coat of grease to the spindle at the outer bearing seat, inner bearing seat, shoulder and seal seat.
17   Put a small quantity of grease inboard of each bearing race inside the hub. Using your finger, form a dam at these points to provide extra grease availability and to keep thinned grease from flowing out of the bearing.
18   Place the grease-packed inner bearing into the rear of the hub and put a little more grease outboard of the bearing.
19   Place a new seal over the inner bearing and tap the seal evenly into place with a hammer and block of wood until it's flush with the hub.
20   Carefully place the hub assembly onto the spindle and push the grease-packed outer bearing into position.
21   Install the washer and spindle nut. Tighten the nut only slightly (no more than 12 ft-lbs of torque).
22   Spin the hub in a forward direction to seat the bearings and remove any grease or burrs which could cause excessive bearing play later.
23   Check to see that the tightness of the spindle nut is still approximately 12 ft-lbs.
24   Loosen the spindle nut until it's just loose, no more.
25   Using your hand (not a wrench of any kind), tighten the nut until it's snug. Install a new cotter pin through the hole in the spindle and spindle nut. If the nut slots don't line up, loosen the nut slightly until they do. From the hand-tight position, the nut should not be loosened more than one-half flat to install the cotter pin.
26   Bend the ends of the cotter pin until they're flat against the nut. Cut off any extra length which could interfere with the dust cap.
27   Install the dust cap, tapping it into place with a hammer.
28   Place the brake caliper near the rotor and carefully remove the wood spacer. Install the caliper (Chapter 9).
29   Install the tire/wheel assembly on the hub and tighten the lug nuts.
30   Grasp the top and bottom of the tire and check the bearings in the manner described earlier in this Section.
31   Lower the vehicle.

36   Cooling system servicing (draining, flushing and refilling)

Refer to illustration 36.4

Warning: *Do not allow antifreeze to come in contact with your skin or painted surfaces of the vehicle. Rinse off spills immediately with plenty of water. Antifreeze is highly toxic if ingested. Never leave antifreeze lying around in an open container or in puddles on the floor; children and pets are attracted by it's sweet smell and may drink it. Check with local authori-*

ties about disposing of used antifreeze. Many communities have collection centers which will see that antifreeze is disposed of safely.

1   Periodically, the cooling system should be drained, flushed and refilled to replenish the antifreeze mixture and prevent formation of rust and corrosion, which can impair the performance of the cooling system and cause engine damage. When the cooling system is serviced, all hoses and the radiator cap should be checked and replaced if necessary.
2   Apply the parking brake and block the wheels. If the vehicle has just been driven, wait several hours to allow the engine to cool down before beginning this procedure.
3   Once the engine is completely cool, remove the radiator cap.
4   Move a large container under the radiator drain fitting to catch the coolant **(see illustration)**. Attach a 3/8-inch diameter hose to the drain fitting to direct the coolant into the container, then open the drain fitting (a pair of pliers may be required to turn it).
5   After the coolant stops flowing out of the radiator, move the container under the engine block drain plug (if so equipped). Remove the plug and allow the coolant in the block to drain.
6   While the coolant is draining, check the condition of the radiator hoses, heater hoses and clamps (refer to Section 9 if necessary).
7   Replace any damaged clamps or hoses.
8   Once the system is completely drained, flush the radiator with fresh water from a garden hose until it runs clear at the drain. The flushing action of the water will remove sediments from the radiator but will not remove rust and scale from the engine and cooling tube surfaces.
9   These deposits can be removed with a chemical cleaner. Follow the procedure outlined in the manufacturer's instructions. If the radiator is severely corroded, damaged or leaking, it should be removed (Chapter 3) and taken to a radiator repair shop.
10   Remove the overflow hose from the coolant recovery reservoir. Drain the reservoir and flush it with clean water, then reconnect the hose.
11   Close and tighten the radiator drain. Install and tighten the block drain plug.
12   Place the heater temperature control in the maximum heat position.
13   Slowly add new coolant (a 50/50 mixture of water and antifreeze) to the radiator until it's full. Add coolant to the reservoir up to the lower mark.
Note: *The HT4100 engine requires antifreeze that meets GM specification 1825M and a special sealer (GM part no. 3634621 or equivalent).*
14   Leave the radiator cap off and run the engine in a well-ventilated area until the thermostat opens (coolant will begin flowing through the radiator and the upper radiator hose will become hot).
15   Turn the engine off and let it cool. Add more coolant mixture to bring the level back up to the lip on the radiator filler neck.
16   Squeeze the upper radiator hose to expel air, then add more coolant mixture if necessary. Replace the radiator cap.

37.2   The PCV valve simply pushes into the valve cover or manifold; place your finger under the valve and pull it out – feel for suction at the end of the valve and shake the valve, listening for a clicking sound

17   Start the engine, allow it to reach normal operating temperature and check for leaks.

37   Positive Crankcase Ventilation (PCV) valve check and replacement

Refer to illustration 37.2

1   The PCV valve is usually located in the rocker arm cover.
2   With the engine idling at normal operating temperature, pull the valve (with hose attached) from the rubber grommet in the cover **(see illustration)**.
3   Place your finger over the valve opening. If there's no vacuum at the valve, check for a plugged hose, manifold port, or the valve itself. Replace any plugged or deteriorated hoses.
4   Turn off the engine and shake the PCV valve, listening for a rattle. If the valve doesn't rattle, replace it with a new one.
5   To replace the valve, pull it from the end of the hose, noting its installed position and direction.
6   When purchasing a replacement PCV valve, make sure it's for your particular vehicle and engine size. Compare the old valve with the new one to make sure they're the same.

FRONT OF CAR

38.2   The evaporative emissions system (charcoal) canister is located at the front of the engine compartment – inspect the various hoses attached to it and the canister itself for any damage

1	Manifold vacuum hose	4	Purge hose
2	Canister hose	5	Canister
3	Fuel vapor hose	6	Purge solenoid

7   Push the valve into the end of the hose until it's seated.
8   Inspect the rubber grommet for damage and replace it with a new one if necessary.
9   Push the PCV valve and hose securely into position.

38   Evaporative emissions control system check

Refer to illustrations 38.2, 38.4 and 38.5

1   The function of the evaporative emissions control system is to draw fuel vapors from the gas tank and fuel system, store them in a charcoal canister and route them to the intake manifold during normal engine operation.
2   The most common symptom of a fault in the evaporative emissions system is a strong fuel odor in the engine compartment. If a fuel odor is detected, inspect the charcoal canister, located in the engine compartment **(see illustration)**. Check the canister and all hoses for damage and deterioration.
3   On earlier models, the filter at the bottom of the canister should be replaced at this time.

38.4   Pull the filter element out from the bottom of the canister

38.5   Make sure the new filter is fully seated all the way around the bottom of the canister

39.2   The diaphragm in the EGR valve (which can be felt by reaching through the hole in the underside of the valve) should move easily with finger pressure

4   Remove the retaining bolts, turn the canister upside-down and pull the old filter from the bottom of the canister **(see illustration)**. If you cannot turn the canister enough for this due to the short length of the hoses, mark the hoses to insure correct installation and disconnect them.
5   Push the new filter into the bottom of the canister, making sure it is seated all the way around **(see illustration)**.
6   Install the canister and connect any hoses which were disconnected.
7   The evaporative emissions control system is explained in more detail in Chapter 6.

---

39   Exhaust Gas Recirculation (EGR) system check

Refer to illustration 39.2
1   The EGR valve is usually located on the intake manifold, adjacent to the carburetor. Most of the time when a problem develops in this emissions system, it's due to a stuck or corroded EGR valve.
2   With the engine cold, to prevent burns, push on the EGR valve diaphragm. Using moderate pressure, you should be able to press the diaphragm in and out within the housing **(see illustration)**.
3   If the diaphragm doesn't move or moves only with much effort, replace the EGR valve with a new one. If in doubt about the condition of the valve, compare the free movement of your EGR valve with a new valve.
4   Refer to Chapter 6 for more information on the EGR system.

---

40   Spark plug replacement

Refer to illustrations 40.2, 40.5a, 40.5b, 40.6 and 40.10
1   Open the hood.
2   In most cases, the tools necessary for spark plug replacement include a spark plug socket which fits onto a ratchet (spark plug sockets are padded inside to prevent damage to the porcelain insulators on the new plugs), various extensions and a gap gauge to check and adjust the gaps on the new plugs **(see illustration)**. A special plug wire removal tool is available for separating the wire boots from the spark plugs, but it isn't absolutely necessary. A torque wrench should be used to tighten the new plugs.
3   The best approach when replacing the spark plugs is to purchase the new ones in advance, adjust them to the proper gap and replace them one at a time. When buying the new spark plugs, be sure to obtain the correct plug type for your particular engine. This information can be found on the Emission Control Information label located under the hood and in the factory owner's manual. If differences exist between the plug specified on the

40.2   Tools required for changing spark plugs

1   **Spark plug socket** – *This will have special padding inside to protect the spark plug's porcelain insulator*
2   **Torque wrench** – *Although not mandatory, using this tool is the best way to ensure the plugs are tightened properly*
3   **Ratchet** – *Standard hand tool to fit the spark plug socket*
4   **Extension** – *Depending on model and accessories, you may need special extensions and universal joints to reach one or more of the plugs*
5   **Spark plug gap gauge** – *This gauge for checking the gap comes in a variety of styles. Make sure the gap for your engine is included.*

40.5a   Spark plug manufacturers recommend using a wire type gauge when checking the gap – if the wire does not slide between the electrodes with a slight drag, adjustment is required

emissions label and in the owner's manual, assume that the emissions label is correct.
4   Allow the engine to cool completely before attempting to remove any of the plugs. While you're waiting for the engine to cool, check the new plugs for defects and adjust the gaps.
5   The gap is checked by inserting the proper thickness gauge between the electrodes at the tip of the plug **(see illustration)**. The gap between the electrodes should be the same as the one specified on the Emissions Control Information label. The wire should just slide between the electrodes with a slight amount of drag. If the gap is incorrect, use the adjuster on the gauge body to bend the curved side electrode slightly until the prop-

40.5b   To change the gap, bend the *side* electrode only, as indicated by the arrows, and be very careful not to crack or chip the porcelain insulator surrounding the center electrode

40.6   When removing the spark plug wires, pull only on the boot and twist it back-and-forth

40.10   A length of 3/16-inch ID rubber hose will save time and prevent damaged threads when installing the spark plugs

er gap is obtained **(see illustration)**. If the side electrode is not exactly over the center electrode, bend it with the adjuster until it is. Check for cracks in the porcelain insulator (if any are found, the plug should not be used).

6   With the engine cool, remove the spark plug wire from one spark plug. Pull only on the boot at the end of the wire – do not pull on the wire. A plug wire removal tool should be used if available **(see illustration)**.

7   If compressed air is available, use it to blow any dirt or foreign material away from the spark plug hole. A common bicycle pump will also work. The idea here is to eliminate the possibility of debris falling into the cylinder as the spark plug is removed.

8   Place the spark plug socket over the plug and remove it from the engine by turning it in a counterclockwise direction.

9   Compare the spark plug to those shown in the color photos on page 65 to get an indication of the general running condition of the engine.

10   Thread one of the new plugs into the hole until you can no longer turn it with your fingers, then tighten it with a torque wrench (if available) or the ratchet. A good idea is to slip a short length of rubber hose over the end of the plug to use as a tool to thread it into place **(see illustration)**. The hose will grip the plug enough to turn it, but will start to slip if the plug begins to cross-thread in the hole – this will prevent damaged threads and the accompanying repair costs.

11   Before pushing the spark plug wire onto the end of the plug, inspect it following the procedures outlined in Section 41.

12   Attach the plug wire to the new spark plug, again using a twisting motion on the boot until it's seated on the spark plug.

13   Repeat the procedure for the remaining spark plugs, replacing them one at a time to prevent mixing up the spark plug wires.

---

41   Spark plug wire check and replacement

1   The spark plug wires should be checked at the recommended intervals and whenever new spark plugs are installed in the engine.

2   The wires should be inspected one at a time to prevent mixing up the order, which is essential for proper engine operation.

3   Disconnect the plug wire from one spark plug. To do this, grab the rubber boot, twist slightly and pull the wire free. Do not pull on the wire itself, only on the rubber boot (see illustration 40.6).

4   Check inside the boot for corrosion, which will look like a white crusty powder. Push the wire and boot back onto the end of the spark plug. It should be a tight fit on the plug. If it isn't, remove the wire and use a pair of pliers to carefully crimp the metal connector inside the boot until it fits securely on the end of the spark plug.

5   Using a clean rag, wipe the entire length of the wire to remove any

built-up dirt and grease. Once the wire is clean, check for holes, burned areas, cracks and other damage. Don't bend the wire excessively or the conductor inside might break.

6   Disconnect the wire from the distributor cap. A retaining ring at the top of the distributor may have to be removed to free the wires. Again, pull only on the rubber boot. Check for corrosion and a tight fit in the same manner as the spark plug end. Reattach the wire to the distributor cap.

7   Check the remaining spark plug wires one at a time, making sure they are securely fastened at the distributor and the spark plug when the check is complete.

8   If new spark plug wires are required, purchase a new set for your specific engine model. Wire sets are available pre-cut, with the rubber boots already installed. Remove and replace the wires one at a time to avoid mix-ups in the firing order. The wire routing is extremely important, so be sure to note exactly how each wire is situated before removing it.

---

42   Distributor cap and rotor check and replacement

Note: *It's common practice to install a new distributor cap and rotor whenever new spark plug wires are installed. On models that have the ignition coil mounted in the cap, the coil will have to be transferred to the new cap.*

Check
Refer to illustrations 42.3a, 42.3b, 42.4, 42.6a and 42.6b

1   To gain access to the distributor cap, especially on a V6 engine, it may be necessary to remove the air cleaner assembly.

2   Loosen the distributor cap mounting screws (note that the screws have a shoulder so they don't come completely out). On most models, the

CARBON DEPOSITS

Symptoms: Dry sooty deposits indicate a rich mixture or weak ignition. Causes misfiring, hard starting and hesitation.

Recommendation: Check for a clogged air cleaner, high float level, sticky choke and worn ignition points. Use a spark plug with a longer core nose for greater anti-fouling protection.

OIL DEPOSITS

Symptoms: Oily coating caused by poor oil control. Oil is leaking past worn valve guides or piston rings into the combustion chamber. Causes hard starting, misfiring and hesition.

Recommendation: Correct the mechanical condition with necessary repairs and install new plugs.

TOO HOT

Symptoms: Blistered, white insulator, eroded electrode and absence of deposits. Results in shortened plug life.

Recommendation: Check for the correct plug heat range, over-advanced ignition timing, lean fuel mixture, intake manifold vacuum leaks and sticking valves. Check the coolant level and make sure the radiator is not clogged.

PREIGNITION

Symptoms: Melted electrodes. Insulators are white, but may be dirty due to misfiring or flying debris in the combustion chamber. Can lead to engine damage.

Recommendation: Check for the correct plug heat range, over-advanced ignition timing, lean fuel mixture, clogged cooling system and lack of lubrication.

HIGH SPEED GLAZING

Symptoms: Insulator has yellowish, glazed appearance. Indicates that combustion chamber temperatures have risen suddenly during hard acceleration. Normal deposits melt to form a conductive coating. Causes misfiring at high speeds.

Recommendation: Install new plugs. Consider using a colder plug if driving habits warrant.

GAP BRIDGING

Symptoms: Combustion deposits lodge between the electrodes. Heavy deposits accumulate and bridge the electrode gap. The plug ceases to fire, resulting in a dead cylinder.

Recommendation: Locate the faulty plug and remove the deposits from between the electrodes.

NORMAL

Symptoms: Brown to grayish-tan color and slight electrode wear. Correct heat range for engine and operating conditions.

Recommendation: When new spark plugs are installed, replace with plugs of the same heat range.

ASH DEPOSITS

Symptoms: Light brown deposits encrusted on the side or center electrodes or both. Derived from oil and/or fuel additives. Excessive amounts may mask the spark, causing misfiring and hesitation during acceleration.

Recommendation: If excessive deposits accumulate over a short time or low mileage, install new valve guide seals to prevent seepage of oil into the combustion chambers. Also try changing gasoline brands.

1

WORN

Symptoms: Rounded electrodes with a small amount of deposits on the firing end. Normal color. Causes hard starting in damp or cold weather and poor fuel economy.

Recommendation: Replace with new plugs of the same heat range.

DETONATION

Symptoms: Insulators may be cracked or chipped. Improper gap setting techniques can also result in a fractured insulator tip. Can lead to piston damage.

Recommendation: Make sure the fuel anti-knock values meet engine requirements. Use care when setting the gaps on new plugs. Avoid lugging the engine.

SPLASHED DEPOSITS

Symptoms: After long periods of misfiring, deposits can loosen when normal combustion temperature is restored by an overdue tune-up. At high speeds, deposits flake off the piston and are thrown against the hot insulator, causing misfiring.

Recommendation: Replace the plugs with new ones or clean and reinstall the originals.

MECHANICAL DAMAGE

Symptoms: May be caused by a foreign object in the combustion chamber or the piston striking an incorrect reach (too long) plug. Causes a dead cylinder and could result in piston damage.

Recommendation: Remove the foreign object from the engine and/or install the correct reach plug.

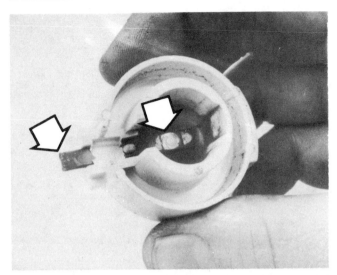

42.3a   Check the distributor rotor contacts (arrows) for wear and burn marks (later model remote coil-type distributor)

42.3b   Carbon tracking on the rotor is caused by a leaking seal between the distributor cap and the ignition coil (always replace both the seal and rotor when this condition is present) (coil in cap-type distributor)

cap is held in place with latches that look like screws – to release them, push down with a screwdriver and turn them about 1/2-turn. Pull up on the cap, with the wires attached, to separate it from the distributor, then position it to one side.

3   The rotor is now visible on the end of the distributor shaft. Check it carefully for cracks and carbon tracks. Make sure the center terminal spring tension is adequate and look for corrosion and wear on the rotor tip (see illustrations). If in doubt about its condition, replace it with a new one.

4   If replacement is required, detach the rotor from the shaft and install a new one. On some models, the rotor is press fit on the shaft and can be pried or pulled off (see illustration). On other models, the rotor is attached to the distributor shaft with two screws.

5   The rotor is indexed to the shaft so it can only be installed one way. Press fit rotors have an internal key that must line up with a slot in the end of the shaft (or vice versa). Rotors held in place with screws have one square and one round peg on the underside that must fit into holes with the same shape.

6   Check the distributor cap for carbon tracks, cracks and other damage. Closely examine the terminals on the inside of the cap for excessive corrosion and damage (see illustrations). Slight deposits are normal. Again, if in doubt about the condition of the cap, replace it with a new one. Be sure to apply a small dab of silicone lubricant to each terminal before installing the cap. Also, make sure the carbon brush (center terminal) is correctly installed in the cap – a wide gap between the brush and rotor will result in rotor burn-through and/or damage to the distributor cap.

Replacement

Conventional distributor

7   On models with a separately mounted ignition coil, simply separate the cap from the distributor and transfer the spark plug wires, one at a time, to the new cap. Be very careful not to mix up the wires!

8   Reattach the cap to the distributor, then tighten the screws or reposition the latches to hold it in place.

42.4   This type of rotor can be pried off the distributor shaft with a screwdriver – other types have two screws which must be removed (be careful not to drop anything into the distributor)

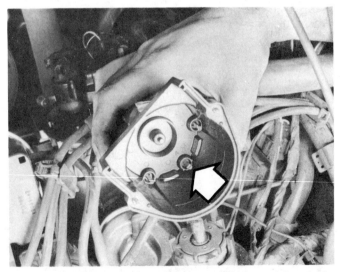

42.6a   Inspect the inside of the cap, especially the metal contacts (arrow) for corrosion and wear

BROKEN
TOWER

CHARRED OR
ERODED TERMINALS

CRACK

CARBON TRACK

CARBON TRACK

WORN OR
DAMAGED
ROTOR
BUTTON

**42.6b   Shown here are some of the common defects to look for when inspecting
the distributor cap (if in doubt about its condition, install a new one)**

1

Coil-in-cap distributor

9   Use your thumbs to push the spark plug wire retainer latches away from the coil cover.

10   Lift the retainer ring away from the distributor cap with the spark plug wires attached to the ring. It may be necessary to work the wires off the distributor cap towers so they remain with the ring.

11   Disconnect the battery/tachometer/coil electrical connector from the distributor cap.

12   Remove the two coil cover screws and lift off the coil cover.

13   There are three small spade connectors on wires extending from the coil into the electrical connector hood at the side of the distributor cap.

Note which terminals the wires are attached to, then use a small screwdriver to push them free.

14   Remove the four coil mounting screws and lift the coil out of the cap.

15   When installing the coil in the new cap, be sure to install a new rubber arc seal in the cap.

16   Install the coil screws, the wires in the connector hood, and the coil cover.

17   Install the cap on the distributor.

18   Plug in the coil electrical connector to the distributor cap.

19   Install the spark plug wire retaining ring on the distributor cap.

Chapter 2 Part A V6 Engine

Contents

Specifications

General

Displacement	4.1 liters
Cylinder numbers (front-to-rear)	
Left bank (driver's side)	1-3-5
Right bank	2-4-6
Firing order	1-6-5-4-3-2

Camshaft

Lobe lift – compare the readings for each intake and	
exhaust valve	Replace the camshaft if readings vary more than 0.003 in.
Journal diameter	1.785 to 1.786 in
Journal-to-bearing (oil) clearance	0.005 to 0.0025 in

Oil pump

Gear-to-pump housing side clearance .... 0.002 to 0.005 in
End clearance .... 0.002 to 0.006 in
Gear length .... 0.8720 to 0.8735 in
Gear diameter .... 1.664 to 1.666 in
Depth of housing .... 0.8677 to 0.8697 in
Diameter of pocket .... 1.671 to 1.674 in

Torque specifications

	Ft-lbs
Camshaft sprocket bolt	20
Crankshaft pulley-to-vibration damper bolts	20
Cylinder head bolts	80
Exhaust manifold bolts	25
Driveplate bolts	60
Intake manifold-to-cylinder head bolts	45
Motor mount-to-cylinder block bolts	55
Oil pan mounting bolts	14
Oil pump cover-to-front cover bolts	10
Main bearing cap bolts	100
Rocker arm shaft-to-cylinder head bolts	30
Tensioner bracket-to-engine block bolts	15
Oil pump cover-to-front cover bolts	10
Front cover-to-block bolts	30
Timing chain tensioner bolts	13
Vibration damper center bolt	225

1 General information

This Part of Chapter 2 is devoted to in-vehicle repair procedures for the V6 engine. All information concerning engine removal and installation and engine block and cylinder head overhaul can be found in Part C of this Chapter.

The following repair procedures are based on the assumption that the engine is installed in the vehicle. If the engine has been removed from the vehicle and mounted on a stand, many of the steps outlined in this Part of Chapter 2 will not apply.

The specifications included in this Part of Chapter 2 apply only to the procedures contained in this Part. Part C of Chapter 2 contains the specifications necessary for cylinder head and engine block rebuilding.

2 Repair operations possible with the engine in the vehicle

Many major repair operations can be accomplished without removing the engine from the vehicle.

Clean the engine compartment and the exterior of the engine with some type of degreaser before any work is done. It will make the job easier and help keep dirt out of the internal areas of the engine.

Depending on the components involved, it may be helpful to remove the hood to improve access to the engine as repairs are performed (refer to Chapter 11 if necessary). Cover the fenders to prevent damage to the paint. Special pads are available, but an old bedspread or blanket will also work.

If vacuum, exhaust, oil or coolant leaks develop, indicating a need for gasket or seal replacement, the repairs can generally be made with the engine in the vehicle. The intake and exhaust manifold gaskets, timing cover gasket, oil pan gasket, crankshaft oil seals and cylinder head gasket are all accessible with the engine in place.

Exterior engine components, such as the intake and exhaust manifolds, the oil pan (and the oil pump), the water pump, the starter motor, the alternator, the distributor and the fuel system components can be removed for repair with the engine in place.

Since the cylinder heads can be removed without pulling the engine, valve component servicing can also be accomplished with the engine in

the vehicle. Replacement of the timing chain, sprockets and camshaft is also possible with the engine in the vehicle.

In extreme cases caused by a lack of necessary equipment, repair or replacement of piston rings, pistons, connecting rods and rod bearings is possible with the engine in the vehicle. However, this practice is not recommended because of the cleaning and preparation work that must be done to the components involved.

3 Top Dead Center (TDC) for number one piston – locating

Refer to illustrations 3.6 and 3.7

1   Top Dead Center (TDC) is the highest point in the cylinder that each piston reaches as it travels up and down when the crankshaft turns. Each piston reaches TDC on the compression stroke and again on the exhaust stroke, but TDC generally refers to piston position on the compression stroke. The timing marks on the vibration damper installed on the front of the crankshaft are referenced to the number one piston at TDC on the compression stroke.

2   Positioning the piston(s) at TDC is an essential part of many procedures such as rocker arm removal, valve adjustment, timing chain and sprocket replacement and distributor removal.

3   In order to bring any piston to TDC, the crankshaft must be turned using one of the methods outlined below. When looking at the front of the engine, normal crankshaft rotation is clockwise. **Warning:** *Before beginning this procedure, be sure to place the transmission in Neutral and unplug the wire connector at the distributor to disable the ignition system (electronic ignition) or remove the center wire from the distributor cap and ground it (conventional ignition).*

 a) The preferred method is to turn the crankshaft with a large socket and breaker bar attached to the vibration damper bolt threaded into the front of the crankshaft.

 b) A remote starter switch, which may save some time, can also be used. Attach the switch leads to the S (switch) and B (battery) terminals on the starter motor. Once the piston is close to TDC, use a socket and breaker bar as described in the previous paragraph.

 c) If an assistant is available to turn the ignition switch to the Start position in short bursts, you can get the piston close to TDC without a remote starter switch. Use a socket and breaker bar as described in paragraph a) to complete the procedure.

3.6   Turn the crankshaft until the line on the vibration damper is directly opposite the zero mark on the timing plate, as shown here

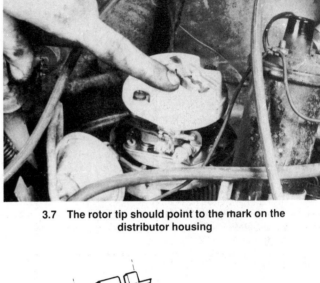

3.7   The rotor tip should point to the mark on the distributor housing

4   Make a mark on the distributor housing directly below the number one spark plug wire terminal on the distributor cap. **Note:** *The terminal numbers may be be marked on the spark plug wires near the distributor.*
5   Remove the distributor cap as described in Chapter 1.
6   Turn the crankshaft (see paragraph 3 above) until the line on the vibration damper is aligned with the zero mark on the timing plate **(see illustration)**. The timing plate and vibration damper are located low on the front of the engine, near the pulley that turns the drivebelt.
7   The rotor should now be pointing directly at the mark on the distributor housing **(see illustration)**. If it isn't, the piston may be at TDC on the exhaust stroke, so follow Step 8.
8   To get the piston to TDC on the compression stroke, turn the crankshaft one complete turn (360-degrees) clockwise. The rotor should now be pointing at the mark. When the rotor is pointing at the number one spark plug wire terminal in the distributor cap (which is indicated by the mark on the housing) and the ignition timing marks are aligned, the number one piston is at TDC on the compression stroke.
9   After the number one piston has been positioned at TDC on the compression stroke, TDC for any of the remaining cylinders can be located by turning the crankshaft 120-degrees at a time for V6 engines (or 90-degrees for V8 engines-see Section 3, Chapter 2B) and following the firing order (refer to the Specifications).

4   Rocker arm cover(s) – removal and installation

Refer to illustration 4.6

Removal

1   Disconnect the negative cable from the battery.
2   Remove the air cleaner assembly (see Chapter 4).
3   Label and disconnect the wires and hoses which would interfere with removal of the rocker arm cover(s).
4   Label and detach the spark plug wires and unclip the wire retainers from the studs.
5   Detach any remaining accessories as necessary. If removal of the air conditioning compressor is required, unbolt the unit and carefully set it aside without disconnecting the refrigerant lines. **Warning:** *The air conditioning system is under high pressure. Do not disconnect any refrigerant line or fitting without first having the system discharged by an air conditioning technician.*
6   Remove the rocker arm cover bolts and detach the cover **(see illustration)**. Note that some of the bolts have studs attached to the ends – you'll have to use a deep socket to remove them. If the cover is stuck, use a

4.6   Rocker arm cover installation details

soft-face hammer or a block of wood and a hammer to dislodge it. If the cover still won't come loose, pry on it carefully with a putty knife, but don't distort the sealing flange surface.
7   Remove all traces of old gasket and sealant with a scraper, then clean the mating surfaces with lacquer thinner or acetone.

Installation

8   On models that use RTV sealant in place of a gasket, apply a 3/16-inch bead of sealant to the cover flange. Be sure to apply it all the way around the bolt holes, or oil will leak past the bolt threads. Apply a bead of sealant to the area where the cylinder head and intake manifold meet. **Caution:** *When applying RTV sealant, keep it out of the bolt holes.*
9   On models that use gaskets, place a small amount of RTV sealant on the seam area where the cylinder head and intake manifold meet, but don't apply sealant to the gasket.
10   Install the cover(s) while the RTV is still wet. Tighten the bolts in 1/4-turn increments until the torque listed in this Chapter's Specifications is reached.
11   Reinstall the remaining parts in the reverse order of removal.
12   Run the engine and check for oil leaks.

5.2   Carefully pull out the nylon rocker arm retainers
with a pair of pliers

5.4   When removing the pushrods, be sure to store them
separately to ensure installation in their original locations

5   Rocker arms, shafts and pushrods – removal, inspection and installation

Removal

Refer to illustration 5.2 and 5.4

1   Refer to Section 4 and detach the rocker arm cover(s) from the cylinder head(s).
2   Remove the nylon rocker arm retainers by pulling them out with a pair of pliers **(see illustration)**.
3   Loosen the rocker arm shaft bolts, a little at a time, to avoid distorting the shaft. Lift off the rocker arms and shafts. If the rocker arms are removed from the shaft, keep them in order so they can be installed in their original positions.
4   Remove the pushrods and store them separately to make sure they don't get mixed up during installation **(see illustration)**.

Inspection

5   Check each rocker arm for wear, cracks and other damage, especially where the pushrods and valve stems contact the rocker arm faces.
6   Make sure the hole at the pushrod end of each rocker arm is open.

7   Check the pivot areas on the rocker arms and shafts for wear, cracks and galling. If the rocker arms and/or shafts are worn or damaged, replace them with new ones.
8   Inspect the pushrods for cracks and excessive wear at the ends. Roll each pushrod across a piece of plate glass to see if it's bent (if it wobbles, it's bent).

Installation

Refer to illustrations 5.11a and 5.11b

9   Lubricate the lower end of each pushrod with clean engine oil or moly-base grease and install them in their original locations. Make sure each pushrod seats completely in the lifter.
10   Apply moly-base grease to the ends of the valve stems and the upper ends of the pushrods.
11   Lubricate the rocker arm shaft and slide the rocker arms onto the shaft, taking care to install them in the correct positions **(see illustrations)**.
12   Set the rocker arms and shafts in place and install the nylon retainers. Install the bolts, tightening them a little at a time until the torque listed in this Chapter's Specifications is reached.
13   Install the rocker arm covers.

2A

5.11a   Carefully note the designation, L or R, stamped on the
rocker arms to insure proper installation

5.11b   Positions of the rocker arms on the shafts

6.4   This is what the air hose adapter that threads into the spark plug hole looks like – they're commonly available from auto parts stores

6.8   Once the spring is depressed, the keepers can be removed with a small magnet or needle-nose pliers (a magnet is preferred to prevent dropping the keepers)

---

6   Valve spring, retainer and seals – replacement in vehicle

---

Refer to illustrations 6.4 and 6.8

Note: *Broken valve springs and defective valve stem seals can be replaced without removing the cylinder heads. Two special tools and a compressed air source are normally required to perform this operation, so read through this Section carefully and rent or buy the tools before beginning the job. If compressed air isn't available, a length of nylon rope can be used to keep the valves from falling into the cylinder during this procedure.*

1   Refer to Section 4 and remove the rocker arm cover from the affected cylinder head. If all of the valve stem seals are being replaced, remove both rocker arm covers.

2   Remove the spark plug from the cylinder which has the defective component. If all of the valve stem seals are being replaced, all of the spark plugs should be removed.

3   Turn the crankshaft until the piston in the affected cylinder is at top dead center (TDC) on the compression stroke (refer to Section 3 for instructions). If you are replacing all of the valve stem seals, begin with cylinder number one and work on the valves for one cylinder at a time. Move from cylinder to cylinder following the firing order sequence (see this Chapter's Specifications).

4   Thread an adapter into the spark plug hole and connect an air hose from a compressed air source to it **(see illustration)**. Most auto parts stores can supply the air hose adapter. **Note:** *Many cylinder compression gauges utilize a screw-in fitting that may work with your air hose quick-disconnect fitting.*

5   Remove the rocker arm shaft and arms and pull out the pushrod for the valve with the defective part. If all of the valve stem seals are being replaced, all of the pushrods should be removed (refer to Section 5).

6   Apply compressed air to the cylinder. The valves should be held in place by the air pressure. If the valve faces or seats are in poor condition, leaks may prevent air pressure from retaining the valves – refer to the alternative procedure below.

7   If you don't have access to compressed air, an alternative method can be used. Position the piston at a point just before TDC on the compression stroke, then feed a long piece of nylon rope through the spark plug hole until it fills the combustion chamber. Be sure to leave the end of the rope hanging out of the spark plug hole so it can be removed easily. Use a large breaker bar and socket to rotate the crankshaft in the normal direction of rotation until slight resistance is felt.

8   Stuff shop rags into the cylinder head holes above and below the valves to prevent parts and tools from falling into the engine, then use a valve spring compressor to compress the spring/damper assembly. Remove the keepers with small needle-nose pliers or a magnet **(see illustration)**.

9   Remove the spring retainer or rotator, oil shield and valve spring assembly, then remove the valve stem O-ring seal and the umbrella-type guide seal (the O-ring seal will most likely be hardened and will probably break when removed, so plan on installing a new one each time the original is removed). **Note:** *If air pressure fails to hold the valve in the closed position during this operation, the valve face and/or seat is probably damaged. If so, the cylinder head will have to be removed for additional repair operations.*

10   Wrap a rubber band or tape around the top of the valve stem so the valve won't fall into the combustion chamber, then release the air pressure. **Note:** *If a rope was used instead of air pressure, turn the crankshaft slightly in the direction opposite normal rotation.*

11   Inspect the valve stem for damage. Rotate the valve in the guide and check the end for eccentric movement, which would indicate that the valve is bent.

12   Move the valve up and down in the guide and make sure it doesn't bind. If the valve stem binds, either the valve is bent or the guide is damaged. In either case, the head will have to be removed for repair.

13   Reapply air pressure to the cylinder to retain the valve in the closed position, then remove the tape or rubber band from the valve stem. If a rope was used instead of air pressure, rotate the crankshaft in the normal direction of rotation until slight resistance is felt.

14   Lubricate the valve stem with engine oil and install a new umbrella-type guide seal.

15   Install the spring/damper assembly and shield in position over the valve.

16   Install the valve spring retainer or rotator. Compress the valve spring assembly and carefully install the new O-ring seal in the lower groove of the valve stem. Make sure the seal isn't twisted – it must lie perfectly flat in the groove.

17   Position the keepers in the upper groove. Apply a small dab of grease to the inside of each keeper to hold it in place if necessary. Remove the pressure from the spring tool and make sure the keepers are seated.

18   Disconnect the air hose and remove the adapter from the spark plug hole. If a rope was used in place of air pressure, pull it out of the cylinder.

19   Refer to Section 5 and install the rocker arm(s) and pushrod(s).

20   Install the spark plug(s) and hook up the wire(s).

21   Refer to Section 4 and install the rocker arm cover(s).

22   Start and run the engine, then check for oil leaks and unusual sounds coming from the rocker arm cover area.

7   Intake manifold – removal and installation

Removal

Refer to illustration 7.12

1   Disconnect the negative cable from the battery.

2   Drain the coolant from the radiator (see Chapter 1).

3   Label and remove the wires, hoses, cables and fuel lines at the carburetor (see Chapter 4).

4   Label and disconnect all wires and hoses connected to the intake manifold.

5   If equipped, unbolt the air conditioning compressor and set it aside without disconnecting the hoses (see Chapter 3).

6   Label and disconnect the spark plug wires from the plugs, then remove the distributor cap (see Chapter 1).

7   Remove the distributor (see Chapter 5).

8   Detach the brake booster vacuum pipe at the manifold.

9   Detach the evaporative emission hoses.

10   Remove the rocker arm covers (see Section 4).

11   Disconnect the upper radiator and heater hoses.

12   Unbolt the intake manifold and lift it off the engine **(see illustration)**. If it's stuck, pry carefully against a protrusion on the manifold. Do not pry between the gasket surfaces.

13   Remove all traces of old gasket material and sealant from the manifold and cylinder head mating surfaces, then clean them with lacquer thinner or acetone. Clean the intake manifold bolt holes in the cylinder head by chasing them with a tap. Compressed air can be used to remove the debris from the holes. **Warning:** *Wear eye protection when using compressed air.*

Installation

Refer to illustrations 7.16 and 7.17

14   Install new seals to the ridges at each end of the block. Apply a 3/16-inch bead of RTV sealant to each of the ridges at the ends of the seals.

15   Install the new one piece intake manifold gasket onto the engine block.

16   Install the intake manifold on the engine and hand tighten the bolts. Install each bolt by size into the designated place **(see illustration)**. Make sure the areas between the block ridges and intake manifold are completely sealed.

7.12   Intake manifold details

7.16   **There are four different length intake manifold bolts – be sure to install them in the proper holes**

7.17   Intake manifold bolt tightening sequence

17 Following the sequence shown **(see illustration)**, tighten the manifold bolts, in several steps, to the torque listed in this Chapter's Specifications.
18 Reinstall the remaining parts in the reverse order of removal.

19 Run the engine, adjust the ignition timing and check for oil and vacuum leaks.

8   Exhaust manifold(s) – removal and installation

Refer to illustration 8.7a and 8.7b
Warning: *Allow the engine to cool completely before performing this procedure.*

Removal

1   Detach the cable from the negative battery terminal.
2   Raise the front of the vehicle and support it securely on jackstands. Apply the parking brake and block the rear wheels to keep the vehicle from rolling.
3   Unbolt the exhaust pipe from the manifold.
4   If you are working on the left side, disconnect the EFE pipe and remove the EFE valve (see Chapter 6).
5   Remove the bottom two exhaust manifold-to-cylinder head bolts.
6   Disconnect the spark plug wires from the spark plugs, labeling them as they're disconnected to simplify installation.
7   Remove the remaining exhaust manifold mounting bolts **(see illustrations)** and separate the manifold from the engine.

Installation

8   Installation is the reverse of removal. Be sure to clean the cylinder head and manifold surfaces thoroughly before installing the manifold. Tighten the bolts to the torque listed in this Chapter's Specifications.

OIL GAGE ROD
ADAPTER

SPARK PLUG
WIRE SHIELD

8.7a   Left exhaust manifold mounting details

9   Cylinder heads – removal and installation

Warning: *Allow the engine to cool completely before performing this procedure.*

Removal

1   Remove the intake manifold (refer to Section 7).
2   Raise the vehicle and support it securely on jackstands.
3   Locate the engine block drain plugs (see Chapter 1). Remove the plugs and allow the coolant to drain.

Right cylinder head
4   Remove the drivebelts (see Chapter 1).
5   Disconnect the electrical connectors from the alternator.
6   If the vehicle is equipped with air conditioning, remove the compressor and mounting bracket and position them out of the way, leaving the hoses connected (see Chapter 3).
7   Remove the alternator with the mounting bracket (see Chapter 5).

Left cylinder head
8   Remove the oil dipstick.
9   Remove the power steering pump with the mounting bracket and move it to the side, without disconnecting the hoses.

Both cylinder heads
10   Disconnect the wires from the spark plugs and remove the spark plug wire clips from the rocker arm cover studs.
11   Remove the exhaust manifold bolts from the cylinder head.
12   Clean the dirt off the cylinder head and the surrounding area **Note:** *It is extremely important to avoid getting dirt into the hydraulic valve lifters.*
13   Loosen the rocker arm nuts and remove the rocker arms, shafts and pushrods (see Section 5).

14   Using a new head gasket, outline the cylinders and bolt pattern on a piece of cardboard **(see illustration 10.13** in Part B). Be sure to indicate the front of the engine for reference. Punch holes at the bolt locations. Loosen the cylinder head bolts in 1/4-turn increments until they can be removed by hand (start at the ends and work toward the center of the head). Store the bolts in the cardboard holder as they're removed – this will ensure that they're reinstalled in their original locations.
15   Lift the head off the engine. If it's stuck, DO NOT pry between the head and block – damage to the mating surfaces will result! To dislodge the head, use a long screwdriver or pry bar under the cast "ears" to pry up on it. Don't damage the cylinder head sealing surface.

Installation
Refer to illustration 9.23

16   If a new cylinder head is being installed, attach the components previously removed from the old head.
17   The mating surfaces of the cylinder head and block must be perfectly clean when the head is installed. Use a gasket scraper to remove all traces of carbon and old gasket material, then clean the mating surfaces with lacquer thinner or acetone. If there's oil on the mating surfaces when the head is installed, the gasket may not seal correctly and leaks could develop. When working on the block, stuff the cylinders with clean shop rags to keep out debris. Use a vacuum cleaner to remove any debris that falls into the cylinders.
18   Check the block and head mating surfaces for nicks, deep scratches and other damage. If damage is slight, it can be removed with a file; if it's excessive, machining may be the only alternative.
19   Use a tap of the correct size to chase the threads in the head bolt holes. Mount each bolt in a vise and run a die down the threads to remove corrosion and restore the threads. Dirt, corrosion, sealant and damaged threads will affect torque readings.
20   Install the gasket over the engine block dowel pins with the mark THIS SIDE UP visible.

2A

8.7b   **Right exhaust manifold mounting details**

9.23   Cylinder head bolt tightening sequence

21   Position the cylinder head over the gasket.
22   Coat the cylinder head bolts with sealant and install them.
23   Tighten the bolts in the recommended sequence **(see illustration)** to the torque listed in this Chapter's specifications. Work up to the final torque in three steps.
24   Install the pushrods and rocker arms as described in Section 5.
25   The remaining installation steps are the reverse of removal.

10   Valve lifters – removal, inspection and installation

1   A noisy valve lifter can be isolated when the engine is idling. Hold a mechanic's stethoscope or a length of hose near the location of each valve while listening at the other end. Another method is to remove the rocker arm cover and, with the engine idling, place a finger on each of the valve spring retainers, one at a time. If a valve lifter is defective, it will be evident from the shock felt at the retainer as the valve seats.
2   The most likely causes of noisy valve lifters are dirt trapped between the plunger and the lifter body or lack of oil flow, viscosity or pressure. Before condemning the lifters, we recommend checking the oil for fuel contamination, correct level, cleanliness and correct viscosity.

Removal

Refer to illustration 10.7

3   Remove the rocker arm cover(s) as described in Section 4.
4   Remove the intake manifold as described in Section 7.
5   Remove the rocker arms, shafts and pushrods (see Section 5).
6   There are several ways to extract the lifters from the bores. A special tool designed to grip and remove lifters is manufactured by many tool companies and is widely available, but it may not be required in every case. On newer engines without a lot of varnish buildup, the lifters can often be removed with a small magnet or even with your fingers. A machinist's scribe with a bent end can be used to pull the lifters out by positioning the point under the retainer ring in the top of each lifter. **Caution:** *Don't use pliers to remove the lifters unless you intend to replace them with new ones (along with the camshaft). The pliers may damage the precision machined and hardened lifters, rendering them useless.*
7   Before removing the lifters, arrange to store them in a clearly labeled box to ensure they can be reinstalled in their original locations. Remove the lifters and store them where they won't get dirty **(see illustration)**.

Inspection and installation

Refer to illustrations 10.9a, 10.9b and 10.9c

8   Clean the lifters with solvent and dry them thoroughly without mixing them up.
9   Check each lifter wall, pushrod seat and foot for pitting, scuffing, score marks and uneven wear **(see illustration)**. Each lifter foot (the surface that rides on the cam lobe) must be slightly convex, although this can be difficult to determine by eye. If the base of the lifter is concave **(see illustration)**, the lifters and camshaft must be replaced. If the lifter walls are

10.7   The lifters on an engine that has accumulated many miles may have to be removed with a special tool – be sure to store the lifters in an organized manner to make sure they are reinstalled in their original locations

damaged or worn (which isn't very likely), inspect the lifter bores in the engine block as well. If the pushrod seats **(see illustration)** are worn, check the pushrod ends.
10   If new lifters are being installed, a new camshaft must also be installed. If the camshaft is replaced, then install new lifters as well (see Section 15). Never install used lifters unless the original camshaft is used and the lifters can be installed in their original locations! When installing lifters, make sure they're coated with moly-base grease or engine assembly lube.
11   Soak new lifters in oil to remove trapped air.
12   The remaining installation steps are the reverse of removal.
13   Run the engine and check for oil leaks.

11   Vibration damper – removal and installation

Removal

Refer to illustration 11.5

1   Remove the bolts and separate the radiator shroud from the radiator.
2   Remove the mounting bolts and detach the cooling fan and the radiator shroud.
3   Loosen the adjusting bolts as necessary, then remove the drivebelts, tagging each one as it's removed to simplify installation.
4   Remove the bolts from the crankshaft pulley (a screwdriver can be used to lock the starter ring gear on the driveplate so the crankshaft won't rotate), then detach the pulley. Remove the vibration damper-to-crankshaft bolt.
5   Attach a puller to the damper and draw it off the crankshaft. Be careful not to drop it as it comes free. A common gear puller should not be used – it may separate the outer portion of the damper from the hub. Use only a puller that bolts to the hub **(see illustration)**.

Installation

6   Coat the oil seal journal on the damper with moly-base grease.
7   Place the damper in position over the key on the crankshaft. Make sure the damper keyway lines up with the key.
8   Using a damper installation tool, push the damper onto the crankshaft. The special tool distributes the pressure evenly around the hub.
9   Remove the installation tool and install the damper bolt. Tighten the bolt to the specified torque.
10   To install the remaining components, reverse the removal procedure.
11   Adjust the drivebelts (refer to Chapter 1).

10.9a   If the bottom of any lifter is worn concave, pitted, scratched or galled, replace the entire set with new lifters

10.9b   The foot of each lifter should be slightly convex – the side of another lifter can be used as a straightedge to check it; if it appears flat, it's worn and must not be reused

10.9c   Check the pushrod seat (arrow) in the top of each lifter for wear

J-24420-A

11.5   Use a puller that applies force to the vibration damper hub – be sure the large puller bolt doesn't damage the crankshaft threads

12   Crankshaft front oil seal – replacement

With front cover installed on engine

Refer to illustration 12.3

1   With the vibration damper removed (see Section 11), pry the old seal out of the cover with a large screwdriver. Be very careful not to damage the seal journal on the crankshaft, or distort the cover.
2   Place the new seal in position with the open end facing toward the inside of the cover.
3   Drive the seal into the cover until it's seated. A special tool (see illustration) is recommended for this purpose. The tool is designed to exert even pressure around the entire circumference of the seal as it's hammered into place. A section of large-diameter pipe or a large socket can also be used. Be careful not to distort the front cover.
4   Reinstall the remaining parts in the reverse order of removal.

With front cover removed from engine

Refer to illustrations 12.7 and 12.9

5   This method is preferred, as the cover can be supported while the old seal is removed and the new one is installed.

12.3   A special tool is recommended for crankshaft front seal installation

2A

12.7   Driving the seal out of the front cover

12.9   Installing the new oil seal with a block of wood and a hammer

13.10   Front cover installation details

6   Remove the front cover (refer to Section 13).

7   Using a large screwdriver, pry the old seal out of the cover bore. As an alternative, support the cover and drive the seal out from the rear **(see illustration)**. Be careful not to damage the cover.

8   With the front of the cover facing up, place the new seal in position with the open end facing toward the inside of the cover.

9   Using a block of wood and hammer, drive the new seal into the cover until it's completely seated **(see illustration)**.

10   Install the front cover by reversing the removal procedure in Section 13.

13   Front cover – removal and installation

Refer to illustration 13.10

Removal

1   Drain the engine coolant (see Chapter 1).

2   Disconnect the heater hose and lower radiator hose from the water pump. Have a drain pan positioned under the vehicle, as some coolant will spill out.

3   Remove the fuel pump (see Chapter 4).

14.8   Timing chain installation details – the timing marks (arrows) on the sprockets should be aligned as shown

4   Remove the radiator fan, pulley and drivebelts (see Chapter 3).

5   Remove the oil filter (see Chapter 1).

6   Loosen the A.I.R pump adjusting bolt and move it out of the way.

7   Loosen the front clamp on the thermostat bypass hose and slide it to the rear.

8   Remove the vibration damper as described in Section 11.

9   Position the engine at TDC for number one cylinder (see Section 3). Remove the distributor (see Chapter 5). Be sure to mark the position of the rotor to the distributor housing and the distributor housing to the front cover to insure proper installation.

10   Place a drain pan under the front of the engine. Remove the front cover-to-engine bolts (be prepared for coolant spillage) and the two oil pan-to-front cover bolts, then separate the cover from the engine **(see illustration)**.

Installation

11   Clean all oil, dirt and old gasket material off the sealing surfaces of the cover and engine block. Replace the oil seal as described in Section 12.

12   Remove the oil pump cover and pack the space around the oil pump gears with petroleum jelly or grease. There must be no air space left inside the pump. Reinstall the cover using a new gasket. This is very important in order to insure immediate oil pressure.

13   Apply a thin coat of RTV sealant to the mating surfaces of the cover and the engine block (except the mating surface where the cover engages the oil pan lip). Apply a bead of RTV sealant to the cover-to-oil pan area. Position a new gasket over the dowel pins.

14   Apply sealant to the threads of the bolts surrounding the water passages. Place the front cover in position on the engine block and install the mounting bolts. Tighten the bolts to the specified torque in a criss-cross pattern (to avoid distorting the cover).

15   The remaining installation steps are the reverse of removal. Be sure to refill the cooling system (see Chapter 1). It's also a good idea to change the engine oil, as coolant may have leaked into the crankcase.

14   Timing chain and sprockets – inspection, removal and installation

Refer to illustrations 14.8, 14.9, 14.10 and 14.12

1   Disconnect the cable from the negative battery terminal.

2   Remove the vibration damper (see Section 11).

3   Remove the front cover (see Section 13).

Inspection

4   Before removing the chain and sprockets, visually inspect the teeth on the sprockets for signs of wear and check the chain for looseness.

5   If either or both sprockets show any signs of wear (edges on the teeth of the camshaft sprocket rounded, bright or blue areas on the teeth of either sprocket, chipping, pitting, etc.), they should be replaced with new ones. Wear in these areas is very common. Failure to replace a worn timing chain and sprockets may result in erratic engine performance, loss of power and lowered gas mileage.

6   If any one component (timing chain or either sprocket) requires replacement, the other two components should be replaced as well.

7   If it's determined the components require replacement, proceed as follows.

Removal

8   Reinstall the vibration damper mounting bolt and use it to turn the crankshaft clockwise until the marks on the camshaft sprocket and crankshaft sprocket are in exact alignment **(see illustration)**. At this point the number one and four pistons will be at top dead center with the number four piston in the firing position (verify by checking the position of the rotor in the distributor, which should point to the number four spark plug wire terminal). **Note:** *Do not attempt to remove either sprocket or the timing chain until this is done and do not turn the crankshaft or camshaft after the sprockets/chain are removed.*

14.9   A screwdriver will keep the camshaft sprocket from turning while loosening the mounting bolts

14.10   A gear puller will be needed to remove the crankshaft sprocket

9   Remove the camshaft sprocket mounting bolts **(see illustration)** and detach the camshaft sprocket, fuel pump eccentric and timing chain from the front of the engine. You may have to tap the sprocket with a soft-face hammer to dislodge it.
10   If you have to remove the crankshaft sprocket, it can be withdrawn with a gear puller **(see illustration)**. The oil slinger can be removed after the sprocket is removed.

Installation

11   Push the crankshaft sprocket onto the crankshaft with the vibration damper bolt and a large washer or washers.
12   Lubricate the thrust (rear) surface of the camshaft sprocket with moly-base grease or engine assembly lube **(see illustration)**. Install the timing chain over the camshaft sprocket with slack in the chain hanging down.
13   With the timing marks aligned, slip the chain over the crankshaft sprocket and then draw the camshaft sprocket into place with the bolts. Do not hammer or attempt to drive the camshaft sprocket into place, as it could dislodge the welch plug at the rear of the engine.
14   With the chain and both sprockets in place, check again to make sure the timing marks on the two sprockets are properly aligned. If not, remove the camshaft sprocket and move the chain until the marks align.
15   Lubricate the chain with engine oil and install the remaining components in the reverse order of removal.

14.12   Lubricate the thrust (rear) surface of the camshaft sprocket before installing it

15   Camshaft and bearings – removal, inspection and installation

Camshaft lobe lift check

Refer to illustration 15.3

1   To determine the extent of cam lobe wear, the lobe lift should be checked prior to camshaft removal. Refer to Section 4 and remove the rocker arm covers.
2   Position the number one piston at TDC on the compression stroke (see Section 3).
3   Beginning with the number one cylinder valves, mount a dial indicator on the engine and position the plunger against the top surface of the first rocker arm. The plunger should be directly above and in-line with the pushrod **(see illustration)**.
4   Zero the dial indicator, then very slowly turn the crankshaft in the normal direction of rotation until the indicator needle stops and begins to move in the opposite direction. The point at which it stops indicates maximum cam lobe lift.
5   Record this figure for future reference, then reposition the piston at TDC on the compression stroke.

15.3   When checking the camshaft lobe lift, the dial indicator plunger must be positioned directly above and in line with the pushrod

15.16   Long bolts can be threaded into the camshaft bolt holes to provide a handle for removal and installation – support the cam near the block as it's withdrawn

15.17   A length of wire with a hook on it can be used to support the camshaft as you guide it out of the block

6   Move the dial indicator to the remaining number one cylinder rocker arm and repeat the check. Be sure to record the results for each valve.
7   Repeat the check for the remaining valves. Since each piston must be at TDC on the compression stroke for this procedure, work from cylinder-to-cylinder following the firing order sequence.
8   After the check is complete, compare the results to the Specifications. If camshaft lobe lift is less than specified, cam lobe wear has occurred and a new camshaft should be installed.

Removal

Refer to illustrations 15.16 and 15.17
9   Disconnect the cable from the negative battery terminal.
10   Drain the coolant (see Chapter 1).
11   Remove the radiator (see Chapter 3).
12   If equipped with air conditioning, remove the condenser (see Chapter 3). **Warning:** *The air conditioning system is under high pressure. Do not loosen any fittings or remove any components until after the system has been discharged by a dealer service department or service station. Always wear eye protection when disconnecting refrigerant fittings.*
13   Remove the rocker arms and shafts, pushrods and lifters, referring to the appropriate Sections in this Chapter.
14   Remove the front cover (see Section 13).
15   Remove the timing chain and camshaft sprocket (see Section 14).
16   Install two long bolts in the end of the camshaft to use as a handle to pull on and support the camshaft **(see illustration)**.
17   Carefully draw the camshaft out of the engine block. Do this very slowly to avoid damage to the camshaft bearings as the lobes pass over them. Support the camshaft with one hand near the engine block and the other with a wire hook at the other end **(see illustration)**.

Inspection and installation

Refer to illustration 15.19
18   Refer to Chapter 2, Part B, for camshaft and bearing inspection procedures.
19   Prior to installing the camshaft, coat each of the lobes and journals with engine assembly lube or moly-base grease **(see illustration)**.
20   Slide the camshaft into the engine block, again taking extra care so you don't damage the bearings.
21   Install the camshaft sprocket and timing chain as described in Section 14.
22   Install the remaining components in the reverse order of removal by referring to the appropriate Chapter or Section.
23   Have the air conditioning system (if equipped) evacuated and recharged. Refill the engine coolant (see Chapter 1).

15.19   Be sure to apply moly-base grease or engine assembly lube to the cam lobes and bearing journals before installing the camshaft

---

16   Oil pan – removal and installation

Refer to illustration 16.7
Note: *The following procedure is based on the assumption the engine is in the vehicle. If its been removed, simply unbolt the oil pan and detach it from the block.*

Removal

1   Disconnect the negative battery cable from the battery.
2   Remove the starter motor (see Chapter 5).
3   Separate the exhaust pipes from the manifolds.
4   Drain the oil (see Chapter 1).
5   Remove the engine mount bolts (see Section 20) and raise the engine using an engine hoist.
6   Remove the oil pan mounting bolts.

2A

16.7   Oil pan installation details – some models use RTV sealant instead of a gasket, but replacement gaskets are available

17.4   Exploded view of the oil pump cover and pressure relief valve

7   Carefully separate the pan from the block **(see illustration)**. Don't pry between the block and pan or damage to the sealing surfaces may result and oil leaks could develop. If the pan sticks, use a block of wood and a hammer to break it loose. You may have to turn the crankshaft slightly to maneuver the front of the pan past the crankshaft counterweights.

Installation

8   Scrape off all traces of old gasket material and sealant. Clean the gasket sealing surfaces with lacquer thinner or acetone. Make sure the bolt holes in the block are clean.
9   Check the oil pan flanges for distortion, particularly around the bolt holes and corners. If necessary, place the pan on a block of wood and use a hammer to flatten and restore the gasket surface. If distortion is severe, install a new oil pan.
10   On models that don't use a gasket, apply a continuous 3/16-inch diameter bead of RTV sealant to the oil pan flange, to the inside of the bolt holes. Install the pan while the sealant is still wet.
11   If a gasket is to be used, place it on the oil pan, using a few dabs or RTV sealant to hold it in place.
12   Carefully position the pan against the block and install the bolts finger-tight. Tighten the bolts in three steps to the torque listed in this Chapter's specifications. Start at the center of the pan and work out toward the ends in a spiral pattern.
13   The remaining steps are the reverse of removal. **Caution:** *Don't forget to refill the engine with oil before starting it (see Chapter 1).*
14   Start the engine and check carefully for oil leaks at the oil pan.

17   Oil pump – removal, inspection and installation

Refer to illustrations 17.4, 17.9a, 17.9b, 17.9c and 17.9d

Removal

1   Remove the oil filter (see Chapter 1).
2   Remove the bolts attaching the oil pump cover assembly to the front cover. Remove the cover assembly and slide out the oil pump gears. If there is a lot of varnish build-up in the engine and the drive gear won't come out, remove the distributor and carefully tap it out from above with a long punch.

Inspection

3   Clean the gears with solvent and inspect them for wear and scoring. If the gears aren't in good condition, replace them as a set.
4   Unscrew the oil pressure relief valve cap, spring and valve **(see illustration)**. Do not remove the oil filter by-pass valve and spring, as they are staked in place.
5   Wash the parts with solvent and inspect the relief valve for wear and scoring. Check to make sure the relief valve spring is not collapsed or worn on its side. Any relief valve spring which is questionable should be replaced with a new one.
6   Check the relief valve in its bore in the cover. It should be an easy slip-fit only, and any side shake that can be felt is too much. The valve and/or cover should be replaced with a new one in this case.
7   The filter by-pass valve should be flat and free of nicks, cracks or warping and scratches.
8   Lubricate the pressure relief valve and spring, and install it in the bore of the oil pump case. Install the cap and gasket, and tighten the cap securely.
9   Install the gears and, using feeler gauges, check the clearance between the gear teeth and the wall of the pump **(see illustration)**. Now, lay a straightedge across the gears and measure the end clearance between the pump gasket surface and the straightedge **(see illustration)**. If either of these two measurements are not within the tolerances listed in this Chapter's Specifications, measure the diameter and length of the gears, and the depth of the pump body, to determine if it is the gears or the pump body that is worn **(see illustrations)**. If the gears are found to be worn, replace them as a set. If the pump body is worn, the front cover must be replaced (see Section 13), in which case a new set of gears would also be installed.
10   If the condition of the pump is satisfactory at this point, remove the gears and pack the pocket full of petroleum jelly. Do not use chassis lube.

Installation

11   Re-install the gears, making sure that petroleum jelly is forced into every cavity of the gear pocket and between the teeth of the gears. The pump may not prime itself when the engine is started if the pump is not packed with the petroleum jelly.
12   Install the pump cover bolts and tighten them to the torque listed in this Chapter's Specifications.
13   Install a new oil filter and check the oil level with the dipstick. Pay close attention to the oil pressure gauge or warning light during the initial startup and driving period. Shut off the engine and inspect all work if a lack of pressure is indicated.

18   Driveplate – removal and installation

Refer to illustrations 18.2 and 18.3

1   Raise the vehicle and support it securely on jackstands, then refer to Chapter 7 and remove the transmission.
2   Use a sharp scribe or a marking pen to draw a line from the driveplate to the end of the crankshaft for correct alignment during reinstallation **(see illustration)**.
3   Remove the bolts that secure the driveplate to the crankshaft flange. If difficulty is experienced in removing the bolts due to movement of the crankshaft, use a screwdriver to keep the driveplate from turning **(see illustration)**.

17.9a   Using feeler gauges, check the clearance between
the gear teeth and the pump wall

17.9b   Check the clearance of the gears using a
straightedge and feeler gauges

2A

LENGTH
OF GEAR

DIAMETER
OF GEAR

17.9c   Measure the length and diameter of the gears
using a micrometer

DEPTH OF POCKET

DIAMETER OF
POCKET

17.9d   A depth micrometer must be used to measure the
depth of the pump body, and a small telescoping gauge or
vernier calipers can be used to measure the diameter of the pocket

18.2   To insure proper balance, mark the driveplate's relation to
the crankshaft

18.3   A large screwdriver wedged in the starter ring gear teeth or
one of the holes in the driveplate can be used to keep the
driveplate from turning as the mounting bolts are removed

4   Remove the driveplate from the crankshaft flange.

5   Check the starter ring gear for cracked or broken teeth. Lay the drive-plate on a flat surface and use a straightedge to check for warpage.

6   Clean the mating surfaces of the driveplate and the crankshaft.

7   Position the driveplate against the crankshaft, matching the alignment marks made during removal. Before installing the bolts, apply a thread locking compound to the threads.

8   Wedge a screwdriver through the driveplate or into the ring gear teeth to keep the crankshaft from turning. Tighten the bolts to the torque listed in this Chapter's Specifications. Working in a criss-cross pattern, tighten the bolts in two or three steps.

9   The remainder of installation is the reverse of the removal procedure.

19   Crankshaft rear oil seal – replacement

The V6 engine installed in the vehicles covered by this manual are equipped with a braided fabric type rear oil seal. Refer to Chapter 2, Part B, for the replacement procedure.

20   Engine mounts – check and replacement

1   Engine mounts seldom require attention, but broken or deteriorated mounts should be replaced immediately or the added strain placed on the driveline components may cause damage.

Check

2   During the check, the engine must be raised slightly to remove the weight from the mounts. Disconnect the negative battery cable from the battery.

3   Raise the vehicle and support it securely on jackstands, then position the jack under the engine oil pan. Place a wood block between the jack head and the oil pan, then carefully raise the engine just enough to take the weight off the mounts.

4   Check the mounts to see if the rubber is cracked, hardened or separated from the metal plates. Sometimes the rubber will split right down the center. Rubber preservative may be applied to the mounts to slow deterioration.

5   Check for relative movement between the mount plates and the engine or frame (use a large screwdriver or pry bar to attempt to move the mounts). If movement is noted, lower the engine and tighten the mount fasteners.

Replacement

Refer to illustration 20.7

6   Remove the fan shroud mounting screws and place the shroud over the fan.

7   Remove the engine mount through-bolts **(see illustration)**.

8   Disconnect the shift linkage where it connects the transmission to the body (Chapter 7).

9   Raise the engine high enough to clear the clevis brackets. Do not force the engine up too high. If it touches anything before the mounts are free, remove the part for clearance. Place a block of wood between the oil pan and crossmember as a safety precaution.

10   Unbolt the mount from the engine block and remove it from the vehicle. **Note:** *On vehicles equipped with self-locking nuts and bolts, replace them with new ones whenever they are disassembled. Prior to assembly, remove hardened residual adhesive from the engine block holes with a proper-size bottoming tap.*

11   Attach the new mount to the engine block and install the fasteners in the appropriate locations. Tighten the fasteners securely.

12   Remove the wooden block and lower the engine into place. Install the through-bolts and tighten the nuts securely.

13   Complete the installation by reinstalling all parts removed to gain access to the mounts.

20.7   V6 engine mount details

Chapter 2 Part B V8 engines

Contents

2B

Specifications

472, 500, 425 and 368 cu in engines

Firing order 1-5-6-3-4-2-7-8

Camshaft
Journal diameter
  472 .... Not available
  500 .... Not available
  368, 425 .... 2.6243 to 2.6250 in
Lobe lift – compare the readings for each intake and
  each exhaust valve ....

Replace the camshaft if readings vary more than 0.003 in.

Torque specifications	**Ft-lbs** (unless otherwise indicated)
Intake manifold bolts	30
Exhaust manifold-to-cylinder head	
Long bolt	35
Short bolt	12
Cylinder head bolts	
425, 368	95
472, 500	115
Driveplate-to-crankshaft bolts	75
Oil pan bolts	14
Oil pump cover bolts	10
Crankshaft pulley-to-hub bolts	17
Rocker arm cover bolts	30 in-lbs
Front cover bolts	
5/16 – 18	10
3/8 – 16	22

Rocker arm shaft bolts
   368, 425 and 500 70
   472 60
Main bearing cap bolts 90

5.7L (350 cu in) Chevrolet engine

Firing order 1-8-4-3-6-5-7-2

Camshaft
Journal diameter .... 1.8682 to 1.8692 in
Runout (limit) .... 0.001 in
Endplay .... 0.004 to 0.012 in
Lobe lift – compare the readings for each intake and
   each exhaust valve .... Replace the camshaft if readings vary more than 0.003 in.

Torque specifications
Ft-lbs (unless otherwise indicated)
Intake manifold bolts 35
Exhaust manifold-to-cylinder head bolts* 25
Camshaft sprocket bolt 21
Camshaft retainer bolt .... 105 in-lbs
Cylinder head bolts 70
Driveplate-to-crankshaft bolts 75
Front cover bolts .... 100 in-lbs
Crankshaft pulley bolts 45
Crankshaft rear seal retainer bolts/nuts .... 132 in-lbs
Oil pan
   Bolts .... 100 in-lbs
   Nuts 17
Oil pump cover bolts .... 80 in-lbs
Rocker arm cover bolts .... 75 in-lbs
Roller lifter guide retainer bolts .... 83 in-lbs
Vibration damper bolt 70
* lightly oil threads

**5.7L (350)
Chevrolet**

350 cu in Oldsmobile engine
Firing order 1-8-4-3-6-5-7-2

Camshaft
Journal diameter
   no. 1 .... 2.0365 to 2.0357 in
   no. 2 .... 2.0165 to 2.0157 in
   no. 3 .... 1.9965 to 1.9957 in
   no. 4 .... 1.9767 to 1.9757 in
   no. 5 .... 1.9565 to 1.9557 in
Endplay .... 0.011 to 0.077 in
Lobe lift – compare the readings for each intake and
   each exhaust valve .... Replace the camshaft if readings vary more than 0.003 in.

Torque specifications
Ft-lbs (unless otherwise indicated)
Intake manifold bolts* 40
Exhaust manifold-to-cylinder head bolts 25
Camshaft sprocket bolt 65
Cylinder head bolts*
   1976 and earlier 85
   1977 on 130
Driveplate bolts 60
Front cover bolts (see illustration 9.8d) 35
   A and B 35
   C, D and G 22
   E 13
Vibration damper-to-crankshaft bolt 310
Oil pan bolts 10
Oil pump cover bolts .... 96 in-lbs
Crankshaft pulley-to-hub bolts 20
Rocker arm cover bolts .... 84 in-lbs
Rocker arm pivot bolts 25
* lightly oil threads

**5.7L (350)
Oldsmobile**

5.0L (307 cu in) Oldsmobile engine
Firing order 1-8-4-3-6-5-7-2

Camshaft

Journal diameter

no. 1	2.0365 to 2.0352 in
no. 2	2.0166 to 2.0152 in
no. 3	1.9965 to 1.9952 in
no. 4	1.9765 to 1.9752 in
no. 5	1.9565 to 1.9552 in
Endplay	0.006 to 0.022 in
Lobe lift – compare the readings for each intake and each exhaust valve	Replace the camshaft if readings vary more than 0.003 in.

Torque specifications

Ft-lbs (unless otherwise indicated)

Intake manifold bolts*	40
Exhaust manifold-to-cylinder head bolts	25
Camshaft sprocket bolt	65
Cylinder head bolts*	
1986	125
1987 and 1988	130
1989 on	
Step 1	40
Step 2	
Positions 1 through 7 and 9	Rotate an additional 120-degrees
Positions 8 and 10	Rotate an additional 95-degrees
Driveplate bolts	60
Vibration damper-to-crankshaft bolt	310
Oil pan bolts	10
Oil pan nuts	17
Oil pump cover bolts	96 in-lbs
Crankshaft pulley-to-hub bolts	20
Rocker arm cover bolts	84 in-lbs
Rocker arm pivot bolt	25
Front cover bolts	35

* lightly oil threads

2B

HT4100 engine

Firing order 1-8-4-3-6-5-7-2

Camshaft

Journal diameter (all)	Not available

Lobe lift – compare the lift readings for each intake and each exhaust valve. Replace the camshaft if readings vary more than 0.003 in.

Torque specifications

Ft-lbs (unless otherwise indicated)

Intake manifold bolts	
Step 1 (bolts 1 through 4)	15
Step 2 (bolts 5 through 16)	20
Step 3 (all bolts, in sequence)	22
Exhaust manifold-to-cylinder head bolts	20
Camshaft sprocket bolt	35
Crankshaft pulley-to-hub bolts	20
Cylinder head bolts	
Step 1	45
Step 2	90
Driveplate-to-crankshaft bolts	35
Oil pan bolts	10
Rocker arm cover bolts	50 in-lbs
Rocker arm pivot-to-support bolts	20
Rocker arm support-to-head bolt nuts	35
Front cover bolts	15

1   General information and engine identification

General information

This Part of Chapter 2 is devoted to in-vehicle repair procedures for the V8 engines. All information concerning engine removal and installation and engine block and cylinder head overhaul can be found in Part C of this Chapter.

Since the repair procedures included in this Part are based on the assumption that the engine is still installed in the vehicle, if they are being used during a complete engine overhaul (with the engine already out of the vehicle and on a stand) many of the steps included here will not apply.

The specifications included in this Part of Chapter 2 apply only to the procedures found here. The specifications necessary for rebuilding the block and cylinder heads are included in Part C.

Engine identification

Until 1977, most engines in Cadillac automobiles were manufactured by Cadillac. However, since that time, Cadillac automobiles come equipped with various engines, supplied by Oldsmobile, Chevrolet and Buick divisions of General Motors.

On 1972 and newer models, a check of the Vehicle Identification Number (VIN) will help you determine which engine your vehicle has. The VIN is stamped onto a small metal plate that is affixed to the cowl bar, visible through the lower left (driver's side) corner of the windshield (see the introductory pages at the front of this manual). The number gives information concerning the engine, the year of the vehicle, and so on. 1972 through 1980 models use a 13 digit number, the fifth position in the VIN being the character that denotes the type of engine. 1981 and newer models use a 17 digit number, the eighth digit of the VIN reveals which engine is installed. Refer to the accompanying chart to determine which engine you have.

There are some differences between the various makes of engines, but overall, repair and maintenance procedures are nearly identical. Where differences occur, they will be noted. A check of the Specifications chart at the beginning of this Chapter will alert the home mechanic to any differences in the various tolerances. Also check the Vehicle Emission Control Information label, located adjacent to the radiator, for additional engine information.

ENGINE IDENTIFICATION

VIN CODE	ENGINE TYPE
R (1974 and earlier)	472
S (1975 and 1976)	500
S,T (1977 to 1979)	425
R (1975 through 1979)	350 Olds
9,6 (1980 only)	368 (carbureted)
9,6 (1981 only)	368 V8-6-4
8 (1982 to 1985)	4.1L (250) Aluminum (HT4100)
Y (1986 to 1990)	5.0L (307) Olds
7 (1990 on)	5.7L (350) Chevy

Cadillac produced two engines that differed from their other conventional V8 engines. In 1981 the 368 V8-6-4, equipped with a Modulated Displacement system, was introduced, but was used for 1981 models only, then dropped. From 1982 through 1985, a 4.1L (250 cu.in.) aluminum engine, commonly referred to as the HT4100, was used.

The 368 Modulated Displacement engine, also known as the V8-6-4, reduces the number of operating cylinders with the use of valve selectors located on the rocker arm assemblies. When energized, these valve selectors deactivate certain cylinders, closing the intake and exhaust valves of those cylinders. As engine load decreases, it will run on six, then four cylinders. When full power is required, the valve selectors are de-energized and all eight cylinders function normally.

The HT4100 engine is constructed of an aluminum block with cast iron cylinder heads. Because the engine is largely aluminum, particular care must be taken to accommodate the characteristics of this metal. Bolts which thread into aluminum must not be over-tightened or the threads may be damaged. The cylinder head tightening procedure must be strictly followed to insure proper sealing of the head gasket. When cleaning the gasket surfaces of the aluminum, use soft wire brushes or dull scrapers. Blow out all debris from the bolt holes to avoid inaccurate torque readings.

2   Repair operations possible with the engine in the vehicle

Many major repair operations can be accomplished without removing the engine from the vehicle.

Clean the engine compartment and the exterior of the engine with some type of degreaser before any work is done. A clean engine will make the job easier and will help keep dirt out of the internal areas of the engine.

Depending on the components involved, it may be a good idea to remove the hood to improve access to the engine as repairs are performed (refer to Chapter 11 if necessary).

If oil or coolant leaks develop, indicating a need for gasket or seal replacement, the repairs can generally be made with the engine in the vehicle. The oil pan gasket, the cylinder head gaskets, intake and exhaust manifold gaskets, timing cover gaskets and the crankshaft oil seals are accessible with the engine in place.

Exterior engine components, such as the water pump, the starter motor, the alternator, the distributor and the fuel system components, as well as the intake and exhaust manifolds, can be removed for repair with the engine in place.

Since the cylinder heads can be removed without pulling the engine, valve component servicing can also be accomplished with the engine in the vehicle.

Replacement of, repairs to, or inspection of the timing chain and sprockets, camshaft and the oil pump are all possible with the engine in place.

In extreme cases, caused by a lack of necessary equipment, repair or replacement of piston rings, pistons, connecting rods and rod bearings is possible with the engine in the vehicle. However, this practice is not recommended because of the cleaning and preparation work that must be performed on the components involved.

3   Top Dead Center (TDC) for number one piston – locating

See Chapter 2, Part A, for this procedure. Be sure to use the firing order in the Specifications in this Part of Chapter 2, where necessary.

4   Rocker arm covers – removal and installation

Refer to illustrations 4.6a, 4.6b and 4.9
1   Disconnect the negative cable from the battery.
2   Remove the air cleaner assembly (see Chapter 4 if necessary).
3   Label and disconnect any emissions or vacuum lines and wires which are routed over the rocker arm cover(s). Note: If you are working on a V8-6-4 engine, disconnect the electrical connectors from the modulated displacement valve selectors.
4   Remove any braces or brackets which block access to the cover(s), noting the way they are mounted to ease reassembly.
5   Detach any remaining accessories as necessary. If removal of the air conditioning compressor is required, unbolt the unit and carefully set it aside without disconnecting the refrigerant lines. **Warning:** *The air conditioning system is under high pressure. Do not disconnect any refrigerant line or fitting without first having the system discharged by an air conditioning technician.*
6   Remove the rocker arm cover bolts **(see illustrations)**.

4.6a   Rocker arm cover installation details (5.7L Chevrolet built engines)

1 Bolt	4 Rocker arm cover (left)
2 Washer	5 Gasket
3 Rocker arm cover (right)	

SCREW
3 REQD.

EGR
SOLENOID
VALVE

SCREW
WITH STUD
3 REQD.

SCREW WITH
THREADED
STUD

REFER TO
FIGURE 1

REFER TO
FIGURE 1

RIGHT SIDE

2B

SEAL

INTAKE
MANIFOLD/
CYLINDER
HEAD

FIGURE 1

VACUUM PIPE
BRACKET

SCREW

SCREW WITH
THREADED STUD
2 REQD.

REFER TO FIGURE 1

SCREW
WITH
STUD
3 REQD.

REFER TO
FIGURE 1

LEFT SIDE

4.6b   Rocker arm cover installation details (HT4100 engine)

Apply a 3/32" bead of R.T.V. (room temperature vulcanizing) sealer on the valve cover as shown

4.9   If your rocker arm covers had RTV sealant instead of a gasket, apply a bead of sealant inside of the bolt holes as shown – install the cover while the sealant is still wet

ROCKER ARM SUPPORT

ROCKER ARMS

5.3a   425 engine rocker arm assembly

5.3b   Rocker arms and related components on a late model 5.0L engine

1	Valve keepers	10	Rocker arms
2	Intake valve seal	11	Pushrods
3	Valve spring	12	Coil spring
4	Dampener spring	13	Rotator body
5	Valve rotator	14	Collar
6	Exhaust valve seal	15	Valve spring
7	Identification pad	16	Flat washer
8	Rocker arm bolts	17	Intake valve
9	Rocker arm pivot	18	Exhaust valve

FRONT OF ENGINE

SELECTOR ASSM.

PIVOT

ARM

SHIELD

PEDESTAL

PIVOT

ARM

SEAL

5.3c   Rocker arm assembly on a V8-6-4 engine

ROCKER
ARM
PIVOT

PUSHROD

ROCKER ARM
SUPPORT

ROCKER ARM
SUPPORT STUD
(HEAD BOLT)

5.3d   HT4100 engine rocker arm assembly

2B

5.4   A perforated cardboard box can be used to store the pushrods to ensure they are reinstalled in their original locations – note the label indicating the front of the engine

7   Remove the rocker arm cover. **Caution:** *Do not pry on the sealing flange. To do so may damage the surface, causing oil leaks. Tap on the sides of the cover with a rubber hammer until it pops loose.*
8   Thoroughly clean the mating surfaces, removing all traces of old gasket material. Use acetone or lacquer thinner and a clean rag to remove any traces of oil.
9   Prepare the cover for installation by applying a continuous bead of RTV sealant **(see illustration)** or a new gasket to the sealing flange. Use

the same sealing method the vehicle had, otherwise new bolts of a different length may be required.
10   Install the cover(s) and bolts and tighten them securely. Do not overtighten them, as the covers may be deformed.
11   Reinstall the remaining parts in the reverse order of removal.
12   Run the engine and check for leaks.

---

5   Rocker arms and pushrods – removal, inspection and installation

---

Removal

Refer to illustrations 5.3a, 5.3b, 5.3c, 5.3d and 5.4

1   Refer to Section 4 and detach the rocker arm cover(s) from the cylinder head(s).
2   Remove each of the rocker arm bolts or nuts (or the rocker shaft bolts). Place them at their correct location in a cardboard box or rack.
3   Remove each rocker arm assembly, placing each component on the numbered box or rack **(see illustrations)**. **Note:** *On HT4100 engines, remove the rocker arm support retaining nuts and lift the rocker arms and support as a single unit* **(see illustration)**. The rocker arms can replaced individually if necessary. Be sure to mark each rocker arm pivot Left or Right to insure proper installation.
4   Remove the pushrods and store them separately to make sure they don't get mixed up during installation **(see illustration)**.

Inspection

5   Check each rocker arm for wear, cracks and other damage, especially where the pushrods and valve stems contact the rocker arm faces.

5.13   To adjust the valves on the 5.7L Chevrolet engine, rotate each pushrod as the rocker arm nut is tightened to determine the point at which all play is removed, then tighten each nut an additional turn

6   Make sure the hole at the pushrod end of each rocker arm is open.
7   Check each rocker arm pivot area for wear, cracks and galling. If the rocker arms are worn or damaged, replace them with new ones and use new pivot balls as well. Be sure to check the rocker shafts, too (where applicable).
8   Inspect the pushrods for cracks and excessive wear at the ends. Roll each pushrod across a piece of plate glass to see if it's bent (if it wobbles, it's bent).

Installation

9   Lubricate the lower end of each pushrod with clean engine oil or moly-base grease and install them in their original locations. Make sure each pushrod seats completely in the lifter.
10   Apply moly-base grease to the ends of the valve stems and the upper ends of the pushrods before positioning the rocker arms over the studs.
11   Set the rocker arms in place, then install the pivots (except engines with rocker shafts) and bolts or nuts. Apply moly-base grease to the pivots or shafts to prevent damage to the mating surfaces before engine oil pressure builds up. On models with nuts (late model Chevrolet-built engines), be sure to install each nut with the flat side against the pivot ball. Also, adjust the valves, as described below.

Valve adjustment (5.7L Chevrolet-built engine only)

Refer to illustration 5.13
Note: *If the valve clearance is excessive on engines other than the 5.7L Chevrolet engine, check that the pivot bolts are tightened securely, then inspect for worn parts.*

12   Refer to Section 3 and bring the number one piston to top dead center on the compression stroke.
13   Tighten the rocker arm nuts (number one cylinder only) until all play is removed at the pushrods. This can be determined by rotating each pushrod between your thumb and index finger as the nut is tightened **(see illustration)**. You'll be able to feel the point at which all play is eliminated because the pushrod will no longer turn.
14   Tighten each nut an additional turn to center the lifters. Valve adjustment for cylinder number one is now complete.
15   With the engine still at TDC for number one cylinder, adjust the exhaust valves for cylinders one, three, four and eight. The intake valves for cylinders one, two, five and seven may also be adjusted.
16   Turn the engine one revolution in the normal direction of rotation, which will bring cylinder number six to TDC on the compression stroke. The exhaust valves for cylinders two, five, six and seven, and the intake valves for cylinders three, four, six and eight can now be adjusted.

7.1a   HT4100 vibration damper installation details

7.1b   This special tool is necessary to remove the hub on the HT4100 engine

17   Refer to Section 4 and install the rocker arm covers. Start the engine, listen for unusual valvetrain noises and check for oil leaks at the rocker arm cover joints.

---

6   Valve spring, retainer and seals – replacement in vehicle

Refer to Chapter 2, Part A, for this procedure. Remove the rocker arm covers, rocker arms and pushrods following the appropriate Sections in this Chapter.

---

7   Vibration damper – removal and installation

Refer to illustrations 7.1a and 7.1b
Refer to Chapter 2, Part A, for this procedure. **Note:** *The HT4100 engine uses a two-piece damper* **(see illustration)**. *The hub of this damper is a very tight press fit on the crankshaft, and requires a special tool (GM tool no. J-21052-02, or equivalent) for removal* **(see illustration)**.

8.2   A puller tool like this should be used to remove the front seal from the front cover, but if one isn't available, a large screwdriver can be used to pry the seal out

8.6   While supporting the cover near the seal bore, drive the old seal out from the inside with a hammer and punch or screwdriver

8   Crankshaft front oil seal – replacement

Neoprene-type seals

Timing cover in place
Refer to illustration 8.2

1   Remove the vibration damper as described in Section 7.
2   Carefully pull the seal out of the cover with a seal removal tool (GM tool nos. J-1859-03, J-21052-4 and J-23129, or equivalent) **(see illustration)** or pry it out with a large screwdriver. Be careful not to distort the cover or scratch the wall of the seal bore. It's a good idea to apply penetrating oil to the seal-to-cover joint and allow it to soak in before attempting to pull the seal out.
3   Clean the bore to remove any old seal material and corrosion. Position the new seal in the bore with the open end of the seal facing IN. A small amount of oil applied to the outer edge of the new seal will make installation easier.
4   Drive the seal into the bore with a large socket and hammer until it's completely seated. Select a socket that's the same outside diameter as the seal (a section of pipe can be used if a socket isn't available).
5   Reinstall the vibration damper.

Timing cover removed
Refer to illustration 8.6

6   Use a punch or screwdriver and hammer to drive the seal out of the cover from the back side. Support the cover as close to the seal bore as possible **(see illustration)**. Be careful not to distort the cover or scratch the wall of the seal bore. If the engine has accumulated a lot of miles, apply penetrating oil to the seal-to-cover joint on each side and allow it to soak in before attempting to drive the seal out.
7   Clean the bore to remove any old seal material and corrosion. Support the cover on blocks of wood and position the new seal in the bore with the open end of the seal facing IN. A small amount of oil applied to the outer edge of the new seal will make installation easier.
8   Drive the seal into the bore with a large socket and hammer until it's completely seated. Select a socket that's the same outside diameter as the seal (a section of pipe can be used if a socket isn't available).

Braided-rope type seals

9   Remove the front cover (see Section 12).

10   Using a punch, drive the old seal and shedder out the back of the front cover.
11   Coil new seal packing around the opening so the ends of the packing are at the top. Drive the shedder in with a punch. Stake the shedder in place in at least three places.
12   Size the packing by rotating a hammer handle or similar tool around the packing until the damper hub can be inserted through the opening.
13   Lubricate the seal and install the vibration damper as described in Section 7.

2B

9   Intake manifold – removal and installation

Removal

1   Disconnect the cable from the negative terminal of the battery.
2   Drain the cooling system (see Chapter 1).
3   Remove the air cleaner assembly.
4   Detach all coolant hoses from the intake manifold.
5   Label and then disconnect any wiring and vacuum, emission and/or fuel lines which attach to the intake manifold.
6   Remove the EGR valve, if necessary (see Chapter 6).
7   On engines with the distributor mounted through the manifold, remove the distributor (see Chapter 5).
8   Remove the carburetor or throttle body unit (see Chapter 4).
9   Remove the intake manifold bolts and any brackets, noting their locations, so they may be reinstalled in the same location.
10   Lift off the manifold. If it is difficult to break loose, carefully pry against a casting protrusion. **Caution:** *Do not pry against a sealing surface.* **Note:** If your engine has a valley cover under the intake manifold, this must be removed to access the valve lifters. Unbolt the cover and lift it out.
11   Stuff rags in the exposed ports and passages. Thoroughly clean all sealing surfaces, removing all traces of gasket material. Check the exhaust crossover passages in the manifold and the cylinder heads for carbon blockage.

Installation
Refer to illustrations 9.13a, 9.13b, 9.14a, 9.14b and 9.14c

12   Position new gaskets and ridge seals, using RTV sealant in the corners to hold them in place. Use plastic gasket retainers, if provided. Follow the gasket manufacturer's instructions.

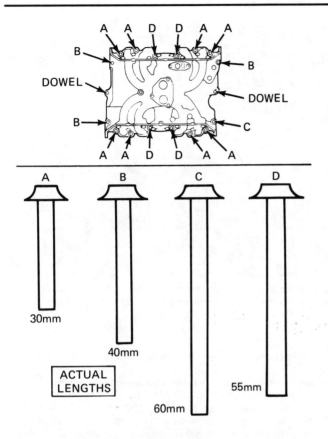

ACTUAL
LENGTHS

30mm

40mm

60mm

55mm

9.13a   Intake manifold bolts on the HT4100 engine

◄ FRONT OF ENGINE

9.13b   Intake manifold bolt tightening sequence on the
HT4100 engine

1. LUBRICATE ENTIRE BOLT IN ENGINE OIL
2. TIGHTEN ALL BOLTS IN SEQUENCE SHOWN

9.14a   Intake manifold bolt tightening sequence on the
5.0L engine

◄ FRT

12   INTAKE MANIFOLD

9.14b   Intake manifold tightening sequence on the 5.7L
Chevy engine

trations). **Warning:** *If the incorrect bolts are used, coolant leaks or
stripped threads may result.*

No mark
This is the 1982 manifold which uses 3 bolt sizes as follows:

40 mm bolt (B)	Bolt locations 1, 2, 3, 4, 12, 13 and 16
30 mm bolt (A)	Bolt locations 5, 6, 7, 8, 9, 10, 11 and 14
60 mm bolt (C)	Bolt location 15

X mark
This manifold uses four bolt sizes as follows:

55 mm bolt (D)	Bolt locations 1, 2, 3 and 4
30 mm bolt (A)	Bolt locations 5, 6, 7, 8, 9, 10, 11 and 14
40 mm bolt (B)	Bolt locations 12, 13 and 16
60 mm bolt (C)	Bolt location 15

Circle with an X inside
*This manifold uses the same bolt locations as the X manifold except for
bolt location 12*

55 mm bolt (D)	Bolt location 12

13   Set the manifold into position. Be sure all the bolt holes are lined up
and start all the bolts by hand before tightening any of them. **Note:** *The
HT4100 engine uses three or four different length intake manifold-to-cylinder head bolts. To determine which intake manifold-to-cylinder head
bolts to use, look for an identifying mark on the intake manifold next to the
manifold air temperature sensor, then refer to the chart below* (see illus-

9.14c Intake manifold torque sequence on the 350 (5.7L)
Olds engine

10.7 Exhaust manifold shrouds on the 307 (5.0L)
Olds engine

10.11a Right exhaust manifold on the HT4100 engine

10.11b Left exhaust manifold on the HT4100 engine

14 Tighten the bolts in three stages, following the appropriate sequence **(see illustrations)** until the specified torque is reached. If the tightening sequence for your engine isn't shown, tighten the bolts carefully and evenly using a similar pattern.

15 The remainder of installation is the reverse of removal. Be sure to refill the cooling system and change the oil and filter (see Chapter 1), as coolant often gets into the oil during manifold removal.

16 Run the engine and check for fluid and vacuum leaks. Adjust the ignition timing, if the distributor was disturbed (see Chapter 1). Road test the vehicle, checking for proper operation of engine and accessories.

10 Exhaust manifolds – removal and installation

Refer to illustrations 10.7, 10.11a, 10.11b and 10.14

Removal

1 Allow the engine to cool completely.
2 Place protective covers on the fenders.
3 Disconnect the negative cable from the battery.
4 Raise the vehicle and support it securely on jackstands.

5 Spray penetrating oil on the threads of fasteners holding the hot air shrouds and the exhaust pipe(s) to the manifold(s) you wish to remove. Go on to the next steps, allowing the penetrating oil to soak in.

6 Remove the air cleaner and hot air duct.

7 Detach the hot air shroud(s) or heat stove assembly from the manifold **(see illustration)**.

8 Label and then remove spark plug and oxygen sensor wires and any hoses such as EFE or AIR, as needed.

9 Unbolt any engine accessories which block access to the manifold(s) such as the alternator, air conditioning compressor or power steering pump. Refer to the appropriate Chapters (5, 3, 10) for further information. When unbolting the air conditioning compressor, leave the refrigerant lines connected and tie the compressor aside without putting a strain on the fittings. **Warning:** *Do not disconnect any air conditioning line or fitting unless the system pressure has been discharged by a qualified air conditioning technician.*

10 Remove the manifold-to-exhaust pipe fasteners. **Note:** *On some models it may be necessary to remove the starter (see Chapter 5), the lower bellhousing cover, and/or a front wheel for access to the manifolds.*

11 Bend back any lock tabs from the manifold bolt heads and remove the bolts and any spark plug heat shields **(see illustrations)**, noting their loca-

2B

10.14   The exhaust manifold gaskets are held in place with a small dab of sealant as the manifold is installed

11.7   To avoid mixing up the head bolts, use a new gasket to transfer the bolt hole pattern to a piece of cardboard, then punch holes to accept the bolts

11.8a   Cylinder head bolt tightening sequence – HT4100 engine (use the reverse of this sequence when loosening the bolts)

5.7L Chevrolet

All others (except HT4100)

11.8b   Cylinder head bolt tightening sequence

tions for reassembly.

12   Remove the manifold(s) from the engine compartment.

Installation

13   Thoroughly clean and inspect the sealing surfaces, removing all traces of old gasket material. Look for cracks and damaged threads. If the gasket was leaking, take the manifold to an automotive machine shop to inspect/correct for warpage.

14   If replacing the manifold, transfer all parts to the new unit. **Note:** *On HT4100 engines, be sure to apply a thin layer of graphite dry film lubricant to the exhaust manifold and cylinder head mating surfaces to prevent the exhaust manifold from cracking.* Using new gaskets (where applicable), install the manifold **(see illustration)** and start the bolts by hand.

15   Working from the center outward, tighten the bolts to the torque listed in this Chapter's Specifications. Bend the lock tabs (if equipped) against the bolt heads.

16   Reinstall the remaining components in the reverse order of removal.

17   Run the engine and check for exhaust leaks.

11   Cylinder heads – removal and installation

Refer to illustrations 11.7, 11.8a, 11.8b, 11.9 and 11.14

Caution: *The engine must be completely cool when the heads are removed. Failure to allow the engine to cool off could result in head warpage.*

Removal

1   Remove the intake manifold (see Section 9).

2   Remove the rocker arm cover(s) as described in Section 4.

3   Remove the rocker arms and pushrods (see Section 5). **Note:** *If any pushrods or head bolts cannot be removed because of interference with components such as the power brake booster, lift them up as far as possible and wrap a rubber band around them to keep them from dropping during head removal. Be sure to do the same during installation.*

4   Remove the exhaust manifolds (see Section 10).

5   Unbolt the engine accessories and brackets as necessary and set

11.9   Cylinder liner holder used on the HT4100 engine

3/4" CONDUIT

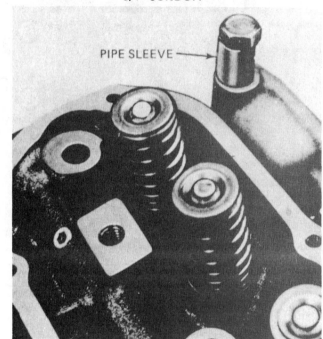

11.15   Before installing a cylinder head on the 368 engine, install the lower rear head bolt, propped up with a sleeve

5   Unbolt the engine accessories and brackets as necessary and set them aside. See Chapter 5 for alternator removal. When removing the power steering pump (see Chapter 10), leave the hoses attached and secure the unit in an upright position. The refrigerant lines should remain attached to the air conditioning compressor (see Chapter 3). **Warning:** *The air conditioning system is under high pressure. Do not loosen any hose or fitting until the refrigerant has been discharged by an auto air conditioning technician.*

6   Recheck to be sure nothing is still connected to the head(s) you intend to remove. Remove anything that is still attached.

7   Using a new gasket, outline the cylinders and bolt pattern on a piece of cardboard **(see illustration)**. Be sure to indicate the front of the engine for reference. Punch holes at the bolt locations.

8   Loosen the head bolts in 1/4-turn increments until they can be removed by hand. Work from bolt to bolt in a pattern that's the reverse of the tightening sequence **(see illustrations)**. Store the bolts in the cardboard holder as they are removed; this will insure the bolts are reinstalled in their original holes.

9   Lift the head(s) off the engine. If excessive resistance is felt, do not pry between the head and block as damage to the mating surfaces may result. To dislodge the head, place a block of wood against the end of it and strike the wood with a hammer, or pry on a casting protrusion. Store the head(s) on their sides to prevent damage to the gasket surface. **Note:** *On HT4100 engines, install a cylinder liner holder (GM tool #J-29775, or equivalent) to the engine block to prevent the liners from shifting in the event the engine is turned over or disturbed* **(see illustration*)**.

10   Cylinder head disassembly and inspection procedures are covered in detail in Chapter 2, Part B.

11   Use a gasket scraper to remove all traces of carbon and old gasket material, then clean the mating surfaces with lacquer thinner or acetone. If there's oil on the mating surfaces when the heads are installed, the gaskets may not seal properly and leaks may develop. When working on the block, cover the lifter valley with shop rags to keep out debris. Use a vacuum cleaner to remove any debris that falls into the cylinders.

12   Check the block and head mating surfaces for nicks, deep scratches and other damage. If damage is slight, it can be removed with a file. If the gasket seemed to be leaking, have the head(s) checked for cracks and warpage by an automotive machine shop. Surface damage or warpage can usually be corrected by machining. Cracks normally require replacement.

Installation

13   Use a tap of the correct size to chase the threads in the head bolt holes. Mount each bolt in a vise and run a die down the threads to remove any corrosion and restore the threads. Dirt, corrosion, sealant and damaged threads will affect torque readings.

14   If an all-metal gasket is used, apply a thin, even coat of sealant such as K & W Copper Coat to both sides prior to installation. Metal gaskets must be installed with the raised bead UP. Most gaskets have "THIS SIDE UP" stamped into them. Composition gaskets must be installed dry – don't use sealant. Follow the gasket manufacturer's instructions, if available. Position a new gasket over the dowel pins in the block.

15   Carefully position the head on the block without denting or disturbing the gasket. **Note:** *If you are working on a 368 cubic inch engine, install the bottom rear head bolt in it's hole, and prop it up with a pipe sleeve* **(see illustration)** *before installing the head (there isn't enough room to install the bolt once the head is in place). After the cylinder head is lowered into place, remove the sleeve.*

16   Be sure the head bolt holes are clean. On the Chevrolet-built engines covered by this manual (5.7L – 350), apply non-hardening sealant such as GM 1052080 to the head bolt threads. Apply a light coating of engine oil to the head bolts of the other engines.

17   Install the bolts in their original locations and tighten them finger tight. Follow the recommended sequence (see illustrations 11.8a and 11.8b) and tighten the bolts in several steps to the torque listed in this Chapter's Specifications.

18   The remaining installation steps are the reverse of removal. Check the index for the appropriate Sections for installation of the various components.

19   Add coolant, change the oil and filter (see Chapter 1), then start the engine and check carefully for leaks.

12.7a   Front cover bolt locations – 368, 425, 472 and 500 engines

| A | 3/8-16 x 1-3/8 | D | 5/16-18 x 5/8 |
| C | 5/16-18 x 1-1/4 | E | 3/8-16 x 5/8 |

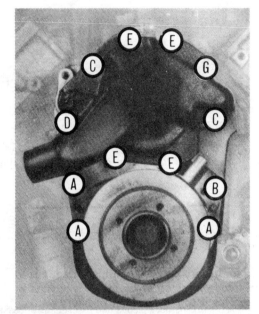

12.7b   Front cover bolt locations – 350 (5.7L) Oldsmobile manufactured engines

A	3/8-16 x 3/4	D	5/16-18 x 2-1/2
B	3/8-16 x 1 (stud head)	E	1/4-20 x 1-1/4
C	5/16-18 x 1-1/2	G	5/16-18 x 1-1/2 (stud head)

12   Front cover, timing chain and sprockets – removal and installation

Removal

Refer to illustrations 12.7a, 12.7b, 12.7c, 12.7d, 12.7e, 12.8, 12.10, 12.11 and 12.12,

1   Disconnect the negative cable from the battery.
2   Remove the alternator and brackets as well as the distributor (if the distributor is mounted to the front cover) (see Chapter 5).
3   Drain the cooling system and disconnect the radiator hoses, heater hose (where applicable) and the small by-pass hose (where applicable).
4   Remove the radiator top support, the fan shroud, the fan and pulley and the radiator (see Chapter 3). **Note:** *On some models it is necessary to remove the staples that secure the upper portion of the fan shroud to the lower portion in order to remove the assembly.*
5   Remove the crankshaft drive pulley and the vibration damper (see Section 7).
6   Remove the water pump (see Chapter 3). Remove the fuel pump (where applicable). Unbolt and set aside any engine accessories which are in the way without disconnecting the hoses. Refer to the appropriate Chapters for further information.
7   Remove the nuts and bolts that attach the cover to the engine, then pull the cover free **(see illustrations)**. If it's stuck, knock it loose with a hammer and a wood block. Don't pry between the mating surfaces, or oil leaks may result. **Note:** *If you are working on a 5.7L Chevrolet-manufactured engine, loosen the front four oil pan bolts on each side to ease removal and installation of the front cover.*
8   Using vise-grip pliers, pull the dowel pins (if equipped) out of the engine block. Grind a chamfer on one end of each pin **(see illustration)**. Thoroughly clean all gasket mating surfaces (do not allow the old gasket material to fall into the oil pan), then wipe them with a cloth soaked in solvent.
9   If equipped, remove the fuel pump drive eccentric by unscrewing the bolt from the end of the camshaft.

12.7c   Front cover retaining bolts on an HT4100 engine

A	M10 x 1.50 x 45	F	M10 x 1.50 x 50
B	M8 x 1.25 x 35	G	M8 x 1.25 x 20
E	M10 x 1.50 (nut)		

10   If equipped, slide the oil slinger off of the end of the crankshaft **(see illustration)**.

CRANK SHAFT AND CAM SPROCKETS ARE TO BE
ASSEMBLED WITH "O" MARK ON CRANKSHAFT
SPROCKET ALIGNED WITH TIMING NOTCH ON CAM
SPROCKET.

12.7d   Front cover and timing chain installation details – 307 (5.0L) Oldsmobile built engines

1	Camshaft	7	Key	13	Button
2	Camshaft flange adapter	8	Plate	14	Fuel pump eccentric
3	Camshaft sprocket	9	Plate	15	Gasket
4	Camshaft sprocket bolt	10	Plug – left hand	16	Front cover
5	Chain	11	Plug – right hand	17	Water pump bolts
6	Crankshaft sprocket	12	Spring	18	Front cover bolts

2B

Chamfer

12.8   Dowel pin chamfer

12.7e   Front cover components on a 350 (5.7L) Chevrolet
built engine

1	Cover	3	Bolt
2	Timing scale	4	Gasket

12.10   Oil slinger installation – typical

12.11   With the number one piston at TDC on the compression stroke and the timing marks on the cam and crankshaft sprockets aligned (except on the HT4100 engine), a straight line should pass through the timing marks and the shaft centers as shown here

12.12   Remove the three bolts from the end of the camshaft (arrows) – Chevrolet built engine shown

11   Turn the crankshaft until the marks on the camshaft and crankshaft sprockets are perfectly aligned (see illustration). DO NOT attempt to remove either sprocket or the chain until this is done. Also, do not turn the camshaft or the crankshaft after the sprockets are removed.
12   Remove the bolts that attach the sprocket to the end of the camshaft (see illustration).
13   Generally speaking, the camshaft sprocket, the crankshaft sprocket and the timing chain can be slipped off the shafts together. If resistance is encountered, it may be necessary to use two screwdrivers to carefully pry the sprockets off of the shafts. If extreme resistance is encountered (which may happen with the crankshaft sprocket), a gear puller will be required. On models with spring loaded timing chain dampers, hold the damper back as you slip the chain off.
14   If the crankshaft and the camshaft are not disturbed while the timing chain and sprockets are out of place, then installation can begin with 17. If the engine is completely dismantled, or if the crankshaft or camshaft are disturbed while the timing chain is off, then the No. 1 piston must be positioned at TDC before the timing chain and sprockets are installed.

Installation
Cadillac-built engines
15   Align the hole in the camshaft sprocket with the dowel pin in the end of the camshaft, then slip the sprocket onto the end of the camshaft. **Note:** *On all engines except the HT4100 engine, with the No. 1 piston at TDC, the timing mark on the camshaft sprocket must be pointed straight up (see illustration 12.11) and aligned with the centerlines of the camshaft and crankshaft.*
16   Slip the crankshaft sprocket onto the end of the crankshaft (make sure the key and keyway are properly aligned), then turn the crankshaft until the timing mark on the sprocket is pointed straight up (all engines).
17   Next, remove the camshaft sprocket from the camshaft and lay the chain over it. Slip the other end of the chain over the crankshaft sprocket (keep the timing marks aligned as this is done) and reinstall the camshaft sprocket.
18   Install the bolts that attach the sprocket to the camshaft, then recheck the alignment of the timing marks. Tighten the bolts to the torque listed in this Chapter's Specifications.

12.21   On Oldsmobile engines, trim the oil pan gasket as shown before installing the front cover

12.22   Trimming the oil pan seal – Oldsmobile engines

12.24 Guide the oil pan seal into place with a small screwdriver – Oldsmobile engines

13.3 When checking the camshaft lobe lift, the dial indicator plunger must be positioned directly above the pushrod

19 The remainder of installation is the reverse of removal. Be sure to clean the mating surfaces of the front cover and cylinder block, and install a new gasket.

20 Be sure to tighten the crankshaft and camshaft sprocket retaining bolts to the specified torque (if applicable).

Oldsmobile-built engines

Refer to illustrations 12.21, 12.22 and 12.24

21 Cut off the excess gasket material at the front of the oil pan until it is flush with the engine block **(see illustration)**.

22 Using a razor knife, trim about 1/8-inch from each end of the new front pan seal **(see illustration)**.

23 Install a new gasket to the engine block and a new front seal on the cover (see Section 8). Use RTV sealant on these gaskets and also at the junction of the cover, block and oil pan.

24 Tilt the cover into place and press down to compress the lower pan seal. Rotate the cover back and forth and guide the pan seal into the cavity using a small screwdriver **(see illustration)**.

25 Apply engine oil to the bolt threads and loosely install two of the bolts to hold the cover in place.

26 Install the dowel pins, chamfered end first, into the engine block.

27 Install the water pump with a new gasket (if removed from cover).

28 Tighten all bolts to the proper torque listed in this Chapter's Specifications and install all components in the reverse order of removal. Apply lubricant to the front hub seal before installing the crankshaft hub.

Chevrolet-built engines

29 Ensure that all gasket surfaces are clean and free of excess gasket material.

30 Use a sharp knife to trim any protruding gasket material at the front of the oil pan.

31 Apply a 1/8-inch bead of RTV gasket sealant to the joint formed at the oil pan and engine block, as well as the front lip of the oil pan.

32 Coat the cover gasket with a non-hardening sealant, position it on the cover, then loosely install the cover. First install the top four bolts loosely, then install two 1/4 – 20 x 1/2 inch long screws at the lower cover holes. Apply a bead of sealant on the bottom of the cover, then install the cover, tightening the screws alternately and evenly and at the same time aligning the dowel pins.

33 Remove the two 1/4 – 20 x 1/2 inch long screws and install the remaining cover bolts. Tighten the bolts to the torque listed in this Chapter's Specifications.

34 Install the water pump using new gaskets (see Chapter 3).

35 The remainder of installation is the reverse of removal.

2B

13 Camshaft, bearings and lifters – removal, inspection and installation

Refer to illustrations 13.3, 13.10, 13.12a, 13.12b, and 13.18

Camshaft lobe lift check

1 In order to determine the extent of cam lobe wear, the lobe lift should be checked prior to camshaft removal. Refer to Section 4 and remove the rocker arm covers.

2 Position the number one piston at TDC on the compression stroke (see Section 3).

3 Beginning with the number one cylinder valves, mount a dial indicator on the engine and position the plunger against the top surface of the first rocker arm. The plunger should be directly above and in line with the pushrod **(see illustration)**.

4 Zero the dial indicator, then very slowly turn the crankshaft in the normal direction of rotation (clockwise) until the indicator needle stops and begins to move in the opposite direction. The point at which it stops indicates maximum cam lobe lift.

5 Record this figure for future reference, then reposition the piston at TDC on the compression stroke.

6 Move the dial indicator to the remaining number one cylinder rocker arm and repeat the check. Be sure to record the results for each valve.

7 Repeat the check for the remaining valves. Since each piston must be at TDC on the compression stroke for this procedure, work from cylinder to cylinder following the firing order sequence (refer to the Specifications).

8 After the check is complete, compare the results to the Specifications. If camshaft lobe lift is less than specified, cam lobe wear has occurred and a new camshaft should be installed.

Note: *On air conditioning equipped models, have the refrigerant discharged and remove the condenser prior to commencing the following procedure (see Chapter 3).*

Removal

9 Refer to the appropriate Sections and remove the intake manifold, the rocker arms, the pushrods and the timing chain and camshaft sprocket. The radiator and air conditioning condenser must be removed as well (see Chapter 3).

13.10   Roller lifter installation details (5.7L Chevrolet built engines only)

1	Lifter	4	Bolts
2	Guide	5	Pushrod
3	Retainer		

13.12a   Removing the camshaft thrust plate

13.12b   A long bolt can be threaded into one of the camshaft bolt holes to provide a handle for removal and installation of the camshaft

10   There are several ways to extract the lifters from the bores. A special tool designed to grip and remove lifters is manufactured by many tool companies and is widely available, but it may not be required in every case. On newer engines without a lot of varnish buildup, the lifters can often be removed with a small magnet or even with your fingers. A machinist's scribe with a bent end can be used to pull the lifters out by positioning the point under the retainer ring in the top of each lifter. **Caution:** *Do not use pliers to remove the lifters unless you intend to replace them with new ones (along with the camshaft). The pliers may damage the precision machined and hardened lifters, rendering them useless.* If you are working on a Chevrolet-built engine with roller lifters, unbolt the lifter guide retainer and remove the lifter guides **(see illustration)**.

11   Before removing the lifters, arrange to store them in a clearly labelled box to ensure that they are reinstalled in their original locations. Remove the lifters and store them where they will not get dirty. Do not attempt to withdraw the camshaft with the lifters in place.

12   Unbolt and remove the thrust plate, if equipped **(see illustration)**. Thread a long bolt of the proper thread into one of the camshaft sprocket bolt holes to use as a handle when removing the camshaft from the block **(see illustration)**.

13   Carefully pull the camshaft out. Support the cam near the block so the lobes do not nick or gouge the bearings as it is withdrawn.

Inspection

Camshaft and bearings

14   After the camshaft has been removed from the engine, cleaned with solvent and dried, inspect the bearing journals for uneven wear, pitting and evidence of seizure. If the journals are damaged, the bearing inserts in the block are probably damaged as well. Both the camshaft and bearings will have to be replaced.

15   Measure the bearing journals with a micrometer to determine if they are excessively worn or out-of-round.

16   Check the camshaft lobes for heat discoloration, score marks, chipped areas, pitting and uneven wear. If the lobes are in good condition and if the lobe lift measurements are as specified, the camshaft can be reused.

Conventional lifters

Caution: *Do not unbolt and remove the lifter carrier assembly on the HT4100 engine. This will destroy the alignment of the lifter bores. Also, don't substitute an incorrect lifter on the HT4100 engine. These special lift-* ers are designed for the valve system on the HT4100 only, and since other types fit the lifter bore, incorrect lifters can easily be installed.

17   Clean the lifters with solvent and dry them thoroughly without mixing them up.

18   Check each lifter wall, pushrod seat and foot for scuffing, score marks and uneven wear. Each lifter foot (the surface that rides on the cam lobe) must be slightly convex, although this can be difficult to determine by eye **(see illustration)**. If the base of the lifter is concave, the lifters and camshaft must be replaced. If the lifter walls are damaged or worn (which is not very likely), inspect the lifter bores in the engine block as well. If the pushrod seats are worn, check the pushrod ends.

19   If new lifters are being installed, a new camshaft must also be installed. If a new camshaft is installed, use new lifters as well. Never install used lifters unless the original camshaft is used and the lifters can be installed in their original locations.

Roller lifters

20   Check the rollers carefully for wear and damage and make sure they turn freely without excessive play. The inspection procedure for conventional lifters also applies to roller lifters.

21   Unlike conventional lifters, used roller lifters can be reinstalled with a new camshaft, and the original camshaft can be used if new lifters are installed.

13.18   The foot of each lifter should be slightly convex – the side of another lifter can be used as a straightedge to check it; if it appears flat, it is worn and must not be reused

14.17a   Tilt the oil pan down (as shown) at the rear to clear the front crossmember

Bearing replacement

22   Camshaft bearing replacement requires special tools and expertise that place it outside the scope of the home mechanic. Take the engine block to an automotive machine shop to ensure that the job is done correctly.

Installation

23   Lubricate the camshaft bearing journals and cam lobes with moly-base grease or engine assembly lube.
24   Slide the camshaft into the engine. Support the cam near the block and be careful not to scrape or nick the bearings.
25   Lubricate and install the thrust plate, if equipped.
26   Refer to Section 12 and install the timing chain and sprockets.
27   Lubricate the lifters with clean engine oil and install them in the block. If the original lifters are being reinstalled, be sure to return them to their original locations. If a new camshaft is being installed, be sure to install new lifters as well (except for engines with roller lifters).
28   The remaining installation steps are the reverse of removal.
29   Before starting and running the engine, change the oil and install a new oil filter (see Chapter 1).

14   Oil pan – removal and installation

Refer to illustrations 14.17a, 14.17b, 14.20a and 14.20b
Warning: *Do not place any part of your body below the engine when it is supported solely by a jack or hoist.*

Removal

1   Disconnect the negative battery cable.
2   Remove the air cleaner assembly and set aside.
3   Remove the distributor cap to prevent breakage as the engine is raised (models with distributor at rear of engine only).
4   Unbolt the radiator shroud from the radiator support and hang the shroud over the cooling fan.
5   If necessary, remove the oil dipstick and dipstick tube.
6   Raise the vehicle and support it securely on jackstands.
7   Drain the engine oil (see Chapter 1).
8   Disconnect the exhaust crossover pipe at the exhaust manifold flanges. Lower the exhaust pipes and suspend them from the frame with wire.
9   Remove the torque converter shield (see Chapter 7).
10   Use the bolt at the center of the vibration damper to rotate the engine until the timing mark is straight down, at the 6 o'clock position. This will

14.17b   Oil pan installation details – HT4100 engine

move the forward crankshaft throw upward, providing clearance at the front of the oil pan.
11   Remove the through bolt at each engine mount.
12   At this time the engine must be raised slightly to enable the oil pan to slide clear of the crossmember. The preferred method is to use an engine hoist, or "cherry picker".
13   An alternative method can be used if extreme care is exercised. Use a floor jack and a block of wood placed under the oil pan. The wood block should spread the load across the oil pan, preventing damage or collapse of the oil pan metal. The oil pump pickup and screen is very close to the oil pan bottom, so any collapsing of the pan may damage the pickup or prevent the oil pump from drawing oil properly.
14   With either method, raise the engine slowly until wood blocks can be placed between the engine mounts on the crossmember and the engine block. The blocks should be approximately three inches thick. Check clearances all around the engine as it is raised. Pay particular attention to the distributor and the cooling fan.
15   Lower the engine onto the wood blocks. Make sure it is firmly supported. If a hoist is being used, keep the lifting chains secured to the engine.
16   Remove the oil pan bolts. Note the different sizes used and their locations.
17   Remove the oil pan by tilting it down at the rear and then working the front clear of the crossmember **(see illustrations)**. It may be necessary to use a rubber mallet to break the seal – don't pry between the pan and the block!

14.20a   Sealant is applied at the area where the front gasket
meets the side gasket (Chevrolet built engine shown)

14.20b   The front oil seal (Chevrolet built engine) has an
indentation which fits into the side gasket

18   Before installing, thoroughly clean the gasket sealing surfaces on the
engine block and on the oil pan. All sealant and gasket material must be
removed.

Installation

19   Apply a thin film of sealant to the new side gaskets and fit them to the
engine block. All bolt holes should line up properly. If you are working on an
HT4100 engine, apply a continuous bead of RTV sealant to the pan, making sure the bead travels around the inside of the bolt holes. Install the pan
while the sealant is still wet.
20   Again using sealant, install the front and rear seals to the engine (except on HT4100 engines). Make sure the ends butt with the ends of the
side gaskets **(see illustrations)**.
21   Lift the pan into position and install all bolts finger-tight. There is no
specific order for tightening the bolts; however, it is a good policy to tighten
the end bolts first.
22   Lower the engine onto its mounts and install the through bolts. Tight-
en the nuts/bolts securely.
23   Follow the removal steps in a reverse order. Fill the engine with the
correct grade and quantity of oil, start the engine and check for leaks.

---

15   Oil pump – removal, inspection and installation

Refer to illustration 15.4

Removal

1   Remove the oil pan as described in Section 14.
2   Remove the bolts securing the oil pump assembly to the main bearing
cap. Remove the oil pump with its pickup tube and screen as an assembly
from the engine block. Once the pump is removed, the oil pump driveshaft
can be withdrawn from the block. **Note:** *On Oldsmobile built engines, do
not attempt to remove the washers from the driveshaft. Note that the end
with the washers fits into the pump.*

Inspection

3   In most cases it will be more practical and economical to replace a
faulty oil pump with a new or rebuilt unit. If it is decided to overhaul the oil
pump, check on internal parts availability before beginning.
4   Remove the pump cover retaining screws **(see illustration)** and the
pump cover (Oldsmobile built engines also have a gasket installed). Index
mark the gear teeth to permit reassembly in the same position.
5   Remove the idler gear, drive gear and shaft from the body.
6   Remove the pressure regulator valve retaining pin, the regulator
valve and the related parts.

7   If necessary, the pick-up screen and pipe assembly can be extracted
from the pump body.
8   Wash all the parts in solvent and thoroughly dry them. Inspect the
body for cracks, wear or other damage. Similarly inspect the gears.
9   Check the drive gear shaft for looseness in the pump body, and the
inside of the pump cover for wear that would permit oil leakage past the
end of the gears.
10   Inspect the pick-up screen and pipe assembly for damage to the
screen, pipe or relief grommet.
11   Apply a gasket sealant to the end of the pipe (pick-up screen and pipe
assembly) and tap it into the pump body, taking care that no damage occurs. If the original press-fit cannot be obtained, a new assembly must be
used to prevent air leaks and loss of pressure.
12   Install the pressure regulator valve and related parts.
13   Install the drive gear and shaft in the pump body, followed by the idler
gear, with the smooth side towards the pump cover opening. **Note:** *On
Oldsmobile built engines, check the gear end clearance by resting a
straightedge on the pump body. Try to slip a feeler gauge between the
ends of the gears and the straightedge. The clearance should be between
0.0025- and 0.0065-inch for the 5.0L Olds and 0.0015 and 0.0085 for the
350. If it is not, the pump should be replaced with a new one. Lubricate the
parts with engine oil.*
14   Install the cover and tighten the screws to the torque listed in this
Chapter's Specifications.
15   Turn the driveshaft to ensure that the pump operates freely.

Installation

16   To install, move the pump assembly into position and align the slot on
the top end of the driveshaft with the drive tang on the lower end of the distributor. The distributor drives the oil pump, so it is essential that these two
components mate properly. On Oldsmobile engines, the driveshaft fits into
the distributor drive gear.
17   Install the bolts and tighten them securely.
18   Make sure the oil pump screen is parallel with the oil rails. The screen
must be in this position to fit into the oil pan properly.

---

16   Driveplate – removal and installation

Refer to illustrations 16.2 and 16.3

Removal

1   Raise the vehicle and support it securely on jackstands, then refer to
Chapter 7 and remove the transmission.

15.4 Typical oil pump assembly – exploded view

2B

2   Use a scribe or a marking pen to draw a line from the driveplate to the end of the crankshaft for correct alignment during reinstallation **(see illustration)**.

3   Remove the bolts that secure the driveplate to the crankshaft rear flange. If difficulty is experienced in removing the bolts due to movement of the crankshaft, wedge a screwdriver to keep the driveplate from turning **(see illustration)**.

16.2 To insure proper balance, mark the driveplate's relation to the crankshaft

16.3 A large screwdriver wedged in the starter ring gear teeth or one of the holes in the driveplate can be used to keep the driveplate from turning as the mounting bolts are removed

17.5   A hammer and brass drift should be used to push the upper seal half around the crankshaft

4   Remove the driveplate from the crankshaft flange.
5   Clean any grease or oil from the driveplate. Check for cracked or broken starter ring gear teeth. Lay the driveplate on a flat surface and use a straightedge to check for warpage.
6   Clean the mating surfaces of the driveplate and the crankshaft.

Installation

7   Position the driveplate against the crankshaft, matching the alignment marks made during removal. Before installing the bolts, apply a thread locking compound to the threads.
8   Wedge a screwdriver through the driveplate or into the ring gear teeth to keep the crankshaft from turning. Tighten the bolts to the torque listed in this Chapter's specifications in two or three steps, working in a criss-cross pattern.
9   The remainder of installation is the reverse of the removal procedure.

---

17   Crankshaft rear oil seal – replacement

Two-piece neoprene type seal

Refer to illustrations 17.5, 17.9, 17.13 and 17.14
1   Always replace both halves of the rear main oil seal as a unit. While the replacement of this seal is much easier with the engine removed from the car, the job can be done with engine in place.

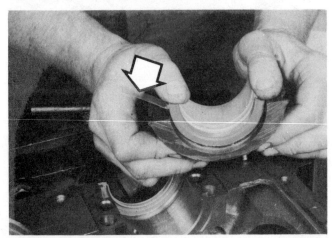

17.13   Use a protector tool (arrow) when pushing the main seal into place

17.9   Neoprene type crankshaft rear oil seal installation tool

---

2   Remove the oil pan and oil pump as described previously in this Chapter.
3   Remove the rear main bearing cap from the engine.
4   Using a screwdriver, pry the lower half of the oil seal from the bearing cap.
5   To remove the upper half of the seal, use a small hammer and a brass pin punch to roll the seal around the crankshaft journal. Tap one end of the seal with the hammer and brass drift (be careful not to strike the crankshaft) until the other end of the seal protrudes enough to pull the seal out with a pair of pliers **(see illustration)**.
6   Clean all seal remnants and foreign material from the bearing cap and block. Do not use an abrasive cleaner for this.
7   Inspect components for nicks, scratches or burrs at all sealing surfaces.
8   Coat the seal lips of the new seal with light engine oil. Do not get oil on the seal mating ends.
9   Included in the purchase of the rear main oil seal should be a small plastic installation tool. If not included, make your own by cutting an old feeler gauge blade or shim stock **(see illustration)**.
10   Position the narrow end of this installation tool between the crankshaft and the seal seat. The idea is to protect the new seal from being damaged by the sharp edge of the seal seat.
11   Raise the new upper half of the seal into position with the seal lips facing towards the front of the engine. Push the seal onto its seat, using the installation tool as a protector against the seal contacting the sharp edge.
12   Roll the seal around the crankshaft, all the time using the tool as a "shoehorn" for protection. When both ends of the seal are flush with the engine block, remove the installation tool, being careful not to withdraw the seal as well.
13   Install the lower half of the oil seal in the bearing cap, again using the installation tool to protect the seal against the sharp edge **(see illustration)**. Make sure the seal is firmly seated, then withdraw the installation tools.
14   Smear a bit of sealant on the bearing cap areas immediately adjacent to the seal ends **(see illustration)**.

17.14   Sealant should be used where the rear main cap touches the engine block

17.16a   Packing tool fabrication details

17.16b   Packing the upper half of the braided fabric type seal
into the block

2B

17.17   Use the bearing cap as a holding fixture when cutting
short sections of the old seal

15   Install the bearing cap (with seal) and torque the attaching bolts to about 10-12 ft-lbs only. Now tap the end of the crankshaft first rearward, then forward to line up the thrust surfaces. Retorque the bearing cap bolts to the torque specified in Chapter 2C.

Braided fabric type seal

Refer to illustrations 17.16a, 17.16b, 17.17, 17.19 and 17.20

16   With the oil pan, oil pump and main bearing cap removed (see previous Sections), insert the special seal packing tool or equivalent **(see illustration)** against the seal. Drive the old seal into its groove until it is packed tight at each end **(see illustration)**.

17   Measure the amount which the seal was driven up, then add 1/16-inch. Cut two pieces that length from the old seal taken from the bearing cap. Use the bearing cap as a guide when cutting **(see illustration)**.

18   Place a drop of sealant on each end of these seal pieces and then pack them into the upper groove to fill the gap made previously.

19   Trim the remaining material perfectly flush with the block **(see illustration)**. Be careful not to harm the bearing surface.

17.19   Using a special tool to trim the ends of the seal

APPLY SEALER
AS INDICATED
INCLUDING ENDS
OF SEAL

17.20   Installing the rear main oil seal in the bearing cap

17.22   The one-piece rear main oil seal fits into a housing bolted to the block

20   Install a new rope seal into the main bearing cap groove and push firmly all around using a hammer handle or special tool **(see illustration)**. Make sure the seal is firmly seated, then trim the ends flush with the bearing cap mating surface.

21   Install cap and remaining components in reverse order, tightening all parts to Specifications.

One-piece neoprene type seal

Refer to illustrations 17.22 and 17.24

22   Later models equipped with a one-piece seal require an entirely different installation procedure. The driveplate must be removed first and then the housing unbolted from the block **(see illustration)**.

23   Check the seal contact surface very carefully for scratches and nicks that could damage the new seal lip and cause oil leaks. If the crankshaft is damaged, the only alternative is a new or different crankshaft.

24   The old seal can be removed from the housing by inserting a large screwdriver into the notches provided and prying it out **(see illustration)**. Be sure to note how far it is recessed into the housing before removing it; the new seal will have to be recessed an equal amount. Be very careful not to scratch or otherwise damage the bore in the housing or oil leaks could develop.

25   Make sure the housing is clean, then apply a thin coat of engine oil to the outer edge of the new seal. The seal must be pressed squarely into the housing bore, so hammering it into place is not recommended. If you do not have access to a press, sandwich the housing and seal between two smooth pieces of wood and press the seal into place with the jaws of a large vise. The pieces of wood must be thick enough to distribute the force evenly around the entire circumference of the seal. Work slowly and make sure the seal enters the bore squarely.

26   The seal lips must be lubricated with clean engine oil before the seal/housing is slipped over the crankshaft and bolted to the block. Use a new gasket – no sealant is required – and make sure the dowel pins are in place before installing the housing.

27   Tighten the nuts/screws a little at a time until they are all snug.

28   Reinstall the remaining parts in the reverse order of removal.

29   Be sure to add oil, then run the engine and check for oil leaks.

---

18   Engine mounts – check and replacement

Refer to illustration 18.7

1   Engine mounts seldom require attention, but broken or deteriorated mounts should be replaced immediately or the added strain placed on the driveline components may cause damage.

17.24   To remove the seal from the housing, insert the tip of the screwdriver into each notch (arrows) and pry the seal out

Check

2   During the check, the engine must be raised slightly to remove the weight from the mounts. Disconnect the negative battery cable from the battery.

3   Raise the vehicle and support it securely on jackstands, then position the jack under the engine oil pan. Place a wood block between the jack head and the oil pan, then carefully raise the engine just enough to take the weight off the mounts.

4   Check the mounts to see if the rubber is cracked, hardened or separated from the metal plates. Sometimes the rubber will split right down the center. Rubber preservative may be applied to the mounts to slow deterioration.

5   Check for relative movement between the mount plates and the engine or frame (use a large screwdriver or pry bar to attempt to move the mounts). If movement is noted, lower the engine and tighten the mount fasteners.

18.7   Engine mount installation details – typical

Replacement

6   Remove the fan shroud mounting screws and place the shroud over the fan.

7   Remove the engine mount through-bolts **(see illustration)**.

8   Disconnect the shift linkage where it connects the transmission to the body (see Chapter 7).

9   Raise the engine high enough to clear the clevis brackets. Do not force the engine up too high. If it touches anything before the mounts are free, remove the part for clearance. Place a block of wood between the oil pan and crossmember as a safety precaution.

10   Unbolt the mount from the engine block and remove it from the ve-hicle. **Note:** *On vehicles equipped with self-locking nuts and bolts, replace them with new ones whenever they are disassembled. Prior to assembly, remove hardened residual adhesive from the engine block holes with a proper-size bottoming tap.*

11   Attach the new mount to the engine block and install the fasteners in the appropriate locations. Tighten the fasteners securely.

12   Remove the wood block and lower the engine into place. Install the through-bolts and tighten the nuts securely.

13   Complete the installation by reinstalling all parts removed to gain access to the mounts.

2B

Chapter 2 Part C
General engine overhaul procedures

Contents

Specifications

V6 engine – VIN code 4

See Chapter 2, Part A, for additional information

General

Oil pressure at 2400 rpm	37 psi
Compression pressure	
Minimum	100 psi
Allowable variation between cylinders	20%

Cylinder head warpage limit .... 0.003 in per 6 inches

Valves

Valve stem diameter	
Intake	0.3412 to 0.3401 in
Exhaust	0.3412 to 0.3405 in
Valve margin width (limit)	1/32 in
Valve spring installed height	1.727 in

Valve stem-to-guide clearance
    Intake . . . .   0.0015 to 0.0035 in
    Exhaust . . . .   0.0015 to 0.0032 in

Engine block

Cylinder bore diameter . . . .   Not available
Cylinder bore taper/out-of-round . . . .   Less than 0.0005 in

Pistons and rings

Piston-to-bore clearance (measured at top of skirt) . . . .   0.0008 to 0.0020 in
Piston ring end gap
    Compression rings . . . .   0.013 to 0.0023 in
    Oil rings . . . .   0.015 to 0.035 in

Crankshaft, connecting rods and bearings

Connecting rod side clearance (total – both rods) . . . .   0.006 to 0.023 in
Connecting rod bearing oil clearance . . . .   0.0005 to 0.0026 in
Rod and main journal taper/out-of-round limit . . . .   0.0015 in
Crankshaft endplay . . . .   0.003 to 0.009 in
Main bearing journal diameter . . . .   2.4995 in
Main bearing oil clearance . . . .   0.0003 to 0.0018 in

Torque specifications*

Ft-lbs
Main bearing cap bolts   100
Connecting rod cap nuts   40

* Note: Refer to Part A for additional torque specifications.

472, 500, 425 and 368 cu in engines – VIN codes R, S, T, 9 and 6

See Chapter 2, Part B, for additional information

General

Oil pressure . . . .   35 psi @ 2600 rpm
Compression pressure
    Allowable variation between cylinders 20%
    Minimum . . . .   100 psi

Cylinder head warpage limit . . . . 0.006 in

Valves

Valve stem diameter
    Intake . . . .   0.3413 to 0.3420 in
    Exhaust
        472 and 500 . . . .   0.3415 to 0.3420 in
        425 and 368 . . . .   0.3413 to 0.3420 in
Valve seat width in head . . . .   1/16 in
Valve spring free length . . . .   2.250 in
Valve stem-to-guide clearance . . . .   0.0010 to 0.0027 in

Engine block

Cylinder bore diameter
    425 cu in
        Letter A . . . .   4.0820 to 4.0824 in
        Letter B . . . .   4.0824 to 4.0828 in.
        Letter C . . . .   4.0828 to 4.0832 in.
        Letter D . . . .   4.0832 to 4.0836 in.
        Letter E . . . .   4.0836 to 4.0840 in.
    472 and 500 cu in.
        Letter A . . . .   4.3000 to 4.3002 in.
        Letter B . . . .   4.3002 to 4.3004 in.
        Letter C . . . .   4.3004 to 4.3006 in.
        Letter D . . . .   4.3006 to 4.3008 in.
        Letter E . . . .   4.3008 to 4.3010 in.
        Letter H . . . .   4.3010 to 4.3012 in.
        Letter J . . . .   4.3012 to 4.3014 in.
        Letter K . . . .   4.3014 to 4.3016 in.
        Letter L . . . .   4.3016 to 4.3018 in.
        Letter M . . . .   4.3018 to 4.3020 in.

2C

368 cu in
    Letter A .... 3.8000 to 3.8004 in.
    Letter B .... 3.8004 to 3.8008 in.
    Letter C .... 3.8008 to 3.8012 in.
    Letter D .... 3.8012 to 3.8016 in.
    Letter E .... 3.8016 to 3.8020 in.
Piston-to-bore clearance (measured at top of skirt)
    425 cu in .... 0.0006 to 0.0014 in
    472 and 500 cu in .... 0.0006 to 0.0010 in
    368 cu in .... Not available

Pistons and rings

Piston size
    425 cu in
        Letter A .... 4.0810 to 4.0814 in.
        Letter B .... 4.0814 to 4.0818 in.
        Letter C .... 4.0818 to 4.0822 in.
        Letter D .... 4.0822 to 4.0826 in.
        Letter E .... 4.0826 to 4.0830 in.
    472 and 500 cu in
        Letter A .... 4.2992 to 4.2994 in.
        Letter B .... 4.2994 to 4.2996 in.
        Letter C .... 4.2996 to 4.2998 in.
        Letter D .... 4.2998 to 4.3000 in.
        Letter E .... 4.3000 to 4.3002 in.
        Letter H .... 4.3002 to 4.3004 in.
        Letter J .... 4.3004 to 4.3006 in.
        Letter K .... 4.3006 to 4.3008 in.
        Letter L .... 4.3008 to 4.3010 in.
        Letter M .... 4.3010 to 4.3012 in.
    368 and 368 V8 6-4 cu in
        Letter A .... 3.7990 to 3.7994 in.
        Letter B .... 3.7994 to 3.7998 in.
        Letter C .... 3.7998 to 3.8002 in.
        Letter D .... 3.8002 to 3.8006 in.
        Letter E .... 3.8006 to 3.8010 in.
Piston ring end gap
    Compression rings .... 0.013 to 0.023 in
    Oil ring .... 0.015 to 0.055 in
Piston ring side clearance
    Compression rings .... 0.0017 to 0.0040 in
    Oil ring .... NONE – side sealing

Crankshaft, connecting rods and main bearings

Rod endplay – (total – both rods)
    425, 368 .... 0.008 to 0.020 in
    472 and 500 .... 0.008 to 0.016 in
Crankshaft endplay (all) .... 0.002 to 0.012 in
Main bearing journal diameter .... 3.250 in
Connecting rod journal diameter .... 2.500 in
Main bearing oil clearance
    425 cu in .... 0.0001 to 0.0026 in
    368 cu in .... 0.0005 to 0.0026 in
    472 and 500 cu in .... 0.0003 to 0.0026
Connecting rod bearing oil clearance .... 0.0005 to 0.0028 in

Torque specifications*

	Ft-lbs
Connecting rod cap nuts	40
Main bearing cap bolts	90

* Note: Refer to Part B for additional torque specifications.

5.7L (350 cu in) Chevrolet-built engine – VIN code 7

See Chapter 2, Part B, for additional information

General

Oil pressure
    At 1000 rpm .... 6 psi
    At 2000 rpm .... 18 psi
    At 4000 rpm .... 24 psi

Compression pressure
    Allowable variation between cylinders 20%
    Minimum . . . .   100 psi

Cylinder head warpage limit . . . .   0.006 in

Valves

Valve seat width
    Intake . . . .   1/32 to 1/16 in
    Exhaust . . . .   1/16 to 3/32 in
Valve spring free length (outer spring) . . . .   2.03 in
Valve spring installed height (all) . . . .   1-23/32 in
Valve stem-to-guide clearance (all) . . . .   0.0011 to 0.0027 in

Engine block

Cylinder bore diameter . . . .   4.000 in
Cylinder bore taper limit . . . .   0.001 in
Cylinder bore out-of-round limit . . . .   0.002 in
Piston-to-bore clearance
    Production . . . .   0.0007 to 0.0021 in
    Service limit . . . .   0.0027 in
Piston ring side clearance
Compression rings . . . .   0.0012 to 0.0032 in
Oil control ring . . . .   0.008 in max

Crankshaft, connecting rods and main bearings

Connecting rod endplay (total – both rods) . . . .   0.006 to 0.014 in
Crankshaft endplay . . . .   0.001 to 0.007 in
Main bearing journal diameter
    No. 1 . . . .   2.4488 to 2.4493 in
    Nos. 2, 3 and 4 . . . .   2.4481 to 2.4490 in
    No. 5 . . . .   2.4481 to 2.4488 in
Connecting rod journal diameter . . . .   2.0893 to 2.0998 in
Journal taper/out-of-round limit . . . .   0.001 in
Main bearing oil clearance wear limits
    No. 1 . . . .   0.0010 to 0.0015 in
    Nos. 2, 3 and 4 . . . .   0.0010 to 0.0025 in
    No. 5 . . . .   0.0025 to 0.0035 in
Connecting rod bearing oil clearance limit . . . .   0.0030 in

Torque specifications*

Ft-lbs
Main bearing cap bolts   75
Connecting rod cap nuts   44
Rear oil seal housing bolts   11
* Note: Refer to Part B for additional torque specifications.

5.0 L (307 cu in) Oldsmobile built engine – VIN code Y
See Chapter 2, Part B, for additional information

General

Oil pressure . . . .   30 psi @ 1500 rpm
Compression pressure
    Allowable variation between cylinders 20%
    Minimum . . . .   100 psi

Cylinder head warpage limit . . . .   0.006 in

Valves

Valve stem diameter
    Intake . . . .   0.3425 to 0.3432 in
    Exhaust . . . .   0.3420 to 0.3427 in
Valve margin width (minimum) . . . .   1/32 in
Valve stem installed height . . . .   Use Tool BT-6428 or J-25289
Valve stem-to-guide clearance
    Intake . . . .   0.0010 to 0.0027 in
    Exhaust . . . .   0.0015 to 0.0032 in

2C

Engine block

Cylinder bore diameter .... 3.800 in
Cylinder bore taper/out-of-round .... 0.0015 in maximum
Piston-to-bore clearance .... 0.00075 to 0.00175 in

Pistons and rings

Piston ring end gap*
   Compression rings .... 0.009 to 0.019 in
   Oil ring .... 0.015 to 0.055 in
*Varies by ring manufacturer – use ring maker's specifications, if different.
Compression ring side clearance .... 0.0018 to 0.0038 in

Crankshaft, connecting rods and main bearings

Connecting rod endplay (side clearance) .... 0.006 to 0.020 in
Crankshaft endplay .... 0.0035 to 0.0135 in
Connecting rod journal diameter .... 2.1238 to 2.1248 in
Main bearing journal diameter
   Front (no.1) .... 2.4988 to 2.4998 in
   All others .... 2.4985 to 2.4995 in
Main bearing oil clearance
   Nos. 1 through 4 .... 0.0005 to 0.0021 in
   No. 5 .... 0.0015 to 0.0031 in
Connecting rod bearing oil clearance (all) .... 0.0004 to 0.0033 in

Torque specifications*   Ft-lbs

Main bearing cap bolts (nos. 1 through 4)
   1988 and earlier 80
   1989 on 70
Main bearing cap bolts (rear – no. 5)
   1988 and earlier 120
   1989 on 105
Connecting rod cap nuts .... 18 plus an additional 70-degrees rotation
* Note: Refer to Part B for additional torque specifications.

HT4100 engine – VIN code 8
See Chapter 2, Part B, for additional information

General

Oil pressure (minimum) .... 30 psi @ 2600 rpm
Compression pressure
   Allowable variation between cylinders 20%
   Minimum .... 100 psi

Cylinder head warpage limit ....   0.006 in

Valves

Valve stem diameter
   Intake .... 0.3420 to 0.3413 in
   Exhaust .... 0.3418 to 0.3411 in
Valve margin width (minimum) .... 1/32 in
Valve spring free length .... 2.087 in
Valve spring installed spring height .... Not available
Valve stem-to-guide clearance (new) .... 0.001 to 0.003 in
Valve stem-to-guide clearance limit .... 0.005 in

Engine block

Cylinder bore diameter .... 3.465 in
Piston-to-bore clearance* .... 0.0010 to 0.0018 in
* Measure pistons at top of skirt, perpendicular to pin

Pistons and rings

Piston ring end gap
   Compression rings .... 0.0090 to 0.0020 in
   Oil rings .... 0.0010 to 0.0050 in
Compression ring side clearance .... 0.0016 to 0.0037 in
Oil ring side clearance .... None (side sealing)

Crankshaft, connecting rods and main bearings

Connecting rod endplay (side clearance)	0.008 to 0.020 in
Crankshaft endplay	
New limits	0.001 to 0.007 in
Worn limits	0.015 in
Main bearing journal diameter	2.640 in
Connecting rod journal diameter	1.930 in
Connecting rod bearing oil clearance	
Production	0.0005 to 0.0028 in
Wear limit	0.0035 in
Connecting rod bearing journal out-of-round limit	0.0004 in
Main bearing oil clearance	
1982 through 1984	0.004 to 0.003 in
1985	
No. 1	0.0008 to 0.0031 in
Nos. 2, 3, 4 and 5	0.0016 to 0.0039 in

Torque specifications*

	Ft-lbs
Main bearing cap bolts	85
Connecting rod bolts	20

Note: Refer to Part B for additional torque specifications.

1   General information

Included in this portion of Chapter 2 are the general overhaul procedures for the cylinder heads and internal engine components.

The information ranges from advice concerning preparation for an overhaul and the purchase of replacement parts to detailed, step-by-step procedures covering removal and installation of internal engine components and the inspection of parts.

The following Sections have been written based on the assumption that the engine has been removed from the vehicle. For information concerning in-vehicle engine repair, as well as removal and installation of the external components necessary for the overhaul, see Part A and B of this Chapter and Section 7 of this Part.

The Specifications included in this Part are only those necessary for the inspection and overhaul procedures which follow. Refer to Part A and B for additional Specifications.

2   Engine overhaul – general information

Refer to illustration 2.4

It's not always easy to determine when, or if, an engine should be completely overhauled, as a number of factors must be considered.

High mileage is not necessarily an indication that an overhaul is needed, while low mileage doesn't preclude the need for an overhaul. Frequency of servicing is probably the most important consideration. An engine that's had regular and frequent oil and filter changes, as well as other required maintenance, will most likely give many thousands of miles of reliable service. Conversely, a neglected engine may require an overhaul very early in its life.

Excessive oil consumption is an indication that piston rings, valve seals and/or valve guides are in need of attention. Make sure that oil leaks aren't responsible before deciding that the rings and/or guides are bad. Perform a cylinder compression check to determine the extent of the work required (see Section 3).

Check the oil pressure with a gauge installed in place of the oil pressure sending unit **(see illustration)** and compare it to the Specifications. If it's extremely low, the bearings and/or oil pump are probably worn out.

Loss of power, rough running, knocking or metallic engine noises, excessive valve train noise and high fuel consumption rates may also point to the need for an overhaul, especially if they're all present at the same time. If a complete tune-up doesn't remedy the situation, major mechanical work is the only solution.

An engine overhaul involves restoring the internal parts to the specifications of a new engine. During an overhaul, the piston rings are replaced and the cylinder walls are reconditioned (rebored and/or honed). If a rebore is done by an automotive machine shop, new oversize pistons will also be installed. The main bearings, connecting rod bearings and camshaft bearings are generally replaced with new ones and, if necessary, the crankshaft may be reground to restore the journals. Generally, the valves are serviced as well, since they're usually in less-than-perfect condition at this point. While the engine is being overhauled, other components, such as the distributor, starter and alternator, can be rebuilt as well. The end result should be a like-new engine that will give many trouble-free miles. **Note:** *Critical cooling system components such as the hoses, drivebelts, thermostat and water pump MUST be replaced with new parts when an engine is overhauled. The radiator should be checked carefully to ensure that it isn't clogged or leaking (see Chapter 3). Also, we don't recommend overhauling the oil pump – always install a new one when an engine is rebuilt.*

2C

2.4   Remove the oil pressure sending unit and install an oil pressure gauge – on some engines, the sending unit is located at the rear of the engine, just behind the intake manifold, while on others, it's near the oil filter

3.5   If your engine has a coil-in-cap distributor, disconnect the wire from the BAT terminal on the distributor cap when checking the compression

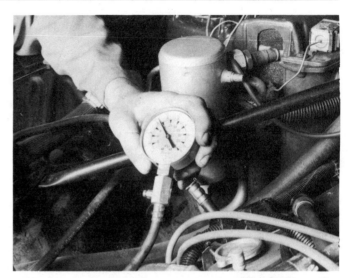

3.6   A compression gauge with a threaded fitting for the plug hole is preferred over the type that requires hand pressure to maintain the seal

Before beginning the engine overhaul, read through the entire procedure to familiarize yourself with the scope and requirements of the job. Overhauling an engine isn't difficult, but it is time consuming. Plan on the vehicle being tied up for a minimum of two weeks, especially if parts must be taken to an automotive machine shop for repair or reconditioning. Check on availability of parts and make sure that any necessary special tools and equipment are obtained in advance. Most work can be done with typical hand tools, although a number of precision measuring tools are required for inspecting parts to determine if they must be replaced. Often an automotive machine shop will handle the inspection of parts and offer advice concerning reconditioning and replacement. **Note:** *Always wait until the engine has been completely disassembled and all components, especially the engine block, have been inspected before deciding what service and repair operations must be performed by an automotive machine shop.* Since the block's condition will be the major factor to consider when determining whether to overhaul the original engine or buy a rebuilt one, never purchase parts or have machine work done on other components until the block has been thoroughly inspected. As a general rule, time is the primary cost of an overhaul, so it doesn't pay to install worn or substandard parts.

As a final note, to ensure maximum life and minimum trouble from a rebuilt engine, everything must be assembled with care in a spotlessly clean environment.

3   Cylinder compression check

Refer to illustrations 3.5 and 3.6

1   A compression check will tell you what mechanical condition the upper end (pistons, rings, valves, head gaskets) of your engine is in. Specifically, it can tell you if the compression is down due to leakage caused by worn piston rings, defective valves and seats or a blown head gasket. **Note:** *The engine must be at normal operating temperature and the battery must be fully charged for this check. Also, the choke valve must be all the way open to get an accurate compression reading (if the engine's warm, the choke should be open).*

2   Begin by cleaning the area around the spark plugs before you remove them (compressed air should be used, if available, otherwise a small brush or even a bicycle tire pump will work). The idea is to prevent dirt from getting into the cylinders as the compression check is being done.

3   Remove all of the spark plugs from the engine (Chapter 1).

4   Block the throttle wide open.

5   On vehicles with "point-type" ignition, detach the coil wire from the center of the distributor cap and ground it on the engine block. Use a jumper wire with alligator clips on each end to ensure a good ground. On elec-

tronic ignition equipped vehicles, the ignition circuit should be disabled by unplugging the "BAT" wire going to the distributor **(see illustration)**. On 5.7L Chevrolet engines disconnect the module connector at the distributor to disable the ignition system.

6   Install the compression gauge in the number one spark plug hole **(see illustration)**.

7   Crank the engine over at least seven compression strokes and watch the gauge. The compression should build up quickly in a healthy engine. Low compression on the first stroke, followed by gradually increasing pressure on successive strokes, indicates worn piston rings. A low compression reading on the first stroke, which doesn't build up during successive strokes, indicates leaking valves or a blown head gasket (a cracked head could also be the cause). Deposits on the undersides of the valve heads can also cause low compression. Record the highest gauge reading obtained.

8   Repeat the procedure for the remaining cylinders and compare the results to the Specifications.

9   Add some engine oil (about three squirts from a plunger-type oil can) to each cylinder, through the spark plug hole, and repeat the test.

10   If the compression increases after the oil is added, the piston rings are definitely worn. If the compression doesn't increase significantly, the leakage is occurring at the valves or head gasket. Leakage past the valves may be caused by burned valve seats and/or faces or warped, cracked or bent valves.

11   If two adjacent cylinders have equally low compression, there's a strong possibility that the head gasket between them is blown. The appearance of coolant in the combustion chambers or the crankcase would verify this condition.

12   If one cylinder is 20 percent lower than the others, and the engine has a slightly rough idle, a worn exhaust lobe on the camshaft could be the cause.

13   If the compression is unusually high, the combustion chambers are probably coated with carbon deposits. If that's the case, the cylinder heads should be removed and decarbonized.

14   If compression is way down or varies greatly between cylinders, it would be a good idea to have a leak-down test performed by an automotive repair shop. This test will pinpoint exactly where the leakage is occurring and how severe it is.

4   Engine removal – methods and precautions

If you've decided that an engine must be removed for overhaul or major repair work, several preliminary steps should be taken.

5.5   Flag each wire and hose to ease reassembly

5.20   Connect the lifting sling or chain to the hoist and take up the slack

Locating a suitable place to work is extremely important. Adequate work space, along with storage space for the vehicle, will be needed. If a shop or garage isn't available, at the very least a flat, level, clean work surface made of concrete or asphalt is required.

Cleaning the engine compartment and engine before beginning the removal procedure will help keep tools clean and organized.

An engine hoist or A-frame will also be necessary. Make sure the equipment is rated in excess of the combined weight of the engine and accessories. Safety is of primary importance, considering the potential hazards involved in lifting the engine out of the vehicle.

If the engine is being removed by a novice, a helper should be available. Advice and aid from someone more experienced would also be helpful. There are many instances when one person cannot simultaneously perform all of the operations required when lifting the engine out of the vehicle.

Plan the operation ahead of time. Arrange for or obtain all of the tools and equipment you'll need prior to beginning the job. Some of the equipment necessary to perform engine removal and installation safely and with relative ease are (in addition to an engine hoist) a heavy duty floor jack, complete sets of wrenches and sockets as described in the front of this manual, wooden blocks and plenty of rags and cleaning solvent for mopping up spilled oil, coolant and gasoline. If the hoist must be rented, make sure that you arrange for it in advance and perform all of the operations possible without it beforehand. This will save you money and time.

Plan for the vehicle to be out of use for quite a while. A machine shop will be required to perform some of the work which the do-it-yourselfer can't accomplish without special equipment. These shops often have a busy schedule, so it would be a good idea to consult them before removing the engine in order to accurately estimate the amount of time required to rebuild or repair components that may need work.

Always be extremely careful when removing and installing the engine. Serious injury can result from careless actions. Plan ahead, take your time and a job of this nature, although major, can be accomplished successfully.

5   Engine – removal and installation

Refer to illustrations 5.5 and 5.20
Warning: *The air conditioning system is under high pressure! Have a dealer service department or service station discharge the system before disconnecting any air conditioning system hoses or fittings.*

Removal

1   Disconnect the negative cable from the battery.

2   Cover the fenders and cowl and remove the hood (see Chapter 11). Special pads are available to protect the fenders, but an old bedspread or blanket will also work.
3   Remove the air cleaner assembly.
4   Drain the cooling system (see Chapter 1).
5   Label the vacuum lines, emissions system hoses, wiring connectors, ground straps and fuel lines, to ensure correct reinstallation, then detach them. Pieces of masking tape with numbers or letters written on them work well **(see illustration)**. If there's any possibility of confusion, make a sketch of the engine compartment and clearly label the lines, hoses and wires.
6   Label and detach all coolant hoses from the engine.
7   Remove the cooling fan, shroud and radiator (see Chapter 3).
8   Remove the drivebelts (see Chapter 1).
9   Warning: Gasoline is extremely flammable, so extra precautions must be taken when working on any part of the fuel system. DO NOT smoke or allow open flames or bare light bulbs near the vehicle. Also, don't work in a garage if a natural gas appliance with a pilot light is present. Disconnect the fuel lines running from the engine to the chassis (see Chapter 4). Plug or cap all open fittings/lines.
10   Disconnect the throttle linkage (and TV linkage/speed control cable, if equipped) from the engine (see Chapter 4 and Chapter 7).
11   On power steering equipped vehicles, unbolt the power steering pump (see Chapter 10). Leave the lines/hoses attached and make sure the pump is kept in an upright position in the engine compartment (use wire or rope to restrain it out of the way).
12   On air conditioned vehicles, unbolt the compressor (see Chapter 3) and set it aside. Do not disconnect the hoses.
13   Drain the engine oil (see Chapter 1) and remove the filter.
14   Remove the starter motor (see Chapter 5).
15   Remove the alternator (see Chapter 5).
16   Unbolt the exhaust system from the engine (see Chapter 4).
17   Refer to Chapter 7 and remove the torque converter-to-driveplate fasteners.
18   Support the transmission with a jack. Position a wood block between them to prevent damage to the transmission. Special transmission jacks with safety chains are available – use one if possible.
19   Attach an engine sling or a length of chain to the lifting brackets on the engine.
20   Roll the hoist into position and connect the sling to it **(see illustration)**. Take up the slack in the sling or chain, but don't lift the engine. **Warning:** *DO NOT place any part of your body under the engine when it's supported only by a hoist or other lifting device.*
21   Remove the transmission-to-engine block bolts.
22   Remove the engine mount-to-frame bolts.

2C

7.3a   4.1L V6 engine – exploded view

23 Recheck to be sure nothing is still connecting the engine to the transmission or vehicle. Disconnect anything still remaining.

24 Raise the engine slightly. Carefully work it forward to separate it from the transmission. Be sure the torque converter stays in the transmission (clamp a pair of vise-grips to the housing to keep the converter from sliding out). Slowly raise the engine out of the engine compartment. Check carefully to make sure nothing is hanging up.

25 Remove the driveplate and mount the engine on an engine stand.

Installation

26 Check the engine and transmission mounts. If they're worn or damaged, replace them.

27 Raise the transmission slightly to accept the angle of the engine when it is lowered into place.

28 Carefully lower the engine into the engine compartment – make sure the engine mounts line up.

29 Guide the torque converter into the crankshaft following the procedure outlined in Chapter 7.

30 Install the transmission-to-engine bolts and tighten them securely. **Caution:** *DO NOT use the bolts to force the transmission and engine together!*

7.3b   Typical V8 engine – exploded view

31 Reinstall the remaining components in the reverse order of removal.
32 Add coolant, oil, power steering and transmission fluid as needed.
33 Run the engine and check for leaks and proper operation of all accessories, then install the hood and test drive the vehicle.
34 Have the air conditioning system recharged and leak tested.

6   Engine rebuilding alternatives

The do-it-yourselfer is faced with a number of options when performing an engine overhaul. The decision to replace the engine block, piston/connecting rod assemblies and crankshaft depends on a number of factors, with the number one consideration being the condition of the block. Other considerations are cost, access to machine shop facilities, parts availability, time required to complete the project and the extent of prior mechanical experience on the part of the do-it-yourselfer.

Some of the rebuilding alternatives include:

Individual parts – If the inspection procedures reveal that the engine block and most engine components are in reusable condition, purchasing individual parts may be the most economical alternative. The block, crankshaft and piston/connecting rod assemblies should all be inspected carefully. Even if the block shows little wear, the cylinder bores should be surface honed.

Short block – A short block consists of an engine block with a crankshaft and piston/connecting rod assemblies already installed. All new bearings are incorporated and all clearances will be correct. The existing camshaft, valve train components, cylinder heads and external parts can be bolted to the short block with little or no machine shop work necessary.

Long block – A long block consists of a short block plus an oil pump, oil pan, cylinder heads, rocker arm covers, camshaft and valve train components, timing sprockets and chain or gears and timing cover. All components are installed with new bearings, seals and gaskets incorporated throughout. The installation of manifolds and external parts is all that's necessary.

Give careful thought to which alternative is best for you and discuss the situation with local automotive machine shops, auto parts dealers and experienced rebuilders before ordering or purchasing replacement parts.

7   Engine overhaul – disassembly sequence

Refer to illustrations 7.3a and 7.3b

1   It's much easier to disassemble and work on the engine if it's mounted on a portable engine stand. A stand can often be rented quite cheaply from an equipment rental yard. Before the engine is mounted on a stand, the flywheel/driveplate should be removed from the engine.
2   If a stand isn't available, it's possible to disassemble the engine with it blocked up on the floor. Be extra careful not to tip or drop the engine when working without a stand.
3   If you're going to obtain a rebuilt engine, all external components must come off first, to be transferred to the replacement engine, just as they will if you're doing a complete engine overhaul yourself. These include:

Alternator and brackets
Emissions control components
Distributor, spark plug wires and spark plugs
Thermostat and housing cover
Water pump
Carburetor or TBI unit
Intake/exhaust manifolds
Oil filter
Engine mounts
Driveplate
Engine rear plate

Note: *When removing the external components from the engine, pay close attention to details that may be helpful or important during installation. Note the installed position of gaskets, seals, spacers, pins, brackets, washers, bolts and other small items* (see illustrations).

8.2   A small plastic bag, with an appropriate label, can be used to store the valve train components so they can be kept together and reinstalled in the correct guide

8.3   Use a valve spring compressor to compress the spring, then remove the keepers from the valve stem

4   If you're obtaining a short block, which consists of the engine block, crankshaft, pistons and connecting rods all assembled, then the cylinder heads, oil pan and oil pump will have to be removed as well. See Engine rebuilding alternatives for additional information regarding the different possibilities to be considered.

5   If you're planning a complete overhaul, the engine must be disassembled and the internal components removed in the following order:

Rocker arm covers
Intake and exhaust manifolds
Rocker arms and pushrods
Valve lifters
Cylinder heads
Timing cover
Timing chain and sprockets
Camshaft
Oil pan
Oil pump
Piston/connecting rod assemblies
Crankshaft and main bearings

6   Before beginning the disassembly and overhaul procedures, make sure the following items are available. Also, refer to Engine overhaul – reassembly sequence for a list of tools and materials needed for engine reassembly.

Common hand tools
Small cardboard boxes or plastic bags for storing parts
Gasket scraper
Ridge reamer
Vibration damper puller
Micrometers
Telescoping gauges
Dial indicator set
Valve spring compressor
Cylinder surfacing hone
Piston ring groove cleaning tool
Electric drill motor
Tap and die set
Wire brushes
Oil gallery brushes
Cleaning solvent

8   Cylinder head – disassembly

Refer to illustrations 8.2, 8.3 and 8.4

Note: *New and rebuilt cylinder heads are commonly available for most engines at dealerships and auto parts stores. Due to the fact that some specialized tools are necessary for the disassembly and inspection procedures, and replacement parts may not be readily available, it may be more practical and economical for the home mechanic to purchase replacement heads rather than taking the time to disassemble, inspect and recondition the originals.*

1   Cylinder head disassembly involves removal of the intake and exhaust valves and related components. If they're still in place, remove the rocker arm nuts, pivot balls and rocker arms from the cylinder head studs. Label the parts or store them separately so they can be reinstalled in their original locations.

2   Before the valves are removed, arrange to label and store them, along with their related components, so they can be kept separate and reinstalled in the same valve guides they are removed from **(see illustration)**.

3   Compress the springs on the first valve with a spring compressor and remove the keepers **(see illustration)**. Carefully release the valve spring compressor and remove the retainer, the spring and the spring seat (if used).

4   Pull the valve out of the head, then remove the oil seal from the guide. If the valve binds in the guide (won't pull through), push it back into the head and deburr the area around the keeper groove with a fine file or whetstone **(see illustration)**.

5   Repeat the procedure for the remaining valves. Remember to keep all the parts for each valve together so they can be reinstalled in the same locations.

6   Once the valves and related components have been removed and stored in an organized manner, the heads should be thoroughly cleaned and inspected. If a complete engine overhaul is being done, finish the engine disassembly procedures before beginning the cylinder head cleaning and inspection process.

9   Cylinder head – cleaning and inspection

1   Thorough cleaning of the cylinder heads and related valve train components, followed by a detailed inspection, will enable you to decide how much valve service work must be done during the engine overhaul. **Note:** *If the engine was severely overheated, the cylinder head is probably warped (see Step 12).*

8.4   If the valve won't pull through the guide, deburr the edge of the stem end and the area around the top of the keeper groove with a file

9.12   Check the cylinder head gasket surface for warpage by trying to slip a feeler gauge under the straightedge (see the Specifications for the maximum warpage allowed and use a feeler gauge of that thickness)

Cleaning

2   Scrape all traces of old gasket material and sealing compound off the head gasket, intake manifold and exhaust manifold sealing surfaces. Be very careful not to gouge the cylinder head. Special gasket removal solvents that soften gaskets and make removal much easier are available at auto parts stores.

3   Remove all built up scale from the coolant passages.

4   Run a stiff wire brush through the various holes to remove deposits that may have formed in them.

5   Run an appropriate size tap into each of the threaded holes to remove corrosion and thread sealant that may be present. If compressed air is available, use it to clear the holes of debris produced by this operation. **Warning:** *Wear eye protection when using compressed air!*

6   Clean the rocker arm pivot stud threads, when equipped, with a wire brush.

7   Clean the cylinder head with solvent and dry it thoroughly. Compressed air will speed the drying process and ensure that all holes and recessed areas are clean. **Note:** *Decarbonizing chemicals are available and may prove very useful when cleaning cylinder heads and valve train components. They are very caustic and should be used with caution. Be sure to follow the instructions on the container.*

8   Clean the rocker arm components and pushrods with solvent and dry them thoroughly (don't mix them up during the cleaning process). Compressed air will speed the drying process and can be used to clean out the oil passages.

9   Clean all the valve springs, spring seats, keepers and retainers (or rotators) with solvent and dry them thoroughly. Do the components from one valve at a time to avoid mixing up the parts.

10   Scrape off any heavy deposits that may have formed on the valves, then use a motorized wire brush to remove deposits from the valve heads and stems. Again, make sure the valves don't get mixed up.

Inspection

Note: *Be sure to perform all of the following inspection procedures before concluding that machine shop work is required. Make a list of the items that need attention.*

Cylinder head

Refer to illustrations 9.12, 9.14a and 9.14b

11   Inspect the head very carefully for cracks, evidence of coolant leakage and other damage. If cracks are found, check with an automotive ma-

9.14a   A dial indicator can be used to determine the valve stem-to-guide clearance (move the valve stem as indicated by the arrows)

chine shop concerning repair. If repair isn't possible, a new cylinder head should be obtained.

12   Using a straightedge and feeler gauge, check the head gasket mating surface for warpage **(see illustration)**. If the warpage exceeds the specified limit, it can be resurfaced at an automotive machine shop. **Note:** *If the heads are resurfaced, the intake manifold flanges will also require machining.*

13   Examine the valve seats in each of the combustion chambers. If they're pitted, cracked or burned, the head will require valve service that's beyond the scope of the home mechanic.

14   Check the valve stem-to-guide clearance by measuring the lateral movement of the valve stem with a dial indicator attached securely to the head **(see illustration)**. The valve must be in the guide and approximately 1/16-inch off the seat. The total valve stem movement indicated by the gauge needle must be divided by two to obtain the actual clearance. After this is done, if there's still some doubt regarding the condition of the valve

2C

VALVE
KEY
GROOVE

10 ÷ .010″ (SERVICE)
6 ÷ .006″ (PRODUCTION)

OVERSIZE MARKING
ON VALVE HEAD
WILL BE MARKED
6 or 10.

9.14b   Some engines are equipped with slightly oversized valves from the factory. Valves with larger diameter stems are available to compensate for guide wear; however, a machine shop must resize the guides

NEW VALVE   WORN VALVE

9.15a   Check for valve wear at the points shown here

1 Valve tip	*4 Stem (most worn area)*
2 Keeper groove	*5 Valve face*
3 Stem (least worn area)	*6 Margin*

9.15b   Valve stem wear patterns

1   Proper tip pattern (rotator functioning properly)
2   No rotation pattern (replace rotator and check rotation)
3   Partial rotation pattern (replace rotator and check rotation)

VALVE MARGIN WIDTH

NO MARGIN

9.16   The margin width on each valve must be as specified (if no margin exists, the valve cannot be reused)

guides they should be checked by an automotive machine shop (the cost should be minimal). Oversize valves may be used to compensate for guide wear **(see illustration)**.

Valves

Refer to illustrations 9.15a, 9.15b and 9.16

15   Carefully inspect each valve face and stem for uneven wear, deformation, cracks, pits and burned areas **(see illustration)**. Check the valve stem for scuffing and galling and the neck for cracks. Rotate the valve and check for any obvious indication that it's bent. Look for pits and excessive wear on the end of the stem **(see illustration)**. The presence of any of these conditions indicates the need for valve service by an automotive machine shop.

16   Measure the margin width on each valve **(see illustration)**. Any valve with a margin narrower than specified will have to be replaced with a new one.

Valve components

Refer to illustrations 9.17, 9.18 and 9.19

17   Check each valve spring for wear (on the ends) and pits. Any springs that are shorter than specified have sagged and should not be reused **(see illustration)**. The tension of all springs should be checked with a special fixture before deciding that they're suitable for use in a rebuilt engine (take the springs to an automotive machine shop for this check).

9.17   Measure the free length of each valve spring with a dial or vernier caliper

9.18   Check each valve spring for squareness

18   Stand each spring on a flat surface and check it for squareness **(see illustration)**. If any of the springs are distorted or sagged, replace all of them with new parts.

19   Check the spring retainers (or rotators) and keepers for obvious wear and cracks. Any questionable parts should be replaced with new ones, as extensive damage will occur if they fail during engine operation. Make sure the rotators operate smoothly with no binding or excessive play **(see illustration)**.

Rocker arm components

20   Check the rocker arm faces (the areas that contact the pushrod ends and valve stems) for pits, wear, galling, score marks and rough spots. Check the rocker arm pivot contact areas and pivot as well. Look for cracks in each rocker arm and nut or bolt.

21   Inspect the pushrod ends for scuffing and excessive wear. Roll each pushrod on a flat surface, like a piece of plate glass, to determine if it's bent.

22   Check the rocker arm studs in the cylinder heads for damaged threads and secure installation.

23   Any damaged or excessively worn parts must be replaced with new ones.

24   If the inspection process indicates that the valve components are in generally poor condition and worn beyond the limits specified, which is usually the case in an engine that's being overhauled, reassemble the valves in the cylinder head and refer to Section 10 for valve servicing recommendations.

2C

9.19   The exhaust valve rotators can be checked by turning the inner and outer sections in opposite directions – feel for smooth movement and excessive play

spring retainers or rotators and keepers (as necessary), replace the valve seals with new ones, reassemble the valve components and make sure the installed spring height is correct. The cylinder head gasket surfaces will also be resurfaced if they're warped.

4   After the valve job has been performed by a professional, the heads will be in like-new condition. When the heads are returned, be sure to clean them again before installation on the engine to remove any metal particles and abrasive grit that may still be present from the valve service or head resurfacing operations. Use compressed air, if available, to blow out all the oil holes and passages.

---

10   Valves – servicing

1   Because of the complex nature of the job and the special tools and equipment needed, servicing of the valves, the valve seats and the valve guides, commonly known as a valve job, should be done by a professional.

2   The home mechanic can remove and disassemble the heads, do the initial cleaning and inspection, then reassemble and deliver them to a dealer service department or an automotive machine shop for the actual service work. Doing the inspection will enable you to see what condition the heads and valvetrain components are in and will ensure that you know what work and new parts are required when dealing with an automotive machine shop.

3   The dealer service department, or automotive machine shop, will remove the valves and springs, recondition or replace the valves and valve seats, recondition the valve guides, check and replace the valve springs,

---

11   Cylinder head – reassembly

Refer to illustrations 11.3, 11.5a, 11.5b, 11.6, 11.8 and 11.9

1   Regardless of whether or not the heads were sent to an automotive repair shop for valve servicing, make sure they are clean before beginning reassembly.

2   If the heads were sent out for valve servicing, the valves and related components will already be in place. Begin the reassembly procedure with Step 8.

11.3   Make sure the new valve stem seals are seated against the tops of the valve guides

1   *Valve seal seated in tool*
2   *Deburr the end of the valve stem before installing the seal*
3   *Seal*
4   *Valve seal installation tool*

11.5a   Typical engine valves and related components – exploded view

1   *Keeper*
2   *Retainer*
3   *Oil shield*
4   *O-ring oil seal*
5   *Umbrella seal*
6   *Damper*
7   *Spring*
8   *Intake valve*
9   *Rotator*
10 *Exhaust valve*

3   Install new seals on each of the intake valve guides. Using a hammer and a deep socket, gently tap each seal into place until it is completely seated on the guide **(see illustration)**. Do not twist or cock the seals during installation or they will not seal properly on the valve stems. The umbrella-type seals are installed over the exhaust valves after the valves are in place. **Note:** *On HT4100 engines, use tool number J-29790 to install the valve stem seals.*

4   Beginning at one end of the head, lubricate and install the first valve. Apply moly-base grease or clean engine oil to the valve stem.

5   Drop the spring seat or shim(s) over the valve guide and set the valve springs, shield and retainer (or rotator) in place **(see illustrations)**.

6   Compress the springs with a valve spring compressor and carefully install the O-ring oil seal in the lower groove of the valve stem. Make sure the seal is not twisted – it must lie perfectly flat in the groove. Position the keepers in the upper groove, then slowly release the compressor and make sure the keepers seat properly. Apply a small dab of grease to each keeper to hold it in place if necessary **(see illustration)**.

7   Repeat the procedure for the remaining valves. Be sure to return the components to their original locations – do not mix them up!

8   Once all the valves are in place in both heads, the valve stem O-ring seals must be checked to make sure they do not leak. This procedure requires a vacuum pump and special adapter (GM tool no. J-23994, or equivalent), so it may be a good idea to have it done by a dealer service department, repair shop or automotive machine shop. The adapter is positioned on each valve retainer or rotator and vacuum is applied with the hand pump **(see illustration)**. If the vacuum cannot be maintained, the seal is leaking and must be checked/replaced before the head is installed on the engine.

9   Check the installed valve spring height with a ruler graduated in 1/32-inch increments or a dial caliper. If the heads were sent out for service work, the installed height should be correct (but don't automatically assume that it is). The measurement is taken from the top of each spring seat or shim(s) to the top of the oil shield (or the bottom of the retainer/rotator, the two points are the same) **(see illustration)**. If the height is greater than

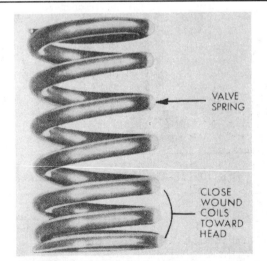

11.5b   If the valve springs are wound closer at one end, install them as shown

VALVE SPRING

CLOSE WOUND COILS TOWARD HEAD

11.6   Before installation, apply a small dab of grease to each keeper as shown here – it will hold them in place on the valve stem as the spring is released

11.8   A special adapter and a vacuum pump are required to check the O-ring valve stem seals for leaks

11.9   Be sure to check the valve spring installed height (the distance from the top of the seat/shims to the top of the shield)

specified, shims can be added under the springs to correct it. **Caution:** *Do not, under any circumstances, shim the springs to the point where the installed height is less than specified.*

10   Apply moly-base grease to the rocker arm faces and the pivots, then install the rocker arms. On 5.7L Chevrolet built engines, thread the nuts on three or four turns only at this time (when the heads are installed, the nuts will be tightened following a specific procedure).

12   Piston/connecting rod assembly – removal

Refer to illustrations 12.1, 12.3 and 12.6

Note: *Prior to removing the piston/connecting rod assemblies, remove the cylinder heads, the oil pan and the oil pump (except externally mounted pumps) by referring to the appropriate Sections in Chapter 2A or 2B.*

1   Use your fingernail to feel if a ridge has formed at the upper limit of ring travel (about 1/4-inch down from the top of each cylinder). If carbon deposits or cylinder wear have produced ridges, they must be completely removed with a special tool **(see illustration)**. Follow the manufacturer's instructions provided with the tool. Failure to remove the ridges before at-

tempting to remove the piston/connecting rod assemblies may result in piston breakage.

2   After the cylinder ridges have been removed, turn the engine upside-down so the crankshaft is facing up.

3   Before the connecting rods are removed, check the endplay with feeler gauges. Slide them between the first connecting rod and the crankshaft throw until the play is removed **(see illustration)**. The endplay is equal to the thickness of the feeler gauge(s). If the endplay exceeds the service limit, new connecting rods will be required. If new rods (or a new crankshaft) are installed, the endplay may fall under the specified minimum (if it does, the rods will have to be machined to restore it – consult an automotive machine shop for advice if necessary). Repeat the procedure for the remaining connecting rods.

4   Check the connecting rods and caps for identification marks. If they aren't plainly marked, use a small center punch to make the appropriate number of indentations on each rod and cap (1, 2, 3, etc., depending on the engine type and cylinder they're associated with).

5   Loosen each of the connecting rod cap nuts 1/2-turn at a time until they can be removed by hand. Remove the number one connecting rod cap and bearing insert. Don't drop the bearing insert out of the cap.

2C

12.1   A ridge reamer is required to remove the ridge from the top of the cylinder – do this before removing the pistons!

12.3   Check the connecting rod endplay with a feeler gauge as shown

12.6   To prevent damage to the crankshaft journals and cylinder walls, slip sections of hose over the rod bolts before removing the pistons

13.1   Checking crankshaft endplay with a dial indicator

6   Slip a short length of plastic or rubber hose over each connecting rod cap bolt to protect the crankshaft journal and cylinder wall as the piston is removed **(see illustration)**.

7   Remove the bearing insert and push the connecting rod/piston assembly out through the top of the engine. Use a wooden hammer handle to push on the upper bearing surface in the connecting rod. If resistance is felt, double-check to make sure that all of the ridge was removed from the cylinder.

8   Repeat the procedure for the remaining cylinders.

9   After removal, reassemble the connecting rod caps and bearing inserts in their respective connecting rods and install the cap nuts finger tight. Leaving the old bearing inserts in place until reassembly will help prevent the connecting rod bearing surfaces from being accidentally nicked or gouged.

10   Don't separate the pistons from the connecting rods (see Section 17 for additional information).

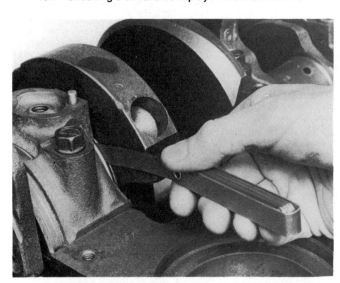

13.3   Checking crankshaft endplay with a feeler gauge

---

13   Crankshaft – removal

Refer to illustrations 13.1, 13.3, 13.4a and 13.4b

Note: *The crankshaft can be removed only after the engine has been removed from the vehicle. It's assumed that the driveplate, vibration damper, timing chain, oil pan, oil pump and piston/connecting rod assemblies have already been removed. If your engine is equipped with a one-piece rear main oil seal, the seal housing must be unbolted and separated from the block before proceeding with crankshaft removal.*

1   Before the crankshaft is removed, check the endplay. Mount a dial indicator with the stem in line with the crankshaft and just touching one of the crank throws **(see illustration)**.

2   Push the crankshaft all the way to the rear and zero the dial indicator. Next, pry the crankshaft to the front as far as possible and check the reading on the dial indicator. The distance that it moves is the endplay. If it's greater than specified, check the crankshaft thrust surfaces for wear. If no wear is evident, new main bearings should correct the endplay.

3   If a dial indicator isn't available, feeler gauges can be used. Gently pry or push the crankshaft all the way to the front of the engine. Slip feeler gauges between the crankshaft and the front face of the thrust main bearing to determine the clearance **(see illustration)**.

4   Check the main bearing caps to see if they're marked to indicate their locations. They should be numbered consecutively from the front of the engine to the rear. If they aren't, mark them with number stamping dies or a center punch **(see illustration)**. Main bearing caps generally have a cast-

in arrow, which points to the front of the engine **(see illustration)**. Loosen the main bearing cap bolts 1/4-turn at a time each, until they can be removed by hand. Note if any stud bolts are used and make sure they're returned to their original locations when the crankshaft is reinstalled.

5   Gently tap the caps with a soft-face hammer, then separate them from the engine block. If necessary, use the bolts as levers to remove the caps. Try not to drop the bearing inserts if they come out with the caps.

6   Carefully lift the crankshaft out of the engine. It may be a good idea to have an assistant available, since the crankshaft is quite heavy. With the bearing inserts in place in the engine block and main bearing caps, return the caps to their respective locations on the engine block and tighten the bolts finger tight.

---

14   Engine block – cleaning

Refer to illustrations 14.1, 14.4 and 14.10

Caution: *The core plugs (also known as freeze or soft plugs) may be difficult or impossible to retrieve if they're driven into the block coolant passages.*

1   Drill a small hole in the center of each core plug and pull them out with an auto body type dent puller **(see illustration)**.

13.4a   Use a center punch or number stamping dies to mark the main bearing caps to ensure that they are reinstalled in their original locations on the block (make the punch marks near one of the bolt heads)

13.4b   The arrow on the main bearing cap indicates the front of the engine

2   Using a gasket scraper, remove all traces of gasket material from the engine block. Be very careful not to nick or gouge the gasket sealing surfaces.

3   Remove the main bearing caps and separate the bearing inserts from the caps and the engine block. Tag the bearings, indicating which cylinder they were removed from and whether they were in the cap or the block, then set them aside.

4   Remove all of the threaded oil gallery plugs from the block. The plugs are usually very tight – they may have to be drilled out and the holes re-tapped. Use new plugs when the engine is reassembled. **Note:** *On HT4100 engines, it is necessary to remove the cylinder liners in order to properly clean the block. Carefully mark the alignment of each liner to the cylinder block* **(see illustration)** *so they can be installed in the same position. If the cylinder wear exceeds the Specifications listed in this Chapter, have the liner replaced at a machine shop* (see Section 17).

5   If the engine is extremely dirty it should be taken to an automotive machine shop to be steam cleaned or hot tanked. On HT4100 engines, be sure to clean the aluminum block with the required solution; as some solvents will corrode the aluminum block.

6   After the block is returned, clean all oil holes and oil galleries one more time. Brushes specifically designed for this purpose are available at most auto parts stores. Flush the passages with warm water until the water runs clear, dry the block thoroughly and wipe all machined surfaces with a light, rust preventive oil. If you have access to compressed air, use it to speed the drying process and to blow out all the oil holes and galleries. **Warning:** *Wear eye protection when using compressed air!*

7   If the block isn't extremely dirty or sludged up, you can do an adequate cleaning job with hot soapy water and a stiff brush. Take plenty of time and do a thorough job. Regardless of the cleaning method used, be sure to clean all oil holes and galleries very thoroughly, dry the block completely and coat all machined surfaces with light oil.

8   The threaded holes in the block must be clean to ensure accurate torque readings during reassembly. Run the proper size tap into each of the holes to remove rust, corrosion, thread sealant or sludge and restore damaged threads. If possible, use compressed air to clear the holes of debris produced by this operation. Now is a good time to clean the threads on the head bolts and the main bearing cap bolts as well.

2C

14.1   Using an auto body dent puller to remove the engine core plugs

14.4   Marking the cylinder liner position on an HT4100 engine

14.10   A large socket on an extension can be used to drive the new core plugs into the bores

15.4a   Measure the diameter of each cylinder just under the wear ridge (A), at the center (B) and at the bottom (C)

9   Reinstall the main bearing caps and tighten the bolts finger tight.

10   After coating the sealing surfaces of the new core plugs with Permatex no. 2 sealant, install them in the engine block **(see illustration)**. Make sure they're driven in straight and seated properly or leakage could result. Special tools are available for this purpose, but a large socket, with an outside diameter that will just slip into the core plug, a 1/2-inch drive extension and a hammer will work just as well. **Warning:** *On HT4100 engines, tap the plugs into the block slowly and gently to avoid cracking the aluminum block.*

11   Apply non-hardening sealant (such as Permatex no. 2 or Teflon pipe sealant) to the new oil gallery plugs and thread them into the holes in the block. Make sure they're tightened securely.

12   If the engine isn't going to be reassembled right away, cover it with a large plastic trash bag to keep it clean.

15.4b   The ability to "feel" when the telescoping gauge is at the correct point will be developed over time, so work slowly and repeat the check until you are satisfied that the bore measurement is accurate

15   Engine block – inspection

Refer to illustrations 15.4a, 15.4b and 15.4c

1   Before the block is inspected, it should be cleaned as described in Section 14.

2   Visually check the block for cracks, rust and corrosion. Look for stripped threads in the threaded holes. It's also a good idea to have the block checked for hidden cracks by an automotive machine shop that has the special equipment to do this type of work. If defects are found, have the block repaired, if possible, or replaced.

3   Check the cylinder bores for scuffing and scoring.

4   Measure the diameter of each cylinder at the top (just under the ridge area), center and bottom of the cylinder bore, parallel to the crankshaft axis **(see illustrations)**.

5   Next, measure each cylinder's diameter at the same three locations across the crankshaft axis. Compare the results to the Specifications.

6   If the required precision measuring tools aren't available, the piston-to-cylinder clearances can be obtained, though not quite as accurately, using feeler gauge stock. Feeler gauge stock comes in 12-inch lengths and various thicknesses and is generally available at auto parts stores.

7   To check the clearance, select a feeler gauge and slip it into the cylinder along with the matching piston. The piston must be positioned exactly as it normally would be. The feeler gauge must be between the piston and cylinder on one of the thrust faces (90 degrees to the piston pin bore).

15.4c   The gauge is then measured with a micrometer to determine the bore size

16.3a   A "bottle brush" hone will produce better results if you have never done cylinder honing before

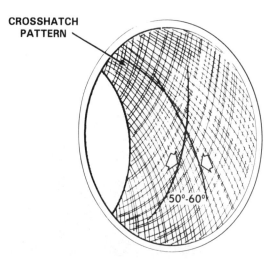

CROSSHATCH PATTERN

50°-60°

16.3b   The cylinder hone should leave a smooth, crosshatch pattern with the lines intersecting at approximately a 60-degree angle

8   The piston should slip through the cylinder (with the feeler gauge in place) with moderate pressure.

9   If it falls through or slides through easily, the clearance is excessive and a new piston will be required. If the piston binds at the lower end of the cylinder and is loose toward the top, the cylinder is tapered. If tight spots are encountered as the piston/feeler gauge is rotated in the cylinder, the cylinder is out-of-round.

10   Repeat the procedure for the remaining pistons and cylinders.

11   If the cylinder walls are badly scuffed or scored, or if they're out-of-round or tapered beyond the limits given in the Specifications, have the engine block rebored and honed at an automotive machine shop. If a rebore is done, oversize pistons and rings will be required.

12   If the cylinders are in reasonably good condition and not worn to the outside of the limits, and if the piston-to-cylinder clearances can be maintained properly, then they don't have to be rebored. Honing is all that's necessary (Section 16).

16   Cylinder honing

Refer to illustrations 16.3a and 16.3b

1   Prior to engine reassembly, the cylinder bores must be honed so the new piston rings will seat correctly and provide the best possible combustion chamber seal. **Note:** *If you don't have the tools or don't want to tackle the honing operation, most automotive machine shops will do it for a reasonable fee.*

2   Before honing the cylinders, install the main bearing caps and tighten the bolts to the specified torque.

3   Two types of cylinder hones are commonly available – the flex hone, or "bottle brush," type and the more traditional surfacing hone with spring-loaded stones. Both will do the job, but for the less experienced mechanic the "bottle brush" hone will probably be easier to use. You'll also need some kerosene or honing oil, rags and an electric drill motor. Proceed as follows:

a)   Mount the hone in the drill motor, compress the stones and slip it into the first cylinder **(see illustration)**. Be sure to wear safety goggles or a face shield!

b)   Lubricate the cylinder with plenty of honing oil, turn on the drill and move the hone up and down in the cylinder at a pace that will produce a fine crosshatch pattern on the cylinder walls. Ideally, the crosshatch lines should intersect at approximately a 60-degree

angle **(see illustration)**. Be sure to use plenty of lubricant and don't take off any more material than is absolutely necessary to produce the desired finish. **Note:** *Piston ring manufacturers may specify a smaller crosshatch angle than the traditional 60-degrees – read and follow any instructions included with the new rings.*

c)   Don't withdraw the hone from the cylinder while it's running. Instead, shut off the drill and continue moving the hone up-and-down in the cylinder until it comes to a complete stop, then compress the stones and withdraw the hone. If you're using a "bottle brush" type hone, stop the drill motor, then turn the chuck in the normal direction of rotation while withdrawing the hone from the cylinder.

d)   Wipe the oil out of the cylinder and repeat the procedure for the remaining cylinders.

4   After the honing job is complete, chamfer the top edges of the cylinder bores with a small file so the rings won't catch when the pistons are installed. Be very careful not to nick the cylinder walls with the end of the file.

5   The entire engine block must be washed again very thoroughly with warm, soapy water to remove all traces of the abrasive grit produced during the honing operation. **Note:** *The bores can be considered clean when a lint-free white cloth – dampened with clean engine oil – used to wipe them out doesn't pick up any more honing residue, which will show up as gray areas on the cloth. Be sure to run a brush through all oil holes and galleries and flush them with running water.*

6   After rinsing, dry the block and apply a coat of light rust preventive oil to all machined surfaces. Wrap the block in a plastic trash bag to keep it clean and set it aside until reassembly.

17   Piston/connecting rod assembly – inspection

Refer to illustrations 17.4a, 17.4b, 17.10 and 17.11

1   Before the inspection process can be carried out, the piston/connecting rod assemblies must be cleaned and the original piston rings removed from the pistons. **Note:** *Always use new piston rings when the engine is reassembled.*

2   Using a piston ring installation tool, carefully remove the rings from the pistons. Be careful not to nick or gouge the pistons in the process.

3   Scrape all traces of carbon from the top of the piston. A handheld wire brush or a piece of fine emery cloth can be used once the majority of the deposits have been scraped away. Do not, under any circumstances, use a wire brush mounted in a drill motor to remove deposits from the pistons. The piston material is soft and may be eroded away by the wire brush.

2C

17.4a   The piston ring grooves can be cleaned with a special tool, as shown here, . . .

17.4b   . . . or a section of a broken ring

4   Use a piston ring groove cleaning tool to remove carbon deposits from the ring grooves. If a tool isn't available, a piece broken off the old ring will do the job. Be very careful to remove only the carbon deposits – don't remove any metal and do not nick or scratch the sides of the ring grooves **(see illustrations)**.

5   Once the deposits have been removed, clean the piston/rod assemblies with solvent and dry them with compressed air (if available). Make sure the oil return holes in the back sides of the ring grooves are clear.

6   If the pistons and cylinder walls aren't damaged or worn excessively, and if the engine block is not rebored, new pistons won't be necessary. Normal piston wear appears as even vertical wear on the piston thrust surfaces and slight looseness of the top ring in its groove. New piston rings, however, should always be used when an engine is rebuilt.

7   Carefully inspect each piston for cracks around the skirt, at the pin bosses and at the ring lands.

8   Look for scoring and scuffing on the thrust faces of the skirt, holes in the piston crown and burned areas at the edge of the crown. If the skirt is scored or scuffed, the engine may have been suffering from overheating and/or abnormal combustion, which caused excessively high operating temperatures. The cooling and lubrication systems should be checked thoroughly. A hole in the piston crown is an indication that abnormal combustion (preignition) was occurring. Burned areas at the edge of the piston crown are usually evidence of spark knock (detonation). If any of the above problems exist, the causes must be corrected or the damage will occur again. The causes may include intake air leaks, incorrect fuel/air mixture, incorrect ignition timing and EGR system malfunctions.

9   Corrosion of the piston, in the form of small pits, indicates that coolant is leaking into the combustion chamber and/or the crankcase. Again, the cause must be corrected or the problem may persist in the rebuilt engine.

10   Measure the piston ring side clearance by laying a new piston ring in each ring groove and slipping a feeler gauge in beside it **(see illustration)**. Check the clearance at three or four locations around each groove. Be sure to use the correct ring for each groove – they are different. If the side clearance is greater than specified, new pistons will have to be used.

11   Check the piston-to-bore clearance by measuring the bore (see Section 15) and the piston diameter. Make sure the pistons and bores are correctly matched. Measure the piston across the skirt, at a 90-degree angle to and in line with the piston pin **(see illustration)** and 3/16-inch below the cross slot. Subtract the piston diameter from the bore diameter to obtain the clearance. If it's greater than specified, the block will have to be rebored and new pistons and rings installed. **Note:** *On HT4100 engines, if the clearances exceed the specifications, then the cylinder liner must be replaced by an automotive machine shop as the installation requires a special tool to set the cylinder liner height.*

17.10   Check the ring side clearance with a feeler gauge at several points around the groove

17.11   Measure the piston diameter at a 90-degree angle to the piston pin and 3/16 of an inch below the cross slot

CRATERS OR POCKETS   BRIGHT (POLISHED) SECTIONS

FATIGUE FAILURE   **IMPROPER SEATING**

SCRATCHES   DIRT IMBEDDED INTO BEARING MATERIAL   OVERLAY WIPED OUT

SCRATCHED BY DIRT   **LACK OF OIL**

OVERLAY GONE FROM ENTIRE SURFACE   RADIUS RIDE

TAPERED JOURNAL   **RADIUS RIDE**

19.1   Typical indications of bearing failure

12   Check the piston-to-rod clearance by twisting the piston and rod in opposite directions. Any noticeable play indicates excessive wear, which must be corrected. The piston/connecting rod assemblies should be taken to an automotive machine shop to have the pistons and rods resized and new pins installed.

13   If the pistons must be removed from the connecting rods for any reason, they should be taken to an automotive machine shop. While they are there have the connecting rods checked for bend and twist, since automotive machine shops have special equipment for this purpose. **Note:** *Unless new pistons and/or connecting rods must be installed, do not disassemble the pistons and connecting rods.*

14   Check the connecting rods for cracks and other damage. Temporarily remove the rod caps, lift out the old bearing inserts, wipe the rod and cap bearing surfaces clean and inspect them for nicks, gouges and scratches. After checking the rods, replace the old bearings, slip the caps into place and tighten the nuts finger tight. **Note:** *If the engine is being rebuilt because of a connecting rod knock, be sure to install new rods.*

18   Crankshaft – inspection

1   Clean the crankshaft with solvent and dry it with compressed air (if available). Be sure to clean the oil holes with a stiff brush and flush them with solvent.

2   Check the main and connecting rod bearing journals for uneven wear, scoring, pits and cracks.

3   Rub a penny across each journal several times. If a journal picks up copper from the penny, it's too rough and must be reground.

4   Remove all burrs from the crankshaft oil holes with a stone, file or scraper.

5   Check the rest of the crankshaft for cracks and other damage. It should be magnafluxed to reveal hidden cracks – an automotive machine shop will handle the procedure.

6   Using a micrometer, measure the diameter of the main and connecting rod journals and compare the results to the Specifications. By measuring the diameter at a number of points around each journal's circumference, you'll be able to determine whether or not the journal is out-of-round. Take the measurement at each end of the journal, near the crank throws, to determine if the journal is tapered.

7   If the crankshaft journals are damaged, tapered, out-of-round or worn beyond the limits given in the Specifications, have the crankshaft reground by an automotive machine shop. Be sure to use the correct size bearing inserts if the crankshaft is reconditioned.

8   Check the oil seal journals at each end of the crankshaft for wear and damage. If the seal has worn a groove in the journal, or if it's nicked or scratched, the new seal may leak when the engine is reassembled. In some cases, an automotive machine shop may be able to repair the journal by pressing on a thin sleeve. If repair isn't feasible, a new or different crankshaft should be installed.

9   Refer to Section 19 and examine the main and rod bearing inserts.

19   Main and connecting rod bearings – inspection

Refer to illustration 19.1

1   Even though the main and connecting rod bearings should be replaced with new ones during the engine overhaul, the old bearings should be retained for close examination, as they may reveal valuable information about the condition of the engine **(see illustration).**

2   Bearing failure occurs because of lack of lubrication, the presence of dirt or other foreign particles, overloading the engine and corrosion. Regardless of the cause of bearing failure, it must be corrected before the engine is reassembled to prevent it from happening again.

3   When examining the bearings, remove them from the engine block, the main bearing caps, the connecting rods and the rod caps and lay them out on a clean surface in the same general position as their location in the engine. This will enable you to match any bearing problems with the corresponding crankshaft journal.

4   Dirt and other foreign particles get into the engine in a variety of ways. It may be left in the engine during assembly, or it may pass through filters or the PCV system. It may get into the oil, and from there into the bearings. Metal chips from machining operations and normal engine wear are often present. Abrasives are sometimes left in engine components after reconditioning, especially when parts are not thoroughly cleaned using the proper cleaning methods. Whatever the source, these foreign objects often end up embedded in the soft bearing material and are easily recognized. Large particles will not embed in the bearing and will score or gouge the bearing and journal. The best prevention for this cause of bearing failure is to clean all parts thoroughly and keep everything spotlessly clean during engine assembly. Frequent and regular engine oil and filter changes are also recommended.

5   Lack of lubrication (or lubrication breakdown) has a number of interrelated causes. Excessive heat (which thins the oil), overloading (which squeezes the oil from the bearing face) and oil leakage or throw off (from excessive bearing clearances, worn oil pump or high engine speeds) all contribute to lubrication breakdown. Blocked oil passages, which usually are the result of misaligned oil holes in a bearing shell, will also oil starve a bearing and destroy it. When lack of lubrication is the cause of bearing failure, the bearing material is wiped or extruded from the steel backing of the bearing. Temperatures may increase to the point where the steel backing turns blue from overheating.

6   Driving habits can have a definite effect on bearing life. Full throttle, low speed operation (lugging the engine) puts very high loads on bearings, which tends to squeeze out the oil film. These loads cause the bearings to flex, which produces fine cracks in the bearing face (fatigue failure). Eventually the bearing material will loosen in pieces and tear away from the steel backing. Short trip driving leads to corrosion of bearings because insufficient engine heat is produced to drive off the condensed water and corrosive gases. These products collect in the engine oil, forming acid and sludge. As the oil is carried to the engine bearings, the acid attacks and corrodes the bearing material.

21.3   When checking piston ring end gap, the ring must be square in the cylinder bore (this is done by pushing the ring down with the top of a piston as shown)

21.4   With the ring square in the cylinder, measure the end gap with a feeler gauge

7   Incorrect bearing installation during engine assembly will lead to bearing failure as well. Tight fitting bearings leave insufficient bearing oil clearance and will result in oil starvation. Dirt or foreign particles trapped behind a bearing insert result in high spots on the bearing which lead to failure.

---

20   Engine overhaul – reassembly sequence

---

1   Before beginning engine reassembly, make sure you have all the necessary new parts, gaskets and seals as well as the following items on hand:
   Common hand tools
   A 1/2-inch drive torque wrench
   Piston ring installation tool
   Piston ring compressor
   Vibration damper installation tool
   Short lengths of rubber or plastic hose
   to fit over connecting rod bolts
   Plastigage
   Feeler gauges
   A fine-tooth file
   New engine oil
   Engine assembly lube or moly-base grease
   Gasket sealant
   Thread locking compound
2   In order to save time and avoid problems, engine reassembly must be done in the following general order:
   New camshaft bearings (must be installed by an auto machine shop)
   Piston rings
   Crankshaft and main bearings
   Piston/connecting rod assemblies
   Oil pump – except external-mount type
   Camshaft and lifters
   Oil pan
   Timing chain and sprockets
   Cylinder heads, pushrods and rocker arms
   Timing cover (and oil pump – external-mount type)
   Intake and exhaust manifolds
   Rocker arm covers
   Engine rear plate
   Driveplate

21.5   If the end gap is too small, clamp a file in a vise and file the ring ends (from the outside in only) to enlarge the gap slightly

---

21   Piston rings – installation

Refer to illustrations 21.3, 21.4, 21.5, 21.9a, 21.9b, 21.12a and 21.12b
1   Before installing the new piston rings, the ring end gaps must be checked. It's assumed that the piston ring side clearance has been checked and verified correct (see Section 17).
2   Lay out the piston/connecting rod assemblies and the new ring sets so the ring sets will be matched with the same piston and cylinder during the end gap measurement and engine assembly. **Note:** *The 425, 500, 472 and 368 V8 engines are stamped on the block with an identification number that designates the size of the piston. The letter is located on the cylinder head face of the cylinder block, directly below the cylinder bore. Refer to the Specifications listed in this Chapter for the correct sizes.*
3   Insert the top (number one) ring into the first cylinder and square it up with the cylinder walls by pushing it in with the top of the piston **(see illustration)**. The ring should be near the bottom of the cylinder, at the lower limit of ring travel.
4   To measure the end gap, slip feeler gauges between the ends of the ring until a gauge equal to the gap width is found **(see illustration)**. The feeler gauge should slide between the ring ends with a slight amount of

21.9a   Installing the spacer/expander in the oil control ring groove

21.9b   DO NOT use a piston ring installation tool when installing the oil ring side rails

drag. Compare the measurement to the Specifications. If the gap is larger or smaller than specified, double-check to make sure you have the correct rings before proceeding.

5   If the gap is too small, it must be enlarged or the ring ends may come in contact with each other during engine operation, which can cause serious damage to the engine. The end gap can be increased by filing the ring ends very carefully with a fine file. Mount the file in a vise equipped with soft jaws, slip the ring over the file with the ends contacting the file face and slowly move the ring to remove material from the ends. When performing this operation, file only from the outside in **(see illustration)**.

6   Excess end gap isn't critical unless it's greater than 0.040-inch. Again, double-check to make sure you have the correct rings for your engine.

7   Repeat the procedure for each ring that will be installed in the first cylinder and for each ring in the remaining cylinders. Remember to keep rings, pistons and cylinders matched up.

8   Once the ring end gaps have been checked/corrected, the rings can be installed on the pistons.

9   The oil control ring (lowest one on the piston) is usually installed first. It's composed of three separate components. Slip the spacer/expander into the groove **(see illustration)**. If an anti-rotation tang is used, make sure it's inserted into the drilled hole in the ring groove. Next, install the lower side rail. Don't use a piston ring installation tool on the oil ring side rails, as they may be damaged. Instead, place one end of the side rail into the groove between the spacer/expander and the ring land, hold it firmly in place and slide a finger around the piston while pushing the rail into the groove **(see illustration)**. Next, install the upper side rail in the same manner.

10   After the three oil ring components have been installed, check to make sure that both the upper and lower side rails can be turned smoothly in the ring groove.

11   The number two (middle) ring is installed next. It's usually stamped with a mark which must face up, toward the top of the piston. **Note:** *Always follow the instructions printed on the ring package or box – different manufacturers may require different approaches. Do not mix up the top and middle rings, as they have different cross sections.*

12   Use a piston ring installation tool and make sure the identification mark is facing the top of the piston **(see illustration)**, then slip the ring into the middle groove on the piston **(see illustration)**. Don't expand the ring any more than necessary to slide it over the piston.

2C

21.12a   Piston ring TOP marks – typical

PERFECT CIRCLE

SEALED POWER

MUSKEGON

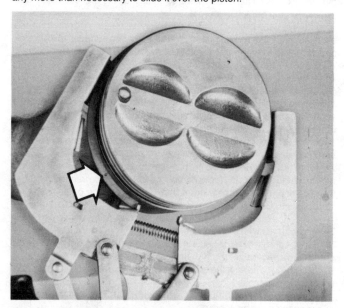

21.12b   Installing the compression rings with a ring expander – the mark (arrow) must face up

MAIN BEARING CAP NUMBERS

FRONT OF ENGINE

22.3   Main bearing cap location markings on an HT4100 engine

22.11   Lay the Plastigage strips (arrow) on the main bearing journals, parallel to the crankshaft centerline

13   Install the number one (top) ring in the same manner. Make sure the mark is facing up. Be careful not to confuse the number one and number two rings.
14   Repeat the procedure for the remaining pistons and rings.

22   Crankshaft – installation and main bearing oil clearance check

Refer to illustrations 22.3, 22.11, 22.15 and 22.16

1   Crankshaft installation is the first step in engine reassembly. It's assumed at this point that the engine block and crankshaft have been cleaned, inspected and repaired or reconditioned.
2   Position the engine with the bottom facing up.
3   Remove the main bearing cap bolts and lift out the caps. Lay them out in the proper order to ensure correct installation. **Note:** *On HT4100 engines, each bearing cap has a cast number (1/8, 2/8, 3/8, 4/8 and 5/8) on the bottom starting from the front of the engine* **(see illustration)***.* Do not mismatch or install the caps upside down as they are manufactured specifically for that particular journal.
4   If they're still in place, remove the original bearing inserts from the block and the main bearing caps. Wipe the bearing surfaces of the block and caps with a clean, lint-free cloth. They must be kept spotlessly clean.

Main bearing oil clearance check

5   Clean the back sides of the new main bearing inserts and lay one in each main bearing saddle in the block. If one of the bearing inserts from each set has a large groove in it, make sure the grooved insert is installed in the block. Lay the other bearing from each set in the corresponding main bearing cap. Make sure the tab on the bearing insert fits into the recess in the block or cap. **Caution:** *The oil holes in the block must line up with the oil holes in the bearing insert.* Do not hammer the bearing into place and don't nick or gouge the bearing faces. No lubrication should be used at this time.
6   The flanged thrust bearing must be installed in the proper cap and saddle.
7   Clean the faces of the bearings in the block and the crankshaft main bearing journals with a clean, lint-free cloth.
8   Check or clean the oil holes in the crankshaft, as any dirt here can go only one way – straight through the new bearings.
9   Once you're certain the crankshaft is clean, carefully lay it in position in the main bearings.
10   Before the crankshaft can be permanently installed, the main bearing oil clearance must be checked.
11   Cut several pieces of the appropriate size Plastigage (they must be slightly shorter than the width of the main bearings) and place one piece on

22.15   Compare the width of the crushed Plastigage to the scale on the container to determine the main bearing oil clearance (always take the measurement at the widest point of the Plastigage); be sure to use the correct scale – standard and metric scales are included

each crankshaft main bearing journal, parallel with the journal axis **(see illustration)**.
12   Clean the faces of the bearings in the caps and install the caps in their respective positions (don't mix them up) with the arrows pointing toward the front of the engine. Don't disturb the Plastigage.
13   Starting with the center main and working out toward the ends, tighten the main bearing cap bolts, in three steps, to the specified torque. Don't rotate the crankshaft at any time during this operation.
14   Remove the bolts and carefully lift off the main bearing caps. Keep them in order. Don't disturb the Plastigage or rotate the crankshaft. If any of the main bearing caps are difficult to remove, tap them gently from side to side with a soft-face hammer to loosen them.
15   Compare the width of the crushed Plastigage on each journal to the scale printed on the Plastigage envelope to obtain the main bearing oil clearance **(see illustration)**. Check the Specifications to make sure it's correct.
16   If the clearance is not as specified, the bearing inserts **(see illustration)** may be the wrong size (which means different ones will be required).

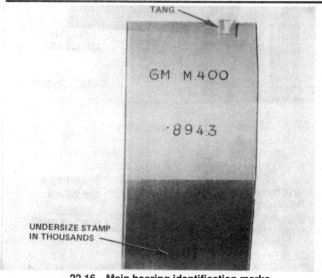

22.16 · Main bearing identification marks

23.3   Using a wood hammer handle for installing the rear main bearing seal

24   Tighten all except the thrust bearing cap bolts to the specified torque (work from the center out and approach the final torque in three steps).
25   Tighten the thrust bearing cap bolts to 10 to 12 ft-lbs.
26   Tap the ends of the crankshaft forward and backward with a lead or brass hammer to line up the main bearing and crankshaft thrust surfaces.
27   Retighten all main bearing cap bolts to the specified torque, starting with the center main and working out toward the ends.
28   Rotate the crankshaft a number of times by hand to check for any obvious binding.
29   The final step is to check the crankshaft endplay with a feeler gauge or a dial indicator as described in Section 13. The endplay should be correct if the crankshaft thrust faces aren't worn or damaged and new bearings have been installed.
30   If you are working on an engine with a one-piece rear main oil seal, refer to Section 23 and install the new seal, then bolt the housing to the block.

23.6   Areas for applying sealer to the main bearing cap

Before deciding that different inserts are needed, make sure that no dirt or oil was between the bearing inserts and the caps or block when the clearance was measured. If the Plastigage was wider at one end than the other, the journal may be tapered (refer to Section 18).
17   Carefully scrape all traces of the Plastigage material off the main bearing journals and/or the bearing faces. Use your fingernail or the edge of a credit card – don't nick or scratch the bearing faces.

Final crankshaft installation
18   Carefully lift the crankshaft out of the engine.
19   Clean the bearing faces in the block, then apply a thin, uniform layer of moly-base grease or engine assembly lube to each of the bearing surfaces. Be sure to coat the thrust faces as well as the journal face of the thrust bearing.
20   Make sure the crankshaft journals are clean, then lay the crankshaft back in place in the block.
21   Clean the faces of the bearings in the caps, then apply lubricant to them.
22   Install the caps in their respective positions with the arrows pointing toward the front of the engine.
23   Install the bolts.

23   Rear main oil seal installation

Split-type (two-piece) fabric seal
Refer to illustrations 23.3 and 23.6
1   Braided fabric seals pressed into grooves formed in the crankcase and rear bearing cap are used to seal against oil leakage around the crankshaft. The crankshaft must be removed for this operation.
2   With the bearing caps and the crankshaft removed, remove the old oil seal and place a new seal in the groove with both ends projecting above the parting surface of the cap.
3   Use a handle of a hammer or similar tool to force the seal into the groove by rubbing down until the seal projects above the groove not more then 1/16-inch (see illustration). Cut the ends of the seal flush with the surface of the cap with a single-edged razor blade.
4   Soak the neoprene seals (if equipped), which go into the grooves in the sides of the bearing cap in kerosene for one to two minutes.
5   Install the neoprene seals (if equipped) in the groove between the bearing cap and the crankcase. The seals are slightly undersized and swell in the presence of heat and oil. They are slightly longer than the groove in the bearing cap and must not be cut to fit.
6   Apply a small amount of RTV sealant at the joint where the bearing cap meets the crankcase to help eliminate oil leakage (see illustration). A very thin coat is all that is necessary.
7   Install the bearing cap in the crankcase. Force the seals up into the bearing cap with a blunt instrument to be sure of a good seal at the upper parting line between the cap and case.

2C

23.9   The rear main oil seal may have two lips – the oil sealing lip (arrow) must point toward the front of the engine, which means that the dust sealing lip will face out, toward the rear of the engine

APPLY SEALANT TO SHADED AREAS ONLY

23.11   Before installing the rear main bearing cap, apply RTV sealant to the shaded areas of the block (or the equivalent areas on the cap)

Split-type (two-piece) neoprene seal

Refer to illustrations 23.9 and 23.11

8   Inspect the rear main bearing cap and engine block mating surfaces, as well as the seal grooves, for nicks, burrs and scratches. Remove any defects with a fine file or deburring tool.

9   Install one seal section in the block with the lip facing the front of the engine (if the seal has two lips, the one with the helix must face the front) **(see illustration)**. Leave one end protruding from the block approximately 1/4- to 3/8-inch and make sure it's completely seated.

10   Repeat the procedure to install the remaining seal half in the rear main bearing cap. In this case, leave the opposite end of the seal protruding from the cap the same distance the block seal is protruding from the block.

11   During final installation of the crankshaft (after the main bearing oil clearances have been checked with Plastigage) as described in Section 22, apply a thin, even coat of RTV sealant to the shaded areas of the cap or block **(see illustration)**. Don't get any sealant on the bearing face, crankshaft journal, seal ends or seal lips. Also,lubricate the seal lips with moly-base grease or engine assembly lube.

One-piece neoprene type oil seal

12   Some models are equipped with a one-piece seal that fits into a housing attached to the block. The crankshaft must be installed first and the main bearing caps bolted in place, then the new seal should be installed in the housing and the housing bolted to the block (see illustration in Chapter 2B).

13   Before installing the crankshaft, check the seal contact surface very carefully for scratches and nicks that could damage the new seal lip and cause oil leaks. If the crankshaft is damaged, the only alternative is a new or different crankshaft.

14   The old seal can be removed from the housing with a screwdriver by prying it out from the front (see illustration in Chapter 2B). Be sure to note how far it's recessed into the housing bore before removing it; the new seal will have to be recessed an equal amount. Be very careful not to scratch or otherwise damage the bore in the housing or oil leaks could develop.

15   Make sure the housing is clean, then apply a thin coat of engine oil to the outer edge of the new seal. The seal must be pressed squarely into the housing bore, so hammering it into place is not recommended. If you don't have access to a press, sandwich the housing and seal between two smooth pieces of wood and press the seal into place with the jaws of a large vise. The pieces of wood must be thick enough to distribute the force evenly around the entire circumference of the seal. Work slowly and make sure the seal enters the bore squarely.

16   The seal lips must be lubricated with moly-base grease or engine assembly lube before the seal/housing is slipped over the crankshaft and bolted to the block. Use a new gasket – no sealant is required – and make sure the dowel pins are in place before installing the housing.

17   Tighten the bolts a little at a time to the torque listed in this Chapter's Specifications.

24   Piston/connecting rod assembly – installation and rod bearing oil clearance check

Refer to illustrations 24.5a, 24.5b, 24.9 and 24.11

1   Before installing the piston/connecting rod assemblies, the cylinder walls must be perfectly clean, the top edge of each cylinder must be chamfered, and the crankshaft must be in place.

2   Remove the cap from the end of the number one connecting rod (refer to the marks made during removal). Remove the original bearing inserts and wipe the bearing surfaces of the connecting rod and cap with a clean, lint-free cloth. They must be kept spotlessly clean.

Connecting rod bearing oil clearance check

3   Clean the back side of the new upper bearing insert, then lay it in place in the connecting rod. Make sure the tab on the bearing fits into the recess in the rod. Don't hammer the bearing insert into place and be very careful not to nick or gouge the bearing face. Don't lubricate the bearing at this time.

4   Clean the back side of the other bearing insert and install it in the rod cap. Again, make sure the tab on the bearing fits into the recess in the cap, and don't apply any lubricant. It's critically important that the mating surfaces of the bearing and connecting rod are perfectly clean and oil-free when they're assembled.

5   Stagger the piston rings as shown in the accompanying illustrations **(see illustrations)**. This will prevent blowby, loss of compression and excessive oil consumption.

6   Slip a section of plastic or rubber hose over each connecting rod cap bolt.

7   Lubricate the piston and rings with clean engine oil and attach a piston ring compressor to the piston. Leave the skirt protruding about 1/4-inch to guide the piston into the cylinder. The rings must be compressed until they're flush with the piston.

8   Rotate the crankshaft until the number one connecting rod journal is at BDC (bottom dead center) and apply a coat of engine oil to the cylinder walls.

9   With the mark or notch on top of the piston **(see illustration)** facing the front of the engine, gently insert the piston/connecting rod assembly into the number one cylinder bore and rest the bottom edge of the ring compressor on the engine block.

10   Tap the top edge of the ring compressor to make sure it's contacting the block around its entire circumference.

OIL RING GAP 90° FROM COMPRESSION RING GAPS AND ON CAMSHAFT SIDE OF PISTON

NOTCH TOWARD FRONT OF ENGINE (LEFT BANK PISTON SHOWN)

TOP COMPRESSION RING GAP OPPOSITE NOTCH ON PISTON

2ND COMPRESSION RING GAP BELOW NOTCH ON PISTON

TOP VIEW OF PISTON

TOP COMPRESSION RING GAP   SECOND COMPRESSION RING GAP

180°

90°   90°

PISTON PIN   OIL RING GAP

CAMSHAFT

24.5a   Position the piston ring gaps as shown (pistons with single-piece oil rings)

ENGINE LEFT   ENGINE FRONT   ENGINE RIGHT

2

3

2

1   4

24.5b   Piston ring gap locations on pistons using multiple-piece oil rings

1	Oil ring spacer gap	3	Second compression ring gap
2	Oil ring rail gaps	4	Top compression ring gap

24.9   The notch in each piston must face the FRONT of the engine as the pistons are installed

24.11   The piston can be driven (gently) into the cylinder bore with the end of a wooden hammer handle

11   Gently tap on the top of the piston with the end of a wooden hammer handle **(see illustration)** while guiding the end of the connecting rod into place on the crankshaft journal. The piston rings may try to pop out of the ring compressor just before entering the cylinder bore, so keep some downward pressure on the ring compressor. Work slowly, and if any resistance is felt as the piston enters the cylinder, stop immediately. Find out what's hanging up and fix it before proceeding. Do not, for any reason, force the piston into the cylinder – you might break a ring and/or the piston.
12   Once the piston/connecting rod assembly is installed, the connecting rod bearing oil clearance must be checked before the rod cap is permanently bolted in place.
13   Cut a piece of the appropriate size Plastigage slightly shorter than the width of the connecting rod bearing and lay it in place on the number one connecting rod journal, parallel with the journal axis.
14   Clean the connecting rod cap bearing face, remove the protective hoses from the connecting rod bolts and install the rod cap. Make sure the mating mark on the cap is on the same side as the mark on the connecting rod.
15   Install the nuts and tighten them to the specified torque, working up to it in three steps. **Note:** *Use a thin-wall socket to avoid erroneous torque readings that can result if the socket is wedged between the rod cap and nut. If the socket tends to wedge itself between the nut and the cap, lift up*

2C

on it slightly until it no longer contacts the cap. Do not rotate the crankshaft at any time during this operation.

16   Remove the nuts and detach the rod cap, being very careful not to disturb the Plastigage.

17   Compare the width of the crushed Plastigage to the scale printed on the Plastigage envelope to obtain the oil clearance. Compare it to the Specifications to make sure the clearance is correct.

18   If the clearance is not as specified, the bearing inserts may be the wrong size (which means different ones will be required). Before deciding that different inserts are needed, make sure that no dirt or oil was between the bearing inserts and the connecting rod or cap when the clearance was measured. Also, recheck the journal diameter. If the Plastigage was wider at one end than the other, the journal may be tapered (refer to Section 18).

Final connecting rod installation

19   Carefully scrape all traces of the Plastigage material off the rod journal and/or bearing face. Be very careful not to scratch the bearing – use your fingernail or the edge of a credit card.

20   Make sure the bearing faces are perfectly clean, then apply a uniform layer of clean moly-base grease or engine assembly lube to both of them. You'll have to push the piston into the cylinder to expose the face of the bearing insert in the connecting rod – be sure to slip the protective hoses over the rod bolts first.

21   Slide the connecting rod back into place on the journal, remove the protective hoses from the rod cap bolts, install the rod cap and tighten the nuts to the specified torque. Again, work up to the torque in three steps.

22   Repeat the entire procedure for the remaining pistons/connecting rods.

23   The important points to remember are:
   a) Keep the back sides of the bearing inserts and the insides of the connecting rods and caps perfectly clean when assembling them.
   b) Make sure you have the correct piston/rod assembly for each cylinder.
   c) The notch or mark on the piston must face the front of the engine.
   d) Lubricate the cylinder walls with clean oil.
   e) Lubricate the bearing faces when installing the rod caps after the oil clearance has been checked.

24   After all the piston/connecting rod assemblies have been properly installed, rotate the crankshaft a number of times by hand to check for any obvious binding.

25   As a final step, the connecting rod endplay must be checked. Refer to Section 12 for this procedure.

26   Compare the measured endplay to the Specifications to make sure it's correct. If it was correct before disassembly and the original crankshaft and rods were reinstalled, it should still be right. If new rods or a new crankshaft were installed, the endplay may be inadequate. If so, the rods will have to be removed and taken to an automotive machine shop for resizing.

---

25   Initial start-up and break-in after overhaul

Warning: *Have a fire extinguisher handy when starting the engine for the first time.*

1   Once the engine has been installed in the vehicle, double-check the engine oil and coolant levels.

2   With the spark plugs out of the engine and the ignition system disabled (see Section 3), crank the engine until oil pressure registers on the gauge or the indicator light goes out.

3   Install the spark plugs, hook up the plug wires and restore the ignition system functions (see Section 3).

4   Start the engine. It may take a few moments for the fuel system to build up pressure, but the engine should start without a great deal of effort. **Note:** *If backfiring occurs through the carburetor or throttle body, recheck the carburetor and ignition timing. If that fails to correct it, check for improper timing chain installation.*

5   After the engine starts, it should be allowed to warm up to normal operating temperature. While the engine is warming up, make a thorough check for fuel, oil and coolant leaks.

6   Shut the engine off and recheck the engine oil and coolant levels.

7   Drive the vehicle to an area with minimum traffic, accelerate at full throttle from 30 to 50 mph, then allow the vehicle to slow to 30 mph with the throttle closed. Repeat the procedure 10 or 12 times. This will load the piston rings and cause them to seat properly against the cylinder walls. Check again for oil and coolant leaks.

8   Drive the vehicle gently for the first 500 miles (no sustained high speeds) and keep a constant check on the oil level. It is not unusual for an engine to use oil during the break-in period.

9   At approximately 500 to 600 miles, change the oil and filter.

10   For the next few hundred miles, drive the vehicle normally. Do not pamper it or abuse it.

11   After 2000 miles, change the oil and filter again and consider the engine broken in.

Chapter 3   Cooling, heating and air conditioning systems

Contents

Specifications

General

Radiator cap pressure rating	14 to 17 psi
Thermostat rating	192 to 199-degrees F

Torque specifications

	Ft-lbs
Water pump mounting fasteners	
V6 engine (all fasteners)	7
V8 engines	
5.0L (all fasteners)	22
HT4100 (see illustration 9.8b)	
A	30
B	15
C	5
D	7
E	30
F	30
425, 472, 500 and 368 (see illustration 9.8c)	
A	22
C	10
D	10
E	22
5.7L (see illustration 9.8d)	
A	35
B	35
C	22
D	22
E	22
G	22
Thermostat housing cover bolts	20
Coolant temperature sending unit	20

1.1   diagram of a typical cooling system – the arrows show the direction of coolant flow

1   General information

Engine cooling system

Refer to illustration 1.1

All vehicles covered by this manual employ a pressurized engine cooling system with thermostatically controlled coolant circulation. An impeller type water pump mounted on the front of the block pumps coolant through the engine. The coolant flows around each cylinder and toward the rear of the engine. Cast-in coolant passages direct coolant around the intake and exhaust ports, near the spark plug areas and in close proximity to the exhaust valve guides **(see illustration)**.

A wax pellet type thermostat is located in the thermostat housing near the front of the engine. During warm up, the closed thermostat prevents coolant from circulating through the radiator. When the engine reaches normal operating temperature, the thermostat opens and allows hot coolant to travel through the radiator, where it is cooled before returning to the engine.

The cooling system is sealed by a pressure type radiator cap. This raises the boiling point of the coolant, and the higher boiling point of the coolant increases the cooling efficiency of the radiator. If the system pressure exceeds the cap pressure relief value, the excess pressure in the system forces the spring-loaded valve inside the cap off its seat and allows the coolant to escape through the overflow tube into a coolant reservoir. When the system cools, the excess coolant is automatically drawn from the reservoir back into the radiator.

The coolant reservoir does double duty as both the point at which fresh coolant is added to the cooling system to maintain the proper fluid level and as a holding tank for overheated coolant.

This type of cooling system is known as a closed design because coolant that escapes past the pressure cap is saved and reused.

Heating system

The heating system consists of a blower fan and heater core located within the heater box, the inlet and outlet hoses connecting the heater core to the engine cooling system and the heater/air conditioning control head on the dashboard. Hot engine coolant is circulated through the heater core. When the heater mode is activated, a flap door opens to expose the heater box to the passenger compartment. A fan switch on the control head activates the blower motor, which forces air through the core, heating the air.

3.9a   The thermostat assembly on a 5.0L V8 engine

Air conditioning system

The air conditioning system consists of a condenser mounted in front of the radiator, an evaporator mounted adjacent to the heater core, a compressor mounted on the engine, a filter-drier (accumulator) which contains a high pressure relief valve and the plumbing connecting all of the above.

A blower fan forces the warmer air of the passenger compartment through the evaporator core (sort of a radiator-in-reverse), transferring the heat from the air to the refrigerant. The liquid refrigerant boils off into low pressure vapor, taking the heat with it when it leaves the evaporator.

2 Antifreeze – general information

Warning: *Do not allow antifreeze to come in contact with your skin or painted surfaces of the vehicle. Rinse off spills immediately with plenty of water. Antifreeze is highly toxic if ingested. Never leave antifreeze lying around in an open container or in puddles on the floor; children and pets are attracted by it's sweet smell and may drink it. Check with local authorities about disposing of used antifreeze. Many communities have collection centers which will see that antifreeze is disposed of safely.*
Caution: *The HT4100 engine requires a special antifreeze supplement to seal against internal and external leakage. Whenever you refill the radiator, add this special sealant – GM #3634621 – (or equivalent) to the radiator. This solution is available at dealer parts departments. Also, make sure the antifreeze meets GM specification 1825-M.*

The cooling system should be filled with a water/ethylene glycol based antifreeze solution, which will prevent freezing down to at least -20 degrees F, or lower if local climate requires it. It also provides protection against corrosion and increases the coolant boiling point.

The cooling system should be drained, flushed and refilled at least every other year (see Chapter 1). The use of antifreeze solutions for periods of longer than two years is likely to cause damage and encourage the formation of rust and scale in the system. If your tap water is "hard", use distilled water with the antifreeze.

Before adding antifreeze to the system, check all hose connections, because antifreeze tends to search out and leak through very minute openings. Engines do not normally consume coolant. Therefore, if the level goes down find the cause and correct it.

The exact mixture of antifreeze-to-water which you should use depends on the relative weather conditions. The mixture should contain at least 50-percent antifreeze, but should never contain more than 70-percent antifreeze. Consult the mixture ratio chart on the antifreeze container before adding coolant.

Hydrometers are available at most auto parts stores to test the ratio of antifreeze to water.

3 Thermostat – check and replacement

Warning: *Do not attempt to remove the radiator cap, coolant or thermostat until the engine has cooled completely.*
Caution: *Do not drive the vehicle without a thermostat. The computer (when equipped) may stay in an open loop and emissions and fuel economy will suffer.*

Check

1   Before assuming the thermostat is to blame for a cooling system problem, check the coolant level (see Chapter 1), drivebelt tension (see Chapter 1) and temperature indicator light operation.
2   If the engine takes a long time to warm up, the thermostat is probably stuck open. Replace the thermostat.
3   If the engine runs hot, use your hand to check the temperature of the upper radiator hose. If the hose is not hot, but the engine is, the thermostat is probably stuck in the closed position, preventing the coolant inside the engine from escaping to the radiator. Replace the thermostat.
4   If the upper radiator hose is hot, it means that the coolant is flowing and the thermostat is open. Consult the Troubleshooting Section at the front of this manual for further diagnosis.

Replacement

Refer to illustrations 3.9a, 3.9b and 3.9c
5   Disconnect the negative battery cable.
6   Drain the cooling system (see Chapter 1).
7   Remove the upper radiator hose from the thermostat housing.
8   If equipped, remove the smaller coolant hose from the thermostat housing.
9   Remove the bolts from the upper thermostat housing and detach the housing **(see illustrations)**. Be prepared for some coolant to spill as the gasket seal is broken.

3

3.9b   The thermostat and housings on an HT4100 engine

3.9c   The thermostat assembly on a V6 engine

**4.4a   A typical radiator
and radiator hoses**

RADIATOR COVER   FAN SHROUD

VIEW A

INSULATOR

RETAINER

RADIATOR
SUPPORT

C, D CARS

4.4b   An early style fan shroud (425 engine shown)

**4.4c   A later style radiator and fan shroud (HT4100
engine shown)**

10   Remove the thermostat, noting the way it was installed.
11   Remove all traces of gasket material from the sealing surfaces. On HT4100 engines, be very careful not to damage the delicate aluminum surface.
12   Install the thermostat, then apply gasket sealer to both sides of a new gasket and position it on the engine.
13   Install the upper thermostat housing and bolts. Tighten the bolts to the torque listed in this Chapter's specifications.
14   Refill the cooling system (see Chapter 1).

4   Radiator – removal and installation

Refer to illustrations 4.4a, 4.4b and 4.4c
Warning: *The engine must be completely cool before beginning this procedure!*

1   Disconnect the negative battery cable.
2   Drain the radiator, referring to Chapter 1.
3   Disconnect the radiator upper and lower hoses and the automatic transmission cooling lines.
4   Disconnect the radiator shroud and hang it over the fan. The shroud is attached with screws going into the radiator (or radiator cover) and clips or staples across the bottom **(see illustrations)**.
5   If equipped, remove the upper metal panel at the top of the radiator.
6   Lift the radiator straight up and out of the engine compartment. Be careful not to scratch the paint on the front nosepiece (if equipped). If coolant drips on any body paint, immediately wash it off with clear water as the antifreeze solution can damage the finish.
7   With the radiator removed, it can be inspected for leaks or damage. If in need of repairs, have a professional radiator shop or dealer perform the work, as special equipment and techniques are required.
8   Bugs and dirt can be cleaned from the radiator by using compressed air and a soft brush. Do not bend the cooling fins as this is done.

9   Inspect the rubber mounting pads which the radiator sits on and re-place as necessary.

10   Lift the radiator into position, making sure it is seated in the mounting pads.

11   Install the upper panel, shroud, hoses and lines in the reverse order of removal.

12   Connect the negative battery cable and fill the radiator as described in Chapter 1.

13   Start the engine and check for leaks. Allow the engine to reach normal operating temperature (upper radiator hose hot) and add coolant until the level reaches the bottom of the filler neck.

14   Install cap with arrows aligned with the overflow tube.

5   Engine cooling fan and clutch – check and replacement

Check

1   Most vehicles covered by this manual are equipped with thermostatically controlled fan clutches. Some models have solid-hub type fans.

2   Begin the clutch check with a lukewarm engine (start it when cold and let it run for two minutes only).

3   Remove the key from the ignition switch for safety purposes.

4   Turn the fan blades and note the resistance. There should be moderate resistance, depending on temperature.

5   Drive the vehicle until the engine is warmed up. Shut it off and remove the key.

6   Turn the fan blades and again note the resistance. There should be a noticeable increase in resistance.

7   If the fan clutch fails this check or is locked up, replacement is indicated. If excessive fluid is leaking from the hub or lateral play over 1/4-inch is noted, replace the fan clutch.

8   If any fan blades are bent, don't straighten them! The metal will be weakened and blades could fly off during engine operation. Replace the fan with a new one.

Replacement

Refer to illustrations 5.10a and 5.10b

9   Remove the upper fan shroud.

10   Remove the fasteners holding the fan assembly to the water pump hub **(see illustrations)**.

5.10a   Typical fan and thermostatic fan clutch installation details – exploded view

5.10b   Typical installation details of a fan without a clutch

3

11   Detach the fan and clutch assembly.
12   Unbolt the fan from the clutch (if equipped).
13   Installation is the reverse of removal.
14   Tighten all fasteners securely.

6   Coolant temperature sending unit – check and replacement

Refer to illustrations 6.1a, 6.1b and 6.1c

Check

1   If the COOLANT TEMPERATURE light doesn't come on when the ignition switch is turned to START, check the bulb. If the light stays on even with the engine cold, unplug the wire at the sending unit **(see illustrations)**. If the light goes off, replace the sending unit. If the light stays on, the wire is grounded somewhere in the harness. **Note:** *Some models are equipped with an additional STOP ENGINE TEMPERATURE light. This is activated when the engine metal temperature sensor located on the cylinder head is heated to an excessive temperature* **(see illustration)**. *Check the STOP ENGINE TEMPERATURE light by opening the driver's door while the ignition is in LOCK or OFF position. The light should glow and the buzzer should sound. The light should not glow when the ignition is in the START mode.*

Replacement

2   Allow the engine to cool completely.
3   Unplug the wire connected to the sending unit.
4   Unscrew the sending unit and quickly install the new unit to prevent loss of coolant.
5   Connect the wire and check indicator operation.

7   Coolant reservoir – removal and installation

1   Disconnect the coolant overflow hose at the radiator neck.
2   Remove the screws attaching the reservoir to the body.
3   Lift the reservoir straight up off the mounting bracket.
4   Installation is the reverse of removal.

6.1a   The location of the coolant temperature sending unit on a typical V8 engine

6.1b   The location of the coolant temperature sending unit on a typical V6 engine

6.1c   The location of the metal temperature warning switch

8   Water pump – check

Refer to illustration 8.3

1   Water pump failure can cause overheating of and serious damage to the engine. There are three ways to check the operation of the water pump while it's installed on the engine. If any one of the three following quick checks indicates water pump failure, it should be replaced immediately.

2   Start the engine and warm it up to normal operating temperature. Squeeze the upper radiator hose. If the water pump is working properly, a pressure surge should be felt as the hose is released.

3   A seal protects the water pump impeller shaft bearing from contamination by engine coolant. If the seal fails, weep holes in the top and bottom of the water pump snout **(see illustration)** will leak coolant under the ve-

hicle. If the weep hole is leaking, shaft bearing failure will follow. Replace the water pump immediately.

4   Besides contamination by coolant after a seal failure, the water pump impeller shaft bearing can also be prematurely worn out by an improperly tensioned drivebelt. When the bearing wears out, it emits a high pitched squealing sound. If noise is coming from the water pump during engine operation, the shaft bearing has failed. Replace the water pump immediately.

5   To identify excessive bearing wear before the bearing actually fails, grasp the water pump pulley and try to force it up and down or from side to side. If the pulley can be moved either horizontally or vertically, the bearing is nearing the end of its service life. Replace the water pump.

9   Water pump – removal and installation

Refer to illustrations 9.6, 9.8a, 9.8b, 9.8c and 9.8d

Note: *It is not economical or practical to overhaul a water pump. If failure occurs, a new or rebuilt unit should be purchased to replace the faulty water pump.*

1   Disconnect the negative battery cable.

2   Drain the radiator, referring to Chapter 1 if necessary.

3   Reaching inside the radiator shroud, remove the bolts which secure the fan to the water pump hub (see Section 5). Remove the fan and spacer (if equipped). **Caution:** *Thermostatic fan clutches must remain in the "in car" position while they are removed from the vehicle.*

4   Remove the radiator shroud for better access to the water pump.

5   It is now necessary to loosen and remove all drivebelts from the water pump pulley. The number of belts will depend upon model, year, and equipment. Loosen the adjusting and pivot bolts of each affected component (air pump, alternator, air conditioning compressor, power steering pump) and push the component toward the engine to loosen the belt enough to be removed from the water pump pulley (see Chapter 1).

6   Disconnect and remove all mounting brackets which are attached to the water pump. These may include on late model vehicles the alternator, air conditioning compressor, and power steering brackets **(see illustration)**.

7   Disconnect the lower radiator hose and, if attached to the pump, the heater and bypass hoses.

3

8.3   Water pump weep hole location

9.6   Note the location and position of all related mounting brackets for ease of reassembly

9.8a   An exploded view of the water pump assembly on a V6 engine

FRONT

9.8b   Water pump bolt locations for HT4100 engines – check this Chapter's Specifications to find the correct torque for each bolt

9.8d   Water pump bolt locations on 5.7L Oldsmobile-built engines – check this Chapter's Specifications to find the correct torque for each bolt

9.8c   Water pump bolt locations on 425, 472, 500 and 368 engines – check this Chapter's Specifications to find the correct torque for each bolt

8   Remove the remaining bolts which secure the water pump to the front cover of the engine. The bolts are different sizes, so be sure to note their locations **(see illustrations)**. Lift the water pump away from the engine. If the pump is stuck to the engine, tap it gently with a soft-face hammer.

9   If installing a new or rebuilt water pump, transfer all fittings and studs to the new water pump.

10   Clean the gasket surfaces of the front cover completely using a gasket scraper or putty knife.

11   Use a thin coat of gasket sealant on the new gasket and install the new water pump. Place the pump into position on the front cover and secure it loosely with the bolts. Do not torque-tighten these bolts until all brackets have been installed to their original position on the water pump.

12   Tighten all water pump bolts to torque listed in this Chapter's Specifications.

10.1a Air conditioning component locations on early models

13   Install the engine components in the reverse order of removal, tightening the fasteners securely.

14   Adjust all drivebelts to the proper tension (see Chapter 1).

15   Connect the negative battery cable and fill the radiator with a mixture of ethylene glycol antifreeze and water in a 50/50 mixture. Start the engine and allow it to idle until the upper radiator hose gets hot. Check for leaks. With the engine hot, fill it with more coolant mixture until the level is at the bottom of the filler neck. Install the radiator cap and check coolant level periodically over the next few miles of driving.

10   Blower motor – removal and installation

Refer to illustrations 10.1a and 10.1b

1   Disconnect the battery negative cable. The motor is accessible from under the hood **(see illustrations)** on the right side of the firewall. Simply disconnect the blower lead wire at the motor and remove the motor attaching screws.

2   Lift the blower motor from the blower/evaporator assembly.

3   Installation is the reverse of the removal procedure.

10.1b The blower motor on 1977 and later models (arrow) is mounted vertically – on 1976 and earlier models, it's mounted horizontally

3

11.8   On 1976 and earlier models, the heater/air conditioning assembly is under the dash

11   Heater core – removal and installation

1   The heater core is contained within the heater/air conditioning assembly. On 1976 and earlier models, this assembly is located inside the passenger compartment under the right side of the instrument panel. On 1977 and later models, the assembly is attached to the right side of the firewall, in the engine compartment.
2   Disconnect the negative battery cable.
3   Drain the cooling system (see Chapter 1).
4   Disconnect the two heater hoses at the firewall.

1970 through 1976

Refer to illustration 11.8

5   Remove the top and bottom portions of the instrument panel (see Chapter 12).
6   Disconnect any wiring connectors or vacuum control lines that are attached to the heater/air conditioning assembly.
7   Disconnect the selector assembly on the dash and set it aside.
8   Remove the nuts that retain the heater/air conditioning assembly to the dash **(see illustration)**.
9   Carefully lower the heater/air conditioning assembly from under the dash.
10   Remove the screws that secure the heater core frame to the heater/air conditioning assembly.
11   Pull the heater core frame with the heater core attached away from the heater/air conditioning assembly.
12   Remove the rubber grommets that are attached to the inlet and outlet fittings.
13   Remove the screws that secure the wire retaining clamps to the heater core frame and remove the heater core.
14   Installation is the reverse of removal.

1977 on

Refer to illustration 11.15

15   Remove the blower motor (see Section 10), the right windshield washer nozzle and any hoses, wires or other components in the way of the heater/air conditioning assembly cover **(see illustration)**.
16   Carefully remove the rubber molding above the plenum (there should be one screw on the right side).
17   Remove the 16 screws securing the heater/air conditioning assembly cover **(see illustration 11.15)**. Remove the cover.
18   Remove the screw and retainer holding the heater core to the frame at the top.

11.15   On 1977 and later models, the heater/air conditioning assembly is in the engine compartment, on the right side of the firewall – remove these screws and pull off the cover for access to the heater core

19   With the temperature valve in the Max Hot position, reach through the heater/air conditioning housing and push the lower forward corner of the heater core away from the housing. Rotate the core parallel to the housing. This causes the core to snap out of the lower clamp. Pull the core out of the housing.
20   Installation is the reverse of removal.

12   Air conditioning system – check and maintenance

Refer to illustrations 12.4a, 12.4b and 12.5

1   The following maintenance steps should be performed on a regular basis to ensure that the air conditioner continues to operate at peak efficiency.

   a) Check the tension of the air conditioning compressor drivebelt and adjust it if necessary (refer to Chapter I).

12.4a   The thermal limiter is usually mounted on the compressor bracket (earlier models without accumulators)

12.4b   Models with accumulators (arrow) do not use a thermal limiter fuse

b) Visually inspect the condition of the hoses, looking for any cracks, hardening and other deterioration. **Note:** *Don't remove any hoses until the system has been discharged.*

c) Make sure the fins of the condenser aren't covered with foreign material, such as leaves or bugs. A soft brush and compressed air can be used to remove them. **Warning:** *Always wear eye protection when using compressed air!*

d) Be sure the evaporator drain is open by slipping a wire into the drain tube occasionally.

2   The air conditioning compressor should be run about 10 minutes at least once every month. This is especially important to remember during the winter months because long-term non-use can cause hardening of the seals.

3   Due to the complexity of the air conditioning system and the special equipment required to effectively work on it, accurate troubleshooting and repair of the system usually cannot be done by a home mechanic and should be left to a professional. In any case, due to the toxic nature of the refrigerant, prior to disconnecting any part of the system, the vehicle should be taken to your dealer or a repair shop to have the system discharged. If the system should lose its cooling action, some causes can be diagnosed by the home mechanic. Look for other symptoms of trouble such as those that follow. In all cases, it's a good idea to have the system serviced by a professional.

4   Most of the earlier (non-accumulator) systems **(see illustration)** use a thermal limiter circuit to protect the compressor. When the thermal limiter fuse burns out, the compressor clutch won't engage. Simply plug in a new one. Later models, with an accumulator, do not use a thermal limiter fuse **(see illustration)**.

5   If bubbles appear in the sight glass (normally located near the top of the receiver-drier or accumulator) **(see illustration)**, this is an indication of either a small refrigerant leak or air in the refrigerant. If air is in the refrigerant, the receiver-dryer or accumulator is probably contaminated with moisture and should be replaced.

6   If the sight glass takes on a mist-like appearance or shows many bubbles, this indicates a large refrigerant leak. In such a case, do not operate the compressor at all until the fault has been corrected.

7   Sweating or frosting of the expansion valve inlet indicates that the expansion valve is clogged or defective. It should be cleaned or replaced as necessary.

8   Sweating or frosting of the suction line (which runs between the suction throttle valve and the compressor) indicates that the expansion valve is stuck open or defective. It should be corrected or replaced as necessary.

9   Frosting on the evaporator indicates a defective suction throttle valve, requiring replacement of the valve.

12.5   Sight glass location – typical

10   Frosting of the high pressure liquid line (which runs between the condenser, accumulator and expansion valve) indicates that either the drier or the high pressure line is restricted. The line will have to be cleared or the accumulator replaced.

11   The combination of bubbles in the sight glass, a very hot suction line and, possibly, overheating of the engine is an indication that either the condenser is not operating properly or the refrigerant is overcharged. Check the tension of the drivebelt and adjust it, if necessary (see Chapter 1). Check for foreign matter covering the fins of the condenser and clean them, if necessary. Also check for proper operation of the cooling system. If no fault can be found in these checks, the condenser may have to be replaced.

3

13.1   A typical receiver-drier system

13   Air conditioning system accumulator/receiver-drier – removal and installation

Refer to illustrations 13.1 and 13.2

Warning: *The air conditioning system is under high pressure. DO NOT disassemble any part of the system (hoses, compressor, line fittings, etc.) until after the system has been depressurized by a dealer service department or service station.*

1   The accumulator/receiver-drier, which acts as a reservoir and filter for the refrigerant, is the canister-shaped object mounted near the right front fenderwell or adjacent to the condenser **(see illustration)** in the engine compartment.
2   Disconnect the two liquid lines from the accumulator or receiver-drier. Cap the open fittings immediately to prevent moisture from entering the system **(see illustration)**.
3   Remove the accumulator or receiver-drier from its bracket.
4   Installation is the reverse of removal.
5   Have the system evacuated, charged and leak tested. If a new accumulator or receiver-drier was installed, add refrigerant oil according to the component manufacturer's instructions.

14   Air conditioning system compressor – removal and installation

Refer to illustrations 14.3, 14.6a and 14.6b

Warning: *The air conditioning system is under high pressure. DO NOT disassemble any part of the system (hoses, compressor, line fittings, etc.) until after the system has been depressurized by a dealer service department or service station.*

1   Have the air conditioning system discharged by a dealer or air conditioning shop.
2   Disconnect the negative battery cable.
3   Disconnect the compressor wiring harness **(see illustration)**.
4   Remove the drivebelt (see Chapter 1).
5   Disconnect the refrigerant lines from the rear of the compressor. Plug the open fittings to prevent entry of dirt and moisture.
6   Unbolt the compressor from the mounting brackets and lift it out of the vehicle **(see illustrations)**.

13.2   Liquid line inlet and outlet and mounting details (models with accumulators)

14.3   All compressors have wiring going to the clutch connector – some have wiring to the rear of the compressor as well

14.6a   The mounting brackets used on early style compressors

14.6b   The mounting brackets used on later style compressors

15.4   Disconnect the refrigerant lines from the condenser – use new O-rings on installation

15.6   Typical condensor mounting details – exploded view

7   If a new compressor is being installed, follow the directions which come with the compressor regarding the draining of excess oil prior to installation.

8   Installation is the reverse of removal. Replace any O-rings with new ones specifically made for the purpose and lubricate them with refrigerant oil.

9   Have the system evacuated, recharged and leak tested by the shop that discharged it.

15   Air conditioning system condenser – removal and installation

Refer to illustrations 15.4 and 15.6

Warning: *The air conditioning system is under high pressure. DO NOT disassemble any part of the system (hoses, compressor, line fittings, etc.) until after the system has been depressurized by a dealer service department or service station.*

1   Have the air conditioning system discharged by a dealer service department or air conditioning shop.

2   Disconnect the negative cable from battery.

3   Drain the cooling system (see Chapter 1).

4   Disconnect the refrigerant lines from the condenser **(see illustration)**.

5   Remove the radiator (see Section 4).

6   Remove the mounting bolts from the condenser brackets **(see illustration)**.

7   Lift the condenser out of the vehicle and plug the lines to prevent dirt and moisture from entering.

8   If the same condenser will be reinstalled, store it with the line fittings on top to prevent oil from draining.

9   If a new condenser is being installed, pour one ounce of refrigerant oil into the new condenser prior to installation.

10   Reinstall the components in the reverse order of removal. Be sure the rubber pads are in place under the condenser. Also, be sure to use new O-rings on the refrigerant lines and lubricate them with a small amount of refrigerant oil.

11   Have the system evacuated, recharged and leak tested by the shop that discharged it.

16   Air conditioner and heater control assembly – general information

Cadillac used many different systems in their vehicles during the years covered by this manual. Automatic Temperature Control and Electronic Climate Control incorporate many different types of computer and automatic devices to regulate the temperature within the vehicle. For repairs to the heater control assembly, take the vehicle to a dealer service department.

Chapter 4   Fuel and exhaust systems

4

Contents

Specifications

Fuel injection system pressure

EFI systems .... 29 to 35 psi
DFI and TBI systems .... 9 to 12 psi

Torque specifications

Ft-lbs

Throttle body mounting bolts 17
Carburetor mounting bolts
   Front 11
   Rear 15

1   General information

Fuel system

The fuel system consists of a fuel tank, an electric or mechanical fuel pump, a fuel pump relay (fuel-injected models), an air cleaner assembly and either a carburetor or one of three fuel injection systems: Digital Fuel Injection (DFI), Throttle Body Injection (TBI) or Electronic Fuel Injection (EFI). The TBI system is used on 1990 and later 5.7L models; the DFI system is used on 1981 through 1985 models; the EFI system is used on some 1975 through 1979 models.

Throttle Body (TBI) and Digital (DFI) injection systems

These systems utilize two injectors, centrally mounted in a carburetor-like throttle body. The injectors are electric solenoid valves, and fuel is delivered to the injectors at a constant pressure level. To maintain the fuel pressure at a constant level, excess fuel is returned to the fuel tank.

A signal from the Electronic Control Unit (ECU) opens the solenoids, allowing fuel to spray through each injector into the throttle body. The amount of time the injector is held open by the ECU determines the fuel/air mixture ratio.

Electronic Fuel Injection (EFI) system

This system utilizes eight injectors of a similar type as TBI and DFI, and the fuel/air ratio is controlled in the same manner. Instead of two injectors mounted in a centrally located throttle body, one injector is installed above each intake port. The throttle body serves only to control the amount of air passing into the system.

Exhaust system

The exhaust system includes two exhaust manifolds, an exhaust oxygen sensor, a catalytic converter, a resonator (some models), an exhaust pipe, and a muffler.

The catalytic converter is an emission control device added to the exhaust system to reduce pollutants. A single or dual-bed converter is used in combination with a three-way (reduction) catalyst. Refer to Chapter 6 for more information regarding the catalytic converter.

2   Fuel pressure relief procedure

Warning: *Gasoline is extremely flammable, so take extra precautions when you work on any part of the fuel system. Don't smoke or allow open flames or bare light bulbs near the work area, and don't work in a garage where a natural gas-type appliance (such as a water heater or clothes dryer) with a pilot light is present. If you spill any fuel on your skin, rinse it off immediately with soap and water. When you perform any kind of work on the fuel tank, wear safety glasses and have a Class B type fire extinguisher on hand.*
Note: *After the fuel pressure has been relieved, it's a good idea to use a shop towel around any fuel connection you're disconnecting to absorb the residual fuel that may spray.*

1   Before servicing any fuel system component, you must relieve the fuel pressure to minimize the risk of fire or personal injury.
2   Remove the cap from the gas tank – this will relieve any pressure built up in the tank.
3   On models with TBI or DFI injection, there is an internal constant bleed feature which relieves fuel system pressure when the engine is turned off.
4   On early models with EFI (no Schrader valve on the fuel rail), cover the fuel rail fitting with a shop towel so that the discharged fuel will be absorbed. Loosen the fuel rail fitting.
5   On later models with EFI, locate the Schrader valve at the rear of the fuel rail. Remove the cap from the valve, place shop towels around the valve and install GM special tool J-5420. Slowly tighten the tool until the fuel pressure is relieved.
6   Disconnect the negative battery cable to avoid any accidental fuel discharge if an attempt is made to start the engine. Dispose of the gasoline-soaked towels in a covered, fire-safe container.

7   After the fuel system has been serviced, reconnect the negative battery cable.

3   Fuel lines and fittings – repair and replacement

Warning: *Gasoline is extremely flammable, so take extra precautions when you work on any part of the fuel system. Don't smoke or allow open flames or bare light bulbs near the work area, and don't work in a garage where a natural gas-type appliance (such as a water heater or clothes dryer) with a pilot light is present. If you spill any fuel on your skin, rinse it off immediately with soap and water. When you perform any kind of work on the fuel tank, wear safety glasses and have a Class B type fire extinguisher on hand.*

1   Always relieve the fuel pressure before servicing fuel lines or fittings (Section 2).
2   The fuel lines extend from the fuel tank to the engine compartment. The lines are secured to the underbody with clip and screw assemblies. Both fuel feed lines must be occasionally inspected for leaks, kinks and dents.
3   If evidence of dirt is found in the system or fuel filter during disassembly, the line should be disconnected and blown out. Check the fuel strainer on the fuel gauge sending unit (see Section 5) for damage and deterioration.

Steel tubing

4   If replacement of a fuel line or emission line is called for, use welded steel tubing meeting GM specification 124-M or its equivalent.
5   Don't use copper or aluminum tubing to replace steel tubing. These materials cannot withstand normal vehicle vibration.
6   Because fuel lines used on fuel injected vehicles are under high pressure, they require special consideration.
7   Most fuel lines have threaded fittings with O-rings. Any time the fittings are loosened to service or replace components:
   a) Use a backup wrench while loosening and tightening the fittings.
   b) Check all O-rings for cuts, cracks and deterioration. Replace any that appear worn or damaged.
   c) If the lines are replaced, always use original equipment parts, or parts that meet the GM standards specified in this Section.

Quick-connect fuel line fittings – removal

8   New quick-connect fuel line fittings were introduced on 1990 models. A special tool (GM J-37008 – fuel line separator) is required to disconnect them.
9   To separate the fuel lines, relieve the fuel system pressure (see Section 2) and insert the fuel line separator tool into the fitting and pull the lines apart.
10   To reattach quick-connect fittings, push the line into the fitting as far as possible, then pull back on it to verify that the connection is secure. **Warning:** *The line must be pushed in and pulled back to verify proper connector engagement – DO NOT rely on an audible click or visual verification to check the assembly of the quick-connect fittings.*

Rubber hose

11   When rubber hose is used to replace a metal line, use reinforced, fuel resistant hose (GM Specification 6163-M) with the word "Fluoroelastomer" imprinted on it. Hose(s) not clearly marked like this could fail prematurely and could fail to meet Federal emission standards. Hose inside diameter must match line outside diameter.
12   Don't use rubber hose within four inches of any part of the exhaust system or within ten inches of the catalytic converter. Metal lines and rubber hoses must never be allowed to chafe against the frame. A minimum of 1/4-inch clearance must be maintained around a line or hose to prevent contact with the frame.

Removal and installation

Refer to illustrations 3.13a, 3.13b, 3.19 and 3.20
Note: *The following procedure and accompanying illustrations are typical for vehicles covered by this manual.*

3.13a Typical fuel return (A), vapor (B) and feed (C) lines (carbureted models)

3.13b Typical fuel return (A), vapor (B) and feed (C) lines (fuel injected models)

13 Relieve the fuel pressure and disconnect the fuel feed, return or vapor line at the fuel tank **(see illustrations)**.
14 Detach the bracket from the rear crossmember.
15 Detach the bracket from the rear end of the left frame member, just in front of the left rear wheel.
16 Detach the three brackets from the left frame member.
17 Detach the bracket from the left front end of the left frame member, just behind the left front wheel.
18 Detach the bracket from the lower left rear corner of the engine compartment.
19 Detach the threaded fitting(s) that attach the metal lines to the engine compartment fuel hoses **(see illustration)**.
20 Installation is the reverse of removal. Be sure to use new O-rings at the threaded fittings **(see illustration)**.

Repair

21 In repairable areas, cut a piece of fuel hose four inches longer than the portion of the line removed. If more than a six inch length of line is removed, use a combination of steel line and hose so hose lengths won't be more than ten inches. Always follow the same routing as the original line.

22 Cut the ends of the line with a tube cutter. Using the first step of a double flaring tool, form a bead on the end of both line sections. If the line is too corroded to withstand bead operation without damage, the line should be replaced.
23 Use a screw type hose clamp. Slide the clamp onto the line and push the hose on. Tighten the clamps on each side of the repair.
24 Secure the lines properly to the frame to prevent chafing.

---

4 Fuel pump/fuel pressure – check

Warning: *Gasoline is extremely flammable, so take extra precautions when you work on any part of the fuel system. Don't smoke or allow open flames or bare light bulbs near the work area, and don't work in a garage where a natural gas-type appliance (such as a water heater or clothes dryer) with a pilot light is present. If you spill any fuel on your skin, rinse it off immediately with soap and water. When you perform any kind of work on the fuel tank, wear safety glasses and have a Class B type fire extinguisher on hand.*

3.19 Typical fuel feed and return line threaded fittings in the left side of the engine compartment

3.20 Always replace the fuel line O-rings

4

Mechanical pump (carbureted models)

1   Disconnect the fuel line from the carburetor and install a T-fitting. Connect a fuel pressure gauge to the T-fitting with a section of fuel hose that's no longer than six inches.

2   Disconnect the gauge from the end of the fuel hose and direct the end of the hose into an approved gasoline container. Operate the starter for a few seconds, until fuel spurts out of the hose, to vent the pump (this eliminates any air in the fuel chamber, which could affect the pressure reading). Reattach the gauge to the fuel hose.

3   Start the engine and allow it to idle. The pressure on the gauge should be about 5 to 6.5 psi, remain constant and return to zero slowly when the engine is shut off.

4   An instant pressure drop indicates a faulty outlet valve. If this occurs, or if the pressure is too high or low, replace the fuel pump with a new one. **Note:** *if the pressure is too high, check the air vent to see if it's plugged before replacing the pump.*

Electric in-tank pump (fuel-injected models)

5   Remove the fuel tank cap and place your ear close to the filler neck. Have an assistant turn the ignition key to On while you listen for the sound of the in-tank pump. It should make a whirring sound. If you don't hear the pump, make the following checks.

6   Relieve the fuel system pressure (see Section 2).

7   Raise the rear of the vehicle and place it securely on jackstands.

8   Lower the fuel tank slightly (see Section 5) and locate the wire harness to the fuel pump (refer to the Wiring Diagrams at the end of the book if you're unable to determine the color of the fuel pump wires).

9   Using a test light or voltmeter, verify that there's voltage to the pump when the key is turned to On and Start.

    a) If there is voltage to the pump, replace it.

    b) If there is no voltage to the pump, refer to the Wiring Diagrams again, locate the fuel pump relay or fuse, check it and replace as necessary.

10   If the pump still doesn't work, have it checked by a dealer service department or a repair shop. Further testing requires special equipment.

Chassis-mounted electric pump (Seville only)

Sevilles are equipped with an additional electric fuel pump mounted on the chassis. The check procedure for the chassis-mounted pump is basically the same as the procedure for the in-tank pump above. To be sure the whirring sound is coming from the chassis-mounted pump, use a long screwdriver as a stethoscope (put the handle to your ear and touch the blade to the pump) and listen for a whirring sound.

Fuel pressure check (TBI and DFI injection systems)

11   Relieve the fuel system pressure (see Section 2).

12   Install a fuel pressure gauge between the fuel feed hose and the inlet fitting of the throttle body.

13   With the ignition OFF, use a fused jumper wire from a 12-volt source to jump the fuel pump test terminal and note the pressure reading (the test terminal is located on the passenger side of the engine compartment).

14   If the pressure is between 9 and 13 psi, no further testing is necessary.

15   If the pressure was higher than specified, check for a restricted fuel return line. If the line is OK, replace the pressure regulator.

16   If the pressure was less than specified, slowly pinch the hose between the gauge and the TBI unit and note the pressure. If the pressure goes above 9 psi, replace the pressure regulator. If the pressure is still below specification, check for a plugged fuel filter, plugged fuel pump inlet filter or a restricted fuel line.

17   After testing is completed, relieve the fuel pressure (see Section 2) and remove the pressure gauge.

---

5   Fuel pump – removal and installation

Warning: *Gasoline is extremely flammable, so take extra precautions when you work on any part of the fuel system. Don't smoke or allow open flames or bare light bulbs near the work area, and don't work in a garage where a natural gas-type appliance (such as a water heater or clothes dryer) with a pilot light is present. If you spill any fuel on your skin, rinse it off immediately with soap and water. When you perform any kind of work on the fuel tank, wear safety glasses and have a Class B type fire extinguisher on hand.*

Mechanical pump

Refer to illustrations 5.1a, 5.1b and 5.1c

1   The fuel pump is bolted to the engine block near the water pump **(see illustrations).**

THERMAC AIR CLEANER

INTAKE MANIFOLD

QUADRAJET CARBURETOR

FUEL LINE

FUEL PUMP

5.1a   Fuel system components (early V8 engines)

5.1b   Fuel pump mounting details (later model V8 engines)

1	Fuel pump	4	Washer
2	Gasket	5	Nut
3	Stud	6	Bolt

2   Place clean rags or newspaper under the fuel pump to catch any gasoline spilled during removal.

3   Carefully unscrew the fuel line fittings and detach the lines from the pump. A flare-nut wrench should be used to prevent damage to the fittings.

4   Unbolt and remove the fuel pump. Using a gasket scraper or putty knife, carefully remove all traces of old gasket material from the engine block and fuel pump (if the same one will be reinstalled).

5   Before installation, coat both sides of the new gasket with RTV sealant, hold the fuel pump in place and install the bolts.

6   Attach the lines to the pump and tighten the fittings securely (use a flare-nut wrench, if available, to prevent damage to the fittings).

7   Run the engine and check for fuel and oil leaks.

Electric in-tank pump (fuel-injected models)

Refer to illustration 5.10

8   Remove the fuel tank (see Section 6).

5.1c   Fuel pump location (V6 engine)

9   Use a hammer and a BRASS punch or hardwood dowel (a steel punch may cause a spark, which could be extremely dangerous when working on the fuel tank!) to remove the fuel pump locking ring. Drive it in a counterclockwise direction until it can be unscrewed.

10   Lift the fuel pump and fuel gage sending unit assembly out of the fuel tank **(see illustration)**.

5.10   In-tank fuel pump details

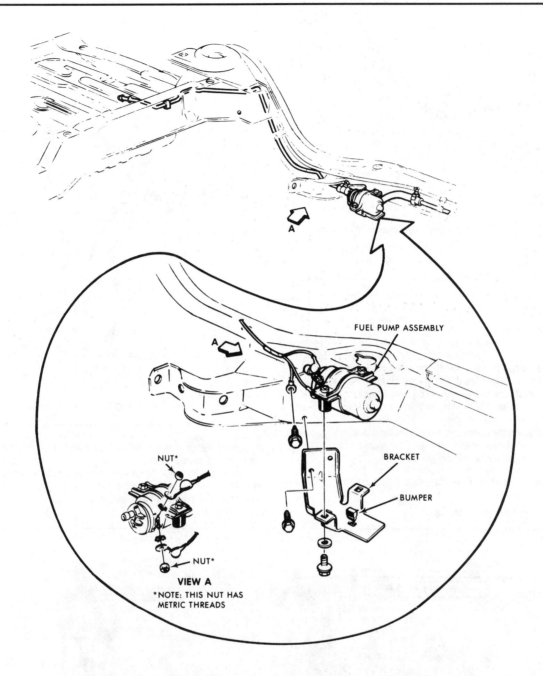

5.14   Mounting details for the chassis-mounted fuel pump used on Seville models

11   Clean the sealing area of the fuel tank and install a new O-ring on the fuel pump. Prior to installation, inspect the fuel inlet sock filter on the fuel pump suction tube for damage and contamination. Replace it with a new one if necessary.
12   Place the fuel pump in position in the tank, install the locking ring and use a hammer and a BRASS punch to lock the pump in place.
13   Install the fuel tank.

Chassis-mounted electric pump (Seville only)
Refer to illustration 5.14

14   Sevilles have an additional electric pump mounted on the chassis of the vehicle. Remove the brackets, electrical connectors and fuel lines from the pump for removal **(see illustration)**.
15   Installation is the reverse of removal.

6   Fuel tank – removal and installation

Warning: *Gasoline is extremely flammable, so take extra precautions when you work on any part of the fuel system. Don't smoke or allow open flames or bare light bulbs near the work area, and don't work in a garage where a natural gas-type appliance (such as a water heater or clothes dryer) with a pilot light is present. If you spill any fuel on your skin, rinse it off immediately with soap and water. When you perform any kind of work on the fuel tank, wear safety glasses and have a Class B type fire extinguisher on hand.*
Refer to illustrations 6.6 and 6.8

1   If the tank is full or nearly full, drive the vehicle to use up the gas.
2   Relieve the fuel pressure (see Section 2).

FRONT OF CAR

6.6   Typical rear fuel lines (1990 5.7L model shown)

1	Fuel feed line	4	Fuel gauge sending
2	Fuel return line		unit assembly
3	Vapor line	5	Fuel tank

3   Detach the cable from the negative terminal of the battery.
4   Raise the vehicle and place it securely on jackstands.
5   Locate the electrical connector for the electric fuel pump and fuel gauge sending unit in front of the tank, and unplug it. If the vehicle doesn't have a connector, see Step 9 below.
6   Disconnect the fuel feed and return lines, the vapor line and the filler neck and vent tubes **(see illustration)**.
7   Support the fuel tank with a floor jack.
8   Disconnect both fuel tank retaining straps **(see illustration)**.
9   Lower the tank enough to disconnect the wires and ground strap from the fuel pump/fuel gauge sending unit, if you haven't already done so.
10   Remove the tank from the vehicle.
11   Installation is the reverse of removal

---

7   Fuel tank cleaning and repair – general information

1   All repairs to the fuel tank or filler neck should be done by an experienced professional – the job is potentially dangerous! Even after cleaning and flushing of the fuel system, explosive fumes can remain and ignite during repair of the tank.
2   If the fuel tank is removed from the vehicle, it shouldn't be stored in an area where sparks or open flames could ignite the fumes coming out of it. Be especially careful inside a garage where a natural gas-type appliance is located, because the pilot light could cause an explosion.

---

8   Carburetor – removal and installation

Warning: *Gasoline is extremely flammable, so take extra precautions when you work on any part of the fuel system. Don't smoke or allow open flames or bare light bulbs near the work area, and don't work in a garage where a natural gas-type appliance (such as a water heater or clothes dryer) with a pilot light is present. If you spill any fuel on your skin, rinse it off immediately with soap and water. When you perform any kind of work on the fuel tank, wear safety glasses and have a Class B type fire extinguisher on hand.*

Removal

1   Remove the fuel tank cap to relieve the tank pressure.
2   Remove the air cleaner from the carburetor. Be sure to label all vacuum hoses attached to the air cleaner housing.

FRONT OF CAR

6.8   Fuel tank mounting details

3   Disconnect the throttle cable from the throttle lever.
4   Disconnect the TV cable from the throttle lever (see Chapter 7).
5   If equipped, disconnect the cruise control actuating lever or chain from the throttle lever.
6   Clearly label all vacuum hoses and fittings, then disconnect the hoses.
7   Disconnect the fuel line from the carburetor.
8   Label the wires and terminals, then unplug all wire electrical connectors.
9   Remove the mounting fasteners and detach the carburetor from the intake manifold. Remove the carburetor mounting gasket. Stuff a shop rag into the intake manifold openings.

Installation

10   Use a gasket scraper to remove all traces of gasket material and sealant from the intake manifold (and the carburetor, if it's being reinstalled), then remove the shop rag from the manifold openings. Clean the mating surfaces with lacquer thinner or acetone.
11   Place a new gasket on the intake manifold.
12   Position the carburetor on the gasket and install the mounting fasteners.
13   To prevent carburetor distortion or damage, tighten the fasteners, in a criss-cross pattern, 1/4-turn at a time, to the torque listed in this Chapter's Specifications.
14   The remaining installation steps are the reverse of removal.
15   Check and, if necessary, adjust the idle speed (see Chapter 1).
16   Refer to Chapter 7, Part B, for the TV cable adjustment procedure.
17   Start the engine and check carefully for fuel leaks.

---

9   Carburetor – adjustments

Note: *Before making any adjustments, make sure the ignition timing and idle speed are correctly adjusted (see Chapter 1).*

Idle mixture adjustment

Refer to illustration 9.9
Note: *Later models are equipped with plugs that cover the mixture adjustment screws. The idle mixture does not need to be adjusted in normal service. If, for some reason, it becomes necessary to access the mixture screws, the plugs on most models can be removed. This should be done by a dealer service department.*

4

9.9   Adjusting the idle mixture on a 425 engine – special tools like the one shown here are often available from larger auto parts stores

1   With the engine off, disconnect the distributor vacuum advance hose and plug the hose to eliminate the possibility of the timing being advanced.
2   Disconnect the parking brake vacuum hose at the vacuum release cylinder (at the top of the parking brake pedal arm) and plug the hose.
3   Connect a tachometer to the engine in accordance with the manufacturer's instructions. Set the parking brake securely so the vehicle cannot move. Place the transmission selector in Neutral.
4   Remove the air cleaner.
5   Make sure the throttle dashpot is not holding the throttle valves open.
6   For the preliminary adjustment, make sure each mixture screw is turned out approximately 6 turns.
7   Start the engine and warm it to normal operating temperature. Be sure the choke is fully off and the carburetor is on slow idle.
8   Turn the air conditioning system off.
9   Using special tool J-22646 or equivalent (equivalent tools are sometimes available at larger auto parts stores and automotive equipment suppliers), turn one idle mixture adjustment screw clockwise **(see illustration)**.
10   Turn the screw until engine speed decreases 10 rpm.
11   Repeat steps 9 and 10 for the other mixture adjustment screw. Turn off the engine.
12   Disconnect the tachometer and connect the vacuum advance and parking brake vacuum hoses. Install the air cleaner assembly.

Fast idle speed adjustment

Refer to illustration 9.17

13   Disconnect the distributor vacuum hose and the EGR vacuum hose. Plug the hose ends.
14   Connect a tachometer in accordance with the manufacturer's instructions.
15   Start the engine and warm it to normal operating temperature in Park with the air conditioning off.
16   Open the throttle and raise the fast idle cam to the middle step of the cam.
17   Turn the fast idle speed screw **(see illustration)** until the engine speed is as specified on the Vehicle Emissions Control Information label in the engine compartment (usually about 1500 rpm) .
18   Reconnect the EGR and distributor vacuum hoses.

---

10   Carburetor diagnosis and overhaul – general information

Warning: *Gasoline is extremely flammable, so take extra precautions when you work on any part of the fuel system. Don't smoke or allow open flames or bare light bulbs near the work area, and don't work in a garage*

FAST IDLE SPEED SCREW

9.17   Location of the fast idle speed screw (typical)

---

where a natural gas-type appliance (such as a water heater or clothes dryer) with a pilot light is present. If you spill any fuel on your skin, rinse it off immediately with soap and water. When you perform any kind of work on the fuel tank, wear safety glasses and have a Class B type fire extinguisher on hand.

Diagnosis

1   A thorough road test and check of carburetor adjustments should be done before any major carburetor service work. Specifications for some adjustments are listed on the Vehicle Emissions Control Information (VECI) label found in the engine compartment.
2   Carburetor problems usually show up as flooding, hard starting, stalling, severe backfiring and poor acceleration. A carburetor that's leaking fuel and/or covered with wet looking deposits definitely needs attention.
3   Some performance complaints directed at the carburetor are actually a result of loose, out-of-adjustment or malfunctioning engine or electrical components. Others develop when vacuum hoses leak, are disconnected or are incorrectly routed. The proper approach to analyzing carburetor problems should include the following items:

a)   Inspect all vacuum hoses and actuators for leaks and correct installation (see Chapter 6).
b)   Tighten the intake manifold and carburetor mounting nuts/bolts evenly and securely.
c)   Perform a cylinder compression test (see Chapter 2).
d)   Clean or replace the spark plugs as necessary (see Chapter1).
e)   Check the spark plug wires (see Chapter 1).
f)   Inspect the ignition primary wires.
g)   Check the ignition timing (follow the instructions printed on the Vehicle Emissions Control Information label).
h)   Check the fuel pump pressure/volume (see Section 3).
i)   Check the heat control valve in the air cleaner for proper operation (see Chapter 1).
j)   Check/replace the air filter element (see Chapter 1).
k)   Check the PCV system (see Chapters 1 and 6).
l)   Check/replace the fuel filter (see Chapter 1). Also, the strainer in the tank could be restricted.
m)   Check for a plugged exhaust system.
n)   Check EGR valve operation (see Chapter 6).
o)   Check the choke – it should be completely open at normal engine operating temperature (see Chapter 1).
p)   Check for fuel leaks and kinked or dented fuel lines (see Chapters 1 and 4)
q)   Check accelerator pump operation with the engine off (remove the air cleaner cover and operate the throttle as you look into the carburetor throat – you should see a stream of gasoline enter the carburetor).
r)   Check for incorrect fuel or bad gasoline.
s)   Check the valve clearances (if applicable) and camshaft lobe lift (see Chapters 1 and 2)
t)   Have a dealer service department or repair shop check the electronic engine and carburetor controls (if equipped).

10.5 Quadrajet 4MV carburetor

4   Diagnosing carburetor problems may require that the engine be started and run with the air cleaner off. While running the engine without the air cleaner, backfires are possible. This situation is likely to occur if the carburetor is malfunctioning, but just the removal of the air cleaner can lean the fuel/air mixture enough to produce an engine backfire. **Warning:** *Don't position any part of your body, especially your face, directly over the carburetor during inspection and servicing procedures. Wear eye protection!*

Overhaul

Refer to illustration 10.5

5   Once it's determined that the carburetor **(see illustration)** needs an overhaul, several options are available. If you're going to attempt to overhaul the carburetor yourself, first obtain a good quality carburetor rebuild kit (which will include all necessary gaskets, internal parts, instructions and a parts list). You'll also need some special solvent and a means of blowing out the internal passages of the carburetor with air.

6   An alternative is to obtain a new or rebuilt carburetor. They're readily available from dealers and auto parts stores. Make absolutely sure the exchange carburetor is identical to the original. A tag is usually attached to the top of the carburetor or a number is stamped on the float bowl. It'll help determine the exact type of carburetor you have. When obtaining a rebuilt carburetor or a rebuild kit, make sure the kit or carburetor matches your application exactly. Seemingly insignificant differences can make a large difference in engine performance.

7   If you choose to overhaul your own carburetor, allow enough time to disassemble it carefully, soak the necessary parts in the cleaning solvent (usually for at least one-half day or according to the instructions listed on

the carburetor cleaner) and reassemble it, which will usually take much longer than disassembly. When disassembling the carburetor, match each part with the illustration in the carburetor kit and lay the parts out in order on a clean work surface. Overhauls by inexperienced mechanics can result in an engine which runs poorly or not at all. To avoid this, use care and patience when disassembling the carburetor so you can reassemble it correctly.

8   Because carburetor designs are constantly modified by the manufacturer in order to meet increasingly more stringent emissions regulations, we cannot include overhaul procedures for all carburetors covered by this manual. You'll receive a detailed, well illustrated set of instructions with any carburetor overhaul kit; they'll apply in a more specific manner to the carburetor on your vehicle.

11   Fuel injection systems – general information

Refer to illustrations 11.4 and 11.5

Electronic fuel injection provides optimum fuel/air mixture ratios at all stages of combustion and offers immediate throttle response characteristics. It also enables the engine to run at the leanest possible fuel/air mixture ratio, reducing exhaust gas emissions.

Cadillac used three different types of fuel injection systems on the vehicles covered by this manual. A port-type system called simply Electronic Fuel Injection (EFI) was used between 1975 and 1979. Digital Fuel Injection (DFI) was used on vehicles between 1981 and 1985. Throttle Body Injection (TBI) was installed on all 1990 5.7L engines. All injection systems use an Electronic Control Unit (ECU) to control pulse width.

11.4   Electronic Fuel Injection (EFI) system components

11.5   Digital Fuel Injection (DFI) system components

The pulse width is the period of time during which the fuel injector is energized (squirts fuel). The Electronic Control Unit (ECU) opens and closes the injector's ground path to control fuel injector pulse width and thus meter the amount of fuel available to the engine. By continually altering the pulse width, the ECU adjusts the air/fuel ratio for varying operating conditions. For more information about the ECU, see Chapter 6.

EFI uses eight fuel injectors which spray a predetermined quantity of fuel into each intake port of the engine (see illustration). This arrangement is commonly called port fuel injection. The injector opening is timed with the engine so that the fuel charge is in place prior to the intake stroke for the particular cylinder.

Instead of using one injector for each cylinder, DFI (see illustration) and TBI systems use two injectors in a carburetor-like throttle body unit mounted on the intake manifold. DFI and TBI systems use identical throttle body units. The primary difference between the two systems is the type and locations of the sensors that send data to the ECU.

On all fuel injection systems, an electric fuel pump (two on Seville models) pumps fuel to the fuel injection system through the fuel feed line and an in-line fuel filter. A pressure regulator keeps fuel available at a constant pressure. Fuel in excess of injector needs is returned to the fuel tank by a separate line.

12   Fuel injection system – check

Warning: *Gasoline is extremely flammable, so take extra precautions when you work on any part of the fuel system. Don't smoke or allow open flames or bare light bulbs near the work area, and don't work in a garage* *where a natural gas-type appliance (such as a water heater or clothes dryer) with a pilot light is present. If you spill any fuel on your skin, rinse it off immediately with soap and water. When you perform any kind of work on the fuel tank, wear safety glasses and have a Class B type fire extinguisher on hand.*

Preliminary checks

1   Check the ground wire connections on the intake manifold for tightness. Check all electrical connectors that are related to the system. Loose connectors and poor grounds can cause many problems that resemble more serious malfunctions.
2   Check to see that the battery is fully charged, as the control unit and sensors depend on an accurate supply voltage in order to properly meter the fuel.
3   Check the air filter element – a dirty or partially blocked filter will severely impede performance and economy (see Chapter 1).
4   If a blown fuse is found, replace it and see if it blows again. If it does, search for a grounded wire in the harness to the fuel pump.
5   Check the condition of the vacuum hoses attached to the throttle body and intake manifold. Vacuum leaks can result in an excessively lean mixture.

DFI and TBI systems

6   Check the fuel system pressure (see Section 4).
7   Set the parking brake, remove the air cleaner top plate and, with the engine idling in Park, observe the operating fuel injectors. The spray pattern should be even and conical in shape. The spray should touch the throttle body bore.
   a) If the spray is weak or uneven, the injector is clogged or faulty. Gasoline additives designed to clean fuel injectors can sometimes clear a clogged injector. If not, a dealer service department has more effective cleaning equipment.
   b) If an injector is not operating at all, check its electrical connector. If the connection is good and the injector is receiving voltage, but the injector still doesn't work, the injector is faulty.

EFI (port-type) systems

8   Check the throttle plates in the throttle body for sticking or binding.

Also, check the throttle body for a build-up of deposits in the throttle bores. These deposits can be cleaned with aerosol carburetor cleaner and a toothbrush.
9   With the engine running, place a screwdriver against each injector, one at a time, and listen through the handle for a clicking sound, indicating operation.

All systems

10   The remainder of the system checks should be left to a dealer service department or other qualified repair shop, as there is a chance that the control unit may be damaged if they are not performed properly.

13   Electronic Fuel Injection (EFI) system – component removal and installation

Warning: *Before servicing an injector, fuel pump, fuel line, fuel rail or pressure regulator, relieve the pressure in the fuel system to minimize the risk of fire and injury (refer to the fuel pressure relief procedure described in Section 2). After servicing the fuel system, cycle the ignition between On and Off several times (wait 10 seconds between cycles) and check the system for leaks.*

Throttle Body

Refer to illustration 13.7

1   Disconnect the cable from the negative terminal of the battery.
2   Remove the air cleaner.
3   If equipped, remove the cruise control chain from the throttle lever.
4   Disconnect the vacuum hoses to the throttle body. Mark the hoses and their associated fittings so you'll be able to attach them correctly on installation.
5   Disconnect the throttle cable (see Section 16).
6   Disengage the downshift switch from the throttle lever and position bracket and move the switch and linkage out of the way.
7   Remove the throttle body bolts and detach the throttle body **(see illustration)**. Using a gasket scraper or putty knife, remove all traces of old gasket material from the mating surfaces on the intake manifold and

13.7   **Throttle body and air cleaner assemblies – exploded view**

13.11   Fuel rail details

throttle body (if the same one is being installed). Be careful not to gouge the mating surfaces.

8   Install the throttle body and gasket and tighten the bolts to the torque listed in this Chapter's Specifications.

9   The remainder of installation is the reverse of removal.

Fuel rail and injectors

Refer to illustration 13.11

Warning: *Before any work is performed on the fuel lines, fuel rail or injectors, the fuel system pressure must be relieved (refer to the fuel pressure relief procedure in Section 2).*

Note: *An eight-digit identification number is stamped on the side of the fuel rail assembly. Refer to this number if servicing or parts replacement is required.*

10   Detach the negative battery cable from the battery.

11   Remove the clamp that secures the pressure regulator hose to the fuel rail **(see illustration)**.

12   Disengage the pressure regulator hose from the fuel rail.

13   Label and unplug the injector electrical connectors. Remove the two screws that hold each injector to the intake manifold.

14   Carefully remove the fuel rail. **Note:** *Some injectors may come out with the fuel rail and others may remain in the manifold.* **Caution:** *Use care when handling the fuel rail assembly to avoid damaging the injectors.*

15   Remove the injectors and O-rings seals.

16   Install the new O-ring seal(s) on the injector(s) and lubricate them with engine oil.

17   Install the injectors on the fuel rail.

18   The remainder of installation is the reverse of removal.

Fuel pressure regulator

Warning: *Relieve the fuel pressure as described in Section 2 before removing any fuel lines.*

19   Remove the vacuum hose from the nipple on top of the pressure regulator.

20   Remove the clamps that secure the fuel line connecting the regulator to the fuel rail and remove the return line.

21   Remove the pressure regulator mounting bolt and remove the pressure regulator.

22   Installation is the reverse of removal.

14   Throttle body unit (DFI and TBI systems) – removal and installation

Refer to illustrations 14.8 and 14.9

Warning: *Gasoline is extremely flammable, so take extra precautions when working on any part of the fuel system. Don't smoke or allow open flames or bare light bulbs in or near the work area, and don't work in a garage where a natural gas-type appliance (such as a water heater or clothes dryer) with a pilot light is present. If you spill fuel on your skin, rinse it off immediately with soap and water. Have a Class B fire extinguisher on hand when working on the fuel system.*

Note: *The fuel injectors, pressure regulator, throttle position sensor and idle air control valve can be replaced without removing the throttle body assembly.*

1   Relieve the fuel system pressure (see Section 2).

2   Disconnect the cable from the negative battery terminal.

3   Remove the air cleaner housing.

4   Unplug the electrical connectors from the idle air control valve, throttle position sensor and fuel injectors.

5   Remove the wiring harness from the injectors.

6   Remove the throttle linkage and return spring, TV cable (see Chapter 7) and cruise control cables (if applicable).

7   Using pieces of numbered tape, mark all of the vacuum hoses to the throttle body and disconnect them.

8   Disconnect the fuel inlet and return lines. Use a back-up wrench on the inlet and return fitting nuts to prevent damage to the throttle body and fuel lines **(see illustration)**. Remove the fuel line nut O-rings and discard them.

9   Remove the throttle body mounting bolts and lift the unit off the intake manifold **(see illustration)**. Stuff a rag into the intake manifold opening and carefully scrape all traces of old gasket material off the intake manifold and throttle body mating surfaces. Scrape carefully so you don't damage the delicate aluminum surfaces.

10   Installation is the reverse of the removal procedure. Be sure to install a new throttle body-to-intake manifold gasket, new fuel line O-rings and tighten the mounting bolts to the torque listed in this Chapter's Specifications.

11   Turn the ignition switch on without starting the engine and check for fuel leaks.

14.8 When disconnecting the fuel inlet and return lines, be sure to use a back-up wrench to prevent damage to the lines

14.9 To detach the throttle body from the intake manifold, remove the bolts (arrows)

12   Check to see if the accelerator pedal is free by depressing it to the floor and releasing it (with the ignition switch off).

15   Throttle body unit (DFI and TBI systems) – component replacement

Warning: *Gasoline is extremely flammable, so take extra precautions when working on any part of the fuel system. Don't smoke or allow open flames or bare light bulbs in or near the work area, and don't work in a garage where a natural gas-type appliance (such as a water heater or clothes dryer) with a pilot light is present. If you spill fuel on your skin, rinse it off immediately with soap and water. Have a Class B fire extinguisher on hand when working on the fuel system.*

Note: *Because of its relative simplicity, the throttle body assembly doesn't have to be removed from the intake manifold or disassembled for component replacement. However, for the sake of clarity, the following procedures are shown with the TBI assembly removed from the vehicle.*

1   Relieve fuel system pressure (see Section 2).
2   Detach the cable from the negative terminal of the battery.
3   Remove the air cleaner housing assembly, adapter and gaskets.

Fuel meter cover/fuel pressure regulator assembly
Refer to illustrations 15.5, 15.6 and 15.7

Note: *The fuel pressure regulator is housed in the fuel meter cover. Whether you are replacing the meter cover or the regulator itself, the entire assembly must be replaced. The regulator must not be removed from the cover.*

4   Unplug the electrical connectors to the fuel injectors.
5   Remove the cover screws **(see illustration on following page)** and detach the fuel meter cover.
6   Remove the fuel meter outlet passage gasket, cover gasket and pressure regulator seal. Carefully remove old gasket material that's stuck with a razor blade **(see illustration)**. **Caution:** *Do not attempt to re-use either of the gaskets.*
7   Inspect the cover for dirt, foreign material and casting warpage. If it's dirty, clean it with a shop rag soaked in solvent. Do not immerse the fuel meter cover in solvent – it could damage the pressure regulator diaphragm and gasket. **Warning:** *Do not remove the four screws **(see illustration)** securing the pressure regulator to the fuel meter cover. The regulator contains a large spring under compression which, if accidentally released, could cause injury. Disassembly might also result in a fuel leak between the diaphragm and the regulator housing. The new fuel meter cover as-*

15.6 Carefully peel away the old outlet passage and cover gaskets with a razor blade

15.7 DO NOT remove the four pressure regulator screws (arrows) from the fuel meter cover

15.5   An Exploded view of a typical throttle body assembly (DFI and TBI systems)

1   Long fuel meter cover attaching screw
2   Short fuel meter cover attaching screw
3   Fuel meter cover
4   Fuel meter cover gasket
5   Fuel meter outlet gasket
6   Pressure regulator seal
7   Pressure regulator
8   Fuel injector
9   Fuel injector inlet filter
10 Lower fuel injector O-ring
11 Upper fuel injector O-ring
12 Fuel injector washer
13 Fuel meter body-to-throttle body attaching screw
14 Fuel meter body
15 Throttle body-to-fuel meter body gasket
16 Air filter gasket
17 Fuel return line O-ring
18 Fuel outlet nut
19 Fuel inlet line O-ring
20 Fuel inlet nut
21 Fuel outlet nut gasket
22 Fuel inlet nut gasket
23 TPS lever attaching screw
24 TPS lever
25 TPS attaching screw
26 TPS attaching screw retainer
27 Throttle Position Sensor (TPS)
28 Idle stop screw plug
29 Idle stop screw
30 Idle stop screw spring
31 Throttle body
32 Flange gasket
33 Idle air control (IAC) valve
34 IAC valve gasket

sembly will include a new pressure regulator.

8   Install the new pressure regulator seal, fuel meter outlet passage gasket and cover gasket.

9   Install the fuel meter cover assembly using Loctite 262 or equivalent on the screws. **Note:** *The short screws go next to the injectors.*

10   Attach the electrical connectors to both injectors.

11   Attach the cable to the negative terminal of the battery.

12   With the engine off and the ignition on, check for leaks around the gasket and fuel line couplings.

13   Install the air cleaner, adapter and gaskets.

Fuel injector assembly

Refer to illustrations 15.16, 15.21, 15.22, 15.23, 15.24 and 15.25

14   To unplug the electrical connectors from the fuel injectors, squeeze the plastic tabs and pull straight up.

15   Remove the fuel meter cover/pressure regulator assembly. **Note:** *Do not remove the fuel meter cover assembly gasket – leave it in place to protect the casting from damage during injector removal.*

16   Use a screwdriver and fulcrum **(see illustration)** to pry out the injector.

15.16   To remove an injector, slip the tip of a standard screwdriver under the lip of the lug on top of the injector and, using another screwdriver as a fulcrum, carefully pry the injector up and out

15.21   Slide the new filter onto the nozzle of the fuel injector

15.22   Lubricate the lower O-ring with transmission fluid, then place it on the shoulder in the bottom of the injector cavity

15.23   Place the steel back-up washer on the shoulder near the top of the injector cavity

17   Remove the upper (larger) and lower (smaller) O-rings and filter from the injector.
18   Remove the steel back-up washer from the top of the injector cavity.
19   Inspect the fuel injector filter for dirt and contamination. If present, check for the presence of dirt in the fuel lines and fuel tank.
20   Be sure to replace the fuel injector with an identical part. Injectors from other models can fit but are calibrated for different flow rates.
21   Slide the new filter into place on the nozzle of the injector (see illustration).
22   Lubricate the new lower (smaller) O-ring with automatic transmission fluid and place it on the small shoulder at the bottom of the fuel injector cavity in the fuel meter body (see illustration).
23   Install the steel back-up washer in the injector cavity (see illustration).
24   Lubricate the new upper (larger) O-ring with automatic transmission fluid and install it on top of the steel back-up washer (see illustration).
Note: The back-up washer and large O-ring must be installed before the injector. If they aren't, improper seating of the large O-ring could cause fuel leakage.

15.24   Lubricate the upper O-ring with transmission fluid, then install it on top of the steel washer

15.25   Make sure the lug is aligned with the groove in the bottom of the fuel injector cavity

15.36   Remove the fuel inlet and outlet nuts from the fuel meter body

36   Unscrew the fuel inlet and return line threaded fittings, detach the lines and remove the O-rings. Remove the fuel inlet and outlet nuts and gaskets from the fuel meter body assembly **(see illustration)**. Note the locations of the nuts to ensure proper reassembly. The inlet nut has a larger passage than the outlet nut.
37   Remove the gasket from the inner end of each fuel nut.
38   Remove the fuel meter body-to-throttle body screws and detach the fuel meter body from the throttle body **(see illustration)**.
39   Install the new throttle body-to-fuel meter body gasket. Match the cutout portions in the gasket with the openings in the throttle body.
40   Install the fuel meter body on the throttle body. Coat the fuel meter body-to-throttle body screws with thread locking compound before installing them.
41   Install the fuel inlet and outlet nuts, with new gaskets, in the fuel meter body and tighten the nuts securely. Install the fuel inlet and return line threaded fittings with new O-rings. Use a back-up wrench to prevent the nuts from turning.
42   Install the fuel injectors.
43   Install the fuel meter cover/pressure regulator assembly.
44   Attach the cable to the negative terminal of the battery.
45   Attach the electrical connectors to the fuel injectors.
46   With the engine off and the ignition on, check for leaks around the fuel meter body, the gasket and around the fuel line nuts and threaded fittings.
47   Install the air cleaner housing assembly, adapters and gaskets.

15.38   Once the fuel inlet and outlet nuts are off, remove the screws and pull the fuel meter body straight up to separate it from the throttle body

25   To install the injector, align the raised lug on the injector base with the groove in the fuel injector cavity **(see illustration)**. Push down on the injector until it's fully seated in the fuel meter body. **Note:** *The electrical terminals should be parallel with the throttle shaft.*
26   Install the fuel meter cover assembly and gasket.
27   Attach the cable to the negative terminal of the battery.
28   With the engine off and the ignition on, check for fuel leaks.
29   Attach the electrical connectors to the fuel injectors.
30   Install the air cleaner housing assembly, adapter and gaskets.

Throttle Position Sensor (TPS)

31   For information on the TPS, see Chapter 6.

Idle Air Control (IAC) valve

32   For information on the IAC valve, see Chapter 6.

Fuel meter body assembly

Refer to illustrations 15.36 and 15.38
33   Unplug the electrical connectors from the fuel injectors.
34   Remove the fuel meter cover/pressure regulator assembly, fuel meter cover gasket, fuel meter outlet gasket and pressure regulator seal.
35   Remove the fuel injectors.

16   Throttle cable – removal and installation

Refer to illustrations 16.2a and 16.2b
1   Disconnect the cable from the negative terminal of the battery.
2   The throttle cable is retained to the throttle linkage by a clip **(see illustrations)**.
3   To remove the retaining clip use a small screwdriver to pop the retaining clip off the post on the throttle lever arm and remove the cable end.
4   To detach the throttle cable and, if equipped, cruise control cables from the cable support bracket, use a pair of needle-nose pliers to squeeze the locking tabs on the top and bottom of the cable retainer, then pull the cable assembly through the bracket.
5   Carefully study the routing of the cable before proceeding.
6   Working inside the vehicle, pull the cable toward you and detach it from the accelerator pedal.
7   Follow the cable with your hand until you locate the locking cable retainer on the passenger compartment side of the firewall. Again, with a pair of needle-nose pliers, squeeze the locking tabs of the retainer together

16.2a   Throttle cable installation details on an EFI-equipped model

16.2b   Throttle cable installation details
on a 5.7L TBI-equipped model

1   Cable assembly
2   Throttle return spring
3   Retainer
4   Throttle body lever
5   Pedal assembly
6   Throttle lever assembly
7   Support plate
8   Screw

4

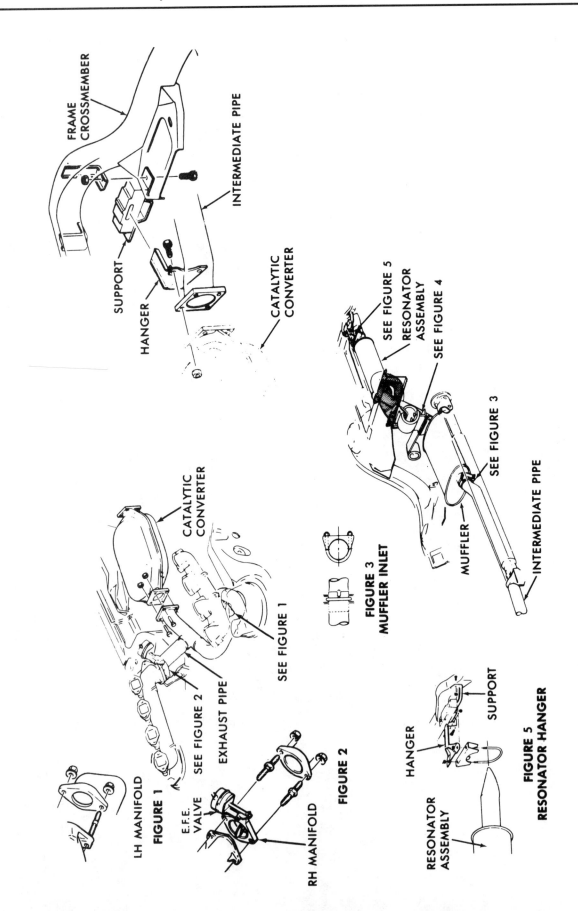

FRAME CROSSMEMBER

INTERMEDIATE PIPE

SUPPORT

HANGER

CATALYTIC CONVERTER

SEE FIGURE 5

RESONATOR ASSEMBLY

SEE FIGURE 4

SEE FIGURE 3

MUFFLER

INTERMEDIATE PIPE

CATALYTIC CONVERTER

SEE FIGURE 1

SEE FIGURE 2

EXHAUST PIPE

LH MANIFOLD

FIGURE 1

E.F.E. VALVE

RH MANIFOLD

FIGURE 2

FIGURE 3
MUFFLER INLET

HANGER

SUPPORT

RESONATOR ASSEMBLY

FIGURE 5
RESONATOR HANGER

17.1a   Typical exhaust system installation details

17.1b   Make sure the exhaust hangers (arrow) are not damaged or cut – this hanger should be replaced

17.4   Apply penetrating oil to the exhaust flange nuts before attempting to remove them

and push the retainer through the firewall.
8 Remove the accelerator cable assembly.
9 Installation is the reverse of removal.

---

17   Exhaust system servicing – general information

Refer to illustrations 17.1a, 17.1b and 17.4

Warning: *Inspection and repair of exhaust system components should be done only after it has cooled completely. Also, when working under the vehicle, make sure it's securely supported on jackstands.*

1 The exhaust system consists of the exhaust manifolds, the catalytic converter, the muffler, the resonator (not all models), the tailpipe and all connecting pipes, brackets, hangers and clamps **(see illustration)**. The exhaust system is attached to the body with mounting brackets and rubber hangers **(see illustration)**. If any of the parts are improperly installed, excessive noise and vibration will be transmitted to the body.

2 Conduct regular inspections of the exhaust system to keep it safe and quiet. Look for any damaged or bent parts, open seams, holes, loose connections, excessive corrosion or other defects which could allow exhaust fumes to enter the vehicle. Deteriorated exhaust system components should not be repaired; they should be replaced with new parts.

3 If the exhaust system components are extremely corroded or rusted together, welding equipment will probably be required to remove them. The convenient way to accomplish this is to have a muffler repair shop remove the corroded sections with a cutting torch. If, however, you want to save money by doing it yourself (and you don't have a welding outfit with a cutting torch), simply cut off the old components with a hacksaw. If you have compressed air, special pneumatic cutting chisels can also be used. If you do decide to tackle the job at home, be sure to wear safety goggles to protect your eyes from metal chips and work gloves to protect your hands.

4 Here are some simple guidelines to follow when repairing the exhaust system:

   a) Work from the back to the front when removing exhaust system components.
   b) Apply penetrating oil to the exhaust system component fasteners to make them easier to remove **(see illustration).**
   c) Use new gaskets, hangers and clamps when installing exhaust system components.
   d) Apply anti-seize compound to the threads of all exhaust system fasteners during reassembly.
   e) Be sure to allow sufficient clearance between newly installed parts and all points on the underbody to avoid overheating the floor pan and possibly damaging the interior carpet and insulation. Pay particularly close attention to the catalytic converter and heat shield.

4

Chapter 5   Engine electrical systems

Contents

1   General information and precautions

The engine electrical systems include all ignition, charging and starting components. Because of their engine-related functions, these components are discussed separately from chassis electrical devices such as the lights, the instruments, etc. (which are included in Chapter 12).

Always observe the following precautions when working on the electrical systems:

a) Be extremely careful when servicing engine electrical components. They are easily damaged if checked, connected or handled improperly.

b) The alternator is driven by an engine drivebelt which could cause serious injury if your hands, hair or clothes become entangled in it with the engine running.

c) Both the alternator and the starter are connected directly to the battery and could arc or even cause a fire if mishandled, overloaded or shorted out.

d) Never leave the ignition switch on for long periods of time with the engine off.

e) Don't disconnect the battery cables while the engine is running.

f) Maintain correct polarity when connecting a battery cable from another source, such as a vehicle, during jump starting.

g) Always disconnect the negative cable first and hook it up last or the battery may be shorted by the tool being used to loosen the cable clamps.

It's also a good idea to review the safety-related information regarding the engine electrical systems located in the Safety First section near the front of this manual before beginning any operation included in this Chapter.

2   Battery – removal and installation

Refer to illustration 2.2

1   **Caution:** *Always disconnect the negative cable first and hook it up last or the battery may be shorted by the tool being used to loosen the cable clamps. Disconnect both cables from the battery terminals.*
2   Remove the battery hold-down clamp **(see illustration)**.
3   Lift out the battery. Use the proper lifting technique – the battery is heavy.
4   While the battery is out, inspect the battery carrier (tray) for corrosion (See Chapter 1).
5   If you are replacing the battery, make sure that you get an identical battery, with the same dimensions, amperage rating, "cold cranking" rating, etc.
6   Installation is the reverse of removal.

3   Battery – emergency jump starting

Refer to the Booster battery (jump) starting procedure at the front of this manual.

4   Battery cables – check and replacement

1   Periodically inspect the entire length of each battery cable for damage, cracked or burned insulation and corrosion. Poor battery cable connections can cause starting problems and decreased engine performance.
2   Check the cable-to-terminal connections at the ends of the cables for cracks, loose wire strands and corrosion. The presence of white, fluffy deposits under the insulation at the cable terminal connection is a sign that the cable is corroded and should be replaced. Check the terminals for distortion, missing mounting bolts and corrosion.
3   When removing the cables, always disconnect the negative cable first and hook it up last or the battery may be shorted by the tool used to loosen the cable clamps. Even if only the positive cable is being replaced, be sure to disconnect the negative cable from the battery first (see Chapter 1 for further information regarding battery cable removal).
4   Disconnect the old cables from the battery, then trace each of them to their opposite ends and detach them from the starter solenoid and ground. Note the routing of each cable to insure correct installation.
5   If you are replacing either or both of the old cables, take them with you when buying new cables. It is vitally important that you replace the cables with identical parts. Cables have characteristics that make them easy to identify: positive cables are usually red, larger in cross-section and have a larger diameter battery post clamp; ground cables are usually black, smaller in cross-section and have a slightly smaller diameter clamp for the negative post.
6   Clean the threads of the solenoid or ground connection with a wire brush to remove rust and corrosion. Apply a light coat of battery terminal corrosion inhibitor, or petroleum jelly, to the threads to prevent future corrosion.
7   Attach the cable to the solenoid or ground connection and tighten the mounting nut/bolt securely.
8   Before connecting a new cable to the battery, make sure that it reaches the battery post without having to be stretched.
9   Connect the positive cable first, followed by the negative cable.

5   Ignition system – general information

1   In order for the engine to run correctly, it is necessary for an electrical spark to ignite the fuel/air mixture in the combustion chamber at exactly the right moment in relation to engine speed and load. The ignition coil converts low tension (LT) voltage from the battery into high tension (HT) voltage, powerful enough to jump the spark plug gap in the cylinder, pro-

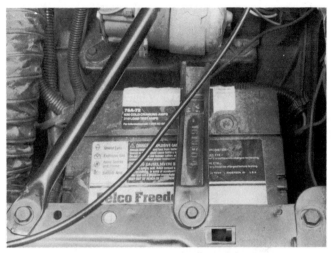

2.2   Typical battery hold-down clamp

viding that the system is in good condition and that all adjustments are correct.
2   The ignition system fitted to all pre-1975 cars as standard equipment is a conventional distributor with mechanical breaker points. On 1975 and later models, a breakerless high energy ignition (HEI) system is used.

Pre-1975 ignition systems

3   The ignition system is divided into the primary (low tension) circuit and the secondary (high tension) circuit.
4   The primary circuit consists of the battery lead to the starter motor, the lead to the ignition switch, the calibrated resistance wire from the ignition switch to the coil primary winding and the lead from the coil low tension windings to the breaker points and condenser in the distributor.
5   The secondary circuit consists of the coil secondary winding, the high tension lead from the coil to the distributor cap, the rotor and the spark plug leads and spark plugs.
6   The system functions in the following manner. Low voltage in the coil is converted into high voltage by the opening and closing of the breaker points in the distributor. This high voltage is carried via the brush in the center of the distributor cap to the rotor arm on the distributor shaft. Every time the end of the rotor passes one of the spark plug wire terminals on the cap, the spark jumps the gap from the rotor arm to the terminal and is carried by the spark plug wire to the spark plug, where it jumps the spark plug gap to ground.
7   Ignition advance is controlled by both mechanical and vacuum operated systems. The mechanical governor mechanism consists of two weights which, due to centrifugal force, move out from the distributor shaft as the engine speed rises. As they move outwards, they rotate the cam relative to the distributor shaft, advancing spark timing. The weights are held in position by two light springs. It is the tension of these springs which determines correct spark advancement.
8   The vacuum control system consists of a diaphragm, one side of which is connected via a vacuum line to the carburetor, the other side to the contact breaker plate. Vacuum in the intake manifold and carburetor varies with engine speed and throttle opening. As the vacuum changes, it moves the diaphragm, which rotates the contact breaker plate slightly in relation to the rotor, thus advancing or retarding the spark. Control is fine-tuned by a spring in the vacuum assembly.
9   On some models, a Transmission Controlled Spark (TCS) system eliminates vacuum advance (see Chapter 6).

HEI ignition systems (1975 through 1980)

10   The high energy ignition (HEI) system is a pulse triggered, transistor controlled, inductive discharge system.
11   A magnetic pick-up inside the distributor contains a permanent magnet, pole-piece and pick-up coil. A toothed wheel, rotating inside the pole piece, induces a voltage in the pick-up coil. When the teeth on the wheel

5

6.2   The ignition system should be checked with a spark tester –
if the ignition system produces a spark that will jump the tester
gap, it's functioning normally

7.5a   After turning the rotor until it is pointing at the terminal for
the number one spark plug, mark the edge of the distributor base
directly beneath it

7.5b   Mark the base of the distributor and the engine block to
insure proper installation

7.6a   Some distributor hold-down bolts can be removed with a
combination wrench . . .

and pole piece line up, a signal passes to the electronic module to open the coil primary circuit. The primary circuit current collapses and a high voltage is induced in the coil secondary winding. This high voltage is directed to the spark plugs by the distributor rotor in a manner similar to a conventional system. A capacitor suppresses radio interference.

12   The HEI system features a longer spark duration than a conventional breaker point ignition system, and the dwell period increases automatically with engine speed. These characteristics are desirable for lean firing and EGR-diluted mixtures.

13   The ignition coil and the electronic module are both housed in the distributor cap on the HEI system. The distributor does not require routine servicing.

14   Spark timing is advanced by mechanical and vacuum devices similar to those used on conventional breaker point distributors (described above). The TCS system is eliminated.

HEI systems (1981 and later)

15   Since 1981, HEI systems have been equipped with electronic spark timing (EST). All spark timing changes are carried out by the Electronic Control Module (ECM), which monitors data from various engine sensors, computes the desired spark timing and signals the distributor to alter spark timing accordingly. Vacuum and mechanical advance is eliminated.

7.6b   . . . others may require a special distributor wrench

16   An Electronic Spark Control (ESC) system utilizes a knock sensor, and the ECM, to allow maximum spark advance without spark knock. The ESC system improves driveability and fuel economy.

FRONT OF ENGINE

℄ OF ENGINE

45.0°
APPROX.

7.6c   On HT4100 engines, position the distributor properly in order to clear the firewall of the engine compartment

---

6   Ignition system – check

Warning: *Because of the very high secondary voltage generated by the ignition system – particularly the High Energy Ignition (HEI) system – extreme care should be taken whenever this check is performed.*

HEI system

Calibrated ignition tester method

Refer to illustration 6.2

1   If the engine turns over but won't start, disconnect the spark plug lead from any spark plug and attach it to a calibrated ignition tester for the HEI system (available at most auto parts stores).

2   Connect the clip on the tester to a ground such as a metal bracket **(see illustration)**, crank the engine and watch the end of the tester to see if bright blue, well-defined sparks occur.

3   If sparks occur, sufficient voltage is reaching the plugs to fire the engine. However, the plugs themselves may be fouled, so remove and check them as described in Chapter 1 or install new ones.

4   If no spark occurs, remove the distributor cap and check the cap and rotor as described in Chapter 1. If moisture is present, use WD-40 (or something similar) to dry out the cap and rotor, then reinstall the cap and repeat the spark test.

5   If there's still no spark, the tester should be attached to the wire from the coil (this cannot be done on vehicles with a coil-in-cap distributor) and the check should be repeated again.

6   If no spark occurs, check the primary wire connections at the coil to make sure they're clean and tight. Make any necessary repairs, then repeat the check again.

7   If sparks now occur, the distributor cap, rotor, plug wire(s) or spark plug(s) may be defective. If there's still no spark, the coil-to-cap wire may be bad. If a substitute wire doesn't make any difference, check the pick-up coil inside the distributor (see Section 11). If it checks out OK, have the system checked by a dealer service department or other repair shop.

Alternative method

Note: *If you're unable to obtain an HEI tester, the following method will enable you to determine whether the ignition system has spark, but it will not*

tell you if there is enough voltage present to actually initiate combustion.

8   Remove the spark plug wire from one of the spark plugs. Slide the boot back and, using an insulated tool, hold the wire about 1/4-inch from a good ground while an assistant cranks the engine.

9   If bright blue, well-defined sparks occur, sufficient voltage is reaching the plugs to fire the engine. However, the plugs themselves may be fouled, so remove and check them as described in Chapter 1 or install new ones.

10   If there's no spark, check another wire in the same manner. A few sparks followed by no spark is the same condition as no spark at all.

11   If no spark occurs, remove the distributor cap and check the cap and rotor as described in Chapter 1. If moisture is present, use WD-40 (or something similar) to dry out the cap and rotor, then reinstall the cap and repeat the spark test.

12   If there's still no spark, disconnect the coil wire from the distributor, hold it about 1/4-inch from a good ground and crank the engine again (this cannot be done on vehicles with a coil-in-cap distributor).

13   If no spark occurs, check the primary wire connections at the coil to make sure they're clean and tight. Make any necessary repairs, then repeat the check again.

14   If sparks now occur, the distributor cap, rotor, plug wire(s) or spark plug(s) may be defective. If there's still no spark, the coil-to-cap wire may be bad. If a substitute wire doesn't make any difference, check the pick-up coil inside the distributor (see Section 11). If it checks out OK, have the system checked by a dealer service department or other repair shop.

Breaker point system

15   Follow the procedure described in Steps 8 through 13 above.

16   If there's still no spark, the coil-to-cap wire may be bad. If a substitute wire doesn't make any difference, proceed as follows.

17   Refer to Chapter 1, remove the distributor cap and check the ignition points.

18   If the points appear to be in good condition and the primary wires are hooked up correctly and undamaged, adjust the points, then repeat the spark check.

19   If the primary circuit is complete (battery voltage is available at the points), the points are clean and properly adjusted and the secondary ignition circuit is functioning correctly, sparks should occur at the plug wires. If there is still no spark, have the system checked by a dealer service department or other repair shop.

---

7   Distributor – removal and installation

Refer to illustrations 7.5a, 7.5b, 7.6a, 7.6b and 7.6c

Removal

1   After disconnecting the negative battery terminal cable, unplug the primary lead from the coil (or distributor cap on coil-in-cap models).

2   Unplug or detach all electrical leads from the distributor. To find the connectors, trace the wires from the distributor.

3   Look for a raised "1" on the distributor cap. This marks the location for the number one cylinder spark plug wire terminal. If the cap does not have a mark for the number one spark plug, locate the number one spark plug and trace the wire back to its corresponding terminal on the cap.

4   Remove the distributor cap (see Chapter 1) and turn the engine over until the rotor is pointing toward the number one spark plug terminal (see locating TDC procedure in Chapter 2).

5   Make a mark on the edge of the distributor base directly below the rotor tip and in line with it **(see illustration)**. Also, mark the distributor base and the engine block to ensure that the distributor is installed correctly **(see illustration)**.

6   Remove the distributor hold-down bolt and clamp **(see illustrations)**, then pull the distributor straight up to remove it. **Caution:** *DO NOT turn the engine while the distributor is removed, or the alignment marks will be useless.* **Note:** *On HT4100 engines, install the distributor into the exact same position in order to allow sufficient clearance against the firewall **(see illustration)**.*

8.4   Apply vacuum to the vacuum advance unit and observe movement of the distributor plate

8.5   To detach the rotor, remove the two screws on top that attach it to the centrifugal advance mechanism

Installation

Note: *If the crankshaft has been moved while the distributor is out, locate Top Dead Center (TDC) for the number one piston (see Chapter 2) and position the distributor and rotor accordingly.*

7   Insert the distributor into the engine in exactly the same relationship to the block that it was in when removed.

8   To mesh the helical gears on the camshaft and the distributor, it may be necessary to turn the rotor slightly. If the distributor doesn't seat completely, the hex shaped recess in the lower end of the distributor shaft is not mating properly with the oil pump shaft. Recheck the alignment marks between the distributor base and the block to verify that the distributor is in the same position it was in before removal. Also check the rotor to see if it's aligned with the mark you made on the edge of the distributor base.

9   Place the hold-down clamp in position and loosely install the bolt.

10   Install the distributor cap.

11   Plug in the module electrical connector (where applicable).

12   Reattach the spark plug wires to the plugs (if removed).

13   Connect the cable to the negative terminal of the battery.

14   Check the ignition timing (see Chapter 1) and tighten the distributor hold-down bolt securely.

8   Vacuum advance – check and replacement

Refer to illustrations 8.4 and 8.5

Check

1   Refer to Chapter 1, Ignition timing check and adjustment, and hook up a timing light as described there.

2   Start the engine and set the speed at approximately 2500 rpm.

3   Observe the timing marks at the front of the engine and remove the vacuum hose from the vacuum advance control unit on the distributor. When the hose is removed, the timing mark on the crankshaft pulley should appear to move closer to the stationary mark on the timing tab. When the hose is reconnected, the mark should move away again.

4   If reconnecting the vacuum hose produces an abrupt increase in advance, or none at all, the vacuum advance control unit is probably defective. **Note:** *Another method to check the vacuum advance assembly is to connect a vacuum pump to the vacuum advance* **(see illustration)** *and observe the distributor plate for the proper movement.*

Replacement

5   Remove the distributor cap and rotor **(see illustration)**.

6   Remove the two screws that retain the vacuum advance mechanism to the distributor housing.

7   Unhook the advance arm from the distributor plate by pushing down on it with a narrow punch, then remove the unit from the distributor.

8   Installation is the reverse of the removal procedure.

9   Centrifugal advance – check and replacement

Refer to illustrations 9.4 and 9.7

Check

1   Refer to Chapter 1, Ignition timing check and adjustment, and hook up a timing light as described there.

2   With the engine running at idle speed and the light properly connected, disconnect and plug the vacuum hose from the vacuum advance control unit on the distributor.

3   Observe the timing marks on the front of the engine and slowly increase engine speed. The timing mark on the crankshaft pulley should appear to move smoothly in a direction away from the stationary mark on the timing tab. Then when the engine is slowed down, the mark should return to its original position.

4   If the above conditions are not met, the advance mechanism inside the distributor should be checked for broken governor springs and sticking weights **(see illustration)**.

9.4 An example of a worn centrifugal advance weight – note the elongated hole

9.7   Remove the centrifugal weight springs (arrows)

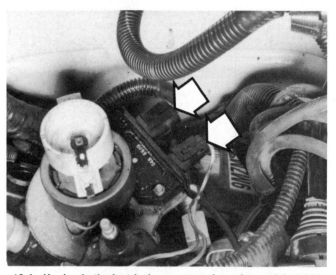

10.4   Unplug both electrical connectors from the module (1990 5.7L Chevrolet-built engine shown)

Replacement

5   Remove the distributor cap.
6   Remove the two screws that retain the rotor (see illustration 8.5).
7   Remove the centrifugal weight springs and carefully lift the weights off the distributor shaft **(see illustration)**.
8   Installation is the reverse of removal.

5   Remove the screws and lift out the module **(see illustration)**. **Note:** *The module can only be tested with special equipment. If you suspect it's malfunctioning, have it checked by a dealer service department.*
6   Installation is the reverse of removal. Be sure to apply the silicone di-electric grease supplied with the new module to the distributor base **(see illustration)** – DO NOT use any other type of grease! If the grease isn't used, the module will overheat and destroy itself.

10   Ignition module – replacement

Refer to illustrations 10.4, 10.5 and 10.6
Note: *It's not necessary to remove the distributor from the engine to re-place the ignition module.*

1   Disconnect the cable from the negative terminal of the battery. Re-move the air cleaner to provide room to work around the distributor.
2   Remove the distributor cap and wires as an assembly and position them out of the way (see Chapter 1).
3   Remove the rotor.
4   Carefully detach the electrical connectors from the module terminals **(see illustration)**.

11   Pick-up coil – check and replacement

Refer to illustrations 11.3, 11.8 and 11.9

Check

1   Later model HEI distributors vary somewhat from those described in Section 9. Most later distributors are not equipped with vacuum advance units, as advance is controlled by electronic control module (ECM).
2   Unplug the electrical connector(s), disengage the latches and re-move the distributor cap.

5

10.5   To remove the ignition module, remove the two mounting screws and unplug the connector from the B and C terminals

MODULE

APPLY SILICONE LUBRICANT

10.6   Apply silicone lubricant to the distributor base in the area under the ignition module – the lubricant dissipates heat and prevents the module from overheating

11.3   To test the pickup coil, connect an ohmmeter between the indicated terminal and ground, then connect it between both terminals

1	Infinite	2	500 – 1500 ohms

3   To test the pick-up coil, remove the rotor and pick-up leads and connect an ohmmeter as shown **(see illustration)**.
4   If the distributor is equipped with a vacuum advance unit, connect a vacuum pump to it.
5   Apply vacuum to the advance unit and verify that the indicated resistance remains steady as vacuum is applied. Replace the advance unit if it is inoperative or the ohmmeter reading changes. Make sure the application of vacuum does not cause the teeth to align (indicated by a jump in the ohmmeter reading).
6   With the ohmmeter attached as shown in Step 1 in the illustrations, the indicated resistance should be infinite. With the ohmmeter attached as shown in Step 2, the reading should be between 500 and 1500 ohms. Replace the coil if it fails either test.

Replacement

7   Place the distributor in a vise, using blocks of wood to protect it.
8   Mark the relative positions of the gear and shaft. Drive the roll pin out **(see illustration)**. Remove the gear and pull the shaft from the distributor housing.
9   Remove the aluminum shield (if equipped) for access to the pick-up coil and module. The pick-up coil can be lifted out after removal of the retaining clip **(see illustration)**.
10   Reassembly is the reverse of the disassembly procedure. After reassembly, spin the distributor shaft to make sure there is no contact between the pick-up coil and the pick-up teeth. Loosen and retighten the teeth to eliminate the contact.

---

12   Ignition coil – check and replacement

Check

1   If the engine is hard to start (particularly when it's already hot), misses at high speed or cuts out during acceleration, the coil may be faulty. First, make sure the battery and the distributor are in good condition, the points (pre-1975 vehicles) are properly adjusted and the plugs and plug wires are in good shape. If the problem persists, perform the following test:

11.8   To remove the distributor shaft, drive the roll pin out of the shaft with a hammer and punch, remove the gear, shim and tanged washer from the shaft, inspect the shaft for any burrs that might prevent its removal, then pull it out (be careful not to lose the washer at the upper end of the shaft)

11.9   To detach the pickup coil from the distributor, remove the retaining clip or C-washer

Separately mounted coils (pre-1975)

2   Before performing any of the following coil electrical checks, make sure that the coil is clean, free of any carbon tracks and that all connections are tight and free of corrosion. Also make sure that both battery terminals are clean and that the cables are securely attached (especially the ground strap at the negative terminal).
3   Detach the coil high tension cable from the distributor cap. Hold the end of the cable about 3/16-inch away from some grounded part of the engine and operate the starter with the ignition turned on. A bright blue spark should jump the gap.
    a) If the spark is weak, yellowish or red, spark voltage is insufficient. If the points, condenser and battery are in good condition, the coil is probably weak. Take it to a dealer and have the output checked. If it tests weak when compared to a new coil of the same specifications, replace it.
    b) If there is no spark at all, try to locate the trouble before replacing the coil. Remove the distributor cap. Turn the engine until the points are open, or separate the points with a small piece of cardboard. Turn on the ignition switch. Using a 12-volt bulb with two test leads,

12.6a   To test the HEI type coil-in-cap, attach the leads of an ohmmeter to the primary terminals and verify that the indicated resistance is zero or very near zero, then, using the high scale, attach one lead to the high tension terminal and the other to each of the primary terminals and verify that both of the readings are not infinite – if the indicated resistance is not as specified, replace the coil

12.6b   To check the ignition coil on the 5.7L Chevrolet-built engine, use an ohmmeter to perform the following three checks

1   *On the high scale, the ohmmeter should read infinity*
2   *On the low scale, the ohmmeter should read very low or zero*
3   *On the high scale the ohmmeter should not read infinity*

attach one lead to ground somewhere on the engine and the other lead to first one of the coil's primary terminals and then the other.

1) If the bulb lights when touched to the primary terminal that leads to the distributor, the coil is getting current and the primary windings are okay.
2) If the bulb lights when touched to the other primary terminal but not when attached to the one leading to the distributor, the primary windings are faulty and the coil is no good.
3) If the light does not go on when connected to either primary connection, the coil is not the problem. Check the ignition switch and starter solenoid.
4) If the bulb lights when touched to both primary terminals (the coil is receiving current at both primary terminals), remove the high-tension cable from the center distributor cap tower and try shorting across the open distributor points with the tip of a clean (no oil) screwdriver.
   (a) If a spark jumps from the coil's high tension secondary wire to a grounded point on the engine as the screwdriver is removed, the points are either contaminated by oil, dirt or water, or they're burned.
   (b) If the screwdriver fails to produce a spark at the high tension wire, disconnect the primary wire that passes between the coil and the distributor and attach a test wire to the coil in its place. Ground the other end of the wire against the engine block, then pull it away (the test wire is simulating the points: grounding the wire is just like closing the points; pulling it away creates the same effect – producing a spark from the coil's high tension wire – as opening the points).
      (1) If a spark jumps from the high-tension cable when the test wire is removed from the ground, the coil is okay. Either the points are grounded or the condenser is shorted.
      (2) If a spark does not jump during this test, the secondary windings of the coil are faulty. Replace the coil.

4   Sometimes, a coil checks out perfectly but the engine is still hard to start and misses at higher speeds. The problem may be inadequate spark voltage caused by reversed coil polarity. If you have recently tuned up the engine or performed any service work involving the coil, it's possible that the primary leads to the coil were accidentally reversed. To check for reversed polarity, remove one of the spark plug leads and hold it about 1/4-inch from the spark plug terminal or any ground point. Then insert the point of a pencil between the ignition lead and the plug while the engine is running (if the plug connector terminals are deeply recessed in a boot or insulating shield, straighten all but one bend in a paper clip and insert the looped end into the plug connector).
   a) If the spark flares on the ground or spark plug side of the pencil, the polarity is correct.
   b) If the spark flares between the ignition lead and the pencil, however, the polarity is wrong and the primary wires should be switched at the coil.

HEI coils (1975 and later vehicles)
Refer to illustrations 12.6a and 12.6b
5   Remove the distributor cap (coil-in-cap models).
6   Attach the two leads of an ohmmeter to the two primary terminals as shown **(see illustrations)**. The indicated resistance should be zero or very near zero. If it isn't, replace the coil.
7   Using the high scale, attach one lead of the ohmmeter to the high tension terminal in the middle of the distributor and the other lead to each of the primary terminals. If both of the readings indicate infinite resistance, replace the coil.

Replacement
Separately mounted coils (non-HEI models)
Refer to illustration 12.10
8   Detach the cable from the negative terminal of the battery.
9   Disconnect the high tension cable from the coil.

12.10   To remove a conventional coil, simply detach the high tension cable and the primary leads and remove the mounting bracket bolts

12.14   To get at the coil, remove the coil cover screws and the cover

10   Detach the primary electrical connectors from the coil. If there is any doubt as to where they go, be sure to mark them before removal to ensure that they are re-installed correctly. Unscrew the mounting bolts then remove the coil **(see illustration)**.

11   Installation is the reverse of removal

Coil-in-cap (HEI) models (1975 through 1990 models)

Refer to Illustrations 12.14, 12.16 and 12.17

12   Detach the cable from the negative terminal of the battery.

13   Disconnect the electrical connectors from the distributor cap.

14   Remove the coil cover screws and the cover **(see illustration)**.

15   Remove the screws securing the coil to the cap.

16   Note the position of each wire, marking them if necessary. Remove the coil ground wire, then push the terminals from the underside of the cap. Remove the coil from the distributor cap **(see illustration)**.

17   Installation is the reverse of the removal procedure. Be sure that the center electrode is in good shape **(see illustration)** and that the leads are connected to their original positions.

Separately mounted coil (1991 and later HEI models)

18   Detach the cable from the negative battery terminal.

19   Mark the distributor base and engine block to ensure the distributor is returned to its original position **(see illustration 7.5b)**.

20   Loosen the distributor clamp bolt and rotate the distributor to gain access to the ignition coil bolt.

21   Disconnect the high-voltage wire from the coil.

22   Detach the primary circuit electrical connectors from the coil. If there is any doubt as to where they go, be sure to mark them before removal to ensure they are reinstalled correctly.

23   Remove the mounting bolts, then remove the coil and bracket.

24   Installation is the reverse of removal.

The fusible link is a short length of insulated wire integral with the engine compartment wiring harness. The link is four wire gauges smaller in diameter than the circuit it protects. Production fusible links and their identification flags are identified by the flag color. See Chapter 12 for additional information regarding fusible links.

The charging system doesn't ordinarily require periodic maintenance. However, the drivebelt, battery and wires and connections should be inspected at the intervals outlined in Chapter 1.

The dashboard warning light should come on when the ignition key is turned to Start, then should go off immediately. If it remains on, there is a malfunction in the charging system (see Section 13). Some vehicles are also equipped with a voltage gauge. If the voltage gauge indicates abnormally high or low voltage, check the charging system (see Section 14).

12.16   To separate the coil from the distributor cap, clearly mark the wires, detach the coil ground wire and push the terminals from the underside of the cap

12.17   Before installing a new coil, make sure that the center electrode is in good condition

13.1   Wiring schematic for a typical charging system

Be very careful when making electrical circuit connections to a vehicle equipped with an alternator and note the following:

a) When reconnecting wires to the alternator from the battery, be sure to note the polarity. Also, never disconnect the battery cables while the engine is running.

b) Before using arc welding equipment to repair any part of the vehicle, disconnect the wires from the alternator and the battery terminals.

c) Never start the engine with a battery charger connected.

d) Always disconnect both battery leads before using a battery charger.

e) The alternator is driven by an engine drivebelt which could cause serious injury if your hands, hair or clothes become entangled in it with the engine running.

f) Because the alternator is connected directly to the battery, it could arc or cause a fire if overloaded or shorted out.

g) Wrap a plastic bag over the alternator and secure it with rubber bands before steam cleaning the engine.

13   Charging system – general information and precautions

Refer to illustration 13.1

The charging system **(see illustration)** includes the alternator, either an internal or an external voltage regulator, a charge indicator, the battery, a fusible link and the wiring between all the components. The charging system supplies electrical power for the ignition system, the lights, the radio, etc. The alternator is driven by a drivebelt at the front (right end) of the engine.

The alternator fitted to all models is a Delco-Remy Delcotron. Several units have been used. Early units, up to and including 1972, use an external voltage regulator. Later units, such as the Series 693 and the Series 697, CS-130 and 27SI, are equipped with an internal voltage regulator. Finally, it should be noted that the CS series alternators cannot be rebuilt. If one becomes inoperative, it must be replaced.

The purpose of the voltage regulator is to limit the alternator's voltage to a preset value. This prevents power surges, circuit overloads, etc., during peak voltage output.

14   Charging system – check

1   If a malfunction occurs in the charging circuit, don't automatically assume that the alternator is causing the problem. First check the following items:

a) Check the drivebelt tension and its condition. Replace it if worn or deteriorated.

b) Make sure the alternator mounting and adjustment bolts are tight.

c) Inspect the alternator wiring harness and the connectors at the alternator and voltage regulator. They must be in good condition and tight.

d) Check the fusible link (if equipped) located between the starter solenoid and the alternator. If it's burned, determine the cause, repair the circuit and replace the link (the vehicle won't start and/or the accessories won't work if the fusible link blows).

e) Start the engine and check the alternator for abnormal noises (a shrieking or squealing sound indicates a bad bushing).

f) Check the specific gravity of the battery electrolyte. If it's low, charge the battery (doesn't apply to maintenance free batteries).

g) Make sure the battery is fully charged (one bad cell in a battery can cause overcharging by the alternator).

h) Disconnect the battery cables (negative first, then positive). Inspect the battery posts and the cable clamps for corrosion. Clean them thoroughly if necessary (see Chapter 1).

i) Reconnect the positive cable to its terminal on the battery. Remove the fuse for the clock, if the vehicle is so equipped. With the key off and the doors closed, insert a test light between the negative battery post and the disconnected negative cable clamp.

   1) If the test light does not come on, reattach the clamp and proceed to the next Step.

   2) If the test light comes on, there is a short in the electrical system of the vehicle. The short must be repaired before the charging system can be checked.

   3) Disconnect the alternator wiring harness.

     a) If the light goes out, the alternator is bad.

     b) If the light stays on, pull each fuse until the light goes out (this will tell you which circuit is shorted).

2   Using a voltmeter, check the battery voltage with the engine off. It should be approximately 12 volts.

3   Start the engine and check the battery voltage again. It should now be approximately 14 to 15 volts.

4   Turn on the headlights. The voltage should drop, and then come back up, if the charging system is working properly.

5   If the voltage reading is less or more than the specified charging voltage, replace the voltage regulator (refer to Section 16).

15   Alternator – removal and installation

Refer to illustrations 15.2, 15.3a and 15.3b

1   Detach the cable from the negative terminal of the battery.

5

15.2   The first step in alternator removal is disconnecting all electrical leads (which will vary somewhat with alternator type and year of manufacture)

15.3a   To remove the drivebelt, loosen the alternator pivot bolt . . .

9   Check the charging voltage to verify proper operation of the alternator (see Section 14).

15.3b   . . . then loosen the adjustment bolt and slip off the belt – finally, remove the pivot and adjustment bolts and remove the alternator

2   Detach the electrical connectors from the alternator **(see illustration)**.
3   Loosen the alternator adjustment and pivot bolts and detach the drivebelt **(see illustrations)**.
4   Remove the adjustment and pivot bolts and separate the alternator from the engine.
5   If you are replacing the alternator, take the old alternator with you when purchasing a replacement unit. Make sure the new/rebuilt unit is identical to the old alternator. Look at the terminals – they should be the same in number, size and location as the terminals on the old alternator. Finally, look at the identification markings – they will be stamped in the housing or printed on a tag or plaque affixed to the housing. Make sure these numbers are the same on both alternators.
6   Many new/rebuilt alternators do not have a pulley installed, so you may have to switch the pulley from the old unit to the new/rebuilt one. When buying an alternator, find out the shop's policy regarding pulleys – some shops will perform this service free of charge.
7   Installation is the reverse of removal.
8   After the alternator is installed, adjust the drivebelt tension (see Chapter 1).

16   Alternator – brush replacement and overhaul

Refer to Illustrations 16.3 and 16.17
Note: *Due to the critical nature of the disassembly and testing of the various alternator components, it may be advisable for the home mechanic to simply replace a faulty unit with a new or factory rebuilt model. If you decide to perform the overhaul procedure yourself, make sure that replacement parts are available before proceeding.*
1   Remove the alternator and pulley (see Section 15).
2   Secure the alternator in the jaws of a vice, applying the pressure to the mounting flange.
3   Remove the through-bolts **(see illustration)** and separate the slip-ring, end frame and stator assembly from the drive-end and rotor assembly. Use a screwdriver to lever them apart and mark the relative position of the end frames to facilitate reassembly.
4   Remove the stator lead securing nuts and separate the stator from the end frame.

Early models (external regulator)

5   Extract the screws and remove the brush holder assembly.
6   Remove the heat sink from the end frame after extracting the BAT and GRD terminals and single securing screws.

Later models (internal regulator)

7   Continue disassembling, by removing the rectifier bridge, securing screw and the BAT terminal screw. Disconnect the capacitor lead and remove the rectifier bridge from the end-frame.
8   Unscrew the two securing screws and remove the brush holder and regulator. Carefully retain the insulating sleeves and washers.
9   Remove the capacitor (one screw) from the end-frame.

All models

10   If the slip ring end-frame bearing is dry or noisy when rotated, it must be replaced (not greased). Greasing will not extend its service life. Press out the old bearing and discard the oil seal. Press in the new bearing, squarely, until the bearing is flush with the outside of the endframe. Install a new oil seal. During these operations, support the endframe adequately to prevent cracking or distorting the frame.
11   Now insert a 5/16-inch Allen wrench into the socket in the center of the shaft at the drive pulley end. Using this to prevent the shaft from rotating, unscrew the pulley retaining nut and remove the washer, pulley, fan and the spacer.

16.3   An exploded view of a typical alternator

1	Slip-ring end frame	7	Rectifier bridge	14	Terminal components	21	Pulley	28	Screw
2	Rotor	8	Brush assembly	15	Seal	22	Fan	29	Screw
3	Stator	9	Brush holder	16	Plate	23	Washer	30	Screw
4	Drive end frame	10	Bearing	17	Collar	24	Washer	31	Screw
5	Regulator	11	Bearing	18	Collar	25	Nut	32	Screw
6	Diode	12	Capacitor	19	Washer	26	Nut	33	Washer
		13	Bracket	20	Through-bolt	27	Screw		

12   Remove the rotor and spacers from the drive end-frame.

13   If the bearing in the drive end-frame is dry or noisy it must be replaced. Do not grease it in the hope that this will extend its life. Access to the bearing is obtained after removing the retainer place bolts and separating the plate/seal assembly. Press the bearing out by using a piece of tube applied to the inner race and press the new one in by applying the tube to the outer race. Make sure that the slinger is correctly located and the recommended grease is applied to the bearing before installation.

14   With the alternator completely dismantled, wipe all components clean (do not use solvent on the stator or rotor windings), and examine for wear or damage. Purchase new components as necessary.

15   If the slip rings are dirty they should be cleaned by spinning the rotor and holding a piece of 400-grain abrasive paper against them. This method will avoid the creation of flat spots on the rings. If the rings are badly scored, out-of-round or otherwise damaged, the complete rotor assembly must be replaced.

16   Check the brushes for wear. If they are worn halfway or more in length, do not re-use them. Purchase new springs only if they appear weak or are distorted.

17   Reassembly is a reversal of disassembly. Observe the following points:

a)   When you are ready to assemble the halves of the alternator, push the brushes into the holder and insert a stiff wire (such as a straightened-out paper clip) through the small hole in the back of the alternator to hold the brushes in a retracted position **(see illustration)**. This will prevent them from catching on the slip rings as the alternator halves are assembled.

b)   Tighten the pulley nut securely. Take great care to position the insulating washers and sleeves correctly on the brush clip screws.

c)   Clean the brush contact surfaces before installing the slip ring end-

frame and hold the brushes up in their holders by passing a thin rod through the opening in the slip ring end-frame to permit the brushes to pass over the slip rings.

d)   Finally, make sure that the marks on the slip ring and drive end-frame (which were made before dismantling) are in alignment.

16.17   To hold the brushes in place during reassembly, insert a straightened paper clip through the hole in the end frame nearest the rotor shaft

17.4   The voltage regulator point and air gap adjustments can be checked with a feeler gauge of the specified thickness (point opening, 0.014-inch; air gap, 0.067-inch)

17   External voltage regulator – check and replacement

Refer to Illustration 17.4

1   A discharged battery will normally be due to a fault in the voltage regulator, but before testing the unit, do the following:

  a) Check the drivebelt tension.
  b) Test the condition of the battery.
  c) Check the charging circuit for loose connections and broken wires.
  d) Make sure that lights or other electrical accessories have not been switched on inadvertently.
  e) Check the generator indicator lamp for normal illumination with the ignition switched on and off, and with the engine idling and stationary.

2   Disconnect the battery ground cable. Disconnect the harness connector from the regulator.

3   Under no circumstances should the voltage regulator or field relay contacts be cleaned since any abrasive materials will destroy the contact material.

4   Voltage regulator point (0.014-inch) and air-gap (0.067-inch) adjustments can be checked with a feeler gauge of the specified thickness. Check the voltage regulator point opening of the upper contacts with the lower contacts just touching. Adjustments are made by carefully bending the upper contact arm. Check the voltage regulator air gap with the lower contacts touching and adjust it, if necessary, by turning the nylon nut **(see illustration)**.

5   The field relay point opening may be adjusted by bending the armature stop. The air gap is checked with the points just touching and is adjusted by bending the flat contact support spring. **Note:** *The field relay will normally operate satisfactorily even if the air-gap is outside the specified limits, and should not be adjusted when the system is functioning satisfactorily.*

6   If the regulator must be replaced, simply remove the mounting screws.

7   Installation is the reverse of the removal procedure. Ensure that the rubber gasket is in place on the regulator base.

18   Starting system – general information and precautions

The sole function of the starting system is to turn over the engine quickly enough to allow it to start.

The starting system consists of the battery, the starter motor, the starter solenoid and the wires connecting them. The solenoid is mounted directly on the starter motor or is a separate component located in the engine compartment.

The solenoid/starter motor assembly is installed on the lower part of the engine, next to the transmission bellhousing.

When the ignition key is turned to the Start position, the starter solenoid is actuated through the starter control circuit. The starter solenoid then connects the battery to the starter. The battery supplies the electrical energy to the starter motor, which does the actual work of cranking the engine.

The starter motor on a vehicle equipped with a manual transmission can only be operated when the clutch pedal is depressed; the starter on a vehicle equipped with an automatic transmission can only be operated when the transmission selector lever is in Park or Neutral.

Always observe the following precautions when working on the starting system:

  a) Excessive cranking of the starter motor can overheat it and cause serious damage. Never operate the starter motor for more than 15 seconds at a time without pausing to allow it to cool for at least two minutes.
  b) The starter is connected directly to the battery and could arc or cause a fire if mishandled, overloaded or shorted out.
  c) Always detach the cable from the negative terminal of the battery before working on the starting system.

19   Starter motor – testing in vehicle

Note: *Before diagnosing starter problems, make sure the battery is fully charged.*

1   If the starter motor does not turn at all when the ignition switch is operated, make sure the shift lever is in Neutral or Park.

2   Make sure that the battery is charged and that all cables, both at the battery and starter solenoid terminals, are clean and secure.

3   If the starter motor spins but the engine is not cranking, the overrunning clutch in the starter motor is slipping and the starter motor must be replaced.

4   If, when the switch is actuated, the starter motor does not operate at all but the solenoid clicks, then the problem lies with either the battery, the main solenoid contacts or the starter motor itself, or the engine is seized.

5   If the solenoid plunger cannot be heard when the switch is actuated, the battery is bad, the fusible link is burned (the circuit is open) or the solenoid itself is defective.

6   To check the solenoid, connect a jumper lead between the battery (positive terminal) and the ignition switch terminal (the small terminal) on the solenoid. If the starter motor now operates, the solenoid is OK and the problem is in the ignition switch, neutral start switch or in the wiring.

7   If the starter motor still does not operate, remove the starter/solenoid assembly for disassembly, testing and repair.

8   If the starter motor cranks the engine at an abnormally slow speed, first make sure that the battery is charged and that all terminal connections are tight. If the engine is partially seized, or has the wrong viscosity oil in it, it will crank slowly.

9   Run the engine until normal operating temperature is reached, then disconnect the coil wire from the distributor cap and ground it on the engine.

10   Connect a voltmeter positive lead to the battery positive post and then connect the negative lead to the negative post.

20.4b   Working from underneath the vehicle (placed securely on jackstands), remove the starter motor mounting bolts . . .

20.4a   Typical starter motor installation details

11   Crank the engine and take the voltmeter readings as soon as a steady figure is indicated. Do not allow the starter motor to turn for more than 15 seconds at a time. A reading of nine volts or more, with the starter motor turning at normal cranking speed, is normal. If the reading is nine volts or more but the cranking speed is slow, the motor is faulty. If the reading is less than nine volts and the cranking speed is slow, the solenoid contacts are probably burned, the starter motor is bad, the battery is discharged or there is a bad connection.

20   Starter motor – removal and installation

Refer to illustrations 20.4a, 20.4b and 20.4c
1   Detach the cable from the negative terminal of the battery.
2   Raise the vehicle and support it securely on jackstands.
3   Clearly label, then disconnect the wires from the terminals on the starter motor and solenoid.
4   Remove the starter motor mounting bolts **(see illustrations)**. Remove the starter.
5   Installation is the reverse of removal.

21   Starter motor solenoid – removal and installation

Refer to illustrations 21.3 and 21.4
1   After removing the starter/solenoid unit (see Section 20), disconnect the connector strap from the solenoid MOTOR terminal.
2   Remove the two screws which secure the solenoid housing to the end-frame assembly.
3   Twist the solenoid in a clockwise direction to disengage the flange key and then withdraw the solenoid **(see illustration)**.

5

20.4c   . . . and remove the starter and solenoid (arrow) as an assembly

21.3   To disengage the solenoid from the starter, turn it in a clockwise direction

4   Remove the nuts and washers from the solenoid terminals and then unscrew the two solenoid end-cover retaining screws and washers and pull off the end-cover **(see illustration)**.

5   Unscrew the nut washer from the battery terminal on the end-cover and remove the terminal.

6   Remove the resistor bypass terminal and contactor.

7   Remove the motor connector strap terminal and solder a new terminal in position.

8   Use a new battery terminal and install it to the end-cover. Install the bypass terminal and contactor.

9   Install the end-cover and the remaining terminal nuts.

10   Install the solenoid to the starter motor by first checking that the return spring is in position on the plunger and then insert the solenoid body into the drive housing and turn the body counter clockwise to engage the flange key.

11   Install the two solenoid securing screws and connect the MOTOR connector strap.

21.4   An exploded view of a typical starter solenoid assembly

Chapter 6   Emissions control systems

Contents

---

1   General information

Refer to illustrations 1.6a and 1.6b

To prevent pollution of the atmosphere from incompletely burned or evaporating gases, and to maintain good driveability and fuel economy, a number of emission control systems, such as the following, are used on your vehicle:

Positive Crankcase Ventilation (PCV) system
Air Injection Reactor (AIR) system
Inlet air temperature control system
*Evaporation Control System (ECS)/ Evaporative Emissions Cont
   System (EECS)*
Exhaust Gas Recirculation (EGR) system
Catalytic converter
Computer Controlled Catalytic Converter (C4) system
Computer Command Control (C3) system
Electronic Spark Timing (EST)

The Sections in this Chapter include general descriptions, checking procedures within the scope of the home mechanic and component replacement procedures (when possible) for each of the systems listed above.

Before assuming that an emissions control system is malfunctioning, check the fuel and ignition systems carefully. The diagnosis of some emission control devices requires specialized tools, equipment and training. If checking and servicing become too difficult or if a procedure is beyond your ability, consult a dealer service department.

This doesn't mean, however, that emission control systems are particularly difficult to maintain and repair. You can quickly and easily perform many checks and do most of the regular maintenance at home with common tune-up and hand tools. **Note:** *Because of a Federally mandated extended warranty which covers the emission control system components, check with your dealer about warranty coverage before working on any emissions-related systems. Once the warranty has expired, you may wish to perform some of the component checks and/or replacement procedures in this Chapter to save money.*

Pay close attention to any special precautions outlined in this Chapter. It should be noted that the illustrations of the various systems may not exactly match the system installed on your vehicle because of changes made by the manufacturer during production or from year to year. Remember – the most frequent cause of emissions problems is simply a loose or broken vacuum hose or wire, so always check the hose and wiring connections first.

The accompanying emission component location schematics **(see illustrations)** will give you a good idea where various emission devices are located on your vehicle. (Unfortunately, these charts are not available for '70's and early-to-mid '80's-era vehicles.) If there is a discrepancy between the included chart and the Vehicle Control Information (VECI) label on your vehicle, always refer to the VECI sticker. The VECI label is located in the engine compartment. This label contains important emissions specifications and adjustment information, and a vacuum hose routing and emission component location schematic. When servicing the engine or emissions systems, the VECI label in your particular vehicle should always be checked for up-to-date information.

6

1.6a   Emission control component locations – 1989 Oldsmobile-built V8 engine

☐ **COMPUTER HARNESS**
C1 Electronic Control Module (ECM)
C2 ALDL diagnostic connector
C3 "SERVICE ENGINE SOON" light
C5 ECM harness ground
C6 Fuse panel
C7 "S.E.S." lamp driver
C10 M/C dwell connector

⋮ **NOT ECM CONNECTED**
N1 Crankcase vent valve (PCV)
N2 EFE valve
N16 Fuel vapor canister valve
N17 Fuel vapor canister
N18 Anti-dieseling solenoid
N20 Anti-dieseling vac. tank

☐ **CONTROLLED DEVICES**
1   Mixture control solenoid
2   Idle load Compensator
5   Trans. Conv. Clutch connector
6   Electronic Spark Timing (EST)connector
9   Air injection divert valve
10 Air injection switching valve
12 Exh. Gas Recirc. vacuum solenoid
13 A/C compressor relay
19 Rear vacuum break solenoid
19a Rear vacuum break
20 ILC Solenoid
21 Canister purge solenoid

◯ **INFORMATION SENSORS**
A Exhaust oxygen
B Throttle position sensor
C Coolant temperature
D Vehicle speed

E ESC module
F Knock sensor
G Pressure sensor

◉ Exhaust Gas Recirculation valve

1.6b   Emission control component locations – 1990 and later Chevrolet-built V8 engine

☐ **COMPUTER HARNESS**
C1 Electronic Control Module (ECM)
C2 ALDL diagnostic connector
C3 "SERVICE ENGINE SOON" light
C5 ECM harness grounds
C6 Fuse panel
C8 Fuel pump test connector
C9 Fuel pump/ECM fuse
C10 Set timing connector

⋮ **NOT ECM CONNECTED**
N1 Crankcase vent valve (PCV)
N4 Power steering pressure switch
N8 Oil pressure switch

☐ **CONTROLLED DEVICES**
1   Fuel injector
2   Idle air control motor
3   Fuel pump relay
5   Torque converter clutch connector
6   EST distributor
6a Remote ignition coil
7   Electronic spark control module
9   AIR port solenoid
10 AIR converter solenoid
12 EGR solenoid
15 Fuel vapor canister solenoid
17 Fuel vapor canister

◉ Exhaust Gas Recirculation valve

◯ **INFORMATION SENSORS**
A Manifold absolute pressure
B Exhaust oxygen
C Throttle position

D Coolant temperature
F Vehicle speed (buffer)
G MAT (in air cleaner)
J ESC knock

CRANKCASE VENTILATION VALVE

PCV CONTROL VALVE

⇨ CLEAN AIR

→ VOLATILE OIL FUMES

--→ MIXTURE OF AIR AND FUMES

2.1 Operation of a typical Positive Crankcase Ventilation (PCV) system

2 Positive Crankcase Ventilation (PCV) system

General description

Refer to illustrations 2.1 and 2.2

1   The positive crankcase ventilation, or PCV as it is more commonly called, reduces hydrocarbon emissions by circulating fresh air through the crankcase to pick up blow-by gases, which are then re-routed through the carburetor or intake manifold to be reburned by the engine **(see illustration)**.

2   The main components of this simple system are vacuum hoses and a PCV valve which regulates the flow of gases according to engine speed and manifold vacuum **(see illustration)**.

Checking

Refer to illustrations 2.6 and 2.9

3   The PCV system can be checked for proper operation quickly and easily. This system should be checked regularly, as carbon and sludge deposited by the blow-by gases will eventually clog the PCV valve and/or system hoses. When the flow of the PCV system is reduced or stopped, common symptoms are rough idling or a reduced engine speed at idle.

4   To check for proper vacuum in the system, remove the top plate of the air cleaner and locate the small PCV filter on the inside of the air cleaner housing.

5   Disconnect the hose leading to this filter. Be careful not to break the molded fitting on the filter.

6   With the engine idling, place your thumb lightly over the end of the hose **(see illustration)**. Leave it there for about 30 seconds. You should feel a slight pull, or vacuum. The suction may be heard as your thumb is

HOSE

CONNECTOR

STUD

Ç OF ENGINE

GASKET NOTE
Install Gasket with colored adhesive side down.

HOSE CLAMP

VALVE ASSEMBLY

GROMMET

CLAMP

GROMMET

2.2 Exploded view of a typical PCV system

2.6 To check for proper vacuum, remove the top plate of the air cleaner housing, locate the small PCV filter on the inside of the air cleaner housing, detach the hose leading to this filter and, with the engine idling, place your thumb lightly over the end of the hose and leave it there for about 30 seconds – you should feel a slight suction

6

2.9   To check for a clogged PCV valve, remove the valve from the rocker arm cover and, with the engine running, place your finger over the end of the valve and feel for suction – it should be fairly strong

released. This will indicate that air is being drawn all the way through the system. If a vacuum is felt, the system is functioning properly. Check that the filter inside the air cleaner housing is not clogged or dirty. If in doubt, replace the filter with a new one, which is an inexpensive safeguard.

7   If there is very little vacuum, or none at all, at the end of the hose, the system is clogged and must be inspected further.

8   Shut off the engine and locate the PCV valve. Carefully pull it from its rubber grommet. Shake it and listen for a clicking sound. If the valve does not click freely, replace the valve with a new one.

9   Now start the engine and run it at idle speed with the PCV valve removed. Place your finger over the end of the valve and feel for suction **(see illustration)**. This should be relatively strong vacuum which will be felt immediately.

10   If little or no vacuum is felt at the PCV valve, turn off the engine and disconnect the vacuum hose from the other end of the valve. Run the engine at idle speed and check for vacuum at the end of the hose just disconnected. No vacuum at this point indicates that the vacuum hose or inlet fitting at the engine is plugged. If it is the hose which is blocked, replace it with a new one or remove it from the engine and blow it out sufficiently with compressed air. A clogged passage at the carburetor or manifold requires that the component be removed and thoroughly cleaned of carbon build-up. A strong vacuum felt going into the PCV valve, but little or no vacuum coming out of the valve, indicates a failure of the PCV valve, requiring replacement with a new one.

11   When purchasing a new PCV valve make sure it is the proper one. Each PCV valve is metered for specific engine sizes and model years. An incorrect PCV valve may pull too much or too little vacuum, possibly causing damage to the engine.

12   Information on removing and installing the PCV valve can be found in Chapter 1.

---

3   Air Injection Reactor (AIR) system

General description

Refer to illustrations 3.1, 3.3a, 3.3b, 3.4a and 3.4b

1   The Air Injection Reactor (AIR) system reduces hydrocarbons in the exhaust by pumping additional oxygen into the exhaust port of the cylinder head, exhaust manifold **(see illustration)**, or the catalytic converter. The oxygen-rich air helps combust the unburned hydrocarbons before they are expelled as exhaust.

2   The AIR system operates at all engine speeds, but it bypasses air for a short time during deceleration and at high speeds, because air added to the over-rich fuel/air mixture present in the exhaust during these conditions can cause backfiring or popping through the exhaust.

3   The AIR system consists of an engine-driven injection pump at the front of the engine, air diverter valve attached to the pump housing **(see illustration)**, the manifold and injection tubes running into each port at the exhaust manifolds, and a check valve for each hose between the pump and the injection tubes on either side of the engine **(see illustration)**.

4   Later versions of the AIR system **(see illustrations)** are under ECM control:

3.1   The Air Injection Reactor (AIR) system reduces hydrocarbons in the exhaust by pumping fresh air directly into the exhaust manifold ports of each cylinder – the fresh oxygen-rich air helps combust the unburned hydrocarbons before they are expelled as exhaust

3.3a   During deceleration and at high speeds, the air diverter valve bypasses air from the air pump and dumps it into the atmosphere to prevent backfiring or popping through the exhaust

3.3b   A typical AIR system installation on a small block V8

3.4a   Air management system operation – cold engine mode

CLOSED LOOP FUEL CONTROL

ECM

DUAL BED CATALYTIC CONVERTER

REDUCING CATALYST

OXIDIZING CATALYST

O^2 SENSOR

CHECK VALVE

CHECK VALVE

AIR SWITCHING VALVE *

ELECTRICAL SIGNALS FROM ECM

AIR PUMP

AIR CONTROL VALVE *

BY-PASS AIR TO AIR CLEANER

* TWO – VALVES OR INTEGRAL

6

3.4b   Air management system operation – warm engine mode

a) When the engine is cold, the ECM energizes an AIR control sole-
    noid. This allows air to flow to an AIR switching valve. The AIR
    switching valve is energized to direct air to the exhaust ports.
b) On a warm engine, or in "closed loop" mode, the ECM de-energizes
    the AIR switching valve, directing air between the beds of the cata-
    lytic converter. This provides extra oxygen for the oxidizing catalyst
    to decrease HC and CO levels, while keeping oxygen levels low in
    the first bed of the converter. This enables the reducing catalyst to
    effectively decrease the levels of oxides of nitrogen (NOx).
c) If the AIR control valve detects a rapid increase in manifold vacuum
    (deceleration) certain operating modes (wide open throttle, for ex-
    ample), or the ECM self-diagnostic system detects a problem in the
    C3 or C4 system, air is diverted (divert mode) to the air cleaner or
    directly to the atmosphere.
d) The divert mode prevents backfiring through the exhaust system.
    Throttle closure at deceleration creates a fuel-air mixture which is
    temporarily too rich to burn completely. This mixture, when it reach-
    es the exhaust, becomes burnable when combined with injected
    air. The next spark would ignite this mixture, causing an exhaust
    backfire, but momentary diverting of injected air prevents it.
e) The air flow and control hoses transmit pressurized air to the cata-
    lytic converter or to the exhaust ports via internal passages in the
    intake manifold, or through external firing.
f) The check valve prevents backflow of exhaust gas into the AIR dis-
    tribution system. The valve prevents backflow when the air pump
    bypasses at high speeds and loads, or when the air pump malfunc-
    tions.

Checking

Note: *The following checks generally apply to all AIR systems. However,
where ECM controlled systems differ in design from older types, diagnosis
is beyond the scope of the home mechanic.*

Refer to illustrations 3.6, 3.7 and 3.8

5   Properly installed and adjusted air injection systems are fairly reliable
and seldom cause problems. However, a malfunctioning system can
cause engine surge, backfiring and over-heated spark plugs. The air

pump is the most critical component of this system and the belt at the front
of the engine which drives the pump should be your first check. If the belt is
cracked or frayed, replace it with a new one. Check the tension of the drive
belt by pressing it with your finger. There should be about 1/2-inch of play
in the belt when pushed halfway between the pulleys. If the belt is too
loose, adjust it (see Chapter 1).
6   To check for proper air delivery from the pump, follow the hoses from
the pump to where they meet the injection tube/manifold assembly on
each side of the engine **(see illustration)**. Loosen the clamps and disconnect the hoses.

**3.6   To check for proper air delivery from the pump,
follow the hoses from the pump to where they meet the
injection tube/manifold assembly on each side of the
engine, loosen the clamps, disconnect the hoses . . .**

3.7 ... start the engine and, with your fingers or a piece of paper, verify that air is flowing out of these hoses, then accelerate the engine and note the air flow, which should increase in relation to engine speed – if it does, the pump is working satisfactorily; if it doesn't, check for crimps in the hoses, a loose drivebelt or a leaky diverter valve

3.8 To check the diverter valve, make sure all hoses are connected, start the engine, locate the muffler (the small perforated canister) on the valve, place your hand near the muffler outlet holes and verify that no air is escaping while the engine is idling, then accelerate the engine and quickly let off the throttle – a momentary blast of air should be felt discharging through the diverter valve muffler

7   Start the engine and, with your fingers or a piece of paper, verify that air is flowing out of these hoses (**see illustration**). Accelerate the engine and observe the air flow, which should increase in relation to engine speed. If this is the case, the pump is working satisfactorily. If air flow was not present, or did not increase, check for crimps in the hoses, proper drivebelt tension and for a leaking diverter valve, which can be heard with the pump operating.

8   To check the diverter valve, sometimes called the "gulp' valve or anti-backfire valve, make sure all hoses are connected and start the engine. Locate the muffler on the valve, which is a canister unit with holes in it (**see illustration**).

9   Being careful not to touch any of the moving engine components, place your hand near the muffler outlet holes and check that no air is escaping with the engine at idle speed. Now have an assistant depress the accelerator pedal to accelerate the engine and then quickly let off the pedal. A momentary blast of air should be felt discharging through the diverter valve muffler.

10   If no air discharge was felt, disconnect the smaller vacuum hose at the diverter valve. Place your finger over the end of the hose and again have your assistant depress the accelerator and let it off. As the engine is decelerating, a vacuum should be felt. If vacuum was felt, replace the diverter valve with a new one. If no vacuum was felt, the vacuum hose or engine vacuum source is plugged, requiring a thorough cleaning to eliminate the problem.

11   Two check valves are located on the air manifold assembly. Their function is to prevent exhaust gases from flowing back into the air pump. To find out if they are functioning properly, disconnect the two air supply hoses where they attach to the check valves. Start the engine and, being careful not to touch any moving engine components, place your hand or a piece of paper over the outlet of the check valve (be careful – if exhaust gas leaks out, it will be hot). No exhaust should flow out of the check valve. The valve can be further checked by turning off the engine, allowing it to cool, and orally blowing through the check valve (toward the air manifold). Then attempt to blow through it in the other direction. If the valve is allowing you to blow through it backwards, it is faulty and should be replaced.

12   Another check for this system is for leaks in the hose connection and/or hoses themselves. Leaks can often be detected by sound or feel with the pump in operation. If a leak is suspected, use a soapy water solution to verify this. Pour or sponge the solution of detergent and water on the

hoses and connections. With the pump running, bubbles will form if a leak exists. The air delivery hoses are of a special design to withstand engine temperatures, so if they are replaced make sure the new hoses are of the proper standards.

Component replacement
Air pump

13   As mentioned earlier, some air pumps share a common drivebelt with the alternator while others use their own belt. The particular layout on the vehicle being serviced will affect the removal and installation procedure somewhat.

14   Disconnect the air delivery hoses at the air pump. Note the position of each hose for assembly.

15   Disconnect the vacuum source hose at the diverter valve.

16   Compress the drivebelt to keep the air pump pulley from turning, and remove the bolts and washers securing the pulley to the pump.

17   To get some slack in the belt, loosen the alternator adjusting bolt and the pivot bolt. Push the alternator inward until the belt and air pump pulley can be removed from the pump.

18   Remove the bolts which secure the air pump to its brackets and then lift the pump and diverter valve assembly from the engine compartment. On some models it may be necessary to first remove the pulley.

19   If the diverter valve is to be installed onto the new air pump, remove the bolts securing it to the pump and separate the two components.

20   Check the pump for evidence that exhaust gas has entered it, indicating a failure of one or both check valves.

21   Install the diverter valve to the new air pump using a new gasket. Tighten the attaching bolts securely.

22   Install the air pump to its engine mounting brackets with the attaching bolts loose. The exception to this is on models where the mounting bolts are inaccessible with the pulley installed. In this case, the pump mounting bolts should be tightened securely at this point.

23   Install the pump pulley with the bolts, only hand tight at this time.

24   Place the drive belt into position on the air pump pulley and adjust the belt by gently prying on the alternator until about 1/2-inch of play is felt in the belt when pushed with your fingers half-way between the pulleys. Tighten the alternator bolts, keeping the belt tension at this point.

25   Keep the pump pulley from turning by compressing the drive belt and tighten the pulley bolts securely.

6

3.36a   To remove the injector tubes, detach the air delivery hoses at the manifold check valves, loosen the threaded connectors on the exhaust manifold at each exhaust port, slide the connectors up on the injection tubes so the threads are out of the exhaust manifold and pull the injection tube/air manifold assembly from the engine exhaust manifold (on some model years, the injection tube extensions leading inside the engine may come out with the assembly)

3.36b   Some models use a head-to-head type of AIR manifold, which injects air into passages in the cylinder head (368 cu. in. engine shown)

26   Connect the hoses to the air pump and diverter valve. Make sure the connections are tight.
27   Tighten the mounting bolts for the pump securely.
28   Check the operation of the air pump as outlined previously.

Diverter valve

29   Disconnect the vacuum signal line and air delivery hoses at the diverter valve. Note the position of each for assembly.
30   Remove the bolts which secure the valve to the air pump and remove the diverter valve from the engine compartment.
31   When purchasing a new diverter or bypass valve, keep in mind that although many of the valves are similar in appearance, each is designed to meet particular requirements of various engines. Therefore, be sure to install the correct valve.
32   Install the new diverter valve to the air pump or pump extension with a new gasket. Tighten the securing bolts.
33   Connect the air delivery and vacuum source hoses and check the operation of the valve as outlined previously.

Air manifold and/or injection tubes

Refer to illustrations 3.36a, 3.36b and 3.38

34   Due to the high temperatures at this area, the connections at the exhaust manifold may be difficult to loosen. Commercial penetrating oil applied to the thread of the injection tubes may help in the removal procedure.
35   Disconnect the air delivery hoses at the manifold check valves.
36   Loosen the threaded connectors on the exhaust manifold at each exhaust port **(see illustration)**. Slide the connectors upwards on the injection tubes so the threads are out of the exhaust manifold. On models with a AIR manifold running between the cylinder heads, remove the accessories on the front of the engine that are in the way, then remove the clamp bolt and clamp from the front of each cylinder head **(see illustration)**.
37   Pull the injection tube/air manifold assembly from the engine exhaust manifold (or cylinder heads) and out of the engine compartment. Depending on the model year, injection tube extensions leading inside the engine may come out with the assembly.
38   On models where the extension tubes remain inside the exhaust manifold, they must be pressed out after the exhaust manifold is removed

3.38   External extension tubes must be pressed out after the exhaust manifold is removed from the engine

from the engine **(see illustration)**. On models with the head-to-head type of AIR manifold, remove the seals from the holes in the cylinder heads and install new ones.
39   If the exhaust manifold was removed from the engine to clean or replace the extensions, reinstall the manifold with extensions to the engine, using a new gasket. Tighten the bolts to the torque listed in the Chapter 2 Specifications Section.
40   Thread each of the injection tube connectors loosely into the exhaust manifold, using an anti-seize compound on the threads. After each of the connectors is sufficiently started, tighten each securely.
41   Connect the air supply hoses to the check valves.
42   Start the engine and check for leaks as previously described.

3.44   To remove the check valve from the air manifold assembly, use two wrenches (one as a backup) on the threaded fittings – be sure that you don't bend or twist the delicate manifold or injection tubes while loosening the check valve

4.2a   Exploded view of a typical vacuum servo type EFE assembly

4.2b   A typical Thermostatic Air Cleaner (THERMAC) system – this design draws warm air from the exhaust manifold directly into the carburetor

4.5   Typical manifold heat valve (or heat riser, as it's known on early models)

Check valve

Refer to illustration 3.44

43   Disconnect the air supply hose at the check valve.

44   Using two wrenches on the flats provided, remove the check valve from the air manifold assembly **(see illustration)**. Be careful not to bend or twist the delicate manifold or injection tubes as this is done.

45   Installation is a reversal of the removal procedure.

---

4   Inlet air temperature control system

General description

Refer to illustrations 4.2a, 4.2b, and 4.5

1   Various versions of this system go by different names, but their purpose is always the same – to improve engine efficiency and reduce hydrocarbon emissions during the initial warm-up period of the vehicle.

2   Two basic methods are used to achieve this goal:

a)   Forced air pre-heat system: Some form of exhaust valve is incorporated inside the exhaust pipe **(see illustration)** to recirculate warm exhaust gases which are then used to pre-heat the carburetor and choke.

b)   Warm air from the exhaust manifold is routed into the air cleaner, then through the carburetor **(see illustration)**.

3   This system has its greatest effect on engine performance and emissions output during the first few miles of driving (depending on the outside temperature). Once the engine reaches its normal operating temperature, the flapper valves in the exhaust pipe and air cleaner open, allowing for normal engine operation.

4   Because of this cold-engine-only function, it is important to periodically check this system to prevent poor cold engine performance and overheating of the fuel mixture once the engine has reached operating temperatures. If either the exhaust heat valve or air cleaner valve sticks in the 'no heat' position, the engine will run poorly, stall and waste gas until it has warmed up on its own. A valve sticking in the 'heat' position causes the engine to run as if it is out of tune, because of the constant flow of hot air to the carburetor.

5   The main component of the initial system is a heat valve **(see illustration)** inside the exhaust pipe on the right side of the engine (called a heat

6

4.10   Typical Early Fuel Evaporation (EFE) system uses manifold vacuum to open and close the heat valve

riser on early models). In 1975, General Motors introduced a new inlet air temperature control system known as the Early Fuel Evaporation (EFE) system. It also has a valve in the exhaust pipe, but uses manifold vacuum to actuate the valve. Instead of a spring and weight, an actuator and Thermal Vacuum Switch TVS control the heat valve. A Thermostatic Air Cleaner (TAC or THERMAC) consisting of a temperature sensor, vacuum diaphragm and heat stove completes the system. Initial checking procedures can be found in Chapter 1.

Checking
Forced air pre-heat system

6   The conventional heat riser, installed on cars built through 1974, should be checked often for free operation. Because of the high exhaust temperatures and its location, which is open to the elements, corrosion frequently keeps the valve from operating freely, or even freezes it in position.

7   To check the heat riser operation, locate it on the exhaust manifold (it can be identified by an external weight and spring), and with the engine cold, try moving the counterweight. The valve should move freely with no binding. Now have an assistant start the engine (still cold) while the counterweight is observed. The valve should move to the closed position and then slowly open as the engine warms.

8   A stuck or binding heat riser valve can usually be loosened by soaking the valve shaft with solvent as the counterweight is moved back and forth. Light taps with a hammer may be necessary to free a tightly stuck valve. If this proves unsuccessful, the heat riser must be replaced with a new one after disconnecting it from the exhaust pipe.

Early Fuel Evaporation (EFE) System

Refer to illustrations 4.10 and 4.11

9   In 1975, General Motors introduced a replacement for the heat riser known as the Early Fuel Evaporation (EFE) system. The EFE system performs the same function as the heat riser but uses manifold vacuum to open and close the heat valve. Some vehicles are equipped with an electrical type EFE, which uses a heater grid located underneath the primary base of the carburetor.

10   To check the EFE system, locate the actuator and rod assembly **(see illustration)** which is located on a bracket attached to the right exhaust manifold. Have an assistant start the engine (it must be cold). Observe the movement of the actuator rod which leads to the heat valve inside the exhaust pipe. It should immediately operate the valve to the closed position. If it does, the system is operating correctly.

11   If the actuator rod doesn't move, disconnect the vacuum hose at the actuator and place your thumb over the open end **(see illustration)**. With the engine cold and at idle, you should feel a suction, indicating proper

vacuum. If there is vacuum at this point, replace the actuator with a new one.

12   If there is no vacuum in the line, this is an indication that either the hose is crimped or plugged, or the thermal vacuum switch threaded into the water outlet is not functioning properly. Replace the hose or switch as necessary.

13   To make sure the Early Fuel Evaporation System is disengaging once the engine has warmed, continue to observe the actuating rod as the engine reaches normal operating temperature (approximately 180-degrees depending on engine size). The rod should again move, indicating the valve is in the open position.

14   If after the engine has warmed, the valve does not open, disconnect the vacuum hose at the actuator and check for vacuum with your thumb. If there is no vacuum, replace the actuator. If there is vacuum, replace the TVS switch on the water outlet housing.

4.11   If the actuator rod is not working properly, you can check the EFE system by disconnecting the vacuum hose at the actuator and placing your thumb over the open end – with the engine cold and at idle, you should feel a suction indicating proper vacuum – if you do, replace the actuator

Thermostatic Air Cleaner (TAC/THERMAC)

15   THERMAC components can be quickly and easily checked for proper operation, (see Chapter 1 for routine checking procedures and illustrations).

16   With the engine off, observe the damper door inside the air cleaner snorkel. If this is difficult because of the direction in which the snorkel is pointing, use a small mirror. The valve should be open (all air flows through the snorkel and none through the exhaust manifold hot-air duct at the underside of the air cleaner housing).

17   Have an assistant start the engine while you observe the flapper door inside the snorkel. With the engine cold and at idle, the damper door should close off all air from the snorkel, allowing heated air from the exhaust manifold to enter the air cleaner intake. As the engine warms to operating temperature, the damper door should move, allowing outside air through the snorkel to be included in the mixture. Eventually, the door should recede to the point where most of the incoming air is through the snorkel and not the exhaust manifold passage.

18   If the damper door does not close off the snorkel to outside air when the cold engine is first started, disconnect the vacuum hose at the snorkel vacuum motor, place your thumb over the hose end and check for vacuum. If there is vacuum to the motor, verify that the damper door and link are not frozen or binding within the air cleaner snorkel. Replace the vacuum motor if the hose routing is correct and the damper door moves freely.

4.35   To replace the air cleaner vacuum motor, drill out the two spot welds which secure the motor retaining strap, remove the attaching strap, lift up the motor, then cock it to one side to unhook the linkage at the control damper assembly

19   If there is no vacuum to the motor in the above test, check the hoses for cracks, crimps or disconnections. If the hoses are clear and in good condition, replace the temperature sensor inside the air cleaner housing.

Component replacement

Actuator and rod assembly

20   Disconnect the vacuum hose from the actuator.
21   Remove the two nuts which attach the actuator to the bracket.
22   Disconnect the rod from the heat valve and remove the actuator and rod from the engine compartment.
23   Installation is the reverse of removal.

Exhaust heat valve

24   Remove the crossover exhaust pipe.
25   Disconnect the actuating rod from the heat valve.
26   Remove the valve from inside the exhaust pipe.
27   Installation is the reverse of removal.

Thermal vacuum switch (TVS)

28   Drain the engine coolant until the fluid level is below the engine water outlet (thermostat) housing. (On some of the V6's, the TVS is located on the engine manifold).
29   Disconnect the hoses from the TVS switch. Note their positions for reassembly.
30   Using a suitable wrench, remove the TVS switch.
31   Apply a soft setting sealant uniformly to the threads of the new TVS switch. Make sure that none of the sealant gets on the sensor end of the switch.
32   Install the switch and tighten it securely.
33   Connect the vacuum hoses to the switch in their original positions and add coolant as necessary.

Air cleaner vacuum motor

Refer to illustration 4.35

34   Remove the air cleaner assembly from the engine and disconnect the vacuum hose from the motor.
35   Drill out the two spot welds **(see illustration)** which secure the vacuum motor retaining strap to the snorkel tube.
36   Remove the motor attaching strap.
37   Lift up the motor, cocking it to one side to unhook the motor linkage at the control damper assembly.
38   To install, drill a 7/64-inch hole in the snorkel tube at the center of the retaining strap.
39   Insert the vacuum motor linkage into the control damper assembly.
40   Using the sheet metal screw supplied with the motor service kit, attach the motor and retaining strap to the snorkel. Make sure the sheet metal screw does not interfere with the operation of the damper door.

41   Connect the vacuum hose to the motor and install the air cleaner assembly.

Air cleaner temperature sensor

42   Remove the air cleaner from the engine and disconnect the vacuum hoses at the sensor.
43   Carefully note the position of the sensor. The new sensor must be installed in exactly the same position.
44   Pry up the tabs on the sensor retaining clip and remove the sensor and clip from the air cleaner.
45   Install the new sensor with a new gasket in the same position as the old one.
46   Press the retaining clip on the sensor, taking care not to damage the control mechanism in the center of the sensor.
47   Connect the vacuum hoses and install the air cleaner on the engine.

---

5   Evaporation Control System (ECS)/Evaporative Emission Control System (EECS)

Refer to illustrations 5.4a and 5.4b

General description

1   The Evaporation Control System is one of the most trouble-free systems in the emissions network. Its function is to reduce hydrocarbon emissions. Basically, this is a closed fuel system which reroutes wasted fuel back to the gas tank and stores fuel vapors instead of venting them to the atmosphere.
2   Because it has few moving parts, the ECS/EECS system requires no periodic maintenance other than replacement of the filter in the bottom the the charcoal canister at the recommended intervals.
3   The strong smell of fuel vapors is a tip-off that the system is not operating properly. So is engine starvation induced by lack of fuel during acceleration.
4   A pressure/vacuum gasoline filler cap must be used on vehicles equipped with ECS/EECS. A standard cap can render the system ineffective and possibly even collapse the fuel tank. The ECS/EECS system consists of a special gas tank with fill limiters and vent connections, a charcoal canister with an integral purge valve and a filter which stores vapor from the fuel tank to be burned by the carburetor, a carburetor bowl vent valve and the system of hoses connecting these components **(see illustrations)**.

5.4a   Typical fuel tank hose routing for the Evaporation Control System (ECS)

6

5.4b Typical underhood hose routing for the Evaporation Control System (ECS)

5   Earlier versions of the purge valve are regulated by coolant temperature: at coolant temperatures below the switching point, canister purge is controlled by an internal orifice in the switch. At coolant temperatures above the switching point, the switch opens, allowing canister purge to be controlled by manifold vacuum from the carburetor port. Later versions of the EECS are equipped with a canister purge valve under ECM control.
6   With the engine cold and at room temperature, disconnect the fuel tank line at the charcoal canister (on all models, the canister is located inside the engine compartment). Each of the hose connections should be labeled. Make sure you label them yourself if they're not already marked, to prevent improper assembly.
7   As this hose is disconnected, check for the presence of liquid fuel in the line. Fuel in this vapor hose is an indication that the vent controls or pressure-vacuum relief valve in the gas cap are not functioning properly.
8   Hook up a pressure suction device on the end of the fuel vapor line. Apply 15 psi pressure to the line and check for excessive loss of pressure.
9   Check for a fuel vapor smell in the engine compartment and around the gas tank.
10   Remove the fuel filler cap and check for pressure in the gas tank.
11   If there is a large loss of pressure or a fuel odor, inspect all lines for leaks or deterioration.
12   With the fuel filler cap removed, apply pressure again and check for obstructions in the vent line.
13   To check the purge valve built into the canister, start the engine, allow it to reach normal operating temperatures, and disconnect the vacuum signal line running from the engine to the canister. With your thumb over the end of the hose, raise the engine speed to about 1500 rpm and check for vacuum. If there is no vacuum signal, check the EGR operation as described in this Chapter. The vacuum signal for the canister and the EGR valve originate from the same source.
14   The purge line to the charcoal canister functions with the PCV vacuum source, so if there is no vacuum when this hose is disconnected from the canister, check the PCV valve vacuum.
15   Checking an ECM-controlled purge valve is beyond the scope of the home mechanic.

Charcoal canister and filter – replacement

16   Chapter 1 contains all information concerning the servicing of the Evaporation Control System, in particular the replacement of the canister filter.

6   Exhaust Gas Recirculation (EGR) system

General description

Refer to illustrations 6.1, 6.2, 6.3a and 6.3b

1   The EGR system **(see illustration)** is used to reduce oxides of nitrogen (NOx) from the exhaust. Formation of these pollutants takes place at very high temperatures; consequently, it occurs during the peak temperature period of the combustion process. To reduce peak temperatures, and thus the formation of NOx, a small amount of exhaust gas is taken from the exhaust system and recirculated in the combustion cycle.

6.1 A typical Exhaust Gas Recirculation (EGR) system

6.2   You can't see much of the EGR exhaust passages, because they are cast into the intake manifold

6.3a   Typical positive backpressure EGR valve diaphragm plate design

6.3b   Typical negative backpressure EGR valve diaphragm plate design

2   To tap this exhaust supply without an extensive array of pipes and connections in the exhaust system, additional exhaust passages are cast into the intricate runner system of the intake manifold **(see illustration)**. Because of this arrangement, most of the EGR routing components are hidden from view under the manifold.

3   Two basic types of EGR valves are used – Vacuum Modulated EGR and Exhaust Back Pressure EGR. When Vacuum Modulated EGR is used, the amount of exhaust gas admitted to the intake manifold depends on a vacuum signal (ported vacuum) which is controlled by throttle position. When the throttle is closed (idle or deceleration), there is no vacuum signal to the EGR valve because the vacuum port is above the closed throttle valve. As the throttle valve is opened, a ported vacuum signal is supplied to the EGR valve, admitting exhaust gas to the intake manifold. The Exhaust Backpressure Modulated EGR uses a transducer located inside the EGR valve to control the operating vacuum signal. The vacuum signal is generated in the same manner as for the Vacuum Modulated EGR system. The integral transducer uses exhaust gas pressure to control an air bleed within the valve to modify the vacuum signal from the carburetor. Two types of backpressure EGR valves are used; positive backpressure **(see illustration)** and negative backpressure **(see illustration)**. The latest versions of the EGR valve are ECM-controlled. EGR flow is regulated by an ECM-controlled solenoid in the vacuum line. The ECM uses data from various combinations of sensors – such as the coolant temperature sensor, throttle position sensor, MAP sensor and distributor signal – to regulate the solenoid.

4   The EGR system does not recirculate gases when the engine is idling or decelerating. The system is also regulated by the thermal vacuum switch, which does not allow the system to operate until the engine has reached normal operating temperature.

5   Common engine problems associated with the EGR system are: rough idling or stalling when at idle, rough engine performance upon light throttle application and stalling on deceleration.

Checking

Refer to illustrations 6.6 and 6.13

6   Locate the EGR valve. The location varies from year to year, but on most models it is located on the intake manifold, adjacent to the right side of the carburetor **(see illustration)**. Initial checking, with illustrations, can be found in Chapter 1.

7   Place your finger under the EGR valve and push upwards on the diaphragm plate. The diaphragm should move freely from the open to the closed position. If it doesn't, replace the EGR valve.

8   Now start the engine and run it at idle speed. With your finger, manually depress the EGR diaphragm. If the valve or adjacent accessories are hot, wear gloves to prevent burning your fingers. When the diaphragm is pressed (valve closed to recirculate exhaust), the engine should lose speed, stumble or even stall. If the engine does not change speed, the EGR passages should be checked for blockage. This will require that the intake manifold be removed (see Chapter 2). Any further checking of the

6.6   On most models, the EGR valve is located on the intake manifold, adjacent to the carburetor

positive backpressure type EGR valve will require special tools, so a questionable valve is best replaced with a new one at this point. Negative backpressure type EGR valves can be further tested as follows:

9   Allow the engine to reach its normal operating temperature. Have an assistant depress the accelerator slightly and hold the engine at a constant speed above idle.

10   Detach the vacuum signal line at the EGR valve and verify that the diaphragm plate moves downward and engine speed increases.

11   Reattach the vacuum line to the valve. The diaphragm plate should move upward with a decrease in engine speed.

12   If the diaphragm doesn't move, make sure the engine is at its normal operating temperature. Repeat the test if in doubt.

6.13   If a check of the EGR valve reveals that it's not working, verify that vacuum is reaching the EGR valve: detach the vacuum hose from the valve and, with the engine running slightly above idle, place your thumb over the end of the hose – if there is vacuum, replace the EGR valve; if there isn't, trace the vacuum hose to its source and look for cracks, breaks or blockage

13   To verify that vacuum is reaching the EGR valve, detach the vacuum hose at the valve and, with the engine running and the throttle slightly opened, verify that there's vacuum at the end of the hose with your thumb **(see illustration)**. If there is vacuum, replace the EGR valve with a new one. If there is no vacuum signal, follow the vacuum hose to its source, inspecting for disconnections, cracks, breaks or blockage in the lines.

14   On all but a few early models, the EGR system uses some kind of vacuum valve to regulate the amount of exhaust gas admitted to the intake air-fuel mixture. Some of the more common valves are the Vacuum Controlled Valve (VCV), which regulates the EGR in accordance with engine intake vacuum; the Thermal Vacuum Switch (TVS) which regulates EGR valve operation in relation to engine temperature; and the electronically operated, ECM-controlled solenoid, which also acts in accordance with engine coolant temperature. Early models without this type of regulation have the vacuum hose routed directly to the carburetor.

15   This vacuum switch opens as the coolant temperature increases, allowing vacuum to reach the EGR valve. The exact temperature varies from year to year, but is indicative of the normal operating temperature of the particular engine.

16   To test a vacuum-actuated switch, check the vacuum signal with a vacuum gauge (if the switch on your vehicle is a solenoid under ECM control, diagnosis should be left to a dealer).

17   Disconnect the vacuum hose at the EGR valve, connect the vacuum gauge to the disconnected end of the hose and start the idle, then have an assistant depress the accelerator slightly and note this reading. As the accelerator is depressed, the vacuum reading should increase.

18   If the gauge does not respond to the throttle opening, disconnect the hose which leads from the carburetor to the vacuum switch. Repeat the test with the vacuum gauge attached to the vacuum hose end of the switch. If the vacuum gauge responds to accelerator opening, the vacuum switch is defective and should be replaced with a new one.

Component replacement
EGR valve
19   If the gauge still does not respond to an increase in throttle opening, check for a plugged hose or a problem with the carburetor.
20   Disconnect the vacuum hose at the EGR valve.
21   Remove the nuts or bolts which secure the valve to the intake manifold.
22   Lift the EGR valve from the engine.
23   Clean the mounting surfaces of the EGR valve. Remove all traces of gasket material.
24   Place the new EGR valve, with a new gasket, on the intake manifold. Install the spacer, if used. Tighten the attaching bolts or nuts.
25   Connect the vacuum signal hose.

Thermal vacuum switch
26   Drain the engine coolant until the coolant level is beneath the switch.
27   Disconnect the vacuum hose at the EGR valve, connect the vacuum gauge to the disconnected end of the hose and start the engine, noting their positions for reassembly.
28   Using a suitable wrench, remove the switch.
29   When installing the switch, apply thread sealer to the threads, being careful not to allow the sealant to touch the bottom of the sensor.
30   Install the switch and tighten it securely.

ECM-controlled EGRs
31   Diagnosis of ECM-controlled EGRs is beyond the scope of the home mechanic.

---

7   Catalytic converter

General description
1   The catalytic converter is an emission control device added to the exhaust system to reduce hydrocarbon and carbon monoxide pollutants. This converter contains beads which are coated with a catalytic substance containing platinum and palladium.
2   It is imperative that only unleaded gasoline be used in a vehicle equipped with a catalytic converter. Unleaded fuel reduces combustion chamber deposits, corrosion and prevents lead contamination of the catalyst.
3   Periodic maintenance of the catalytic converter is not required; however, if the car is raised for other service it is advisable to inspect the overall condition of the catalytic converter and related exhaust components.
4   If the catalytic converter has been ruled by an official inspection station to be ineffective, the converter can be replaced with a new one, or the coated beads drained and replaced. Physical damage and the use of leaded fuels are the main causes of a malfunctioning catalytic converter.
5   It should be noted that the catalytic converter can reach very high temperatures in operation. Because of this, any work performed to the converter or in the general area where it is located should be done only after the system has sufficiently cooled. Also, caution should be exercised when lifting the vehicle with a hoist, as the converter can be damaged if the lifting pads are not properly positioned.
6   There are no functional tests which the home mechanic can make to determine if the catalytic converter is performing its task.

Component replacement
Catalytic converter
Refer to illustration 7.8
7   Raise the car and support it firmly with jackstands. The converter and exhaust system should be cool before proceeding.
8   Disconnect the converter at the front and rear **(see illustration)**. On

7.8   An exploded view of a typical catalytic converter assembly

7.17   A typical catalytic converter service fill plug assembly

13   Bead replacement is more easily done with the converter removed from the car (see above).

14   With the converter on a workbench, remove the pressed fill plug. This is done by driving a small chisel between the converter shell and the fill plug lip. Deform the lip until pliers can be used to remove the plug. Be careful not to damage the converter shell surface where the plug seals.

15   Once the plug is removed, drain the beads into a container for disposal. Shake the converter vigorously to remove all beads.

16   To fill the catalytic converter with new beads, raise the front of the converter to approximately 45-degrees and pour the beads through the fill hole. Tapping lightly on the converter seam with a hammer as the beads are poured in will help to settle them. Continue tapping and pouring until the converter is full.

17   A special service fill plug will be required to replace the stock one which was removed. This consists of a bridge, bolt and fill plug (**see illustration**) and is installed as follows:

    a) Install the bolt into the bridge and put the bridge into the converter opening. Move it back and forth to loosen the beads across the opening (bolt centered).

    b) Remove the bolt from the bridge and put the washer and fill plug, dished side out, over the bolt.

    c) While holding the fill plug and washer against the bolt head, thread the bolt four or five turns into the bridge.

    d) After fill plug has seated against the converter housing, tighten the bolt to 28 ft-lbs.

18   Install the converter, start the engine and check for leaks.

most models a flange is used with four bolts and nuts to secure the converter to its mating exhaust pipes. If the fasteners are frozen in place due to high temperatures and corrosion, apply a penetrating oil liberally and allow it to soak in. As a last resort, the fasteners will have to be carefully cut off with a hacksaw.

9   Gently separate the inlet and outlet converter flanges from the exhaust pipes and remove the converter from under the vehicle.

10   Installation is a reversal of the removal process; however, always use new nuts and bolts.

Catalyst

Refer to illustration 7.17

11   Two types of catalytic converters are used on the vehicles covered in this manual. The monolith converter has coated rods which cannot be serviced. If failure occurs, the entire converter must be replaced with a new one. The catalyst in bead type converters can be changed by draining and filling the beads through a plug at the bottom of the converter.

12   With specialized equipment, the beads can be replaced with the converter still positioned under the car. This is definitely a job for a dealer who has the equipment and training necessary to perform this operation.

8   Computer Controlled Catalytic Converter (C4)/ Computer Command Control (C3 or CCC) system and information sensors

General description

Refer to illustrations 8.1a and 8.1b

1   The C4 system first became available on 1980 models. In 1981, the C4 system was replaced by the Computer Command Control (CCC or C3) System. Both systems control exhaust emissions while retaining driveability by maintaining a continuous interaction between all of the emissions systems on your vehicle (**see illustrations**). A malfunction in the

6

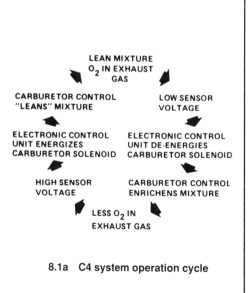

8.1a   C4 system operation cycle

8.1b   C4 system component diagram

8.5   An exploded view of a typical oxygen sensor installation on a 5.0-liter V8 – on V6 engines, the sensor is located just behind the junction of the two exhaust manifold pipes

system is signaled by a Check Engine or Service Engine Soon light on the dash. On the C4 system, the Check Engine light will remain on as long as the engine is running. With the CCM diagnostic system activated, this same lamp will flash the trouble code related to the cause of the malfunction. On the C3 system, the Check Engine or Service Engine Soon light will remain on until the problem is identified and repaired and the code is erased from memory. In other words, the C3 system stores trouble codes in its memory, but the C4 system doesn't.

2   The C4/C3 System requires special tools for maintenance and repair, so most service work on it should be left to your dealer or a qualified technician. Although it seems complex, the system is easily understood in terms of its various components and their functions.

Electronic control module (ECM)

3   The electronic control module (ECM) is essentially a small on-board computer (located under the dash on most vehicles) which monitors numerous engine functions and controls many engine-related systems. The ECM contains a Programmable Read Only Memory (PROM) calibration unit which tailors each ECM's performance to conform to the vehicle. The PROM is programmed with the vehicle's particular design, weight, axle ratio, etc., and cannot be used in another ECM in a car which differs in any way.

4   The ECM receives continuous data from the various information sensors, processes it in accordance with PROM instructions, then sends electronic signals to system components, modifying their performance (see next Section).

Oxygen (02) sensor

Refer to illustration 8.5

5   The oxygen sensor (**see illustration**) is mounted in the exhaust pipe, upstream of the catalytic converter. It monitors the exhaust stream and sends information to the ECM on how much oxygen is present. The oxygen level is determined by how rich or lean the fuel mixture is.

Mixture Control (M/C) solenoid

6   The M/C solenoid controls the fuel flow through the carburetor idle and main metering circuits. The solenoid cycles ten times per second, constantly adjusting the fuel/air mixture. The ECM energizes the solenoid to keep emissions within limits based on information it receives from the oxygen sensor.

Coolant temperature sensor

7   This sensor monitors coolant temperature and sends this information to the ECM. The ECM alters the air fuel ratio accordingly for conditions

such as cold starting. The ECM also performs various switching functions on the EGR, EFE and AIR management systems, depending on engine temperature. This feedback from the coolant sensor can also activate the hot temperature light.

Pressure sensors

Refer to illustrations 8.9a and 8.9b

8   The ECM uses information from the Barometric Pressure Sensor (BARO) and Manifold Absolute Pressure (MAP) sensor, or the Differential Pressure Sensor (DPS or VAC) to adjust engine performance. The BARO sensor senses ambient pressure changes that occur as a result of changes in the weather and the altitude of the vehicle. It then sends an electronic signal to the ECM that is used to adjust the air fuel ratio and spark timing.

9   The MAP or DPS/VAC sensor (**see illustrations**) measures changes in manifold pressure and provides this information to the ECM. The pressure changes reflect the need for adjustments in air-fuel mixture, spark timing (EST), etc., that are needed to maintain good vehicle performance under various driving conditions.

10   The DPS also measures engine load. It produces a low voltage when manifold vacuum is low and a high voltage when manifold vacuum is high. It's called a differential pressure sensor because it measures the difference between atmospheric pressure and manifold pressure.

8.9a   Typical MAP sensor installation details (on some vehicles, the MAP sensor is located on the firewall or behind the glovebox – check the VECI label for the location of the MAP sensor on your vehicle)

8.9b   A typical firewall installation of a pressure differential (DPS or VAC) sensor assembly – check the VECI label for the location of the DPS/VAC sensor on your vehicle

Manifold Air Temperature (MAT) sensor

11   The MAT sensor, mounted on the intake manifold ahead of the throttle body, measures the temperature of the incoming air/fuel mixture and sends this information to the ECM. When it senses a low temperature, its resistance is high. When it senses a high temperature, its resistance is low.

Throttle position sensor (TPS)

12   Mounted on the carburetor body, the TPS is actuated by the throttle plate and sends a variable voltage signal to the ECM: when the throttle plate is closed, the voltage signal is low, but as the throttle plate is opened, the voltage increases. The ECM uses this voltage signal to recognize throttle position.

Idle speed control (ISC)

13   The idle speed control maintains a low idle speed without stalling under changing conditions. The ECM controls the idle speed control motor on the carburetor to adjust the idle.

Electronic spark timing (EST)

14   The High Energy Ignition (HEI) distributor used with the C4/C3 system does not use centrifugal or vacuum advance. Spark timing is controlled electronically by the ECM, except under certain conditions, such as cranking the engine.

Transmission Converter Clutch/Torque Converter Clutch (TCC)

15   The ECM controls an electric solenoid mounted in the automatic transmission. When the vehicle reaches a specified speed, the ECM energizes the solenoid and allows the torque converter to mechanically couple the engine to the transmission. When operating conditions indicate the transmission should operate as a normal, fluid-coupled transmission (deceleration, passing, etc.), the solenoid is de-energized. The transmission also returns to normal (fluid-coupled) automatic operation when the brake pedal is depressed.

Air Injection Reactor (AIR)

16   When the engine is cold, the ECM energizes an air switching valve which allows air to flow to the exhaust ports to lower carbon monoxide (CO) and hydrocarbon (HC) levels in the exhaust.

Exhaust gas recirculation (EGR)

17   The ECM controls ported vacuum to the EGR with a solenoid valve. When the engine is cold, the solenoid is energized to block vacuum to the EGR valve until the engine is warm.

Evaporative emission system (ECS/EECS)

18   When the engine is cold or idling, the ECM solenoid blocks vacuum to the valve at the top of the charcoal canister. When the engine is warm and at a specified rpm, the ECM de-energizes the valve, releasing the collected vapors into the intake manifold.

Early fuel evaporation (EFE)

19   The ECM controls a valve which shuts off the system until the engine is warm.

9   C4/C3 system and trouble codes

Refer to illustration 9.4

The C4/C3 system is analogous to the central nervous system in the human body. The sensors (nerve endings) constantly relay information to the ECM (brain), which processes the data and, if necessary, sends out a command to change the operating parameters of the engine (body).

9.4   Typical Assembly Line Data Link (ALDL) terminal – (Assembly Line Communications Link, or ALCL, terminals similar)

A Ground	E Serial data (special tool
B Diagnostic terminal	required – do not use)
C AIR (if used)	F TCC (if used)
D Check Engine (or Service	G Fuel pump (if used)
Engine Soon) light	H Brake sensor speed input

Here's a specific example of how one portion of this system operates: An oxygen sensor, located in the exhaust manifold, constantly monitors the oxygen content of the exhaust gas. If the percentage of oxygen in the exhaust gas is incorrect, an electrical signal is sent to the ECM. The ECM takes this information, processes it and then sends a command to the fuel injection system, telling it to change the air/fuel mixture. This happens in a fraction of a second and it goes on continuously when the engine is running. The end result is an air/fuel ratio which is constantly maintained at a predetermined ratio, regardless of driving conditions.

One might think that a system which uses an on-board computer and electrical sensors would be difficult to diagnose. This is not necessarily the case. The C4/C3 system has a built-in diagnostic feature which indicates a problem by flashing a Check Engine or Service Engine Soon light on the instrument panel. When this light comes on during normal vehicle operation, a fault in one of the information sensor circuits or the ECM itself has been detected. More importantly, the source of the malfunction is stored in the ECM's memory.

1980 V8 engines, 1982 and earlier V6 engines and 1986 and later V8 engines

To retrieve this information from the ECM memory, you must use a short jumper wire to ground a diagnostic terminal. On some early models, this terminal is located under the dash on the driver's side near the kick panel, and is identified by a green plastic connector. Attach one end of the jumper wire to the terminal and the other end to ground, then turn the ignition On. On others it is part of a wiring connector known as the Assembly Line Communications Link (ALCL) or Assembly Line Data Link (ALDL) **(see illustration)**. The ALCL/ALDL is located underneath the dashboard, just below the instrument panel and to the left of the center console. Connect a jumper wire between terminals A and B to enter the diagnostic mode.

When the diagnostic mode has been entered, the ECM will display a Code 12 by flashing the light, indicating that the system is operating. A Code 12 is simply one flash, followed by a brief pause, then two flashes in quick succession. This code will be flashed three times. If no other codes are stored, Code 12 will continue to flash until the diagnostic terminal ground is removed.

After flashing Code 12 three times, the ECM will display any stored trouble codes. Each code will be flashed three times, then Code 12 will be flashed again, indicating that the display of any stored trouble codes has been completed.

When the ECM sets a trouble code, the light will come on and a trouble code will be stored in memory. If the problem is intermittent, the light will go out after ten seconds, when the fault goes away. However, the trouble code will stay in the ECM memory until the battery voltage to the ECM is interrupted. Removing battery voltage for ten seconds will clear all stored trouble codes. Trouble codes should always be cleared after repairs have been completed. **Caution:** *To prevent damage to the ECM, the ignition switch must be Off when disconnecting power to the ECM.*

6

1981 to 1985 V8 engines

The system on these models operates in a similar manner, but a different procedure is used to enter the diagnostic mode. The Off and Warmer buttons on the climate control panel must be pressed simultaneously, with the ignition On. The system will then begin to reveal any stored trouble codes on the climate control numerical display.

Trouble codes

Following is a list of the typical trouble codes which may be encountered while diagnosing these systems. Also included are simplified troubleshooting procedures. If the problem persists after these checks have been made, more detailed service procedures will have to be done by a dealer service department.

Trouble code	Circuit or system	Probable cause
Code 12	Distributor-to-ECM	This is the normal code when the engine isn't running. It is not stored in memory. If additional codes are stored in the ECM, they will appear after this code has flashed three times. If the code appears while the engine is running, no reference pulses from the distributor are reaching the ECM. Check the HEI module and wiring between the associated wiring.
Code 13	Oxygen sensor	The engine must run up to five minutes at part throttle under road load before this code will set. Check for a sticking or misadjusted throttle position sensor. Check the oxygen sensor wires and connectors. Replace the oxygen sensor if necessary.
Code 14	Coolant sensor	This code indicates a shorted coolant sensor circuit. The engine must run up to two minutes before this code will set. If the engine is experiencing overheating problems, the problem must be rectified before continuing. Check all wiring and connectors associated with the coolant temperature sensor. Replace the sensor if necessary.
Code 13 and 14 at same time	Coolant sensor	See Code 43.
Code 13 and 43 at same time	Coolant sensor	See Code 43.
Code 15	Coolant sensor	The temperature sensor circuit is open. The engine must run for five minutes under 800 rpm to set this code. See Code 14 probable cause, then check the wiring connections at the ECM.
Code 16	Alternator voltage out of range	See Chapter 5 for alternator checks. Could also be an ECM malfunction.
Code 17	Crank signal circuit	Crank signal circuit shorted. Check 3-amp crank fuse – if it's blown, the ECM is probably faulty. If it's not blown, check the wire between the fuse and the orange connector at the ECM for a short to ground.
Code 18	Crank signal circuit	Crank signal circuit open. Check the fuse – if it's blown, repair the short circuit condtion in the wire between the ignition switch and the fuse or between the fuse and the ECM. If it's not blown, check the same wires for an open circuit condition. If the circuit is OK, the ECM is probably malfunctioning.
Code 19	Fuel pump circuit	Fuel pump circuit shorted. Check oil pressure switch, fuel pump relay and associated wiring harnesses. Check electrical connectors at ECM. May be a faulty ECM.
Code 20	Fuel pump circuit	Check fuel pump fuse, oil pressure switch, fuel pump relay and associated wiring. ECM may be malfunctioning.
Code 21	WOT switch	The Wide Open Throttle (WOT) switch is shorted or the closed throttle switch (if equipped) is open. On some year models, Code 21 may refer to the TPS switch (see below) or to both WOT and TPS switches.
Code 21	TPS switch	Check for a sticking or misadjusted Throttle Position Sensor (TPS) plunger. The engine must run for at least 10 seconds at 800 rpm, or at the specified curb idle, to set the code. Check all wiring and connectors between the TPS and the ECM. Adjust or replace the TPS if necessary.
Code 22	TPS switch	The engine must run 20 seconds at the specified curb idle to set this code. Check the Throttle Position Sensor (TPS) adjustment. Check the ECM connector. Replace the TPS.
Code 23 (carbureted models)	M/C solenoid	The Mixture Control (MC) solenoid is open or grounded.
Code 23 (DFI models)	EST/bypass circuit problem	Check for an open 'set timing' connector. Check electrical connectors at the distributor and the ECM. Check all associated wiring. Could be defective HEI module or ECM.
Code 23 (5.7L Chevy engines)	MAT sensor circuit	Low manifold air temperature indicated. Check wiring from sensor to ECM. Could be faulty sensor or ECM.
Code 24	VSS	A fault in the Vehicle Speed Sensor (VSS) circuit should appear only when the vehicle is in motion and the engine has run at least five minutes. Disregard this code if it is set when the drive wheels are not turning. Check the connectors at the ECM. Check the TPS adjustment.

Trouble code	Circuit or system	Probable cause
Code 25 (V8-6-4 only) ...	Modulated displacement failure .	Take the vehicle to a dealer service department or other repair shop for diagnosis.
Code 25 (HT4100 only) ..	EST circuit problem	See DFI code 23.
Code 25 .... (5.7L Chevy engines)	MAT sensor circuit	High manifold air temperature indicated. See probable cause for code 23.
Code 26.	Throttle switch circuit	Throttle switch circuit shorted. Check wiring to TPS. Check wiring and connectors to ECM and firewall connector. Could be faulty TPS or ECM.
Code 27	Throttle switch circuit.	Throttle switch circuit open. See above.
Code 28.	Open fourth gear circuit	Check electrical connectors at transmission. Check wiring between TCC connector and ECM. Could be faulty fourth gear pressure switch or malfunctioning ECM. Take the vehicle to a dealer service department or other repair shop for further diagnosis and possible repair.
Code 29	Shorted fourth gear circuit	See above.
Code 30	ISC circuit problem	Check TPS adjustment. Check ISC motor – motor may be burned out or gears may be stripped. Check the wiring between the ISC motor and the ECM. ECM may be defective.
Code 31 (DFI models) ...	MAP sensor circuit.	MAP sensor circuit shorted. Check wiring between the sensor and the ECM. May be faulty MAP sensor or ECM.
Code 31 .... (1988, 1989 models)	Canister purge solenoid circuit. .	Measure the resistance of the canister purge solenoid – it should be more than 20 ohms. Check the wiring between the solenoid and the ECM. Could be faulty ECM.
Code 32 (DFI models) ...	MAP sensor circuit	MAP sensor circuit open. See DFI code 31.
Code 32 (carbureted models)	BARO sensor	The Barometric Pressure (BARO) sensor circuit output voltage is low.
Code 32 .... (5.7L Chevy engines).	EGR circuit	Check EGR valve with a vacuum pump – it should hold vacuum for at least 20 seconds. Check wiring between EGR solenoid and ECM. Could be malfunctioning EGR solenoid, valve, or ECM.
Code 33 (DFI models). ...	MAP/BARO sensor correlation	Check the wiring between the MAP and BARO sensors and the ECM. Check the hose between the MAP sensor and the manifold. The sensor(s) could be defective or the ECM may be faulty.
Code 34	Vacuum sensor or MAP sensor .	This code will set when the signal voltage from the Manifold Absolute Pressure (MAP) sensor circuit signal is too high. The engine must idle for up to five minutes to set this code. The ECM will substitute a fixed MAP value and use the TPS to control fuel delivery. Replace the MAP sensor.
Codes 33 and or 34 .... (5.7L Chevy engines)	MAP sensor circuit	See DFI codes 31 and 32.
Code 35 (DFI models) ...	BARO sensor circuit	BARO sensor circuit shorted. Check wiring between BARO sensor and ECM. Could be faulty BARO sensor or defective ECM.
Code 35 (1986 on)	ISC switch.	The Idle Speed Control (ISC) switch is shorted. It takes at least two seconds at half throttle to set this code. Replace the ISC switch.
Code 36	BARO sensor circuit	BARO sensor circuit open. See DFI code 35.
Code 37	MAT sensor circuit.	MAT sensor circuit shorted. Check wiring between sensor and ECM. Could be faulty MAT sensor or ECM. Remove sensor from intake manifold – if it appears burned, replace it.
Code 38.	MAT sensor circuit	MAT sensor circuit open. See above.
Code 39	TCC engagement problem	Check the electrical connectors at the transmission. Check the wiring between the transmission electrical connectors and the ECM. Take the vehicle to a dealer service department or other repair shop.
Code 41	EST circuit.	No distributor reference pulses to the ECM at specified engine vacuum (about 8 inches Hg). This code will store in memory. Also, see below
Code 41	EST circuit.	The Electronic Spark Timing (EST) bypass circuit or the EST circuit is grounded or open. A malfunctioning HEI module can set this code.
Code 41 (1987 to 1989) ..	No distributor reference pulse ..	See code 12.
Code 42	EST circuit	Electronic Spark Timing bypass circuit or EST circuit is grounded or open. A malfunctioning HEI module can cause this code.
Code 43	ESC unit	The Electronic Spark Control (ESC) retard signal has been on for too long or the voltage is too low.

6

Trouble code	Circuit or system	Probable cause
Code 44	Oxygen sensor	The exhaust is lean. Indicated by the oxygen sensor after the engine has run in closed loop, part throttle at road load up to five minutes. Check the ECM wiring connectors. Check for vacuum leakage at the base gasket, vacuum hoses or the intake manifold gasket. Replace the oxygen sensor.
Code 45	Oxygen sensor	The exhaust is rich. Indicated by the oxygen sensor after the vehicle has run in closed loop, part throttle at road load up to five minutes. Check the evaporative charcoal canister and its components for the presence of fuel. Replace the oxygen sensor. **Note:** A Code 33 or 34 may also cause a Code 45 – so check them first.
Code 44 and 45 . . . . at same time	Oxygen sensor	Indicates a faulty oxygen sensor circuit.
Code 51	PROM unit.	Faulty Programmed Read Only Memory (PROM) or improper PROM installation. Make sure that the PROM or MEM-CAL is properly in the ECM. Replace the PROM or MEM-CAL.
Code 52	ECM unit	Faulty ECM. Replace the ECM.
Code 52 . . . . (5.7L Chevy engines)	CALPAK error	Check CALPAK installation. If OK, ECM may be faulty.
Code 53 (V6 models)	ECM unit	Faulty ECM.
Code 53 . . . . (1983 and later HT4100)	Distributor signal interrupt	See code 12.
Code 53 (1986 on)	EGR valve	Exhaust Gas Recirculation (EGR) valve vacuum sensor is receiving improper vacuum signal. The EGR valve is faulty. Replace the EGR.
Code 52 and 53 . . . . at same time	ECM unit	If the Check Engine light is off, there is an intermittent ECM problem. If the Check Engine light is on, the ECM is faulty. Replace it.
Code 54	M/C solenoid	The Mixture Control (M/C) solenoid voltage is high at the ECM because of a shorted M/C solenoid circuit and/or faulty ECM.
Code 54 . . . . (5.7L Chevy engines)	Fuel pump circuit	See Code 19.
Code 55	ECM or oxygen sensor	Make sure that the ECM ground connectors are tight. If they are, either the ECM or the oxygen sensor is faulty. Replace the ECM and/or the oxygen sensor.
Code 60	Transmission not in drive	Clear the code, drive the vehicle and see if it sets (cruise control circuit) again. If it does, take the vehicle to a dealer service department or other repair shop for further diagnosis.
Code 63	Car and set speed tolerance . . . exceeded (cruise control circuit)	See probable cause for code 60.
Code 65	Coolant temperature exceeds . . limit (cruise control circuit)	See probable cause for code 60.
Code 66	Engine rpm exceeds . . . . maximum limit (cruise control circuit)	See probable cause for code 60.
Code 72	Throttle switch circuit	Check for a binding throttle linkage or stuck ISC plunger. Replace ISC motor. Check wiring from ISC motor to ECM. Could be defective ECM.

Note: *Where replacement of one of the above systems, units or devices is recommended, it should be recognized that simply replacing some of the above components will not always solve the problem. For this reason, you may want to seek professional advice before purchasing any replacement parts.*

---

10   Electronic Control Module (ECM)/Programmable Read Only Memory (PROM) (1980 and later models)/CALPAK (1990 and later models)

1   The Electronic Control Module (ECM) is located under the dash, on the right side, behind the glove box.
2   To remove it, disconnect the negative battery cable from the battery.
3   Remove the screws from the under-dash panel on the right side. Remove the panel.
4   Remove the glove box.
5   Remove the retaining bolts and carefully slide the ECM out far enough to unplug the electrical connector.

6   Unplug both electrical connectors from the ECM. **Caution:** *The ignition switch must be Off when pulling out or plugging in the connectors, to prevent damage to the ECM.*

PROM

Refer to illustration 10.7
7   To allow one model of ECM to be used for many different vehicles, a device called a PROM (Programmable Read Only Memory) is used. To access the PROM, remove the cover. The PROM **(see illustration)** is located inside the ECM and contains information on the vehicle's weight, engine, transmission, axle ratio, etc. One ECM part number can be used by many GM vehicles but the PROM is very specific and must be used only in the vehicle for which it was designed.

10.7   The CALPAK (top right) and PROM (bottom right) inside an ECM for a 1990 Chevrolet-built engine (others similar)

8   For this reason, it is essential to check the latest parts book and Service Bulletin information for the correct part number when replacing a PROM. An ECM purchased at the dealer is purchased without a PROM. The PROM from the old ECM must be carefully removed and installed in the new ECM.

CALPAK (1990 and later Chevrolet-built engines)

9   A device known as a CALPAK (see illustration 10.7) is used to allow fuel delivery if other parts of the ECM are damaged. The CALPAK has an access door in the ECM, and replacement is the same as that described for the PROM.

ECM/PROM/CALPAK replacement

Refer to illustrations 10.12, 10.14 and 10.17

10   Turn the ECM so that the bottom cover is facing up and place it on a clean work surface.
11   Remove the PROM/PAK access cover.
12   Using a PROM removal tool (usually supplied with new ECMs), grasp the PROM carrier at the narrow ends (see illustration). Gently rock the carrier from end to end while carefully pulling up.
13   The PROM carrier and PROM should lift off the PROM socket easily. **Caution:** *The PROM carrier should only be removed with the special PROM removal tool. Removal without this tool or with any other type of tool may damage the PROM or the PROM socket.*
14   Note the reference end of the PROM carrier (see illustration) before setting it aside.
15   If you are replacing the ECM, remove the new ECM from its container and check the service number to make sure that it is the same as the number on the old ECM.
16   If you are replacing the PROM, remove the new PROM from its container and check the service number to make sure that it is the same as the number of the old PROM.
17   Position the PROM/PROM carrier assembly squarely over the PROM socket with the small notched end of the carrier aligned with the small notch in the socket at the pin on one end. Press on the PROM carrier until it seats firmly in the socket (see illustration)
18   If the PROM is new, make sure that the notch in the PROM is matched to the small notch in the carrier. **Caution:** *If the PROM is installed backwards and the ignition switch is turned on, the PROM will be destroyed.*
19   Using the tool, install the new PROM carrier in the PROM socket of the ECM. The small notch of the carrier should be aligned with the small notch in the socket. Press on the PROM carrier until it is firmly seated in the socket. **Caution:** *Do not press on the PROM – press only on the carrier.*
20   Attach the access cover to the ECM and tighten the two screws.
21   Install the ECM in the support bracket, plug in the electrical connectors to the ECM and install the hush panel.

22   Start the engine.
23   Enter the diagnostic mode (see Section 9). If no trouble codes occur, the PROM is correctly installed.
24   If Trouble Code 51 occurs, or if the Check Engine/Service Engine Soon light comes on and remains constantly lit, the PROM is not fully seated, is installed backwards, has bent pins or is defective.
25   If the PROM is not fully seated, pressing firmly on both ends of the carrier should correct the problem.
26   If the pins have been bent, remove the PROM, straighten the pins and reinstall the PROM. If the bent pins break or crack when you attempt to straighten them, discard the PROM and replace it with a new one.
27   If careful inspection indicates that the PROM is fully seated, has not been installed backwards and has no bent pins, but the Check Engine/Service Engine Soon light remains lit, the PROM is probably faulty and must be replaced.

10.12   Using a PROM removal tool, grasp the PROM carrier at the narrow ends and gently rock the removal tool until the PROM is unplugged from the socket

10.14   Note how the notch in the PROM is matched up with the smaller notch in the carrier

6

10.17   Press only on the ends of the PROM carrier – pressure on the area in between could result in bent or broken pins or damage to the PROM itself

11   Electronic Spark Timing (EST) (1981 and later models)

General description

1   To provide improved engine performance, fuel economy and control of exhaust emissions, the Electronic Control Module (ECM) controls distributor spark advance (ignition timing) with the Electronic Spark Timing (EST) system.

2   The ECM receives a reference pulse from the distributor, which indicates both engine rpm and crankshaft position. The ECM then determines the proper spark advance for the engine operating conditions and sends an EST pulse to the distributor.

Checking

3   The ECM will set spark timing at a specified value when the diagnostic test terminal in the ALCL connector is grounded. To check for EST operation, the timing should be checked at 2000 rpm with the terminal ungrounded. Then ground the test terminal. If the timing changes at 2000 rpm, the EST is operating. A fault in the EST system will usually set a trouble code.

Setting base timing

4   To set the initial base timing, locate, then disconnect the timing connector (the location and wire color of the timing connector is on the VECI label).

5   Set the timing as specified on the VECI label. This will cause a trouble code to be stored in the ECM memory. Be sure to clear the memory after setting the timing (see Section 9).

6   For further information regarding the testing and component replacement procedures for the distributor, refer to Chapter 5.

Chapter 7 Automatic transmission

Contents

Specifications

Torque specifications   Ft-lbs

Transmission-to-engine bolts	35 to 40
Torque converter-to-driveplate bolts	
1970 through 1985	30 to 35
1986 on	46

7

---

1 General information

All vehicles covered in this manual come equipped with an automatic transmission.

Due to the complexity of the automatic transmissions covered in this manual and the need for specialized equipment to perform most service operations, this Chapter contains only general diagnosis, routine maintenance, adjustment and removal and installation procedures.

If the transmission requires major repair work, it should be left to a dealer service department or an automotive or transmission repair shop. You can, however, remove and install the transmission yourself and save the expense, even if the repair work is done by a transmission shop.

2 Diagnosis – general

Note: *Automatic transmission malfunctions may be caused by five general conditions: poor engine performance, improper adjustments, hydraulic malfunctions, mechanical malfunctions or malfunctions in the computer or its signal network (models equipped with computer-controlled transmissions). Diagnosis of these problems should always begin with a check of the easily repaired items: fluid level and condition (see Chapter 1), shift linkage adjustment and throttle linkage adjustment. Next, perform a road test to determine if the problem has been corrected or if more diagnosis is necessary. If the problem persists after the preliminary tests and corrections are completed, additional diagnosis should be done by a dealer ser-*

vice department or transmission repair shop. Refer to the Troubleshooting Section at the front of this manual for information on symptoms of transmission problems.

Preliminary checks

1   Drive the vehicle to warm the transmission to normal operating temperature.
2   Check the fluid level as described in Chapter 1:
   a) If the fluid level is unusually low, add enough fluid to bring the level within the designated area of the dipstick, then check for external leaks (see below).
   b) If the fluid level is abnormally high, drain off the excess, then check the drained fluid for contamination by coolant. The presence of engine coolant in the automatic transmission fluid indicates that a failure has occurred in the internal radiator walls that separate the coolant from the transmission fluid (see Chapter 3).
   c) If the fluid is foaming, drain it and refill the transmission, then check for coolant in the fluid or a high fluid level.
3   Check the engine idle speed. **Note:** *If the engine is malfunctioning, do not proceed with the preliminary checks until it has been repaired and runs normally.*
4   If equipped, check the throttle valve cable for freedom of movement. Adjust it if necessary (see Section 6). **Note:** *The throttle cable may function properly when the engine is shut off and cold, but it may malfunction once the engine is hot. Check it cold and at normal engine operating temperature.*
5   Inspect the shift linkage (see Section 3). Make sure it's properly adjusted and that the linkage operates smoothly.

Fluid leak diagnosis

6   Most fluid leaks are easy to locate visually. Repair usually consists of replacing a seal or gasket. If a leak is difficult to find, the following procedure may help.
7   Identify the fluid. Make sure it's transmission fluid and not engine oil or brake fluid (automatic transmission fluid is a deep red color).
8   Try to pinpoint the source of the leak. Drive the vehicle several miles, then park it over a large sheet of cardboard. After a minute or two, you should be able to locate the leak by determining the source of the fluid dripping onto the cardboard.
9   Make a careful visual inspection of the suspected component and the area immediately around it. Pay particular attention to gasket mating surfaces. A mirror is often helpful for finding leaks in areas that are hard to see.
10   If the leak still cannot be found, clean the suspected area thoroughly with a degreaser or solvent, then dry it.
11   Drive the vehicle for several miles at normal operating temperature and varying speeds. After driving the vehicle, visually inspect the suspected component again.
12   Once the leak has been located, the cause must be determined before it can be properly repaired. If a gasket is replaced but the sealing flange is bent, the new gasket will not stop the leak. The bent flange must be straightened.
13   Before attempting to repair a leak, check to make sure the following conditions are corrected or they may cause another leak. **Note:** *Some of the following conditions cannot be fixed without highly specialized tools and expertise. Such problems must be referred to a transmission repair shop or a dealer service department.*

Gasket leaks

14   Check the pan periodically. Make sure the bolts are tight, no bolts are missing, the gasket is in good condition and the pan is flat (dents in the pan may indicate damage to the valve body inside).
15   If the pan gasket is leaking, the fluid level or the fluid pressure may be too high, the vent may be plugged, the pan bolts may be too tight, the pan sealing flange may be warped, the sealing surface of the transmission housing may be damaged, the gasket may be damaged or the transmission casting may be cracked or porous. If sealant instead of gasket material has been used to form a seal between the pan and the transmission housing, it may be the wrong sealant.

Seal leaks

16   If a transmission seal is leaking, the fluid level or pressure may be too high, the vent may be plugged, the seal bore may be damaged, the seal itself may be damaged or improperly installed, the surface of the shaft protruding through the seal may be damaged or a loose bearing may be causing excessive shaft movement.
17   Make sure the dipstick tube seal is in good condition and the tube is properly seated. Periodically check the area around the speedometer gear or sensor for leakage. If transmission fluid is evident, check the O-ring for damage.

Case leaks

18   If the case itself appears to be leaking, the casting is porous and will have to be repaired or replaced.
19   Make sure the oil cooler hose fittings are tight and in good condition.

Fluid comes out vent pipe or fill tube

20   If this condition occurs, the transmission is overfilled, there is coolant in the fluid, the case is porous, the dipstick is incorrect, the vent is plugged, the transmission is overheated or the drain back holes are plugged.

---

3   Shift linkage – check and adjustment

Refer to illustrations 3.2a, 3.2b and 3.2c

1   A common indication of an improperly adjusted shift linkage is the ability to shift into Low or Reverse without first having to lift the shift lever so it can pass over the mechanical stop.
2   If adjustment is required, loosen the control rod clamp, working underneath the vehicle **(see illustrations)**. **Warning:** *Be sure the vehicle is safely supported on jackstands before crawling under it!*
3   Place the steering column shift lever in the Neutral position.
4   Position the shift lever on the transmission in the Neutral detent, which is two detentes back from the Park position (all the way forward).

3.2a   Typical early model shift linkage details (except Seville)

3.2b   Typical late model shift linkage details (except Seville)

5   Hold the clamp flush against the equalizer lever and tighten the clamp screw or nut finger tight. Make sure that no force is exerted in either direction on the rod or equalizer lever while the screw or nut is tightened.
6   Tighten the screw or nut securely.
7   Check that the ignition key can be moved freely to the Lock position when the shift lever is in Park and not in any other position.

4   Turbo Hydra-Matic 400 downshift (detent) switch – adjustment

Refer to illustrations 4.3a and 4.3b

1   On models other than Seville, remove the air cleaner assembly and make sure the carburetor (if equipped) is adjusted properly. Locate the detent switch on the throttle linkage
2   On Seville models, locate the detent switch on the accelerator pedal.
3   Loosen the mounting screws and insert a #42 (0.094-inch) wire gage into the calibrating hole **(see illustrations)**. The shank of a properly sized drill bit will work if a gage is not available.

4.3a   Typical Turbo Hydra-Matic 400 downshift switch mounting details (except Seville)

3.2c   Typical Seville shift linkage details

4.3b   Typical Turbo Hydra-Matic 400 downshift switch mounting details (Seville only)

5.2   To check for free operation, pull forward on the throttle valve (TV) inner cable, feeling for smooth operation through the full range of travel – the cable should retract evenly and rapidly when released

4   Adjust the position of the switch so the lever just touches the accelerator relay rod or the throttle lever or arm.
5   With the switch positioned, tighten the mounting screws.

5   Turbo Hydra-Matic 200 4R, 350 and 700 4R throttle valve (TV) cable – inspection and adjustment

Inspection
Refer to illustration 5.2
1   Inspection should be made with the engine running at idle speed with the shift lever in Neutral. Set the parking brake firmly and block the wheels to prevent any vehicle movement. As an added precaution, have an assistant in the driver's seat applying the brake pedal.
2   Grab the inner cable a few inches behind where it attaches to the throttle linkage and pull the cable forward. It should easily slide through the cable housing with no binding or jerky operation (see illustration).
3   Release the cable. It should return to its original location with the cable stop against the cable terminal.
4   If the TV cable does not operate as above, the cause is a defective or misadjusted cable or damaged components at either end of the cable.

Adjustment
Note: *Two types of cables are used on these models: a manual adjusting cable and a self adjusting cable. To determine which type the vehicle has, inspect the TV cable assembly. If there's a re-adjust tab like the one shown in illustration 5.9, it's a self adjusting cable. If not, it's a manual adjusting cable.*

Manual adjusting cable
Refer to illustration 5.5
Note: *The engine should NOT be running during this adjustment.*
5   Insert a screwdriver on each side of the snap lock and pry it out to release it (see illustration).
6   Compress the locking lugs and disconnect the snap lock assembly from its bracket.
7   Manually set the throttle in the fully open position with the throttle lever fully against its stop.
8   With the throttle in the fully open position, push the snap lock into the locked position and release the throttle lever.

5.5   Adjustment details for manual adjusting TV cables

Self adjusting cable
Refer to illustration 5.9
Note: *the engine should NOT be running during this adjustment.*
9   Depress the re-adjust tab and move the slider back through the fitting away from the throttle linkage until the slider stops against the fitting (see illustration).

5.9   On self adjusting cables, depress the throttle valve (TV) cable re-adjust tab and pull the slider back (arrow) until it rests on its stop – release the tab and open the throttle completely

7.1   To check the transmission mount for wear, place a large screwdriver or prybar between the crossmember and the extension housing – try to pry up on the transmission; it shouldn't move much

10   Release the re-adjust tab.
11   Turn the throttle lever to the wide open throttle (WOT) position, which will automatically adjust the cable. Release the throttle lever.
 Caution: *Don't use excessive force at the throttle lever to adjust the TV cable. If great effort is required to adjust the cable, disconnect the cable at the transmission end and check for free operation. If it's still difficult, replace the cable. If it's now free, suspect a bent TV link in the transmission or a problem with a throttle lever.*
12   After adjustment check for proper operation.

6   Neutral start switch – removal and installation (1970 through 1973 models only)

Note: *1974 and later models do not have a neutral start switch. A mechanical block in the steering column prevents the engine from cranking in positions other than Park or Neutral.*

Removal

Refer to illustration 6.4

1   When the switch is operating properly, the engine should crank with the shift lever in Park or Neutral only. Also, the back-up lights should come on when the lever is in Reverse.
2   Set the shift lever against the Neutral gate by rotating the lower lever on the shift tube counterclockwise as viewed from the driver's seat.
3   Remove the screw from the mounting bracket and carefully remove the switch from the bottom of the steering column. If the switch is going to be reused, be very careful not to disturb the position of the contact carrier.
4   Mark the position of the contact carrier **(see illustration)**.
5   Remove the vacuum hose and the electrical connectors.

Installation

6   If a new switch is being installed, the switch will be secured in Neutral by a shear pin. Don't break the pin.
7   Locate the switch actuating tang in the shifter tube slot and then tighten the securing screw.
8   Connect the electrical connectors and vacuum hose to the switch and check that the starter motor will actuate.

9   If the switch operates correctly, move the shift lever out of Neutral, which will cause the alignment pin to shear.

7   Transmission mount – check and replacement

Refer to illustration 7.1

1   Insert a large screwdriver or prybar into the space between the transmission extension housing and the crossmember and pry up **(see illustration)**.
2   The transmission should not move away from the insulator much at all.
3   To replace the mount, remove the nuts attaching the insulator to the crossmember and the bolts attaching the insulator to the transmission.
4   Raise the transmission slightly with a jack and remove the insulator, noting which holes are used in the crossmember for proper alignment during installation.
5   Installation is the reverse of the removal procedure.

8   Oil seal – replacement

Refer to illustrations 8.5 and 8.7

1   Oil leaks frequently occur due to wear of the extension housing oil seal and bushing (if equipped), and/or the speedometer driven gear oil seal and O-ring. Replacement of these seals is relatively easy, since the repairs can usually be performed without removing the transmission from the vehicle.
2   The extension housing oil seal is located at the extreme rear of the transmission, where the driveshaft is attached. If leakage at the seal is suspected, raise the vehicle and support it securely on jackstands. If the seal is leaking, transmission fluid will be built up on the front of the driveshaft and may be dripping from the rear of the transmission.
3   Refer to Chapter 8 and remove the driveshaft.
4   Using a soft-faced hammer, carefully tap the dust shield (if equipped) to the rear and remove it from the transmission. Be careful not to distort it.

7

8.5   Use a prybar or a long screwdriver to carefully pry the seal out of the rear of the transmission

8.7   A large socket or pice of pipe works well for installing the seal – the socket should come in contact with the outer edge of the seal

5   Using a screwdriver or prybar, carefully pry the oil seal out of the rear of the transmission **(see illustration)**. Take care not to damage the splines on the transmission output shaft.

6   If the oil seal cannot be removed with a screwdriver or prybar, a special oil seal removal tool (available at auto parts stores) will be required.

7   Using a large section of pipe or a very large deep socket as a drift, install the new oil seal **(see illustration)**. Drive it into the bore squarely and make sure it's completely seated.

8   Reinstall the dust shield by carefully tapping it into place. Lubricate the splines of the transmission output shaft and the outside of the driveshaft sleeve yoke with lightweight grease, then install the driveshaft. Be careful not to damage the lip of the new seal.

9   The speedometer cable and driven gear housing is located on the side of the extension housing. Look for transmission fluid around the cable housing to determine if the seal and O-ring are leaking.

10   Disconnect the speedometer cable.

11   Using a hook, remove the seal.

12   Using a small socket as a drift, install the new seal.

13   Install a new O-ring in the driven gear housing and reinstall the driven gear housing and cable assembly on the extension housing.

***

9   Automatic transmission – removal and installation

Refer to illustrations 9.5 and 9.6

Removal

1   Disconnect the negative cable at the battery.

2   Raise the vehicle and support it securely.

3   Drain the transmission fluid (see Chapter 1).

4   Remove the torque converter cover.

5   Mark the relationship of the flywheel to the torque converter with white paint so they can be reinstalled in the same position **(see illustration)**.

6   Remove the torque converter-to-flywheel bolts **(see illustration)**. Turn the crankshaft bolt for access to each bolt in turn.

7   Remove the starter motor (see Chapter 5).

9.5   Mark the relationship of the torque converter to the flywheel with white paint

9.6   Remove the torque converter-to-flywheel bolts (here, a flywheel wrench is being used to prevent the flywheel from turning, but a wrench on the crankshaft vibration damper will also work)

8   Remove the driveshaft (see Chapter 8).

9   Disconnect the speedometer cable.

10   Disconnect the electrical connectors from the transmission.

11   On models so equipped, disconnect the vacuum hoses.

12   Remove any exhaust component which will interfere with transmission removal (see Chapter 4).

13   Disconnect the TV linkage rod or cable.

14   Disconnect the shift linkage.

15   Support the engine using a jack and a block of wood under the oil pan to spread the load.

16   Support the transmission with a jack – preferably a jack made for this purpose. Safety chains will help steady the transmission on the jack.

17   Remove the rear mount-to-crossmember attaching bolts and the crossmember-to-frame attaching bolts.

18   Remove the two engine rear support-to-transmission extension housing attaching bolts.

19   Raise the transmission sufficiently to allow removal of the crossmember.

20   Remove the bolts securing the transmission to the engine.

21   Lower the transmission slightly and disconnect and plug the transmission cooler lines.

22   Remove the transmission fluid filler tube.

23   Move the transmission to the rear to disengage it from the engine block dowel pins and make sure the torque converter is detached from the flywheel. Secure the torque converter to the transmission so that it will not fall out during removal. Lower the transmission from the vehicle.

Installation

24   Make sure prior to installation that the torque converter hub is secure-ly engaged in the pump.

25   With the transmission secured to the jack, raise the transmission into position, making sure to keep it level so the torque converter does not slide forward. Connect the transmission cooler lines.

26   Turn the torque converter to line up the torque converter and flywheel bolt holes. The white paint mark on the torque converter and the stud made during Step 5 must line up.

27   Move the transmission carefully forward until the dowel pins are engaged and the torque converter is engaged.

28   Install the transmission housing-to-engine bolts. Tighten the bolts to the specified torque.

29   Install the torque converter-to-flywheel nuts. Tighten the nuts to the specified torque.

30   Install the transmission mount crossmember, bolts and nuts. Tighten the bolts and nuts securely.

31   Remove the jacks supporting the transmission and the engine.

32   Install the fluid filler tube.

33   Install the starter.

34   Connect the vacuum hose(s) (if equipped).

35   Connect the shift and TV linkage.

36   Plug in the transmission electrical connectors.

37   Install the torque converter cover.

38   Connect the driveshaft.

39   Connect the speedometer.

40   Adjust the shift linkage.

41   Install any exhaust system components which were removed.

42   Lower the vehicle.

43   Fill the transmission with the specified fluid (see Chapter 1), run the vehicle and check for fluid leaks.

7

Chapter 8   Driveshafts and rear axles

Contents

Specifications

Pinion bearing preload (used bearings) ....   8 to 12 in-lbs

Torque specifications   **Ft-lbs**

Driveshaft
Universal joint strap bolts   15
Universal joint U-bolt nuts   15
Universal joint flange bolts   65

Rear axle
Differential cover bolts   20
Pinion shaft lock bolt   25
Differential yoke-to-pinion nut ....   See Section 9

---

1   General information

Refer to illustrations 1.2a and 1.2b

The information in this Chapter deals with the components from the rear of the engine to the rear wheels, except for the transmission, which is dealt with in the previous Chapter. For the purposes of this Chapter, these components are grouped into two categories; driveshaft and rear axle. Separate Sections within this Chapter offer general descriptions and checking procedures for components in each of these groups.

Cadillac offers two optional types of rear ends from 1970 through 1990, Controlled Differential and Limited Slip Differential. The Controlled Differ-

ential's basic advantage is that the major driving force is always directed to the wheel having the greater traction **(see illustration)**. This unit is not a positive lock type. It will release before an excessive amount of torque is directed to one rear wheel. The main purpose of the Controlled Differential is to reduce the possibility of the vehicle getting stuck while driving under slippery conditions. The Limited Slip Differential **(see illustration)** responds in the same manner as the Controlled Differential except that the Limited Slip Differential incorporates clutch discs instead of cones to control the movement of the axle.

Since nearly all the procedures covered in this Chapter involve working under the vehicle, make sure it's securely supported on sturdy jackstands or on a hoist where the vehicle can be easily raised and lowered.

GEAR CASE
LEFT HALF

LEFT SIDE GEAR

SPRINGS

THRUST WASHER

LEFT CONE
CLUTCH

PINION GEAR

INNER SPRING RETAINER

PINION GEAR

UPPER SPRING RETAINER

RIGHT CONE
CLUTCH

CROSS-SHAFT

SPRINGS

THRUST WASHER

RIGHT SIDE GEAR

GEAR CASE
RIGHT HALF

1.2a Exploded view of a
Controlled Differential

RING GEAR BOLT

CASE

RING
GEAR

SIDE BEARING

LOCK
SCREW

PRELOAD SPRING

THRUST
WASHER

PINION GEAR

PINION
SHAFT

CLUTCH DISC S GUIDE

SHIMS

1.2b Exploded view
of a Limited
Slip Differential

SPRING
RETAINER

SIDE
GEAR

CLUTCH PLATES

8

SNAP RING
BEARING CUP
BALL SEAT
SMALL WASHER
LARGE WASHER
BALL STUD
SPRING
SEAL
CENTERING BALL
BALL SUPPORT YOKE
BALL TUBE YOKE
LINK YOKE

2.4a   Double Cardan universal Joint – exploded view

22 N•m
16 Ft. LBS.
RETAINER
PINION
FLANGE

SLIP
YOKE
SOLID TUBE
RUBBER
ELEMENT

2.4b   Typical Driveshaft and U-joint
assembly (later model shown)

2 Driveshaft and universal joints – description and check

Refer to illustrations 2.4a and 2.4b

1   The driveshaft is a tube running between the transmission and the rear end. Universal joints are located at either end of the driveshaft and permit power to be transmitted to the rear wheels at varying angles.

2   The driveshaft features a splined yoke at the front, which slips into the extension housing of the transmission. This arrangement allows the driveshaft to slide back and forth within the transmission as the vehicle is in operation.

3   An oil seal is used to prevent leakage of fluid at this point and to keep dirt and contaminants from entering the transmission. If leakage is evident at the front of the driveshaft, replace the oil seal, referring to the procedures in Chapter 7.

4   The driveshaft assembly requires very little service. The universal joints are lubricated for life and must be replaced if problems develop. The driveshaft must be removed from the vehicle for this procedure. The early models employed the Double Cardan Joint at each end of the shaft **(see illustration)**, while the later models used a single U-joint at each end **(see illustration)**.

5   Since the driveshaft is a balanced unit, it's important that no undercoating, mud, etc., be allowed to stay on it. When the vehicle is raised for service it's a good idea to clean the driveshaft and inspect it for any obvious damage. Also check that the small weights used to originally balance the driveshaft are in place and securely attached. Whenever the driveshaft is removed it's important that it be reinstalled in the same relative position to preserve this balance.

6   Problems with the driveshaft are usually indicated by a noise or vibration while driving the vehicle. A road test should verify if the problem is the driveshaft or another vehicle component:

   a) On an open road, free of traffic, drive the vehicle and note the engine speed (rpm) at which the problem is most evident.
   b) With this noted, drive the vehicle again, this time manually keeping the transmission in 1st, then 2nd, then 3rd gear ranges and running the engine up to the engine speed noted.
   c) If the noise or vibration occurs at the same engine speed regardless of which gear the transmission is in, the driveshaft is not at fault because the speed of the driveshaft varies in each gear.
   d) If the noise or vibration decreased or was eliminated, visually inspect the driveshaft for damage, material on the shaft which would effect balance, missing weights and damaged universal joints. Another possibility for this condition would be tires which are out of balance.

7   To check for worn universal joints:

   a) On an open road, free of traffic, drive the vehicle slowly until the transmission is in High gear. Let off on the accelerator, allowing the vehicle to coast, then accelerate. A clunking or knocking noise will indicate worn universal joints.

   b) Drive the vehicle at a speed of about 10 to 15 mph and then place the transmission in Neutral, allowing the vehicle to coast. Listen for abnormal driveline noises.
   c) Raise the vehicle and support it securely on jackstands. With the transmission in Neutral, manually turn the driveshaft, watching the universal joints for excessive play.

3 Driveshaft – removal and installation

Refer to illustration 3.3 and 3.4

Removal

1   Disconnect the negative cable from the battery.

2   Raise the vehicle and support it securely on jackstands. Place the transmission in Neutral with the parking brake off.

3   Using a sharp scribe, white paint or a hammer and punch, place marks on the driveshaft and the differential flange in line with each other **(see illustration)**. This is to make sure the driveshaft is reinstalled in the same position to preserve the balance.

4   Disconnect the rear universal joint by unscrewing and removing the nuts from the U-bolts or strap retaining bolts, or by removing the flange bolts. Turn the driveshaft (or tires) as necessary to bring the bolts into the most accessible position **(see illustration)**.

3.3   Before removing the driveshaft, mark the relationship of the driveshaft yoke to the differential flange – to prevent the driveshaft from turning when loosening the strap bolts, insert a screwdriver through the yoke

8

3.4   Driveshaft attachment methods

A   Strap   B   Flange   C   U-bolt

4.1   Cleveland type universal joint repair kit

1   *Trunnion*   4   *Cap*
2   *Seal*   5   *Snap-ring*
3   *Bearings*

5   Tape the bearing caps to the spider to prevent the caps from coming off during removal.
6   Lower the rear of the driveshaft and then slide the front out of the transmission. On models equipped with a center support bearing, unbolt the bearing mount from the underside of the vehicle.
7   To prevent loss of fluid and protect against contamination while the driveshaft is out, wrap a plastic bag over the transmission housing and hold it in place with a rubber band.

Installation

8   Remove the plastic bag on the transmission and wipe the area clean. Inspect the oil seal carefully. Procedures for replacement of this seal can be found in Chapter 7.
9   Slide the front of the driveshaft into the transmission.
10   Raise the rear of the driveshaft into position, checking to be sure that the marks are in alignment. If not, turn the rear wheels to match the pinion flange and the driveshaft. If the driveshaft has a center support bearing, raise it into position and install the bolts, tightening them securely.
11   Remove the tape securing the bearing caps and install the straps and bolts. Tighten the bolts to the specified torque.

---

4   Universal joints – replacement

Note: *A press or large vise will be required for this procedure. It may be advisable to take the driveshaft to a local dealer or machine shop where the universal joints can be replaced for you, normally at a reasonable charge.*

Cleveland type joint

Refer to illustrations 4.1 and 4.2
1   Clean away all dirt from the ends of the bearings on the yokes so that the snap-rings can be removed using a pair of needle-nose or snap-ring pliers **(see illustration)**. If the snap-rings are very tight, tap the end of the bearing cup (inside the snap–ring) to relieve the pressure.
2   Support the trunnion yoke on a short piece of tube or the open end of a socket, then use a suitably sized socket to press out the cross (trunnion) by means of a vise **(see illustration)**.
3   Press the trunnion through as far as possible, then grip the bearing cup in the jaws of a vise to fully remove it. Repeat the procedure for the remaining cups.
4   On some models, the slip yoke at the transmission end has a vent hole. When disassembling, check to make sure this vent hole is not plugged up.
5   A universal joint repair kit will contain a new trunnion, seals, bearings, cups and snap-rings. Some replacement universal joints are often equipped with grease fittings. Be sure it is offset in the proper direction (toward the driveshaft).

4.2   To press the universal joint out of the driveshaft, set it up in a vise with the small socket (on the left) pushing the joint and bearing cap into the large socket

6   Begin reassembly by packing each of the reservoirs at the trunnion ends with grease.
7   Make sure that the dust seals are correctly located on the trunnion, so that the cavities in the seals are nearer the trunnion.
8   Using a vise, press one bearing cup into the yoke so that it enters not more than 1/4-inch.
9   Using a thick grease, stick each of the needle rollers inside the cup.
10   Insert the trunnion into the partially installed bearing cup, taking care not to displace the needle rollers.
11   Stick the needle bearings into the opposite cup and then, holding the trunnion in correct alignment, press both cups in completely with the jaws of the vise.
12   Install the new snap-rings.
13   Repeat the operations on the other two bearing cups.
14   In extreme cases of wear or neglect, it is possible that the bearing cup housings in the yoke will have worn so much that the cups are a loose fit in the yokes. In such cases, replace the complete driveshaft assembly.
15   Always check the wear in the sliding sleeve splines and replace the sleeve if worn.

Saginaw type joint

Refer to illustrations 4.16 and 4.18
16   Where a Saginaw joint is to be disassembled, the procedure given in the previous Section for pressing out the bearing cup is applicable. If the joint has been previously repaired it will be necessary to remove the snap-rings inboard of the yokes **(see illustration)**; if this is to be the first time

4.16   Saginaw type universal joint repair kit

4.18   To relieve stress produced by pressing the bearing caps into the yokes, strike the yoke in the area shown

4.19   CV joint alignment marks made before disassembly

that servicing has been carried out, there are no snap-rings to remove, but the pressing operation in the vise will shear the plastic molding material.

17   Having removed the cross (trunnion), remove the remains of the plastic material from the yoke. Use a small punch to remove the material from the injection holes.

18   Reassembly is similar to that given for the Cleveland type joint except that the snap-rings are installed inside the yoke. If difficulty is encountered, strike the yoke firmly with a hammer to assist in seating (see illustration).

Double Cardan type constant velocity joint

Refer to illustrations 4.19 and 4.21

19   An inspection kit containing two bearing cups and two retainers is available to permit the joint to be dismantled to the stage where the joint can be inspected. Before any dismantling is started, mark the flange yoke and coupling yoke so that they can be reassembled in the same relative position (see illustration).

20   Dismantle the joint by removing the bearing cups in a similar way to that described in the preceding Section, according to type.

21   Disengage the flange yoke and trunnion from the centering ball. Pry the seal from the ball socket and remove the washers, springs and three ball seats (see illustration).

4.21   CV joint centering ball mechanism

22   Clean the ball seat insert bushing and inspect for wear. If evident, the flange yoke and trunnion assembly must be replaced.

23   Clean the seal, ball seats, spring and washers and inspect for wear. If excessive wear is evident or parts are broken, a replacement service kit must be used.

24   Remove all plastic material from the groove of the coupling yoke (if this type of joint is used).

25   Inspect the centering ball; if damaged, it must be replaced.

26   Withdraw the centering ball from the stud using a suitable extractor. Provided that the ball is not to be re-used, it will not matter if it is damaged.

27   Press a new ball onto the stud until it seats firmly on the stud shoulder. It is extremely important that no damage to the ball occurs during this stage, and suitable protection must be given to it.

28   Using the grease provided in the repair kit, lubricate all the parts and insert them into the ball seat cavity in the following order: spring, washer (small OD), three ball seats (largest opening outwards to receive the ball), washer (large OD) and the seal.

29   Lubricate the seal lips and press it (lip inwards) into the cavity. Fill the cavity with the grease provided.

30   Install the flange yoke to the centering ball, ensuring that the alignment marks are correctly positioned.

31   Install the trunnion caps as described previously for the Cleveland or Saginaw types.

---

5   Rear axle – description and check   **8**

Refer to illustration 5.3

Description

1   The rear axle assembly is a hypoid, semi-floating type (the centerline of the pinion gear is below the centerline of the ring gear). The differential carrier is a casting with a pressed steel cover, and the axle tubes are made of steel, pressed and welded into the carrier.

2   An optional locking rear axle, either the Controlled Differential or the Limited Slip Differential, is also available. This type of differential allows for normal differential operation until one wheel loses traction. The unit utilizes cone clutches or multi-disc clutch packs and a speed sensitive engagement mechanism which locks both axleshafts together, applying equal rotational power to both wheels.

3   In order to undertake certain operations, particularly replacement of the axleshafts, it's important to know the axle identification number. It's lo-

AXLE ASSEMBLY PART NO. CODE
LABEL ON REVERSE SIDE OF
R. H. CALIPER SUPPORT PLATE

CODE

LAST 2 DIGITS OF
MODEL YEAR

3.00'' APPROX.

CALIPER SUPPORT PLATE

AXLE IDENTIFICATION STAMP
ON TUBE:
    — DATE OF MFG.
    — SOURCE IDENT.
    — AXLE ASSEMBLY PART NO. CODE
    — LAST DIGIT OF MODEL YEAR

WITH DISC BRAKES

AXLE ASSEMBLY PART NO. CODE
LABEL ON R. H. BRAKE DRUM SURFACE

3.00'' APPROX.

CODE

LAST 2 DIGITS
OF MODEL YEAR

BRAKE DRUM

AXLE IDENTIFICATION STAMP
ON TUBE:
    — DATE OF MFG.
    — SOURCE IDENT.
    — AXLE ASSEMBLY PART NO. CODE
    — LAST DIGIT OF MODEL YEAR

WITH DRUM BRAKES

5.3   **Location of the rear axle identification numbers**

cated on the rear face of the right side axle tube **(see illustration)**. The second and third letter of the code identifies the axle assembly part number code. This is important, as axle design varies slightly among manufacturers.

Check

4   Many times a fault is suspected in the rear axle area when, in fact, the problem lies elsewhere. For this reason, a thorough check should be performed before assuming a rear axle problem.

5   The following noises are those commonly associated with rear axle diagnosis procedures:

    a) Road noise is often mistaken for mechanical faults. Driving the vehicle on different surfaces will show whether the road surface is the cause of the noise. Road noise will remain the same if the vehicle is under power or coasting.

    b) Tire noise is sometimes mistaken for mechanical problems. Tires which are worn or low on pressure are particularly susceptible to emitting vibrations and noises. Tire noise will remain about the same during varying driving situations, where rear axle noise will change during coasting, acceleration, etc.

    c) Engine and transmission noise can be deceiving because it will travel along the driveline. To isolate engine and transmission noises, make a note of the engine speed at which the noise is most pronounced. Stop the vehicle and place the transmission in Neutral and run the engine to the same speed. If the noise is the same, the rear axle is not at fault.

6   Overhaul and general repair of the rear axle is beyond the scope of the home mechanic due to the many special tools and critical measurements required. Thus, the procedures listed here will involve axleshaft removal and installation, axleshaft oil seal replacement, axleshaft bearing replacement and removal of the entire unit for repair or replacement.

6   Axleshaft (standard differential) – removal and installation

Refer to illustrations 6.3a, 6.3b, 6.4 and 6.5

Removal

1   Loosen the rear wheel lug nuts, raise the rear of the vehicle and support it securely on jackstands. Remove the wheel and brake drum (refer to Chapter 9).

2   Remove the cover from the differential carrier and allow the lubricant to drain into a container.

3   Remove the lock bolt from the differential pinion shaft. Remove the pinion shaft **(see illustrations)**.

6.3a   **Remove the pinion shaft lock bolt . . .**

6.3b . . . then carefully remove the pinion shaft from the differential carrier (don't turn the wheels or the carrier after the shaft has been removed, or the spider gears may fall out)

6.4 Push the axle flange in, then remove the C-lock from the inner end of the axleshaft

4   Push the outer (flanged) end of the axleshaft in and remove the C-lock from the inner end of the shaft **(see illustration)**.

5   Withdraw the axleshaft, taking care not to damage the oil seal in the end of the axle housing as the splined end of the axleshaft passes through it **(see illustration)**.

Installation

6   Installation is the reverse of removal. Tighten the pinion shaft lock bolt to the specified torque.

7   Always use a new cover gasket and tighten the cover bolts to the specified torque.

8   Refill the axle with the correct quantity and grade of lubricant (see Chapter 1).

---

7   Axleshaft oil seal (standard differential) – replacement

Refer to illustrations 7.2 and 7.3

1   Remove the axleshaft as described in the preceding Section.

2   Pry the old oil seal out of the end of the axle housing, using a large screwdriver or the inner end of the axleshaft itself as a lever **(see illustration)**.

3   Using a large socket as a seal driver, tap the seal into position so that the lips are facing in and the metal face is visible from the end of the axle

6.5 Carefully pull the axleshaft from the housing to avoid damaging the seal

housing **(see illustration)**. When correctly installed, the face of the oil seal should be flush with the end of the axle housing. Lubricate the lips of the seal with gear oil.

4   Installation of the axleshaft is described in the preceding Section.

7.2 The axleshaft oil seal can sometimes be pried out with the end of the axle

7.3 A large socket can be used to install the new seal squarely

8

8.3   A slide hammer with a special bearing puller attachment is required to pull the axleshaft bearing from the axle housing

8.4   A special bearing driver is needed to install the axleshaft bearing without damaging it

8   Axleshaft bearing (standard differential) – replacement

Refer to illustrations 8.3 and 8.4

1   Remove the axleshaft (refer to Section 6) and the oil seal (refer to Section 7).
2   A bearing puller will be required, or a tool which will engage behind the bearing will have to be fabricated.
3   Attach a slide hammer and pull the bearing from the axle housing **(see illustration)**.
4   Clean out the bearing recess and drive in the new bearing using GM tool no. J8902 and J23765 or equivalent **(see illustration)**. **Caution:** *Failure to use this tool could result in bearing damage. Lubricate the new bearing with gear lubricant. Make sure the bearing is tapped into the full depth of its recess and that the numbers on the bearing are visible from the outer end of the housing.*
5   Discard the old oil seal and install a new one, then install the axleshaft.

9   Pinion oil seal – replacement

Refer to illustrations 9.6a and 9.6b

1   A pinion oil seal failure results in the leakage of differential gear lubricant past the seal and onto the driveshaft yoke or flange. The seal is replaceable without removing or disassembling the differential.
2   Loosen the rear wheel lug nuts, raise the vehicle and place it on jackstands.

3   Remove the rear wheels and brake drums. On models with rear disc brakes, remove the calipers and hang them out of the way.
4   Disconnect the driveshaft from the pinion shaft yoke (see Section 3).
5   Using a beam-type torque wrench, slowly turn the pinion shaft nut and measure the torque required to turn the pinion.
6   If the pinion nut is staked into a slot in the pinion shaft, unstake it using a narrow chisel. Mark the relationship of the pinion shaft to the pinion shaft yoke **(see illustration)**. Hold the pinion shaft yoke with a large pair of adjustable pliers, then remove the nut **(see illustration)**.
7   Remove the pinion shaft yoke from the shaft, using a puller if necessary.
8   After noting what the visible side of the oil seal looks like, carefully pry it out of the differential with a screwdriver or pry bar. Be careful not to damage the splines on the pinion shaft.
9   Lubricate the new seal lip with multi-purpose grease or differential lubricant and carefully install it in position in the differential. Using a seal driver or a short section of pipe of the proper diameter and a hammer, carefully drive the seal into place.
10   Clean the sealing lip contact surface of the pinion shaft yoke. Apply a thin coat of moly-based grease to the seal contact surface and the shaft spines then install the yoke, making sure the match-marks line up.
11   Coat the threads of a new pinion shaft nut with multi-purpose grease and, holding the flange stationary, tighten the nut just enough to eliminate all end-play in the pinion shaft.
12   Turn the pinion shaft yoke several times to seat the bearing.

9.6a   Mark the relationship of the pinion shaft to the yoke

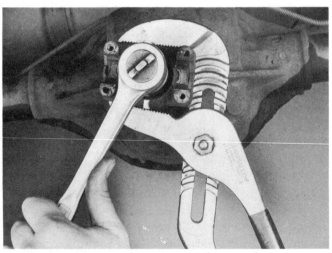

9.6b   Hold the yoke in place and loosen the nut

13   Using a torque wrench, see how much torque is required to turn the pinion shaft. The desired preload is the previously recorded torque value plus five inch-pounds. If the preload is less than desired, retighten the nut in small increments until the desired preload is reached. If the nut is tightened too much and the desired preload figure is accidently exceeded, the bearing spacer must be replaced by a repair shop. **Note:** *Do not back off the pinion nut to reduce the preload.*
14   Connect the driveshaft to the pinion shaft yoke (see Section 3).
15   Install the brake drums (or calipers) and wheels, lower the vehicle to the ground and tighten the lug nuts to the specified torque.
16   Test drive the vehicle and check around the differential pinion shaft yoke for evidence of leakage.

10   Rear axle assembly – removal and installation

1   Raise the rear of the vehicle and support it securely on stands placed under the body frame rails.
2   Position an adjustable floor jack under the differential housing and just take up the weight. Do not raise the jack sufficiently to take the weight of the vehicle from the frame stands.
3   Disconnect the lower shock absorber mounts (see Chapter 10).
4   Remove the driveshaft (see Section 3).
5   Remove the rear wheels and brake drums. See Chapter 9 for information if difficulty is experienced in removing the brake drums.
6   Disconnect the hydraulic brake lines from their clips on the axle housing.
7   Unbolt and remove the differential cover, allowing the fluid to drain into a container.
8   Remove the axleshafts as described in Section 6 of this Chapter.
9   Depending on axle type, unbolt the brake backing plates, carefully withdraw the brake assemblies and wire them up to the frame without bending the hydraulic lines or disconnecting them.
10   Remove the leaf springs or coil springs as described in Chapter 10.
11   Withdraw the axle assembly from under the vehicle.
12   Installation is a reversal of removal, but tighten all suspension bolts and nuts to the specified torque (refer to Chapters 9 and 10). Fill the axle assembly with the proper grade and amount of lubricant (see Specifications, Chapter 1).

8

Chapter 9   Brakes

Contents

Specifications

Brake fluid type . . . .   See Chapter 1

Disc brakes

Minimum brake pad thickness . . . .   See Chapter 1
Disc discard thickness . . . .   Refer to minimum thickness cast into rotor
Lateral runout . . . .   0.004 in maximum
Disc thickness variation (parallelism) . . . .   0.0005 in

Drum brakes

Minimum brake lining thickness . . . . See Chapter 1
Drum maximum diameter . . . . Refer to diameter cast into drum
Drum out-of-round . . . . 0.006 in maximum
Drum taper . . . . 0.003 in maximum

Parking brake travel

1970 through 1976 . . . . 4 to 5 in
1977 on
    Drum rear brakes . . . . 5 1/4 to 6 3/4 in
    Disc rear brakes
        Seville . . . . 6 3/4 to 7 3/4 in
        Full size . . . . 5 1/4 to 6 3/4 in

Torque specifications

	Ft-lbs
Master cylinder mounting nuts	20
Power booster mounting nuts	20
Caliper mounting bolts	
1970 to 1980	30
1981, 1982	25 to 30
1983 on	35 to 38
Wheel cylinder mounting bolts	13
Brake hose-to-caliper inlet fitting bolt	30
Wheel lug nuts	See Chapter 1

1   General information

The vehicles covered by this manual are equipped with hydraulically operated front and rear brake systems. The front brakes are disc type and the rear brakes are drum type with some models available with discs. Both the front and rear brakes are self adjusting. The disc brakes automatically compensate for pad wear, while the drum brakes incorporate an adjustment mechanism which is activated as the brakes are applied when the vehicle is driven in Reverse.

Some later models are equipped with Anti-Lock Brakes (ABS) to maintain vehicle control under severe braking conditions. The ABS system monitors the rotational speed of each wheel and controls the brake line pressure to prevent wheel lock-up.

Hydraulic system

The hydraulic system consists of two separate circuits. The master cylinder has separate reservoirs for the two circuits and in the event of a leak or failure in one hydraulic circuit, the other circuit will remain operative. A visual warning of circuit failure or air in the system is given by a warning light activated by displacement of the piston in the pressure differential switch portion of the combination valve from its normal "in balance" position.

Combination valve

A combination valve, located in the engine compartment below the master cylinder, consists of three sections providing the following functions. The metering section limits pressure to the front brakes until a predetermined front input pressure is reached and until the rear brakes are activated. There is no restriction at inlet pressures below three psi, allowing pressure equalization during non-braking periods. The proportioning section proportions outlet pressure to the rear brakes after a predetermined rear input pressure has been reached, preventing early rear wheel lock-up under heavy brake loads. The valve is also designed to assure full pressure to one brake system should the other system fail. The pressure differential warning switch incorporated into the combination valve is de-

signed to continuously compare the front and rear brake pressure from the master cylinder and energize the dash warning light in the event of either a front or rear brake system failure. The design of the switch and valve are such that the switch will stay in the "warning" position once a failure has occurred. The only way to turn the light off is to repair the cause of the failure and apply a brake pedal force of 450 psi.

Power brake booster

The power brake booster, utilizing engine manifold vacuum and atmospheric pressure to provide assistance to the hydraulically operated brakes, is mounted on the firewall in the engine compartment.

Parking brake

The parking brake operates the rear brakes only, through cable actuation. It's activated by a pedal mounted on the left side kick panel.

Service

After completing any operation involving disassembly of any part of the brake system, always test drive the vehicle to check for proper braking performance before resuming normal driving. When testing the brakes, perform the tests on a clean, dry flat surface. Conditions other than these can lead to inaccurate test results.

Test the brakes at various speeds with both light and heavy pedal pressure. The vehicle should stop evenly without pulling to one side or the other. Avoid locking the brakes, because this slides the tires and diminishes braking efficiency and control of the vehicle.

Tires, vehicle load and front-end alignment are factors which also affect braking performance.

2   Disc brake pads – replacement

Warning: *Disc brake pads must be replaced on both front or rear wheels at the same time – never replace the pads on only one wheel. Also, the dust created by the brake system may contain asbestos, which is harmful*

9

2.5   Using a large C-clamp, push the piston back into the caliper bore – note that one end of the clamp is on the flat area near the brake hose fitting and the other end (screw end) is pressing against the outer brake pad

2.6a   Remove the two caliper-to-steering knuckle mounting bolts (arrows) (this will require the use of an Allen head or Torx head socket wrench)

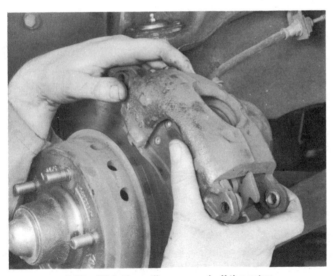

2.6b   Slide the caliper up and off the rotor

2.6c   Pull the inner pad straight out, disengaging the retainer spring from the caliper piston

to your health. Never blow it out with compressed air and don't inhale any of it. An approved filtering mask should be worn when working on the brakes. Do not, under any circumstances, use petroleum-based solvents to clean brake parts. Use brake cleaner or denatured alcohol only!

Note: When servicing the disc brakes, use only high quality, nationally recognized name-brand pads.

1   Remove the cover from the brake fluid reservoir.
2   Loosen the wheel lug nuts, raise the vehicle and support it securely on jackstands.
3   Remove the wheels. Work on one brake assembly at a time, using the assembled brake for reference if necessary.
4   Inspect the brake disc carefully as outlined in Section 4. If machining is necessary, follow the information in that Section to remove the disc, at which time the pads can be removed from the calipers as well.

Front brake

Refer to illustrations 2.5 and 2.6a through 2.6g

5   Push the piston back into the bore to provide room for the new brake pads. A C-clamp can be used to accomplish this **(see illustration)**. As the piston is depressed to the bottom of the caliper bore, the fluid in the master cylinder will rise. Make sure it doesn't overflow. If necessary, siphon off some of the fluid.
6   Follow the accompanying illustrations, beginning with 2.6a, for the actual pad replacement procedure. Be sure to stay in order and read the caption under each illustration.
7   When reinstalling the caliper, be sure to tighten the mounting bolts to the specified torque. After the job has been completed and before driving the vehicle, firmly depress the brake pedal a few times to bring the pads into contact with the disc.

2.6d   Transfer the retainer spring from the old inner pad to the new one – hook the end of the spring in the hole at the top of the pad, then insert the two prongs of the spring into the slot on the pad backing plate

2.6e   Lubricate the caliper mounting ears with multi-purpose grease

2.6f   Push the mounting bolt sleeves out of the bores, remove the old bushings and install the new ones supplied with the brake pads

1	Caliper	3	Bushings
2	Sleeves	4	Bushings

2.6g   Slide the caliper assembly over the rotor, install the mounting bolts, then use large pliers to clinch the ears of the outer brake pad to eliminate all play between the pad and caliper

9

Rear brake

Refer to illustrations 2.14 and 2.17

Caution: *Operation of the rear disc brake adjuster mechanism is critical on these models. If any problems with rear brake adjustment are encountered, take the vehicle to a dealer or properly equipped shop for diagnosis and repair.*

8   Install one of the wheel nuts with the flat side toward the disc to hold the disc in place.

9   Loosen the parking brake cable tension at the equalizer and detach the cable from the brake lever. Remove the spring and cable conduit from the bracket.

10   Detach the spring, then hold the parking brake lever in place while removing the locknut, anti-friction washer, seal and lever. Carefully clean around the lever seal.

11   Push the piston back into bore using a C-clamp **(see illustration 2.5)**. Lubricate the caliper housing surface under the lever seal with silicone grease before removing the C-clamp.

12   Using a new anti-friction washer and lever seal, install the lever with the hex on the arm pointing down. Rotate the lever toward the front of the vehicle, hold it there and install the locknut securely, then rotate the lever back to the stop. Install the return spring and remove the C-clamp.

13   Disconnect the brake line from the caliper and plug the openings.

BOLT
(DO NOT LUBRICATE)
SLEEVE
(DO NOT LUBRICATE)

AXLE

COVER

PLATE

CALIPER [B]

[A]

ROTOR

PLATE

CALIPER
"0" RING
BOLT

"0" RING

SLEEVE

ROTOR
PAD

SECTION THRU PIN
& CALIPER ASSEMBLY

[A] WEAR INDICATOR POSITION:
     BROUGHAM: LH ON BOTTOM OF CALIPER
                RH ON TOP OF CALIPER

     SEVILLE: LH ON TOP OF CALIPER
               RH ON BOTTOM OF CALIPER

[B] SEVILLE CALIPER MOUNTED FORWARD
    OF AXLE. BROUGHAM CALIPER MOUNTED
    REARWARD OF AXLE.

L.H. SIDE OF CAR

2.14   Rear disc brake details

J-7624
SPANNER WRENCH

PISTON

"D" SHAPED
LOCATOR

2.17   Screw the piston into the caliper with a spanner wrench or
needle-nose pliers

14   Remove the mounting bolts **(see Illustration 2.6a).** Lift the caliper,
complete with pads, from the brake assembly **(see illustration).**
15   Detach the pads from the caliper.
16   Replace the mounting bolt sleeves and bushings **(see illustration
2.6f).** Remove and discard the piston check valve and install a new one.
Lubricate the bolts and sleeves with silicone grease.
17   Install the new brake pads with the "D" shaped locater tab on the inner
pad fitting into the indentation in the piston. To provide clearance for the
new, thicker inner pad it will probably be necessary to first rotate the piston
fully into the bore using needle-nose pliers or factory spanner wrench tool
J-7624 **(see illustration).**
18   Lower the caliper into position over the disc and install the mounting
bolts. Tighten the mounting bolts to the torque specified in this Chapter's
Specifications.
19   Connect the fluid lines.
20   Clinch the brake pad ears with locking pliers so there is no play between the pad ears and the caliper **(see illustration 2.6g).**

3.4   It's easier to remove the brake hose inlet fitting bolt (arrow) before removing the caliper mounting bolts

3.8   With the caliper padded to catch the piston, use compressed air to force the piston out of the bore – make sure your hands or fingers are not between the piston and caliper!

3.9   When prying the dust boot out of the caliper, be very careful not to scratch the bore surface

21   Connect the parking brake cables and adjust them (see Section 11). After adjustment make sure the parking brake levers are against their stops on the caliper housings, adjusting as necessary. Apply the parking brake several times until the travel specified at the beginning of this Chapter is achieved.
22   Bleed the rear brakes (Section 10). Apply the brake pedal approximately 30 times to automatically adjust the parking brake mechanism. The brake pedal travel should be approximately 2 3/4 inches.
Note: *If any problem is encountered with achieving the specified foot or parking brake pedal travel, take the vehicle to a dealer or properly equipped brake shop because there could be a problem with the adjuster mechanism inside the rear disc brake caliper.*

---

3   Disc brake caliper – removal, overhaul and installation

Warning: *Dust created by the brake system may contain asbestos, which is harmful to your health. Never blow it out with compressed air and don't*

inhale any of it. An approved filtering mask should be worn when working on the brakes. Do not, under any circumstances, use petroleum-based solvents to clean brake parts. Use brake cleaner or denatured alcohol only!

Note: *If an overhaul is indicated (usually because of fluid leakage) explore all options before beginning the job. New and factory rebuilt calipers are available on an exchange basis, which makes this job quite easy. If it's decided to rebuild the calipers, make sure a rebuild kit is available before proceeding. Always rebuild the calipers in pairs – never rebuild just one of them. Because of the special tools required, rear brake calipers should not be rebuilt by the home mechanic. This job should be left to a dealer service department or brake shop.*

Removal
Refer to illustration 3.4
1   Remove the cover from the brake fluid reservoir, siphon off two thirds of the fluid into a container and discard it.
2   Loosen the wheel lug nuts, raise the front of the vehicle and support it securely on jackstands. Remove the front wheels.
3   Bottom the piston in the caliper bore **(see illustration 2.5)**.
4   **Note:** *Do not remove the brake hose from the caliper if you are only removing the caliper. Remove the brake hose inlet fitting bolt and detach the hose* **(see illustration)**. *Have a rag handy to catch spilled fluid and wrap a plastic bag tightly around the end of the hose to prevent fluid loss and contamination.*
5   Remove the two mounting bolts and detach the caliper from the vehicle (refer to Section 2 if necessary).

Overhaul
Refer to illustrations 3.8, 3.9, 3.10, 3.11, 3.15, 3.16, 3.17 and 3.18
6   Refer to Section 2 and remove the brake pads from the caliper.
7   Clean the exterior of the caliper with brake cleaner or denatured alcohol. Never use gasoline, kerosene or petroleum-based cleaning solvents. Place the caliper on a clean workbench.
8   Position a wood block or several shop rags in the caliper as a cushion, then use compressed air to remove the piston from the caliper **(see illustration)**. Use only enough air pressure to ease the piston out of the bore. If the piston is blown out, even with the cushion in place, it may be damaged.
Warning: *Never place your fingers in front of the piston in an attempt to catch or protect it when applying compressed air, as serious injury could occur.*
9   Carefully pry the dust boot out of the caliper bore **(see illustration)**.

3.10   Remove the piston seal with a wooden or plastic tool to avoid scratching the bore and seal groove – a pencil will do the job

10   Using a wood or plastic tool, remove the piston seal from the groove in the caliper bore **(see illustration)**. Metal tools may cause bore damage.
11   Remove the caliper bleeder screw, then remove and discard the sleeves and bushings from the caliper ears. Discard all rubber parts **(see illustration)**.
12   Clean the remaining parts with brake system cleaner or denatured al-

cohol, then blow them dry with compressed air.
13   Carefully examine the piston for nicks and burrs and loss of plating. If surface defects are present, the parts must be replaced.
14   Check the caliper bore in a similar way. Light polishing with crocus cloth is permissible to remove light corrosion and stains. Discard the mounting bolts if they're corroded or damaged.
15   When assembling, lubricate the piston bores and seal with clean brake fluid. Position the seal in the caliper bore groove **(see illustration)**.
16   Lubricate the piston with clean brake fluid, then install a new boot in the piston groove with the fold toward the open end of the piston **(see illustration)**.
17   Insert the piston squarely into the caliper bore, then apply force to bottom it **(see illustration)**.
18   Position the dust boot in the caliper counterbore, then use a drift to drive it into position **(see illustration)**. Make sure the boot is recessed evenly below the caliper face.
19   Install the bleeder screw.
20   Install new bushings in the mounting bolt holes and fill the area between the bushings with the silicone grease supplied in the rebuild kit. Push the sleeves into the mounting bolt holes.

Installation

Refer to illustration 3.23

21   Inspect the mounting bolts for excessive corrosion.
22   Place the caliper in position over the rotor and mounting bracket, install the bolts and tighten them to the specified torque.
23   Check to make sure the total clearance between the caliper and the bracket stops is between 0.005 and 0.012-inch **(see illustration)**.
24   Install the brake hose and inlet fitting bolt, using new copper washers, then tighten the bolt to the specified torque.

3.11   An exploded view of the disc brake caliper components

25 If the line was disconnected, be sure to bleed the brakes (see Section 10).
26 Install the wheels and lower the vehicle.
27 After the job has been completed, firmly depress the brake pedal a few times to bring the pads into contact with the disc.
28 Check brake operation before driving the vehicle in traffic.

---

4 Brake disc – inspection, removal and installation

Inspection

Refer to illustrations 4.3, 4.4a, 4.4b and 4.5

1 Loosen the wheel lug nuts, raise the vehicle and support it securely on jackstands. Remove the wheel.
2 Remove the brake caliper as outlined in Section 2 (rear brake) and Section 3 (front brake). Remove caliper mounting bracket on models so equipped. It's not necessary to disconnect the brake hose on front brakes. After removing the caliper bolts, suspend the caliper out of the way with a piece of wire. Don't let the caliper hang by the hose and don't stretch or twist the hose. On rear disc brakes, install two lug nuts with the flat sides against the disc to hold it in place during inspection.

3.15   Position the seal in the caliper bore groove, making sure it isn't twisted

3.16   Install the new dust boot in the piston groove (note that the folds are at the open end of the piston)

3.17   Install the piston squarely in the caliper bore then bottom it by pushing down evenly

3.18   Seat the boot in the counterbore (a seal driver is being used in this photo, but a drift punch will work if care is exercised)

CLEARANCE BETWEEN CALIPER AND BRACKET STOPS SHALL BE 0.13-0.30 MM (0.005-0.012 IN.) THREE PLACES

9

3.23   The dimension between each caliper stop and the caliper should be 0.005 to 0.012-inch

4.3   Check the disc for deep grooves and score marks (be sure to inspect both sides of the disc)

4.4a   Check disc runout with a dial indicator – if the reading exceeds the maximum allowable runout, the disc will have to be resurfaced or replaced

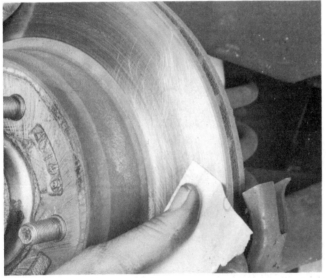

4.4b   Using a swirling motion, remove the glaze from the rotor with emery cloth or sandpaper

4.5   A micrometer is used to measure disc thickness – this can be done on the vehicle (as shown) or on the bench (the minimum thickness is cast into the inside of the disc)

3   Visually check the disc surface for score marks and other damage. Light scratches and shallow grooves are normal after use and may not always be detrimental to brake operation, but deep score marks – over 0.015-inch (0.38 mm) – require disc removal and refinishing by an automotive machine shop. Be sure to check both sides of the disc **(see illustration)**. If pulsating has been noticed during application of the brakes, suspect disc runout. Be sure to check the wheel bearings to make sure they're properly adjusted (front brakes).

4   To check disc runout, place a dial indicator at a point about 1/2-inch from the outer edge of the disc **(see illustration)**. Set the indicator to zero and turn the disc. The indicator reading should not exceed the specified allowable runout limit. If it does, the disc should be refinished by an automotive machine shop. **Note:** *Professionals recommend resurfacing of brake discs regardless of the dial indicator reading (to produce a smooth, flat surface that will eliminate brake pedal pulsations and other undesirable symptoms related to questionable discs). At the very least, if you elect not to have the discs resurfaced, deglaze them with emery cloth or sand-*

paper (use a swirling motion to ensure a nondirectional finish) **(see illustration)**.

5   The disc must not be machined to a thickness less than the specified minimum refinish thickness. The minimum wear (or discard) thickness is cast into the inside of the disc. The disc thickness can be checked with a micrometer **(see illustration)**.

Removal

6   On front disc brakes, refer to Chapter 1, Front wheel bearing check, repack and adjustment for the hub/disc removal procedure. On rear disc brakes, remove the two lug nuts that were installed to hold the disc in place and pull the disc over the wheel studs and off the hub.

Installation

7   On front disc brakes, install the disc and hub assembly and adjust the wheel bearing (see Chapter 1). On rear disc brakes, slide the disc into place over the wheel studs.

5.4a   An exploded view of the drum brake components

1	Hold down pins	10	Return spring
2	Backing plate	11	Hold down spring
3	Parking brake lever	12	Lever pivot
4	Secondary shoe	13	Lever return spring
5	Shoe guide	14	Strut spring (rear only)
6	Parking brake strut	15	Adjusting screw assembly
7	Actuator lever	16	Adjusting screw spring
8	Actuator link	17	Primary shoe
9	Return spring		

8   Install the caliper and brake pad assembly over the disc and position it on the steering knuckle (refer to Section 2 and Section 3 for the caliper installation procedure, if necessary). Tighten the caliper bolts to the specified torque.

9   Install the wheel, then lower the vehicle to the ground. Depress the brake pedal a few times to bring the brake pads into contact with the disc. On front brakes, bleeding of the system will not be necessary unless the brake hose was disconnected from the caliper. On rear disc brakes, refer to the procedure in Section 2. Check the operation of the brakes carefully before placing the vehicle into normal service.

5   Drum brake shoes – replacement

Refer to illustrations 5.4a through 5.4v

Warning: *Drum brake shoes must be replaced on both wheels at the same time – never replace the shoes on only one wheel. Also, the dust created by the brake system may contain asbestos, which is harmful to your health. Never blow it out with compressed air and don't inhale any of it. An approved filtering mask should be worn when working on the brakes. Do not, under any circumstances, use petroleum-based solvents to clean brake parts. Use brake cleaner or denatured alcohol only!*

Caution: *Whenever the brake shoes are replaced, the retractor and hold-down springs should also be replaced. Due to the continuous heating/cooling cycle that the springs are subjected to, they lose their tension over a period of time and may allow the shoes to drag on the drum and wear at a much faster rate than normal. When replacing the rear brake shoes, use only high quality nationally recognized brand-name parts.*

1   Loosen the wheel lug nuts, raise the rear of the vehicle and support it securely on jackstands. Block the front wheels to keep the vehicle from rolling.

2   Release the parking brake.

3   Remove the wheel. **Note:** *All four rear brake shoes must be replaced at the same time, but to avoid mixing up parts, work on only one brake assembly at a time.*

4   Follow the accompanying photos **(illustrations 5.4a through 5.4v)**

5.4b   Remove the shoe return springs – the spring tool shown here is available at most auto parts stores and makes this job much easier and safer

9

5.4c Pull the bottom of the actuator lever toward the secondary brake shoe, compressing the lever return spring – the actuator link can now be removed

5.4d Pry the actuator lever spring out with a large screwdriver

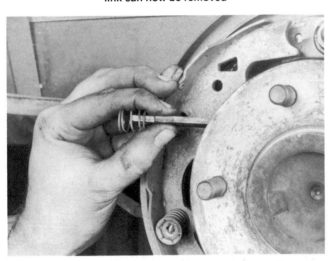

5.4e Slide the parking brake strut out from between the axle flange and primary shoe

5.4f Remove the hold-down springs and pins – the hold-down spring tool shown here is available at most auto parts stores

5.4g Remove the actuator lever and pivot – be careful not to let the pivot fall out of the lever

5.4h Spread the top of the shoes apart and slide the assembly around the axle

5.4i   Unhook the parking brake lever from the secondary shoe

5.4j   Spread the bottom of the shoes apart and remove the adjusting screw assembly

5.4k   Clean the adjusting screw with solvent, dry it off and lubricate the threads and end with multi-purpose grease; then reinstall the adjusting screw assembly between the new brake shoes

5.4l   Lubricate the shoe contact points on the backing plate with high-temperature brake grease

5.4m   Insert the parking brake lever into the opening in the secondary brake shoe (arrow)

5.4n   Spread the shoes apart and slide them into position on the backing plate

9

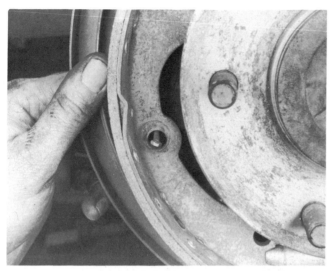

5.4o   Install the hold-down pin and spring through the backing plate and primary shoe

5.4p   Insert the lever pivot into the actuator lever, place the lever over the secondary shoe hold-down pin and install the hold-down spring

5.4q   Guide the parking brake strut behind the axle flange and engage the rear end of it in the slot on the parking brake lever – spread the shoes enough to allow the other end to seat against the primary shoe

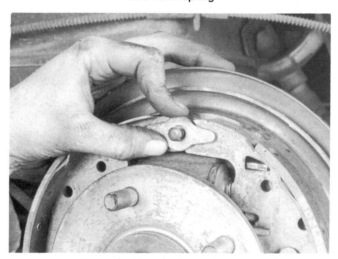

5.4r   Place the shoe guide over the anchor pin

5.4s   Hook the lower end of the actuator link to the actuator lever, then loop the top end over the anchor pin

5.4t   Install the lever return spring over the tab on the actuator lever, then push the spring up onto the brake shoe

5.4u Install the primary and secondary shoe return springs

5.4v Pull out on the actuator lever to disengage it from the adjusting screw wheel, turn the wheel to adjust the shoes in or out as necessary – the brake drum should slide over the shoes and turn with a very slight amount of drag

for the inspection and replacement of the brake shoes. Be sure to stay in order and read the caption under each illustration. **Note:** *If the brake drum cannot be easily pulled off the axle and shoe assembly, make sure that the parking brake is completely released, then apply some penetrating oil at the hub-to-drum joint. Allow the oil to soak in and try to pull the drum off. If the drum still cannot be pulled off, the brake shoes will have to be retracted. This is accomplished by first removing the plug from the backing plate (or brake drum on early models). With the plug removed, pull the lever off the adjusting star wheel with one small screwdriver while turning the adjusting wheel with another small screwdriver, moving the shoes away from the drum. The drum should now come off.*

5   Before reinstalling the drum it should be checked for cracks, score marks, deep scratches and hard spots, which will appear as small discolored areas. If the hard spots cannot be removed with fine emery cloth or if any of the other conditions listed above exist, the drum must be taken to an automotive machine shop to have it turned. **Note:** *Professionals recommend resurfacing the drums whenever a brake job is done. Resurfacing will eliminate the possibility of out-of-round drums. If the drums are worn so much that they can't be resurfaced without exceeding the maximum allowable diameter (stamped into the drum), then new ones will be required. At the very least, if you elect not to have the drums resurfaced, remove the glazing from the surface with emery cloth or sandpaper using a swirling motion.*

6   Install the brake drum on the axle flange.

7   Mount the wheel, install the lug nuts, then lower the vehicle.

8   Make a number of forward and reverse stops to adjust the brakes until satisfactory pedal action is obtained.

9   Check brake operation before driving the vehicle in traffic.

---

6   Wheel cylinder – removal, overhaul and installation

Note: *If an overhaul is indicated (usually because of fluid leakage or sticky operation) explore all options before beginning the job. New wheel cylinders are available, which makes this job quite easy. If it's decided to rebuild the wheel cylinder, make sure that a rebuild kit is available before proceeding. Never overhaul only one wheel cylinder – always rebuild both of them at the same time.*

6.4 Completely loosen the brake line fitting (A) then remove the two wheel cylinder mounting bolts (B)

Removal

Refer to illustration 6.4

1   Raise the rear of the vehicle and support it securely on jackstands. Block the front wheels to keep the vehicle from rolling.

2   Remove the brake shoe assembly (see Section 5).

3   Remove all dirt and foreign material from around the wheel cylinder.

4   Unscrew the brake line fitting **(see illustration)**. Don't pull the brake line away from the wheel cylinder.

5   Remove the wheel cylinder mounting bolts.

6   Detach the wheel cylinder from the brake backing plate and place it on a clean workbench. Immediately plug the brake line to prevent fluid loss and contamination. **Note:** *If the brake shoe linings are contaminated with brake fluid, install new brake shoes.*

9

6.7   An exploded view of the wheel cylinder components

1	Bleeder valve	4	Boot
2	Seal	5	Spring assembly
3	Piston		

7.2   Disconnect the brake lines from the master cylinder – a flare-nut wrench should be used

7.4   Pull the combination valve forward, being careful not to bend or kink the lines, then slide the master cylinder off the mounting studs

Overhaul

Refer to illustration 6.7

7   Remove the bleeder screw, cups, pistons, boots and spring assembly from the wheel cylinder body **(see illustration)**.

8   Clean the wheel cylinder with brake fluid, denatured alcohol or brake system cleaner. **Warning:** *Do not, under any circumstances, use petroleum based solvents to clean brake parts!*

9   Use compressed air to remove excess fluid from the wheel cylinder and to blow out the passages.

10   Check the cylinder bore for corrosion and score marks. Crocus cloth can be used to remove light corrosion and stains, but the cylinder must be replaced with a new one if the defects cannot be removed easily, or if the bore is scored.

11   Lubricate the new cups with brake fluid.

12   Assemble the wheel cylinder components. Make sure the cup lips face in **(see illustration)**.

Installation

13   Place the wheel cylinder in position and install the bolts.

14   Connect the brake line and tighten the fitting. Install the brake shoe assembly.

15   Bleed the brakes (see Section 10).

16   Check brake operation before driving the vehicle in traffic.

---

7   **Master cylinder – removal, overhaul and installation**

Removal

Refer to illustrations 7.2 and 7.4

Note: *Before deciding to overhaul the master cylinder, investigate the availability and cost of a new or factory rebuilt unit and also the availability of a rebuild kit.*

1   Place rags under the brake line fittings and prepare caps or plastic bags to cover the ends of the lines once they are disconnected. **Caution:** *Brake fluid will damage paint. Cover all body parts and be careful not to spill fluid during this procedure.*

2   Loosen the tube nuts at the ends of the brake lines where they enter the master cylinder. To prevent rounding off the flats on these nuts, a flare-nut wrench, which wraps around the nut, should be used **(see illustration)**.

3   Pull the brake lines away from the master cylinder slightly and plug the ends to prevent contamination.

4   Remove the two master cylinder mounting nuts. If there is a bracket retaining the combination valve, move it forward slightly, taking care not to bend the hydraulic lines running to the combination valve, and remove the master cylinder from the vehicle **(see illustration)**.

5   Remove the reservoir covers and reservoir diaphragms, then discard any fluid remaining in the reservoir.

Overhaul

Plastic reservoir master cylinder

Refer to illustrations 7.7a, 7.7b, 7.8, 7.9, 7.14, 7.15a, 7.15b, 7.15c, 7.15d and 7.16

6   Mount the master cylinder in a vise. Be sure to line the vise jaws with blocks of wood to prevent damage to the cylinder body.

7.7b   Push the primary piston in and remove the lock ring

7.8   Pull the primary piston and spring assembly out of the bore

7.7a   Exploded view of a plastic master cylinder assembly

1	Reservoir cover	8	Primary piston assembly
2	Reservoir diaphragm	9	Secondary seal
3	Reservoir cover	10	Spring retainer
4	Reservoir diaphragm	11	Primary seal
5	Reservoir	12	Secondary piston
6	Reservoir grommet	13	Spring
7	Lock ring	14	Cylinder body

7   Remove the primary piston lock ring by depressing the piston and prying the ring out with a screwdriver (**see illustrations**).

8   Remove the primary piston assembly from the cylinder bore (**see illustration**).

9   Remove the secondary piston assembly from the cylinder bore. It may be necessary to remove the master cylinder from the vise and invert it, carefully tapping it against a block of wood to expel the piston (**see illustration**).

10   Pry the reservoir from the cylinder body with a screwdriver. Remove the grommets.

11   Do not attempt to remove the quick take-up valve from the master cylinder body – it's not serviceable.

12   Inspect the cylinder bore for corrosion and damage. If any corrosion or damage is found, replace the master cylinder body with a new one, as abrasives cannot be used on the bore.

13   Lubricate the new reservoir grommets with silicone lubricant and press them into the master cylinder body. Make sure they're properly seated.

9

7.9   To remove the secondary piston, tap the cylinder against a block of wood

7.14   Lay the reservoir face down on the bench, with the secondary reservoir propped up on a block of wood – push the master cylinder straight down over the reservoir tubes using a rocking motion

7.15a   Pry the secondary piston spring retainer off with a small screwdriver, then remove the seal

7.15b   Remove the secondary seals from the piston (some only have one seal)

14   Lay the reservoir on a hard surface and press the master cylinder body onto the reservoir, using a rocking motion **(see illustration)**.

15   Remove the old seals from the secondary piston assembly and install the new secondary seals with the lips facing away from each other **(see illustrations)**. The lip on the primary seal must face in **(see illustration)**.

16   Attach the spring retainer to the secondary piston assembly **(see illustration)**.

17   Lubricate the cylinder bore with clean brake fluid and install the spring and secondary piston assembly.

18   Install the primary piston assembly in the cylinder bore, depress it and install the lock ring.

19   Inspect the reservoir cover and diaphragm for cracks and deformation. Replace any damaged parts with new ones and attach the diaphragm to the cover.

20   **Note:** *Whenever the master cylinder is removed, the complete hydraulic system must be bled. The time required to bleed the system can be reduced if the master cylinder is filled with fluid and bench bled (refer to Steps 35 through 39) before the master cylinder is installed on the vehicle.*

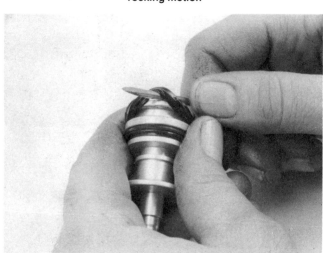

7.15c   Install the secondary seals with the lips facing away from each other (on the single seal design, the seal lip should face away from the center of the piston)

7.15d   Install a new primary seal on the secondary piston with the seal lip facing in the direction shown

7.16 Install a new spring retainer over the end of the secondary piston and push it into place with a socket

Cast iron master cylinder

Refer to illustrations 7.22a, 7.22b, 7.23, 7.26a, 7.26b, 7.27, 7.29a, 7.29b and 7.30

21 Drain all fluid from the master cylinder and place the unit in a vise. Use wood blocks to cushion the jaws of the vise.

22 Remove the secondary stop bolt from the bottom of the front fluid reservoir (Delco Moraine) or from the base of the master cylinder body (Bendix) **(see illustrations)**.

23 Remove the retaining ring from the groove and take out the primary piston assembly **(see illustration)**. Following the primary piston out of the bore will be the secondary piston, spring and retainer. Tap the cylinder against a wood block to eject the secondary piston assembly.

24 Examine the inside surface of the master cylinder and the secondary piston. If there is evidence of scoring or "bright' wear areas, the entire master cylinder should be replaced with a new one.

25 If the components are in good condition, wash them in clean brake fluid or brake cleaner. Discard all the rubber components and the primary piston. Purchase a rebuild kit which will contain all the necessary parts for the overhaul.

26 Inspect the line seats which are located in the master cylinder body where the lines connect. If they appear damaged they should be replaced with new ones, which come in the overhaul kit. They are forced out of the body by threading a screw into the tube and then prying out **(see illustration)**. The new ones are forced into place using a spare brake line nut **(see**

7.22a Typical cast iron master cylinder – exploded view

7.22b Removing the secondary stop bolt

7.23 Removing the retaining ring

7.26a Removing the line seats

9

7.26b   Installing a new line seat (note the cone-shaped end is installed facing up)

7.27   Seals correctly installed on the piston

7.29a   Assembling the retainer and spring

7.29b   Assembling the spring and piston

7.30   Pushing the piston into the master cylinder bore

illustration). All parts necessary for this should be included in the rebuild kit.

27   Place the new secondary seals in the grooves of the secondary piston **(see illustration)**.

28   Assemble the primary seals and seal protector over the end of the secondary piston.

29   Lubricate the cylinder bore and secondary piston with clean brake fluid. Insert the spring retainer into the spring then place the retainer and spring over the end of the secondary piston **(see illustrations)**. The retainer should locate inside the primary seal lips.

30   With the master cylinder vertical, push the secondary piston into the bore to seat its spring **(see illustration)**.

31   Coat the seals of the primary piston with brake fluid and fit it into the cylinder bore. Hold it down while the retaining ring is installed in the cylinder groove.

32   Continue to hold the piston down while the stop screw is installed.

33   Install the reservoir diaphragm into the reservoir cover plate, making sure it is fully collapsed inside the recess lid.

34   **Note:** *Whenever the master cylinder is removed, the complete hydraulic system must be bled. The time required to bleed the system can be reduced if the master cylinder is filled with fluid and bench bled (refer to Step 35 through 39) before the master cylinder is installed on the vehicle.*

Bench bleeding

35   Insert threaded plugs of the correct size into the cylinder outlet holes and fill the reservoirs with brake fluid. The master cylinder should be supported in such a manner that brake fluid will not spill during the bench bleeding procedure.
36   Loosen one plug at a time and push the piston assembly into the bore to force air from the master cylinder. To prevent air from being drawn back into the cylinder, the appropriate plug must be replaced before allowing the piston to return to its original position.
37   Stroke the piston three or four times for each outlet to ensure that all air has been expelled.
38   Since high pressure is not involved in the bench bleeding procedure, an alternative to the removal and replacement of the plugs with each stroke of the piston assembly is available. Before pushing in on the piston assembly, remove one of the plugs completely. Before releasing the piston, however, instead of replacing the plug, simply put your finger tightly over the hole to keep air from being drawn back into the master cylinder. Wait several seconds for the brake fluid to be drawn from the reservoir to the piston bore, then repeat the procedure. When you push down on the piston it will force your finger off the hole, allowing the air inside to be expelled. When only brake fluid is being ejected from the hole, replace the plug and go on to the other port.
39   Refill the master cylinder reservoirs and install the diaphragm and cover assembly. **Note:** *The reservoirs should only be filled to the top of the reservoir divider to prevent overflowing when the cover is installed.*

Installation

40   Carefully install the master cylinder by reversing the removal steps, then bleed the brakes (refer to Section 10).

8   Combination valve – check and replacement

Check

1   Disconnect the wire from the pressure differential switch. **Note:** *When unplugging the connector, squeeze the side lock releases, moving the inside tabs away from the switch, then pull up. Pliers may be used as an aid if necessary.*
2   Using a jumper wire, connect the switch wire to a good ground, such as the engine block.
3   Turn the ignition key to the On position. The warning light in the instrument panel should light.
4   If the warning light does not light, either the bulb is burned out or the electrical circuit is defective. Replace the bulb (refer to Chapter 12) or repair the electrical circuit as necessary.
5   When the warning light functions correctly, turn the ignition switch off, disconnect the jumper wire and reconnect the wire to the switch terminal.
6   Make sure the master cylinder reservoirs are full, then attach a bleeder hose to one of the rear wheel bleeder valves and immerse the other end of the hose in a container partially filled with clean brake fluid.
7   Turn the ignition switch On.
8   Open the bleeder valve while a helper applies moderate pressure to the brake pedal. The brake warning light on the instrument panel should light.
9   Close the bleeder valve before the helper releases the brake pedal.
10   Reapply the brake pedal with moderate to heavy pressure. The brake warning light should go out.
11   Attach the bleeder hose to one of the front brake bleeder valves and repeat Steps 8 through 10. The warning light should react in the same manner as in Steps 8 and 10.
12   Turn the ignition switch Off.
13   If the warning light did not come on in Steps 8 and 11, but does light when a jumper is connected to ground, the warning light switch portion of the combination valve is defective and the combination valve must be replaced with a new one since the components of the combination valve are not individually serviceable.

Replacement

14   Place a container under the combination valve and protect all painted surfaces with newspapers or rags.
15   Disconnect the hydraulic lines at the combination valve, then plug the lines to prevent further loss of fluid and to protect the lines from contamination.
16   Disconnect the electrical connector from the pressure differential switch.
17   Remove the bolt holding the valve to the mounting bracket and remove the valve from the vehicle.
18   Installation is the reverse of the removal procedure.
19   Bleed the entire brake system.

9   Brake hoses and lines – inspection and replacement

Inspection

1   About every six months, with the vehicle raised and supported securely on jackstands, the rubber hoses which connect the steel brake lines with the front and rear brake assemblies should be inspected for cracks, chafing of the outer cover, leaks, blisters and other damage. These are important and vulnerable parts of the brake system and inspection should be complete. A light and mirror will be helpful for a thorough check. If a hose exhibits any of the above conditions, replace it with a new one.

Replacement
Front brake hose
Refer to illustration 9.2
2   Using a back-up wrench, disconnect the brake line from the hose fitting, being careful not to bend the frame bracket or brake line (**see illustration**).
3   Use a pair of pliers to remove the U-clip from the female fitting at the bracket, then detach the hose from the bracket.
4   Unscrew the brake hose from the caliper. At the caliper end of the hose, remove the bolt from the fitting block, then remove the hose and the copper washers on either side of the fitting block.
5   To install the hose, first thread it into the caliper, tightening it securely. When installing the hose, always use new copper washers on either side of the fitting block and lubricate all bolt threads with clean brake fluid before installation.
6   With the fitting engaged with the caliper locating ledge, attach the hose to the caliper, tightening the fitting bolt to the specified torque.
7   Without twisting the hose, install the female fitting in the hose bracket. It will fit the bracket in only one position.

9.2   Place a wrench on the hose fitting to prevent it from turning and disconnect the line with a flare-nut wrench

9

TO CENTER   REAR
BRAKE PIPE   BRAKE
HOSE

9.13   Rear brake line details

10.9   When bleeding the brakes, a hose is connected to the bleeder valve and then submerged in brake fluid – air will be seen as bubbles in the container and the hose

8   Install the U-clip retaining the female fitting to the frame bracket.
9   Using a back-up wrench, attach the brake line to the hose fitting.
10   When the brake hose installation is complete, there should be no kinks in the hose. Make sure the hose doesn't contact any part of the suspension. Check this by turning the wheels to the extreme left and right positions. If the hose makes contact, remove it and correct the installation as necessary. Bleed the system (see Section 10).

Rear brake hose

Refer to illustration 9.13

11   Using a back-up wrench, disconnect the hose at the frame bracket, being careful not to bend the bracket or steel lines.
12   Remove the U-clip with a pair of pliers and separate the female fitting from the bracket.
13   Disconnect the two hydraulic lines at the junction block, then unbolt and remove the hose **(see illustration)**.
14   Bolt the junction block to the axle housing and connect the lines, tightening them securely. Without twisting the hose, install the female end of the hose in the frame bracket.
15   Install the U-clips retaining the female end to the bracket.
16   Using a back-up wrench, attach the steel line fittings to the female fittings. Again, be careful not to bend the bracket or steel line.
17   Make sure the hose installation did not loosen the frame bracket. Tighten the bracket if necessary.
18   Fill the master cylinder reservoir and bleed the system (see Section 10).

Metal brake lines

19   When replacing brake lines be sure to use the correct parts. NEVER use copper tubing for any brake system components. Purchase steel brake lines from a dealer or auto parts store.
20   Prefabricated brake line, with the tube ends already flared and fittings installed, is available at auto parts stores and dealers. These lines are also bent to the proper shapes.
21   If prefabricated lines are not available, obtain the recommended steel tubing and fittings to match the line to be replaced. Determine the correct length by measuring the old brake line (a piece of string can usually be used for this) and cut the new tubing to length, allowing about 1/4 -inch extra for flaring the ends.
22   Install the fitting over the cut tubing and flare the ends of the line with a flaring tool. A double-flare is the only acceptable type for automotive brake system applications.
23   If necessary, carefully bend the line to the proper shape. A tube bender is recommended for this **Warning:** *Do not crimp or damage the line.*
24   When installing the new line make sure it's securely supported in the brackets and has plenty of clearance between moving or hot components.
25   After installation, check the master cylinder fluid level and add fluid as necessary. Bleed the brake system as outlined in the next Section and test the brakes carefully before driving the vehicle in traffic.

10   Brake system bleeding

Refer to illustration 10.8
Warning: *Wear eye protection when bleeding the brake system. If the fluid comes in contact with your eyes, immediately rinse them with water and seek medical attention.*
Note: *Bleeding the hydraulic system is necessary to remove any air that manages to find its way into the system when it's been opened during removal and installation of a hose, line, caliper or master cylinder.*
1   It will probably be necessary to bleed the system at all four brakes if air has entered the system due to low fluid level, or if the brake lines have been disconnected at the master cylinder.
2   If a brake line was disconnected only at a wheel, then only that caliper or wheel cylinder must be bled.
3   If a brake line is disconnected at a fitting located between the master cylinder and any of the brakes, that part of the system served by the disconnected line must be bled.
4   Remove any residual vacuum from the brake power booster by applying the brake several times with the engine off.
5   Remove the master cylinder reservoir cover and fill the reservoir with brake fluid. Reinstall the cover. **Note:** *Check the fluid level often during the bleeding operation and add fluid as necessary to prevent the fluid level from falling low enough to allow air bubbles into the master cylinder.*
6   Have an assistant on hand, as well as a supply of new brake fluid, a clear container partially filled with clean brake fluid, a length of 3/16-inch plastic, rubber or vinyl tubing to fit over the bleeder valve and a wrench to open and close the bleeder valve.
7   On early models equipped with the Trackmaster ABS system, the modulator (located on top of the master cylinder) must be bled first, using the procedure described below, before proceeding.
8   Beginning at the right rear wheel, loosen the bleeder valve slightly, then tighten it to a point where it is snug but can still be loosened quickly and easily.
9   Place one end of the tubing over the bleeder valve and submerge the other end in brake fluid in the container **(see illustration)**.
10   Have the assistant pump the brakes slowly a few times to get pressure in the system, then hold the pedal firmly depressed.
11   While the pedal is held depressed, open the bleeder valve just enough to allow a flow of fluid to leave the valve. Watch for air bubbles to exit the submerged end of the tube. When the fluid flow slows after a couple of seconds, close the valve and have your assistant release the pedal.

11.3   To adjust the parking brake cable, turn the adjusting nut on the equalizer while preventing the cable from turning with a pair of locking pliers clamped to the cable stud (later model cable)

12.4   To disconnect the cable end from the parking brake lever, pull back on the return spring and maneuver the cable out of the slot in the lever (drum brake)

12   Repeat Steps 10 and 11 until no more air is seen leaving the tube, then tighten the bleeder valve and proceed to the left rear wheel, the right front wheel and the left front wheel, in that order, and perform the same procedure. Be sure to check the fluid in the master cylinder reservoir frequently.
13   Never use old brake fluid. It contains moisture which will deteriorate the brake system components.
14   Refill the master cylinder with fluid at the end of the operation.
15   Check the operation of the brakes. The pedal should feel solid when depressed, with no sponginess. If necessary, repeat the entire process.
Warning: *Do not operate the vehicle if you are in doubt about the effectiveness of the brake system.*

11   Parking brake – adjustment

Refer to illustration 11.3
1   The adjustment of the parking brake cable may be necessary whenever the rear brake cables have been disconnected or the parking brake cables have stretched due to age and stress.
2   On models equipped with rear drum brakes, depress the parking brake pedal approximately 1 1/2 inches (1970 through 1986 models) or 3 clicks (1987 on). On rear disc brake equipped models, the parking brake must be in the released position. Raise the car for access underneath, supporting it securely on jackstands.

Rear drum brake equipped models
3   Tighten the adjusting nut until light drag is felt on either wheel when turned forward (1970 through 1986 models). On 1987 and later models, the left rear tire should just barely be turned in a rearward motion (**see illustration**). The tire should be completely locked from moving in a forward rotation.
4   Carefully release the parking brake pedal and check that the tire is able to rotate freely in either direction. It is important that there is no drag on the rear brakes with the pedal released.

Rear disc brake equipped models
5   Tighten the adjusting nut until all slack is removed from the parking brake cables. The parking brake caliper levers must be in contact their stops after adjustment. If they are off the stops, loosen the adjuster as necessary.

1970 through 1986 models
6   Depress the parking brake pedal with approximately 125 lbs of force and make sure the pedal travel is as specified in this Chapter's Specifications.

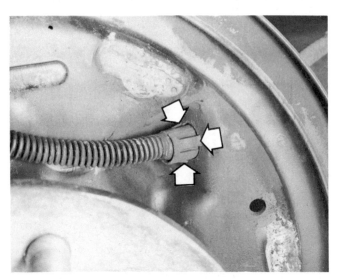

12.5   Depress the retention tangs (arrows) to free the cable and housing from the backing plate (drum brake)

12   Parking brake cables – replacement

Rear cables
Refer to illustrations 12.4 and 12.5
1   Loosen the wheel lug nuts, raise the rear of the vehicle and support it securely on jackstands. Remove the wheel(s).
2   Loosen the equalizer nut to slacken the cables, then disconnect the cable to be replaced from the equalizer.
3   Remove the brake drum from the axle flange. See Section 5 if any difficulty is encountered.
4   Remove the drum brake shoe assembly far enough to disconnect the cable end from the parking brake lever (**see illustration**).
5   Depress the tangs on the cable housing retainer and push the housing and cable through the backing plate (**see illustration**).
6   To install the cable, reverse the removal procedure and adjust the cable as described in the preceding Section.

9

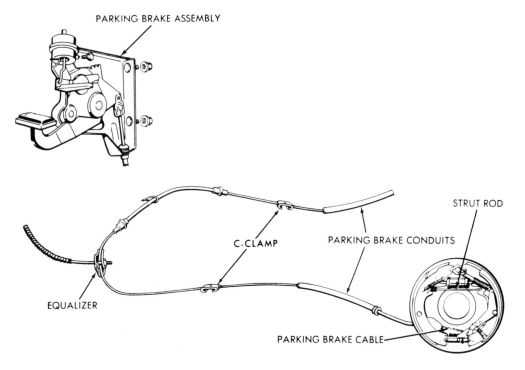

12.9a   Typical early model parking brake cable routing

12.9b   Typical later model parking brake cable layout

12.9c   Seville parking brake cable layout

Front cable

Refer to illustrations 12.9a, 12.9b and 12.9c

7   Raise the vehicle and support it securely on jackstands.
8   Loosen the equalizer assembly to provide slack in the cable.
9   Disconnect the front cable from the cable joiner near the equalizer **(see illustrations)**.
10   Disconnect the cable from the pedal assembly.
11   Free the cable from the routing clips and push the cable and grommet through the firewall.
12   To install the cable, reverse the removal procedure and adjust the cable as described in the preceding Section.

---

13   Power brake booster – inspection, removal and installation

---

1   The power brake booster unit requires no special maintenance apart from periodic inspection of the vacuum hose and the case.

2   Dismantling of the power unit requires special tools and is not ordinarily done by the home mechanic. If a problem develops, install a new or factory rebuilt unit.
3   Remove the nuts attaching the master cylinder to the booster and carefully pull the master cylinder forward until it clears the mounting studs. Don't bend or kink the brake lines.
4   Disconnect the vacuum hose where it attaches to the power brake booster.
5   From the passenger compartment, disconnect the power brake push-rod from the top of the brake pedal.
6   Also from this location, remove the nuts attaching the booster to the firewall.
7   Carefully lift the booster unit away from the firewall and out of the engine compartment.
8   To install, place the booster in position and tighten the nuts to the Specifications. Connect the brake pedal.
9   Install the master cylinder and vacuum hose.
10   Carefully test the operation of the brakes before placing the vehicle in normal service.

9

14.1   Typical brake light switch installation

BRAKE PEDAL
MOUNTING BRACKET

TUBULAR
CLIP

STOPLIGHT
SWITCH
(WITHOUT CRUISE)

STOPLIGHT
SWITCH
(WITH CRUISE)

14   Brake light switch – removal, installation and adjustment

Refer to illustration 14.1

1   This switch is located on a flange or bracket protruding from the brake pedal support **(see illustration)**.

2   With the brake pedal in the fully released position, the plunger on the body of the switch should be fully pressed in. When the pedal is pushed in, the plunger releases and sends electrical current to the stop lights at the rear of the car.

3   Electrical contact should be made when the pedal is depressed 0.38- to 0.64-inch. If this is not the case, the switch can be adjusted by turning it in or out as required.

4   To replace the switch if it is faulty, disconnect the electrical coupler (two couplers if car is equipped with cruise control) and loosen the switch locknut until the switch can be unscrewed from the bracket. Installation is a reversal of this procedure.

15   Anti-lock Braking System (ABS) – general information

Refer to illustration 15.3

Two types of ABS were available on these models; the Trackmaster type used on some early models and the Bosch II system introduced in 1990. ABS is designed to maintain vehicle control under severe braking conditions. The system performs this function by monitoring the rotational speed of the wheels and controlling the brake line pressure to prevent wheel lockup.

The Trackmaster system controls the rear wheels only. It consists of a speed sensor mounted in the transmission, a modulator and modulator activator, a solenoid valve and an electronic controller. The Trackmaster system operates by pulsing the brake fluid pressure by energizing the modulator which varies the pressure to the rear brakes, preventing them from locking and causing a skid.

The more sophisticated Bosch II system uses wheel speed sensors located on the front hubs and another sensor in the differential housing to monitor wheel speed **(see illustration)**. The electrical signal from these sensors is processed by the Electronic Brake Control Module (EBCM) to operate the hydraulic modulator valve to maintain or reduce to the brake fluid pressure to keep the wheels from locking.

Due to the rather complicated nature of ABS, particularly the Bosch II system, all repair work must be performed by a dealer service department or other repair shop.

15.3   Bosch II ABS system components

1   *Front wheel toothed speed sensors*
2   *Hydraulic modulator*
3   *Front brake caliper*
4   *Brake master cylinder and booster*
5   *Brake pedal*
6   *Rear drum brake*
7   *Rear axle speed sensor and toothed sensor ring*
8   *ABS warning lamp*
9   *Electronic Brake Control Module (ECBM)*

Chapter 10
Suspension and steering systems

Contents

Specifications

Torque specifications

	Ft-lbs
Front suspension	
Stabilizer bar link nuts	15
Stabilizer bar bracket-to-frame bolts	25
Shock absorber upper stud nut	8 to 11
Shock absorber-to-lower control arm bolts	20
Upper control arm-to-frame nuts	80 to 90
Upper balljoint stud-to-steering knuckle nut	
Seville	62
All others	
Through 1976	60
1977 on	40

Torque specifications (continued)

Lower balljoint stud-to-steering knuckle nut   80
Lower control arm-to-frame pivot bolt nut   90
Tie strut-to-lower control arm bolts   55

Rear suspension

Shock absorber lower mount bolts
    Seville   45
    All others   65
Shock absorber upper mount bolts   15
Stabilizer bar-to-suspension bolts   50
Stabilizer bar link bolt nuts (Seville only)   30
Control arm pivot bolts (models except Seville)
    Through 1976 (all bolts)   75
    1977 on
        Lower arm-to-axle bolt   120
        All other bolts . . . .   80 to 90
Leaf spring (Seville only)
    U-bolt nuts   45
    Front through-bolt nut   105
    Front mounting bracket bolts   30
    Rear shackle pin nuts   50

Steering

Steering wheel-to-steering shaft nut   30
Tie-rod end-to-steering knuckle nut   30
Tie-rod adjuster sleeve clamp nut   20
Steering gear-to-frame bolts   70
Pitman shaft nut   185
Pitman arm-to-intermediate rod nut . . . .   40 to 50
Tie-rod end-to-intermediate rod nut
    Seville   35
    All others   50
Idler arm-to-intermediate rod nut
    Seville   40
    All others   35
Idler arm-to-frame nuts
    Seville   50
    All others   40
Intermediate shaft pinch bolts   50
Steering damper nut   35

---

1   General information

Refer to illustration 1.1

Caution: *Whenever any suspension or steering fasteners are loosened or removed they must be inspected and, if necessary, replaced with new ones of the same part number or of original equipment quality and design. Cotter keys, used extensively on steering components, should never be reused – always replace them with new ones. Torque specifications must be followed for proper reassembly and component retention. Never attempt to heat, straighten or weld any steering or suspension component. Always replace bent or damaged parts with new ones.*

Each front wheel is connected to the frame by upper and lower control arms (A-frames), through a steering knuckle and upper and lower balljoints. 1970 through 1975 models also have a tie strut connecting the lower control arm to the frame. A coil spring is installed between the lower control arm and the frame, and a telescopic shock absorber is positioned inside the coil spring. A stabilizer bar connected to the frame rails and to the lower control arms on each side aids in controlling body roll **(see illustration)**.

The rear suspension on full-size models consists of a solid axle located by upper and lower control arms, with coil springs supplying the suspension. On Seville models the control arms and coil springs are replaced with multi-leaf springs. All models utilize telescopic shock absorbers installed between the spring mounts or seats and the frame rails.

The steering system consists of the steering wheel and column, an articulated intermediate shaft, a recirculating ball steering gear and the steering linkage. Power steering is standard on all models.

Frequently, when working on the suspension or steering system components, you may come across fasteners which seem impossible to loosen. These fasteners on the underside of the vehicle are continually subjected to water, road grime, mud, etc., and can become rusted or "frozen," making them extremely difficult to remove. In order to unscrew these stubborn fasteners without damaging them (or other components), be sure to use lots of penetrating oil and allow it to soak in for a while. Using a wire brush to clean exposed threads will also ease removal of the nut or bolt and prevent damage to the threads. Sometimes a sharp blow with a hammer and punch is effective in breaking the bond between a nut and bolt threads, but care must be taken to prevent the punch from slipping off the fastener and ruining the threads. Heating the stuck fastener and surrounding area with a torch sometimes helps too, but isn't recommended because of the obvious dangers associated with fire. Long breaker bars and extension, or "cheater," pipes will increase leverage, but never use an extension pipe on a ratchet – the ratcheting mechanism could be damaged. Sometimes, turning the nut or bolt in the tightening (clockwise) direction first will help to break it loose. Fasteners that require drastic measures to unscrew should always be replaced with new ones.

Since most of the procedures that are dealt with in this chapter involve jacking up the vehicle and working underneath it, a good pair of jackstands will be needed. A hydraulic floor jack is the preferred type of jack to lift the vehicle, and it can also be used to support certain components during various operation. **Warning:** *Never, under any circumstances, rely on a jack to support the vehicle while working on it.*

1.1 Front suspension components – typical

1 Idler arm
2 Stabilizer bar
3 Steering damper
4 Intermediate rod
5 Pitman arm
6 Steering gear
7 Lower balljoint
8 Shock absorber lower mount
9 Lower control arm
10 Steering knuckle
11 Tie-rod

10

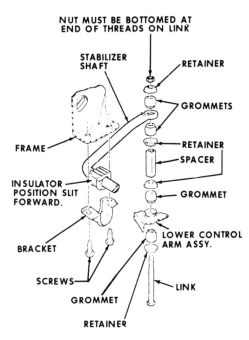

2.2   Typical front stabilizer bar mounting details

2.3   Remove the brackets and rubber bushings on each side which attach the stabilizer bar to the frame

2   Front stabilizer bar – removal and installation

Refer to illustrations 2.2 and 2.3

Removal

1   Raise the vehicle and support it securely on jackstands. Apply the parking brake.
2   Remove the stabilizer bar link nuts, noting how the grommets and retainers are positioned **(see illustration)**. Clamp a pair of locking pliers to the stabilizer bar link to prevent it from turning.
3   Remove the stabilizer bar bracket bolts and detach the bar from the vehicle **(see illustration)**.
4   Pull the brackets off the stabilizer bar and inspect the bushings for cracks, hardening and other signs of deterioration. If the bushings are damaged, cut them from the bar and replace them.

Installation

5   Position the stabilizer bar bushings on the bar with the slits facing the front of the vehicle. **Note:** *The offset in the bar must face down.*
6   Push the brackets over the bushings and raise the bar up to the frame. Install the bracket bolts but don't tighten them completely at this time.
7   Install the stabilizer bar link nuts, washers and rubber bushings and tighten the nuts securely.
8   Tighten the bracket bolts.

3   Front shock absorbers – removal and installation

Refer to illustration 3.1

Removal

1   Remove the upper shock absorber stem nut **(see illustration)**. Use an open end wrench to keep the stem from turning. If the nut won't loosen because of rust, squirt some penetrating oil on the stem threads and allow it to soak in for awhile. It may be necessary to keep the stem from turning with a pair of locking pliers, since the flats provided for a wrench are quite small.

3.1   Typical front shock absorber mounting details – exploded view

2   Loosen the wheel lug nuts, raise the vehicle and support it securely on jackstands. Apply the parking brake. Remove the wheel.
3   Remove the through bolt (early models) or two lower shock mount bolts (later models) and pull the shock absorber out through the bottom of the lower control arm. Remove the retainers and the rubber grommets from the top of the shock absorber.

Installation

4   Extend the new shock absorber as far as possible. Position a new retainer and rubber grommet on the stem and guide the shock up through the coil spring and into the upper mount.

4.4   A special GM tool (J-23742) is used to push the balljoint out of the steering knuckle, but an alternative tool can be fabricated from a large bolt, nut, washer and socket

5   Install the upper rubber grommet and retainer and wiggle the stem back-and-forth to ensure that the grommets are centered in the mount. Tighten the stem nut securely.
6   Install the lower mounting bolts and tighten them securely.

---

4   Balljoints – replacement

Upper balljoint (1977 and later models only)

Refer to illustrations 4.4, 4.5 and 4.8

Note: *On 1970 through 1976 models, the upper balljoint is welded to the control arm. In the event that the upper balljoint becomes badly worn, the upper control arm will have to be replaced.*

1   Loosen the wheel lug nuts, raise the vehicle and support it securely on jackstands. Apply the parking brake. Remove the wheel.
2   Place a floorjack under the lower control arm. Raise the jack far enough to just begin to compress the coil spring. **Note:** *The jack must remain under the control arm during removal and installation of the balljoint to hold the spring and control arm in position.*
3   Remove the cotter pin from the upper balljoint stud and back off the nut two turns.
4   Separate the balljoint from the steering knuckle (use GM tool no. J-23742 or equivalent to press the balljoint out of the steering knuckle). An equivalent tool can be fabricated from a large bolt, nut, washer and socket **(see illustration)**. Countersink the center of the bolt head with a large drill bit to prevent the tool from slipping off the balljoint stud. Install the tool as shown in the illustration, hold the bolt head with a wrench and tighten the nut against the washer until the balljoint pops out. Notice that the balljoint nut hasn't been completely removed.
5   Using a 1/8-inch drill bit, drill a 1/4-inch deep hole in the center of each rivet head **(see illustration)**.
6   Using a 1/2-inch diameter drill bit, drill off the rivet heads.
7   Use a punch to knock the rivet shanks out, then remove the balljoint from the control arm.
8   Position the new balljoint on the control arm and install the bolts and nuts supplied in the kit **(see illustration)**. Be sure to tighten the nuts to the torque specified on the balljoint kit instruction sheet.
9   Insert the balljoint stud into the steering knuckle and install the nut, tightening it to the torque listed in this Chapter's Specifications.
10   Install a new cotter pin, tightening the nut slightly if necessary to align a slot in the nut with the hole in the balljoint stud.
11   Install the balljoint grease fitting and fill the joint with grease.

4.5   To remove the upper balljoint on 1977 and later models, drill pilot holes into the heads of the balljoint rivets with a 1/8-inch bit, then use a 1/2-inch bit to cut the rivet heads off – be careful not to enlarge the holes in the control arm

4.8   Install the replacement balljoint in the upper control arm with the nuts on top

---

12   Install the wheel, tightening the lug nuts to the torque specified in Chapter 1.
13   Drive the vehicle to an alignment shop to have the front end alignment checked and, if necessary, adjusted.

Lower balljoint

14   The lower balljoint is a press fit in the lower control arm and requires special tools to remove and replace it. Refer to Section 6, remove the lower control arm and take it to an automotive machine shop to have the old balljoint pressed out and the new balljoint pressed in.

10

---

5   Front upper control arm – removal and installation

Refer to illustrations 5.4a, 5.4b and 5.4c

Removal

1   Loosen the wheel lug nuts, raise the front of the vehicle and support it securely on jackstands. Apply the parking brake. Remove the wheel.

INNER SHAFT MOUNTING BOLTS

HEAT SHIELD
(RIGHT SIDE ONLY)

UPPER CONTROL ARM

FLATWASHER

INNER SHAFT

FLATWASHER

BUSHING

NUT

NUT

BUSHING

UPPER
SPHERICAL
JOINT

NUT

RETAINER

BUSHING

WASHERS

STABILIZER
LINK

CAMBER
ECCENTRIC

RETAINER

SPECIAL FLATWASHER

STEERING KNUCKLE

NUTS

GROMMET

GROMMET

STABILIZER BAR

SPACER

NUT

RETAINER

COIL SPRING

GROMMET

LOWER CONTROL ARM

FLAT WASHER

LOWER SPHERICAL JOINT

PIVOT BOLT

TIE STRUT

SHOCK
ABSORBER

GROMMET

RETAINER

NUT

SHOCK ABSORBER
LOWER MOUNTING BOLT

LOCKNUT

NUT

RETAINER

BUSHING

FRAME

BUSHING

SPACER

RETAINER

NUT

STRUT

5.4a   Typical front suspension components (1970 through 1976, except Seville) – exploded view

2   Support the lower control arm with a floorjack. The support point must be as close to the balljoint as possible to give maximum leverage on the lower control arm.

3   Disconnect the upper balljoint from the steering knuckle (refer to Section 4). **Note:** *DO NOT use a "pickle fork" type balljoint separator – it will damage the balljoint seal.*

4   Remove the control arm shaft-to-frame nuts and bolts, recording the position of any alignment shims. They must be reinstalled in the same location to maintain wheel alignment **(see illustrations).**

5   Detach the control arm from the vehicle. **Note:** *The control arm bushings are pressed into place and require special tools for removal and installation. If the bushings must be replaced, take the control arm to a*

dealer service department or an automotive machine shop to have the old bushings pressed out and the new ones pressed in.

Installation

6   Position the control arm on the frame and install the bolts and nuts. Install any alignment shims that were removed. Tighten the nuts to the torque listed in this Chapter's Specifications.

7   Insert the balljoint stud into the steering knuckle and tighten the nut to the torque listed in this Chapter's Specifications. Install a new cotter pin, tightening the nut slightly, if necessary, to align a slot in the nut with the hole in the balljoint stud.

UPPER
SUSPENSION
ARM

BUSHING

RETAINER

SPHERICAL
JOINT

NUT

SHIM

SHAFT

UPPER BUMPER

STABILIZER
BAR

BUSHING

COIL SPRING

SHOCK ABSORBER

LOWER SUSPENSION ARM

SPHERICAL JOINT

BRAKE CALIPER

BRACKET

FITTING

STEERING KNUCKLE

GASKET

SPLASH SHIELD

SEAL

BEARING

HUB & ROTOR
ASSEMBLY

BEARING

WASHER

CAP

LINK BOLT

WHEEL ASM.

10

5.4b   Typical front suspension components (1977 and later models, except Seville) – exploded view

SHIM
SHAFT
SPHERICAL JOINT
UPPER SUSPENSION ARM
BUSHING
WASHER
NUT
BUMPER
COIL SPRING
SPLASH SHIELD
BRAKE CALIPER
BUSHING
FRAME
STABILIZER BAR
STEERING KNUCKLE
NUT
CAP
SPHERICAL JOINT
HUB AND ROTOR ASSEMBLY
BEARING CUP
BEARING
WASHER
LINK BOLT
SHOCK ABSORBER

5.4c Seville front suspension components – exploded view

8   Install the wheel and lug nuts and lower the vehicle. Tighten the lug nuts to the torque specified in Chapter 1.
9   Drive the vehicle to an alignment shop to have the front end alignment checked and, if necessary, adjusted.

6   Front lower control arm – removal and installation

Removal

1   Loosen the wheel lug nuts, raise the vehicle and support it securely on jackstands. Apply the parking brake. Remove the wheel.
2   Unbolt the shock absorber from the lower control arm and push it up into the coil spring.
3   Disconnect the stabilizer bar from the lower control arm (Section 2).
4   Remove the coil spring as described in Section 8.
5   Remove the cotter pin and back off the lower control arm balljoint stud nut two turns. Separate the lower balljoint from the steering knuckle (Section 4). On 1970 through 1976 models, remove the tie strut-to-lower control arm bolts **(Refer to illustration 5.4a)**.
6   Separate the control arm from the vehicle **(Refer to illustration 5.4a, 5.4b or 5.4c)**. **Note:** *The control arm bushings are pressed into place and require special tools for removal and installation. If the bushings must be replaced, take the control arm to a dealer service department or an automotive machine shop to have the old bushings pressed out and the new ones pressed in.*

Installation

7   Insert the balljoint stud into the steering knuckle, tighten the nut to the torque listed in this Chapter's Specifications and install a new cotter pin. If necessary, tighten the nut slightly to align a slot in the nut with the hole in the balljoint stud.
8   Install the coil spring (Section 8) and the lower control arm pivot bolts and nuts, but don't completely tighten them at this time. On 1970 through 1976 models, install the tie strut bolts and nuts and tighten them to the torque listed in this Chapter's Specifications.
9   Connect the stabilizer bar to the lower control arm (Section 2). Install the wheel and lug nuts, lower the vehicle and tighten the lug nuts to the torque specified in Chapter 1.
10   With the vehicle at normal ride height, tighten the lower control arm pivot bolt nuts to the torque listed in this Chapter's Specifications.
11   Drive the vehicle to an alignment shop to have the front end alignment checked and, if necessary, adjusted.

7   Steering knuckle – removal and installation

Refer to illustration 7.4

Removal

1   Loosen the wheel lug nuts, raise the vehicle and support it securely on jackstands placed under the frame. Apply the parking brake. Remove the wheel.
2   Remove the brake caliper and suspend it with a piece of wire (Chapter 9). Do not let it hang by the brake hose!

**7.4 A typical steering knuckle and
hub assembly – exploded view**

3   Remove the brake hub and disc assembly (see Chapter 1).
4   Remove the splash shield from the steering knuckle **(see illustration)**.
5   Separate the tie-rod end from the steering knuckle (see Section 19).
6   If the steering knuckle must be replaced, remove the dust seal from the spindle by prying it off with a screwdriver. If it's damaged, replace it with a new one.
7   Position a floor jack under the lower control arm and raise it slightly to take the spring pressure off the suspension stop. The jack must remain in this position throughout the entire procedure.
8   Remove the cotter pins from the upper and lower balljoint studs and back off the nuts two turns each.
9   Break the balljoints loose from the steering knuckle with a balljoint separator (Section 4). **Note:** *A pickle fork type balljoint separator will damage the balljoint seals.*
10   Remove the nuts from the balljoint studs, separate the control arms from the steering knuckle and remove the knuckle from the vehicle.

Installation

11   Place the knuckle between the upper and lower control arms and insert the balljoint studs into the knuckle, beginning with the lower balljoint. Install the nuts and tighten them to the torques listed in this Chapter's Specifications. Install new cotter pins, tightening the nuts slightly to align the slots in the nuts with the holes in the balljoint studs, if necessary.
12   Install the splash shield.
13   Connect the tie-rod end to the steering arm and tighten the nut to the torque listed in this Chapter's Specifications. Be sure to use a new cotter pin.
14   Install the brake rotor and adjust the wheel bearings following the procedure outlined in Chapter 1.
15   Install the brake caliper.

16   Install the wheel and lug nuts. Lower the vehicle to the ground and tighten the nuts to the torque specified in Chapter 1.

8   Front coil springs – removal and installation

Removal

1   Loosen the wheel lug nuts, raise the vehicle and support it securely on jackstands placed under the frame. Apply the parking brake. Remove the wheel.
2   Remove the shock absorber (Section 3).
3   Disconnect the stabilizer bar from the lower control arm (Section 2). On 1970 through 1976 models, unbolt the tie strut from the lower control arm **(see illustration 5.4a)**.
4   Position a jack under the inner edge of the lower control arm. Make sure the jack is centered from front to rear.
5   Loop a length of safety chain up through the control arm and coil spring and bolt the ends of the chain together. Make sure there's enough slack in the chain so it won't inhibit spring extension when the control arm is lowered.
6   Raise the jack slightly to relieve spring pressure from the control arm pivot bolt(s) and remove the nut(s) and bolt(s). If the bolts are hard to remove, drive them out with a long, narrow drift.
7   Slowly lower the jack until the coil spring is fully extended.
8   Unbolt the safety chain and maneuver the coil spring out. Do not apply downward pressure on the lower control arm as it may damage the balljoint. If the upper coil spring insulator is not on the top of the spring, reach up in the spring pocket and retrieve it.

10

Installation

9   Place the insulators on the top and bottom of the coil spring (the top of the spring is flat on the end, with a gripper notch near the end of the spring coil).

10   Install the top of the spring into the spring pocket and the bottom in the lower control arm. The end of the lower spring coil must be seated in the lowest recessed portion of the spring seat.

11   Place the jack under the lower control arm, install the safety chain and slowly raise the control arm into place. When the bolt holes are aligned, install the bolt(s). If there are two bolts, make sure the bolt heads face towards the center of the control arm. It may be necessary to insert a punch through the mounting bracket and into the control arm bushing to align the holes. Do not completely tighten the nuts at this time.

12   Install the shock absorber (Section 3). On 1970 through 1976 models, connect the tie strut to the lower control arm and install the nuts and bolts. Tighten the nuts to the torque specified at the beginning of this Chapter.

13   Attach the stabilizer bar to the lower control arm (Section 2).

14   Install the wheel and lug nuts. Lower the vehicle and tighten the lug nuts to the torque specified in Chapter 1.

9.2   On all models except Seville, the rear stabilizer bar bolts to the lower control arm on each side (right side shown – left side opposite)

9.6   Typical Seville rear stabilizer bar installation details

10.3b   Typical Seville shock absorber mounting

FRAME

SHOCK ABSORBER ASM.

INSTALL IN LOWER
HOLE IN BRACKET

REAR
AXLE
ASM.

10.3a   Typical shock absorber mounting details (models
except Seville)

15   Reach under the vehicle and tighten the lower control arm pivot bolt nuts to the torque listed in this Chapter's Specifications.
16   Drive the vehicle to an alignment shop to have the front end alignment checked and, if necessary, adjusted.

9   Rear stabilizer bar – removal and installation

All models except Seville

Refer to illustration 9.2
1   Raise the rear of the vehicle and support it securely on jackstands.
2   Remove the two nuts and bolts on each side securing the stabilizer bar to the lower control arms **(see illustration)**.
3   Remove the stabilizer bar and, if present, the shims installed between the bar and lower control arm on each side.
4   Installation is the reverse of the removal procedure, being sure to re-place the shims (if any were removed) and tightening the nuts and bolts to the torque listed in this Chapter's Specifications.

Seville

Refer to illustration 9.6
5   Raise the rear of the vehicle and support it securely on jackstands.
6   Disconnect the nut from each link bolt. Disconnect the stabilizer bar clamp bolts from each spring anchor plate and lower the stabilizer bar from the vehicle **(see illustration)**.
7   Installation is the reverse of the removal procedure. Do not tighten the fasteners completely until the vehicle is lowered and at normal ride height.
Note: *When installing the insulators on the stabilizer bar, the slit in the in-sulator should face the front of the vehicle.*

10   Rear shock absorbers – removal and installation

Refer to illustrations 10.3a and 10.3b
1   Raise the rear of the vehicle and support it securely on jackstands. On Automatic Level Control (ALC) equipped models, disconnect the air fit-tings at the shock absorber.
2   On Seville models, remove the wheel and tire.
3   On models where the lower end of the shock absorber is retained to the axle by a stud, remove the nut and washer **(see illustrations)**.
4   On models where the lower end of the shock absorber is retained to the axle by a through-bolt, remove the nut, lockwasher and bolt.
5   Remove the two upper bolts securing the shock absorber to the frame and remove the shock absorber from the vehicle.
6   Installation is the reverse of the removal procedure.
7   On ALC equipped models, inflate the ALC reservoir. This is done on 1970 through 1983 models through the fitting on the reservoir (make sure to use dry air – moisture will damage the system). On 1984 and later mod-els the reservoir fills automatically when the ignition is turned to On.
8   On ALC equipped models, inflate the shock absorbers. On 1970 through 1981 models this is accomplished by disconnecting the leveling arm at the axle bracket and pushing the arm up, allowing air to enter the shock absorbers, then reconnecting the lever. On electronic ALC systems used on 1982 through 1983 models, turn the ignition On and move the shift lever from Park to Reverse and back to Park. On 1984 and later models, turn the ignition On and ground the compressor test lead.

11   Rear coil springs – removal and installation

Refer to illustration 11.8
Note: *This procedure does not apply to Seville models.*
1   Raise the rear of the vehicle and support it securely on jackstands un-der the frame rails.
2   Remove the rear wheels and stabilizer bar (see Section 2). On ALC equipped models, disconnect the leveling arm link.
3   Place a floor jack under the center of the differential housing and raise the axle until the coil springs just start to compress. **Warning:** *When the springs are removed, the floor jack will be the sole support for the rear axle assembly, so be sure the jack is positioned correctly.*
4   Disconnect the lower ends of both shock absorbers from the rear axle.
5   Remove the bolt attaching the brake line to the frame crossmember and disconnect the brake lines from the clips on the axle.
6   Disconnect the driveshaft and hang it out of the way on a piece of wire.
7   Remove the upper control arm pivot bolts (see Section 12).

10

11.8   Typical rear coil spring and insulator details

12.3   Typical rear upper and lower control arms used on all models except Seville

8   Carefully lower the jack just enough to remove the spring and rubber insulator (on top of the spring on later models) **(see illustration)**. **Note:** *When removing the spring make note of the position of the coil ends, top and bottom. The spring must be reinstalled with the coil ends in the same position.*
9   Installation is the reverse of the removal procedure.

12   Rear control arms – removal and installation

Refer to illustration 12.3
Note: *This procedure does not apply to Seville models.*
1   Raise the vehicle and support it securely with jackstands placed under the axle housing.

Upper arm

2   Support the nose of the differential with a floor jack to keep the axle housing from pivoting when the control arms are removed. On ALC equipped models, disconnect the leveling arm link.
3   Remove the pivot bolt holding the rear of the control arm to the ear on the axle housing **(see illustration)** and pry the control arm upwards until it clears the ear.
4   Remove the control arm pivot bolt at the frame.
5   Remove the control arm.
6   Installation is the reverse of the removal procedure. Do not tighten the bolts completely until the vehicle is lowered to the ground.
7   Lower the vehicle to the ground and tighten all control arm bolts to the torque listed in this Chapter's Specifications. On ALC equipped models, connect the leveling arm link.

Lower arm

8   Remove the pivot bolt holding the rear of the control arm to the lower spring seat and pry the control arm down until it clears the spring seat flanges.

9   Remove the control arm pivot bolt at the frame rail.
10   Remove the control arm.
11   Installation is the reverse of the removal procedure. Do not tighten the bolts completely until the vehicle is lowered to the ground.
12   Lower the vehicle to the ground and tighten all control arm bolts to the torque listed in this Chapter's Specifications.

13   Leaf springs (Seville only) – removal and installation

Refer to illustration 13.5
1   Raise the vehicle and support it securely on jackstands placed beneath the frame rails, just in front of the front spring mounts. On ALC equipped models, disconnect the leveling link and hold the lever down to depressurize the shock absorbers.
2   Remove the lower shock absorber mounting nut or bolt and compress the shock absorber up to move it out of the way.
3   Loosen the parking brake cable (see Chapter 9) and detach the cable from the leaf springs.
4   Place a floor jack under the axle housing and lift the axle housing slightly.
5   Loosen the spring front through-bolt nut **(see illustration)**.
6   Remove the front spring bracket-to-frame bolts, lower the jack sufficiently for access and remove the through-bolt and the bracket.
7   Remove the U-bolt and T-bolt nuts and withdraw the anchor plate and lower spring cushion.
8   Use the floor jack to lift the axle off the spring and remove the upper spring cushion.
9   Loosen the upper and lower shackle pin nuts at the rear of the spring.
10   Remove the lower shackle pin from the rear of the spring and withdraw the spring from the vehicle.

VIEW A

7°

HORIZONTAL
LINE

TIGHTEN EYE BOLT NUT WITH
SPRING AT APPROX. 7° OR WITH
VEHICLE WEIGHT ON SPRINGS

NOTE: SHACKLES AND PINS MUST
BE INSTALLED IN DIRECTION SHOWN.

UNDERBODY

U-BOLT

T-BOLT

FLOOR PAN
REINFORCEMENT

SIDE RAIL

UPPER CUSHION

BUSHING

NOTE: TIGHTEN NUT WITH VEHICLE
WEIGHT ON SPRINGS.

SLOT

BRACKET

LOWER CUSHION

SHOCK ABSORBER
LOWER LOCATION

DAMPER

CUSHION

TAB

PLATE

FRONT OF CAR

SPRING
FRONT EYE

CLAMP SCREW
MUST BE OUTBOARD
OF SPRING

13.5   Typical leaf spring mounting details (Seville)

11   Installation is the reverse of the removal procedure. Do not tighten the front spring through bolt and shackle pin nuts completely until the vehicle is lowered to the ground and at normal ride height. On ALC equipped models, hold the leveling link lever up to inflate the shock absorbers, then connect the link.

12   Lower the vehicle to the ground and tighten the front spring through bolt and shackle pin nuts to the torques listed in this Chapter's Specifications.

14   Steering wheel – removal and installation

Refer to illustrations 14.3, 14.4 and 14.5

1   Disconnect the cable from the negative terminal of the battery.

2   Remove the cover from the steering wheel spoke. Most are secured with screws at the back of the steering wheel. Pull the cover from the steering wheel and disconnect the wire to the horn switch.

3   If equipped, remove the safety clip from the end of the steering shaft **(see illustration)**.

14.3   Snap-ring pliers are used to remove the safety clip from the steering shaft (not all models)

10

14.4   Check to be sure there are alignment marks on the steering shaft and steering wheel (arrow) – if there aren't, or they don't line up, scribe or paint new marks

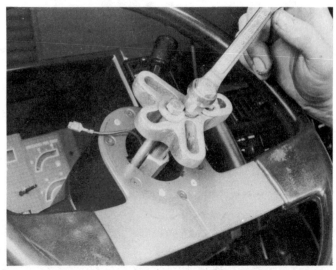

14.5   Remove the steering wheel from the shaft with a puller – do not hammer on the shaft!

15.2   Mark the relationship of the intermediate shaft to the steering shaft (arrow) and the steering gear input shaft

4   Remove the steering wheel retaining nut, then mark the relationship of the steering shaft to the hub (if marks don't already exist or don't line up) to simplify installation and ensure steering wheel alignment **(see illustration)**.

5   Use a puller to disconnect the steering wheel from the shaft **(see illustration)**.

6   To install the wheel, align the mark on the steering wheel hub with the mark on the shaft and slip the wheel onto the shaft. Install the hub nut and tighten it to the torque listed in this Chapter's Specifications. Install the safety clip.

7   Connect the horn wire and install the cover.

8   Connect the negative battery cable.

---

15   Intermediate shaft – removal and installation

Refer to illustrations 15.2 and 15.3

1   Turn the front wheels to the straight ahead position.

2   Using white paint, mark the relationship of the intermediate shaft to the steering shaft and the steering gear input shaft **(see illustration)**.

3   Remove the upper and lower universal joint pinch bolts **(see illustration)**. Some models require the steering gear to be lowered for shaft removal.

4   Pry the intermediate shaft out of the steering shaft universal joint with a large screwdriver, then pull the shaft from the steering gearbox. **Note:** *On some models, you must unhook the plastic coupling shield from the steering gear return line nut before separating the shaft from the steering gear.*

5   Installation is the reverse of the removal procedure. Be sure to align the marks and tighten the pinch bolts to the torque listed in this Chapter's Specifications.

---

16   Steering gear – removal and installation

Refer to illustrations 16.4 and 16.5

Removal

1   Raise the front of the vehicle and support it securely on jackstands. Apply the parking brake.

2   Place a drain pan under the steering gear. Remove the power steering pressure and return lines and cap the ends to prevent excessive fluid loss and contamination.

3   Mark the relationship of the lower intermediate shaft universal joint to the steering gear input shaft. Remove the lower intermediate shaft pinch bolt.

4   Mark the relationship of the pitman arm to the shaft so it can be installed in the same position **(see illustration)**. Remove the nut and washer.

5   Remove the Pitman arm from the shaft with a two-jaw puller **(see illustration)**.

6   Support the steering gear and remove the steering gear-to-frame mounting bolts from inside the left wheel well. Lower the unit, separate the intermediate shaft from the steering gear input shaft and remove the steering gear from the vehicle.

Installation

7   Raise the steering gear into position and connect the intermediate shaft, aligning the marks.

8   Install the mounting bolts and washers and tighten them to the torque listed in this Chapter's Specifications.

15.3   Typical intermediate shaft installation details

INTERMEDIATE SHAFT

INTERMEDIATE SHAFT

COUPLING SHIELD

STEERING GEAR

INSTALLATION OF COUPLING SHIELD TO RETURN PIPE NUT

16.4   Paint alignment marks on the pitman arm and the steering gear output shaft, then remove the nut and washer

16.5   Use a puller to remove the pitman arm from the steering gear output shaft

10

9   Slide the pitman arm onto the pitman shaft, ensuring that the marks are aligned. Install the washer and nut and tighten the nut to the torque listed in this Chapter's Specifications.
10   Install the lower intermediate shaft pinch bolt and tighten it to the torque listed in this Chapter's Specifications.
11   Connect the power steering pressure and return hoses to the steering gear and fill the power steering pump reservoir with the recommended fluid (Chapter 1).
12   Lower the vehicle and bleed the steering system as outlined in Section 18.

17   Power steering pump – removal and installation

Refer to illustration 17.3
1   Disconnect the hydraulic lines from either the pump or the steering gear and support them in a raised position to keep the fluid from draining. If you disconnect the lines at the pump, plug the fittings at the pump so the reservoir won't drain.
2   Loosen the pump mounting bolts and pivot the pump in (towards the engine) until the drivebelt can be removed.

17.3   Typical power steering pump
mounting details

3   Remove the pump mounting bolts and braces and remove the pump
(see illustration).
4   Reinstall the pump by reversing the removal procedure. Before installing the drivebelt, prime the pump by filling the reservoir with fluid, then
turn the pulley in the opposite direction to normal rotation until no more air
bubbles are observed in the reservoir.
5   Install the drivebelt (see Chapter 1) and bleed the system as described in Section 18.

18   Power steering system – bleeding

1   Following any operation in which the power steering fluid lines have
been disconnected, the power steering system must be bled to remove all
air and obtain proper steering performance.
2   With the front wheels in the straight ahead position, check the power
steering fluid level and, if low, add fluid until it reaches the Cold mark on the
dipstick.
3   Start the engine and allow it to run at fast idle. Recheck the fluid level
and add more if necessary to reach the Cold mark on the dipstick.
4   Bleed the system by turning the wheels from side-to-side, without hit-
ting the stops. This will work the air out of the system. Keep the reservoir
full of fluid as this is done.
5   When the air is worked out of the system, return the wheels to the
straight ahead position and leave the vehicle running for several more
minutes before shutting it off.
6   Road test the vehicle to be sure the steering system is functioning
normally and noise free.
7   Recheck the fluid level to be sure it is up to the Hot mark on the dipstick while the engine is at normal operating temperature. Add fluid if necessary (see Chapter 1).

19   Steering linkage – inspection, removal and installation

Warning: *Whenever any of the suspension or steering fasteners are loosened or removed they must be inspected and, if necessary, replaced with
new ones of the same part number or of original equipment quality and design. Torque specifications must be followed for proper reassembly and
component retention. Never attempt to heat, straighten or weld any suspension or steering component. Instead, replace any bent or damaged
part with a new one.*
Caution: *DO NOT use a "pickle fork" type separator when disconnecting
the tie-rod ends – it may damage the tie-rod seals.*

Inspection
Refer to illustrations 19.1 and 19.5
1   The steering linkage connects the steering gear to the front wheels
and keeps the wheels in proper relation to each other **(see illustration)**.
The linkage consists of the pitman arm, fastened to the steering gear
shaft, which moves the intermediate rod back-and-forth. The intermediate
rod is supported on one end by a frame-mounted idler arm. The back-and-
forth motion of the intermediate rod is transmitted to the steering knuckles
through a pair of tie-rod assemblies. Each tie-rod is made up of an inner
and outer tie-rod end (pivot), a threaded adjuster tube and two clamps.
Some later models are equipped with a shock absorber-like damper
mounted between the linkage and the frame to cushion steering system
shocks.
2   Set the wheels in the straight ahead position and lock the steering
wheel by turning the steering wheel to the OFF position.
3   Raise one side of the vehicle until the tire is approximately 1-inch off
the ground. Be sure the vehicle is supported securely.
4   Mount a dial indicator with the needle resting on the outside edge of
the wheel, at the rear. Grasp the front and rear of the tire and, using light

19.1 Typical steering linkage details

pressure, wiggle the wheel back-and-forth and note the dial indicator reading. The reading should be less than 0.108-inch. If the play in the steering system is more than specified, inspect each steering linkage pivot points (such as the tie-rod ends and idler arm) for looseness. Replace parts if necessary.

5   Raise the vehicle and support it on jackstands. Push up, then pull down on the intermediate rod end of the idler arm, exerting a force of approximately 25 pounds each way. Measure the total distance the end of the arm travels **(see illustration)**. If the play is greater than 1/4-inch, replace the idler arm.

6   Check for torn tie-rod end boots, oil leaking from the steering damper, frozen joints and bent or damaged linkage components.

Removal and installation

Tie-rod

Refer to illustrations 19.9, 19.11 and 19.13

7   Loosen the wheel lug nuts, raise the vehicle and support it securely on jackstands. Apply the parking brake. Remove the wheel.

8   Remove the cotter pin and loosen, but do not remove, the castellated nut from the ball stud.

9   Using a two-jaw puller, separate the tie-rod end from the steering knuckle **(see illustration)**. Remove the castellated nut and pull the tie-rod end from the knuckle.

19.5   To check for excessive idler arm play, apply approximately 25 lbs. of force up and down (B) on the idler arm – if the total movement (A) is greater than 1/4-inch, replace the idler arm

19.9   Use a puller to press the tie-rod end out of the steering knuckle

10

19.11   Measure the distance from the adjuster tube to the ball stud centerline so the new tie-rod end can be set to the same length

19.13   It may be necessary to force the ball stud into the tapered hole to keep it from turning while the nut is tightened

10   Remove the nut securing the inner tie-rod end to the intermediate rod. Separate the inner tie-rod end from the intermediate rod in the same manner as in Step 9.

11   If the inner or outer tie-rod end must be replaced, measure the distance from the end of the adjuster tube to the center of the ball stud and record it **(see illustration)**. Loosen the adjuster tube clamp and unscrew the tie-rod end.

12   Lubricate the threaded portion of the tie-rod end with chassis grease. Screw the new tie-rod end into the adjuster tube and adjust the distance from the tube to the ball stud to the previously measured dimension. The number of threads showing on the inner and outer tie-rod ends should be equal within three threads. Don't tighten the clamp yet.

13   To install the tie-rod, insert the inner tie-rod end ball stud into the intermediate rod until it's seated. Install the nut and tighten it to the torque listed in this Chapter's Specifications. If the ball stud spins when attempting to tighten the nut, force it into the tapered hole with a large pair of pliers **(see illustration)**.

14   Connect the outer tie-rod end to the steering knuckle and install the castellated nut. Tighten the nut to the torque listed in this Chapter's Specifications and install a new cotter pin. If necessary, tighten the nut slightly to align a slot in the nut with the hole in the ball stud.

15   Tighten the clamp nuts. The center of the bolt should be nearly horizontal and the adjuster tube slot must not line up with the gap in the clamps.

16   Install the wheel and lug nuts, lower the vehicle and tighten the lug nuts to the torque listed in this Chapter's Specifications. Drive the vehicle to an alignment shop to have the front end alignment checked and, if necessary, adjusted.

Idler arm

17   Raise the vehicle and support it securely on jackstands. Apply the parking brake.

18   Loosen but do not remove the idler arm-to-intermediate rod nut.

19   Separate the idler arm from the intermediate rod with a two-jaw puller (see illustration 19.9). Remove the nut.

20   Remove the idler arm-to-frame bolts.

21   To install the idler arm, position it on the frame and install the bolts, tightening them to the torque listed in this Chapter's Specifications.

22   Insert the idler arm ball stud into the intermediate rod and install the nut. Tighten the nut to the torque listed in this Chapter's Specifications. If the ball stud spins when attempting to tighten the nut, force it into the tapered hole with a large pair of pliers.

Intermediate rod

23   Raise the vehicle and support it securely on jackstands. Apply the parking brake.

METRIC TIRE SIZES
P 185 / 80 R 13

TIRE TYPE
P – PASSENGER
T – TEMPORARY
C – COMMERCIAL

SECTION WIDTH
(MILLIMETERS)
185
195
205
ETC

ASPECT RATIO
(SECTION HEIGHT)
(SECTION WIDTH)
70
75
80

RIM DIAMETER
(INCHES)
13
14
15

CONSTRUCTION TYPE
R – RADIAL
B – BIAS – BELTED
D – DIAGONAL (BIAS)

SECTION WIDTH

SECTION HEIGHT

20.1   Metric tire size code

24   Separate the two inner tie-rod ends from the intermediate rod.

25   Separate the pitman arm from the intermediate rod.

26   Separate the idler arm from the intermediate rod.

27   Installation is the reverse of the removal procedure. If the ball studs spin when attempting to tighten the nuts, force them into the tapered holes with a large pair of pliers. Be sure to tighten all of the nuts to the torques listed in this Chapter's Specifications.

Steering damper

28   Remove the bolts and nuts and detach the damper from the steering linkage and frame mounting bracket.

29   Installation is the reverse of removal.

Pitman arm

30   Refer to Section 16 of this Chapter for the pitman arm removal procedure.

20   Wheels and tires – general information

Refer to illustration 20.1

Most vehicles covered by this manual are equipped with metric-sized fiberglass or steel belted radial tires **(see illustration)**. Use of other size or type of tires may affect the ride and handling of the vehicle. Don't mix different types of tires, such as radials and bias belted, on the same vehicle as handling may be seriously affected. It's recommended that tires be replaced in pairs on the same axle, but if only one tire is being replaced, be sure it's the same size, structure and tread design as the other.

Because tire pressure has a substantial effect on handling and wear, the pressure of all tires should be checked at least once a month or before any extended trips (see Chapter 1).

Wheels must be replaced if they are bent, dented, leak air, have elongated bolt holes, are heavily rusted, out of vertical symmetry or if the lug nuts won't stay tight. Wheel repairs that use welding or peening are not recommended.

Tire and wheel balance is important in the overall handling, braking and performance of the vehicle. Unbalanced wheels can adversely affect handling and ride characteristics as well as tire life. Whenever a tire is installed on a wheel, the tire and wheel should be balanced by a shop with the proper equipment.

21   Front end alignment – general information

Refer to illustration 21.1

A front end alignment refers to the adjustments made to the front wheels so they are in proper angular relationship to the suspension and the ground. Front wheels that are out of proper alignment not only affect steering control, but also increase tire wear. The front end adjustments normally required are camber, caster and toe-in **(see illustration)**.

Getting the proper front wheel alignment is a very exacting process, one in which complicated and expensive machines are necessary to perform the job properly. Because of this, you should have a technician with the proper equipment perform these tasks. We will, however, use this space to give you a basic idea of what is involved with front end alignment so you can better understand the process and deal intelligently with the shop that does the work.

Toe-in is the turning in of the front wheels. The purpose of a toe specification is to ensure parallel rolling of the front wheels. In a vehicle with zero toe-in, the distance between the front edges of the wheels will be the same as the distance between the rear edges of the wheels. The actual amount of toe-in is normally only a fraction of an inch. Toe-in adjustment is controlled by the tie-rod end position on the inner tie-rod. Incorrect toe-in will cause the tires to wear improperly by making them scrub against the road surface.

Camber is the tilting of the front wheels from the vertical when viewed from the front of the vehicle. When the wheels tilt out at the top, the camber is said to be positive (+). When the wheels tilt in at the top the camber is negative (-). The amount of tilt is measured in degrees from the vertical and this measurement is called the camber angle. This angle affects the amount of tire tread which contacts the road and compensates for changes in the suspension geometry when the vehicle is cornering or travelling over an undulating surface.

Caster is the tilting of the top of the front steering axis from the vertical. A tilt toward the rear is positive caster and a tilt toward the front is negative caster.

Caster is adjusted by moving shims from one end of the upper control arm mount to the other.

22   Automatic Level Control (ALC) system – general information

Some models are equipped with Automatic Level Control (ALC). The ALC system automatically adjusts the height of the rear of the vehicle, maintaining a preset height, regardless of load. The system consists of an air compressor, air reservoir and regulator located at the front of the vehicle; a height control sensor valve and leveling arm link connected to the rear suspension; and two air adjustable rear shock absorbers.

The system operates with the ignition On when weight is added or removed from the rear of the vehicle. The leveling arm moves with the suspension, turning the compressor on or off as necessary or releasing air from the shock absorbers to maintain a constant height.

Because of the special equipment and techniques required to work on this system, servicing should be performed by a dealer service department.

**Camber Angle
Front View**

**Caster Angle
Side View**

**Toe-In
Top View**

21.1   Typical front end alignment details

A minus B = C (degrees camber)
D = caster (measured in degrees)
E minus F = toe-in (measured in inches)
G = toe-in (expressed in degrees)

10

Chapter 11   Body

Contents

1   General information

All models covered by this manual have a separate frame and body, with the exception of the Seville, which is of unibody construction. Certain components are particularly vulnerable to accident damage and can be unbolted and repaired or replaced. Among these parts are the body moldings, bumpers, the hood and trunk lids and all glass.

Only general body maintenance practices and body panel repair procedures within the scope of the do-it-yourselfer are included in this Chapter.

2   Body – maintenance

1   The condition of your vehicle's body is very important, because the resale value depends a great deal on it. It's much more difficult to repair a neglected or damaged body than it is to repair mechanical components. The hidden areas of the body, such as the wheel wells, the frame and the engine compartment, are equally important, although they don't require as frequent attention as the rest of the body.

2   Once a year, or every 12,000 miles, it's a good idea to have the underside of the body steam cleaned. All traces of dirt and oil will be removed and the area can then be inspected carefully for rust, damaged brake lines, frayed electrical wires, damaged cables and other problems. The front suspension components should be greased after completion of this job.

3   At the same time, clean the engine and the engine compartment with a steam cleaner or water soluble degreaser.

4   The wheel wells should be given close attention, since undercoating can peel away and stones and dirt thrown up by the tires can cause the paint to chip and flake, allowing rust to set in. If rust is found, clean down to the bare metal and apply an anti-rust paint.

5   The body should be washed about once a week. Wet the vehicle thoroughly to soften the dirt, then wash it down with a soft sponge and plenty of clean soapy water. If the surplus dirt is not washed off very carefully, it can wear down the paint.

6   Spots of tar or asphalt thrown up from the road should be removed with a cloth soaked in solvent.

7   Once every six months, wax the body and chrome trim. If a chrome cleaner is used to remove rust from any of the vehicle's plated parts, remember that the cleaner also removes part of the chrome, so use it sparingly.

3   Vinyl trim – maintenance

Don't clean vinyl trim with detergents, caustic soap or petroleum-based cleaners. Plain soap and water works just fine, with a soft brush to clean dirt that may be ingrained. Wash the vinyl as frequently as the rest of the vehicle.

After cleaning, application of a high quality rubber and vinyl protectant will help prevent oxidation and cracks. The protectant can also be applied to weatherstripping, vacuum lines and rubber hoses, which often fail as a result of chemical degradation, and to the tires.

4   Upholstery and carpets – maintenance

1   Every three months remove the carpets or mats and clean the interior of the vehicle (more frequently if necessary). Vacuum the upholstery and carpets to remove loose dirt and dust.
2   Leather upholstery requires special care. Stains should be removed with warm water and a very mild soap solution. Use a clean, damp cloth to remove the soap, then wipe again with a dry cloth. Never use alcohol, gasoline, nail polish remover or thinner to clean leather upholstery.
3   After cleaning, regularly treat leather upholstery with a leather wax. Never use car wax on leather upholstery.
4   In areas where the interior of the vehicle is subject to bright sunlight, cover leather seats with a sheet if the vehicle is to be left out for any length of time.
5   Use of an interior-type windshield sun deflector is also recommended.

5   Body repair – minor damage

See color photo sequence

Repair of minor scratches

1   If the scratch is superficial and does not penetrate to the metal of the body, repair is very simple. Lightly rub the scratched area with a fine rubbing compound to remove loose paint and built up wax. Rinse the area with clean water.
2   Apply touch-up paint to the scratch, using a small brush. Continue to apply thin layers of paint until the surface of the paint in the scratch is level with the surrounding paint. Allow the new paint at least two weeks to harden, then blend it into the surrounding paint by rubbing with a very fine rubbing compound. Finally, apply a coat of wax to the scratch area.
3   If the scratch has penetrated the paint and exposed the metal of the body, causing the metal to rust, a different repair technique is required. Remove all loose rust from the bottom of the scratch with a pocket knife, then apply rust-inhibiting paint to prevent the formation of rust in the future. Using a rubber or nylon applicator, coat the scratched area with glaze-type filler. If required, the filler can be mixed with thinner to provide a very thin paste, which is ideal for filling narrow scratches. Before the glaze filler in the scratch hardens, wrap a piece of smooth cotton cloth around the tip of a finger. Dip the cloth in thinner and then quickly wipe it along the surface of the scratch. This will ensure that the surface of the filler is slightly hollow. The scratch can now be painted over as described earlier in this Section.

Repair of dents

4   When repairing dents, the first job is to pull the dent out until the affected area is as close as possible to its original shape. There is no point in trying to restore the original shape completely as the metal in the damaged area will have stretched on impact and cannot be restored to its original contours. It is better to bring the level of the dent up to a point which is about 1/8-inch below the level of the surrounding metal. In cases where the dent is very shallow, it is not worth trying to pull it out at all.
5   If the back side of the dent is accessible, it can be hammered out gently from behind using a soft-face hammer. While doing this, hold a block of wood firmly against the opposite side of the metal to absorb the hammer blows and prevent the metal from being stretched.
6   If the dent is in a section of the body which has double layers, or some other factor makes it inaccessible from behind, a different technique is required. Drill several small holes through the metal inside the damaged area, particularly in the deeper sections. Screw long, self-tapping screws into the holes just enough for them to get a good grip in the metal. Now the dent can be pulled out by pulling on the protruding heads of the screws with locking pliers.
7   The next stage of repair is the removal of paint from the damaged area and from an inch or so of the surrounding metal. This is easily done with a wire brush or sanding disk in a drill motor, although it can be done just as effectively by hand with sandpaper. To complete the preparation for filling, score the surface of the bare metal with a screwdriver or the tang of a file, or drill small holes in the affected area. This will provide a good grip for the filler material. To complete the repair, see the Section on filling and painting.

Repair of rust holes or gashes

8   Remove all paint from the affected area and from an inch or so of the surrounding metal using a sanding disk or wire brush mounted in a drill motor. If these are not available, a few sheets of sandpaper will do the job just as effectively.
9   With the paint removed, you will be able to determine the severity of the corrosion and decide whether to replace the whole panel, if possible, or repair the affected area. New body panels are not as expensive as most people think, and it is often quicker to install a new panel than to repair large areas of rust.
10   Remove all trim pieces from the affected area except those which will act as a guide to the original shape of the damaged body, such as headlight shells, etc. Using metal snips or a hacksaw blade, remove all loose metal and any other metal that is badly affected by rust. Hammer the edges of the hole inward to create a slight depression for the filler material.
11   Wire brush the affected area to remove the powdery rust from the surface of the metal. If the back of the rusted area is accessible, treat it with rust-inhibiting paint.
12   Before filling is done, block the hole in some way. This can be done with sheet metal riveted or screwed into place, or by stuffing the hole with wire mesh.
13   Once the hole is blocked off, the affected area can be filled and painted. See the following subsection on filling and painting.

Filling and painting

14   Many types of body fillers are available, but generally speaking, body repair kits which contain filler paste and a tube of resin hardener are best for this type of repair work. A wide, flexible plastic or nylon applicator will be necessary for imparting a smooth and contoured finish to the surface of the filler material. Mix up a small amount of filler on a clean piece of wood or cardboard (use the hardener sparingly). Follow the manufacturer's instructions on the package, otherwise the filler will set incorrectly.
15   Using the applicator, apply the filler paste to the prepared area. Draw the applicator across the surface of the filler to achieve the desired contour and to level the filler surface. As soon as a contour that approximates the original one is achieved, stop working the paste. If you continue, the paste will begin to stick to the applicator. Continue to add thin layers of paste at 20-minute intervals until the level of the filler is just above the surrounding metal.
16   Once the filler has hardened, the excess can be removed with a body file. From then on, progressively finer grades of sandpaper should be used, starting with a 180-grit paper and finishing with 600-grit wet-or-dry paper. Always wrap the sandpaper around a flat rubber or wooden block, otherwise the surface of the filler will not be completely flat. During the sanding of the filler surface, the wet-or-dry paper should be periodically rinsed in water. This will ensure that a very smooth finish is produced in the final stage.
17   At this point, the repair area should be surrounded by a ring of bare metal, which in turn should be encircled by the finely feathered edge of good paint. Rinse the repair area with clean water until all of the dust produced by the sanding operation is gone.
18   Spray the entire area with a light coat of primer. This will reveal any imperfections in the surface of the filler. Repair the imperfections with fresh filler paste or glaze filler and once more smooth the surface with sandpaper. Repeat this spray-and-repair procedure until you are satisfied that the surface of the filler and the feathered edge of the paint are perfect. Rinse the area with clean water and allow it to dry completely.
19   The repair area is now ready for painting. Spray painting must be carried out in a warm, dry, windless and dust-free atmosphere. These conditions can be created if you have access to a large indoor work area, but if you are forced to work in the open, you will have to pick the day very carefully. If you are working indoors, dousing the floor in the work area with water will help settle the dust which would otherwise be in the air. If the repair area is confined to one body panel, mask off the surrounding panels. This will help minimize the effects of a slight mismatch in paint color. Trim pieces such as chrome strips, door handles, etc., will also need to be

11

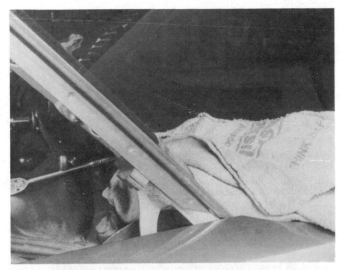

9.1   Pad the back corners of the hood with cloths so the windshield won't be damaged if the hood accidentally swings rearward

10.2   Typical hood latch mounting details

masked off or removed. Use masking tape and several thicknesses of newspaper for the masking operations.

20   Before spraying, shake the paint can thoroughly, then spray a test area until the spray painting technique is mastered. Cover the repair area with a thick coat of primer. The thickness should be built up using several thin layers of primer rather than one thick one. Using 600-grit wet-or-dry sandpaper, rub down the surface of the primer until it is very smooth. While doing this, the work area should be thoroughly rinsed with water and the wet-or-dry sandpaper periodically rinsed as well. Allow the primer to dry before spraying additional coats.

21   Spray on the top coat, again building up the thickness by using several thin layers of paint. Begin spraying in the center of the repair area and then, using a circular motion, work out until the whole repair area and about two inches of the surrounding original paint is covered. Remove all masking material 10 to 15 minutes after spraying on the final coat of paint. Allow the new paint at least two weeks to harden, then use a very fine rubbing compound to blend the edges of the new paint into the existing paint. Finally, apply a coat of wax.

6   Body repair – major damage

1   Major damage must be repaired by a properly equipped auto body shop. These shops have the specialized equipment required to do the job properly.

2   If the damage is extensive, the body must be checked for proper alignment or the vehicle's handling characteristics may be adversely affected and other components may wear at an accelerated rate.

3   Due to the fact that all of the major body components (hood, fenders, etc.) are separate and replaceable units, any seriously damaged components should be replaced rather than repaired. Sometimes the components can be found in a wrecking yard that specializes in used vehicle components, often at considerable savings over the cost of new parts.

7   Hinges and locks – maintenance

Once every 3000 miles, or every three months, the hinges and latch assemblies on the doors, hood and trunk should be given a few drops of light oil or lock lubricant. The door latch strikers should also be lubricated with a thin coat of grease to reduce wear and ensure free movement. Lubricate the door and trunk locks with spray-on graphite lubricant.

8   Fixed glass – replacement

Replacement of the windshield and fixed glass requires the use of special fast-setting adhesive/caulk materials and some specialized tools and techniques. These operations should be left to a dealer service department or a shop specializing in glass work.

9   Hood – removal, installation and adjustment

Refer to illustration 9.1

Note: *The hood is extremely heavy and somewhat awkward to remove and install – at least two people should perform this procedure.*

Removal and installation

1   Use blankets or pads to cover the fenders and rear of the hood **(see illustration)**. This will protect the windshield and body and paint as the hood is lifted off.

2   Use a felt-tip marker or scribe to make alignment marks around the bolt heads to insure proper alignment during installation.

3   Disconnect any cables or wire harnesses which will interfere with removal.

4   Have an assistant support the weight of the hood. Remove the hinge-to-hood nuts or bolts.

5   Lift off the hood.

6   Installation is the reverse of removal.

Adjustment

7   Fore-and-aft and side-to-side adjustment of the hood is done by moving the hood in relation to the hinge plate after loosening the bolts or nuts.

8   Scribe a line around the entire hinge plate so you can judge the amount of movement.

9   Loosen the bolts or nuts and move the hood into correct alignment. Move it only a little at a time. Tighten the hinge bolts or nuts and carefully lower the hood to check the alignment.

10   If necessary after installation, the entire hood latch assembly can be adjusted up and down as well as from side to side on the radiator support so the hood closes securely and is flush with the fenders. To do this, scribe a line around the hood latch mounting bolts to provide a reference point (Section 10). Then loosen the bolts and reposition the latch assembly as necessary. Following adjustment, retighten the mounting bolts.

11   Finally, adjust the hood bumpers on the radiator support so the hood, when closed, is flush with the fenders.

12   The hood latch assembly, as well as the hinges, should be periodically lubricated with white lithium-base grease to prevent sticking and wear.

11.3   Use a felt-tip marker or scribe to mark around the trunk lid attaching bolts before loosening them

12.1   Remove the lock cylinder cover (not all models)

10   Hood latch mechanism – removal and installation

Refer to illustration 10.2
1   Disconnect the hood release cable.
2   Scribe a line around the latch to aid alignment when installing, then remove the screws retaining it to the radiator support **(see illustration)**. Remove the latch.
3   Installation is the reverse of the removal procedure. Adjust the latch so the hood engages securely when closed and the hood bumpers are slightly compressed.

11   Trunk lid – removal, installation and adjustment

Refer to illustrations 11.3
1   Open the trunk lid and cover the edges of the trunk compartment with pads or cloths to protect the painted surfaces when the lid is removed.
2   Disconnect any cables or wire harness connectors attached to the trunk lid that would interfere with removal. On some models it will be necessary to remove the bolts and detach the cover for access to the attaching bolts.

3   Use a felt-tip marker or scribe to make alignment marks around the trunk lid attaching bolt heads **(see illustration)**.
4   While an assistant supports the lid, remove the hinge bolts from both sides and lift it off.
5   Installation is the reverse of removal. **Note:** *When reinstalling the trunk lid, align the hinge bolt heads with the marks made during removal.*
6   After installation, close the lid and see if it's in proper alignment with the surrounding panels. Fore-and-aft and side-to-side adjustments of the lid are controlled by the position of the hinge bolts in the slots. To adjust it, loosen the hinge bolts, reposition the lid and retighten the bolts.
7   The height of the lid in relation to the surrounding body panels when closed can be adjusted by loosening the lock striker bolts, repositioning the striker and retightening the bolts.

12   Trunk lid lock cylinder – removal and installation

Refer to illustrations 12.1, 12.2 and 12.3
1   Open the trunk. On some models it will be necessary to remove the cover for access to the lock cylinder **(see illustration)**
2   Remove the retaining nuts or rivets and remove the emblem so the lock cylinder can be withdrawn **(see illustration)**.

12.2   Remove the retaining nuts or rivets and detach the emblem assembly

11

3   Pull the retainer down or away from the lock cylinder and remove the cylinder from the body (see illustration).
4   Installation is the reverse of removal.

13   Trunk lid latch and striker – removal and installation

Refer to illustrations 13.2a, 13.2b and 13.4

1   On models with electrically operated automatic closing units, disconnect the negative cable from the battery. Unplug any electrical connectors and detach any cables from the lock assembly.
2   The lid latch is retained by bolts which can readily be removed with a wrench on some models, while on others rivets are used which must be drilled out and replaced with nuts and bolts during installation (see illustrations).

12.3   Pull off the lock cylinder retainer

13.2a   Early model trunk latch details

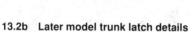

13.2b   Later model trunk latch details

1	Screw	5	Screws
2	Electrical connector	6	Rivets
3	Solenoid	7	Bolt
4	Latch assembly		

13.4   Typical trunk lid striker

1	Striker	4	Tab
2	Stud	5	Support
3	Nut		

3   When installing, ensure that the lid latch is correctly aligned before finally tightening the bolts.

4   The striker is retained with bolts or screws. Before removing a striker, scribe around the adjacent panel to facilitate installation in the original position **(see illustration)**. If necessary, adjustment can be made by repositioning.

14   Door trim panel – removal and installation

Refer to illustrations 14.2a, 14.2b, 14.3a and 14.3b

1   Disconnect the negative cable from the battery.

2   Remove all door trim panel retaining screws, door handles and door pull/armrest assemblies **(see illustrations)**.

14.2a   Typical door handle installation details

CADILLAC "C" STYLES

OPENED FOR ATTACHING SCREW ACCESS

14.2b   Typical door pull strap installation details

11

14.3a   Typical manual window crank installation details

14.3b   Typical power window switch assembly
installation details

3   On manual window regulator equipped models, remove the window
crank (see illustration). On power regulator models, remove the retaining
screws (if equipped) and pry out the switch assembly and unplug it (see
illustration).
4   Insert a putty knife between the trim panel and the door and disengage the retaining clips. Work around the outer edge until the panel is free.
5   Once all of the clips are disengaged, detach the trim panel, unplug
any wire harness connectors and remove the trim panel from the vehicle.
6   For access to the inner door, carefully peel back the plastic water-
shield.
7   Prior to installation of the door panel, be sure to reinstall any clips in
the panel which may have come out during the removal procedure and remain in the door itself.
8   Plug in the wire harness connectors and place the panel in position in
the door. Press the door panel into place until the clips are seated and install the armrest/door pulls. Install the manual regulator window crank or
power window switch assembly.

**15   Door latch and lock cylinder assembly – removal
and installation**

Front door

Refer to illustrations 15.1a and 15.1b

1   To remove the lock cylinder, remove the trim panel and the water deflector. If equipped, unplug the electrical or fiber optic connector from the
lock cylinder. Raise the window, then use a screwdriver to slide the lock
cylinder retainer out of engagement (see illustrations). Installation is the
reverse of the removal procedure.
2   To remove the latch assembly, raise the window and remove the trim
panel and water deflector (see Section 14).
3   Working through the large access hole, disengage the remote con-
trol-to-lock connecting rod (spring clip). On coupe models it may be necessary to disengage the inside locking rod from the latch, which can be
achieved by sliding the plastic retaining sleeves toward each other.
4   Remove the screws securing the latch to the door, then remove the
assembly from the door. On some four-door models, the inside locking rod
must be removed from the latch after removal of the latch assembly.
5   Installation is the reverse of removal.

Rear door

6   Raise the door glass fully and remove the trim panel.
7   Working through the access hole, disengage the latch connecting
rods and then remove the latch securing screws. Withdraw the latch.
8   Installation is the reverse of removal.

16   Door outside handle – removal and installation

Refer to illustration 16.3

1   Different designs of outside door handles are used according to vehicle model and date of production, but removal is similar for all types.
2   Raise the window completely, remove the door trim and peel away the
upper corner of the water deflector in order to gain access to the outside
handle mounting nuts or bolts.
3   Unscrew the nuts or bolts and remove the handle and gaskets (see
illustration).
4   Installation is the reverse of removal.

17   Front door glass – removal and installation

Refer to illustration 17.3

1   Remove the door trim panel and water deflector (see Section 14).

ILLUMINATED ENTRY AND ANTITHEFT OPTIONS

FIBER OPTIC

ANTITHEFT
WIRE CONNECTOR

VIEW A

VIEW B

15.1a   On later models, unplug the connectors from the lock cylinder

SEALING
GASKET

BOTTOM DRAIN HOLE

LOCK
CYLINDER
ASSEMBLY

RETAINER

LOCK
EXTENSION

15.1b   Typical door lock cylinder installation details

2   Remove the weatherstrip clips, the travel stops and the stabilizer guide assembly.

3   Set the window to the half-raised position and remove the lower sash channel nuts **(see illustration)**. Now raise the window glass completely and remove the nut.

4   Mark the position of the bolts and remove them, disengage the guide from the roller and rest the guide in the bottom of the door.

5   Tilt the top of the glass until the rear roller is clear of the inner panel and then lift the glass from the door.

6   Installation is the reverse of removal, but adjust the channels, guides and stops as necessary to give smooth operation before finally tightening their mounting nuts.

DOOR OUTSIDE HANDLE

DOOR OUTSIDE HANDLE
SCREWS

16.3   Typical outside handle installation details

17.3   Typical front door window glass component layout

1	Glass	5	Plastic washer
2	Bellcrank assembly	6	Nut
3	Bushing	7	Window roller
4	Inner panel cam bolt	8	Metal washer

11

These photos illustrate a method of repairing simple dents. They are intended to supplement *Body repair - minor damage* in this Chapter and should not be used as the sole instructions for body repair on these vehicles.

1   If you can't access the backside of the body panel to hammer out the dent, pull it out with a slide-hammer-type dent puller. In the deepest portion of the dent or along the crease line, drill or punch hole(s) at least one inch apart . . .

2   . . . then screw the slide-hammer into the hole and operate it. Tap with a hammer near the edge of the dent to help 'pop' the metal back to its original shape. When you're finished, the dent area should be close to its original contour and about 1/8-inch below the surface of the surrounding metal

3   Using coarse-grit sandpaper, remove the paint down to the bare metal. Hand sanding works fine, but the disc sander shown here makes the job faster. Use finer (about 320-grit) sandpaper to feather-edge the paint at least one inch around the dent area

4   When the paint is removed, touch will probably be more helpful than sight for telling if the metal is straight. Hammer down the high spots or raise the low spots as necessary. Clean the repair area with wax/silicone remover

5   Following label instructions, mix up a batch of plastic filler and hardener. The ratio of filler to hardener is critical, and, if you mix it incorrectly, it will either not cure properly or cure too quickly (you won't have time to file and sand it into shape)

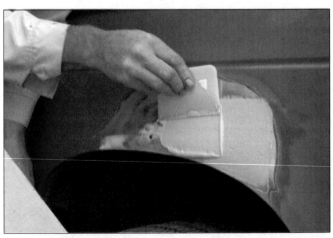

6   Working quickly so the filler doesn't harden, use a plastic applicator to press the body filler firmly into the metal, assuring it bonds completely. Work the filler until it matches the original contour and is slightly above the surrounding metal

7   Let the filler harden until you can just dent it with your fingernail. Use a body file or Surform tool (shown here) to rough-shape the filler

8   Use coarse-grit sandpaper and a sanding board or block to work the filler down until it's smooth and even. Work down to finer grits of sandpaper - always using a board or block - ending up with 360 or 400 grit

9   You shouldn't be able to feel any ridge at the transition from the filler to the bare metal or from the bare metal to the old paint. As soon as the repair is flat and uniform, remove the dust and mask off the adjacent panels or trim pieces

10   Apply several layers of primer to the area. Don't spray the primer on too heavy, so it sags or runs, and make sure each coat is dry before you spray on the next one. A professional-type spray gun is being used here, but aerosol spray primer is available inexpensively from auto parts stores

11   The primer will help reveal imperfections or scratches. Fill these with glazing compound. Follow the label instructions and sand it with 360 or 400-grit sandpaper until it's smooth. Repeat the glazing, sanding and respraying until the primer reveals a perfectly smooth surface

12   Finish sand the primer with very fine sandpaper (400 or 600-grit) to remove the primer overspray. Clean the area with water and allow it to dry. Use a tack rag to remove any dust, then apply the finish coat. Don't attempt to rub out or wax the repair area until the paint has dried completely (at least two weeks)

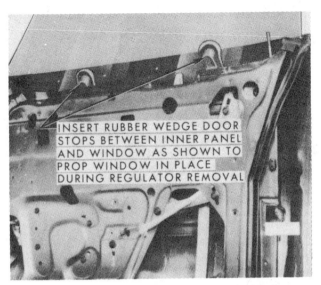

INSERT RUBBER WEDGE DOOR
STOPS BETWEEN INNER PANEL
AND WINDOW AS SHOWN TO
PROP WINDOW IN PLACE
DURING REGULATOR REMOVAL

18.2   Use rubber doorstops to hold the glass in the raised position

18   Front door window regulator – removal and installation

Refer to illustration 18.2
1   Remove the door trim panel and water deflector (see Section 14).
2   Raise the window completely and prop it in this position by inserting two rubber doorstops between the glass and the door panel **(see illustration)**.
3   Mark the position of the cam attaching bolts and remove the regulator bolts.
4   With electrically-operated regulators, disconnect the wiring harness. **Warning:** *On gear driven sector-type electrically operated regulators the control arms are under pressure and can cause serious injury if the motor is removed without locking the sector gear as described in Chapter 12, Section 25.*
5   Slide the front regulator upper arm from the sash, then slide the rear lift arm forward from the sash cam.
6   Slide the regulator to the rear and withdraw it through the lower rear access hole.
7   Installation is the reverse of removal.

19   Rear door glass – removal and installation

1   Remove top section of the door trim panel.
2   Remove the front and rear travel stop and the weatherstrip retainers.
3   Raise the window almost to the fully up position and then remove the lower sash guide plate-to-glass mounting nuts.
4   Tilt the upper edge of the glass to disengage the glass from the sash plate and then withdraw the glass by lifting it straight up.
5   Installation is the reverse of removal.

20   Rear door window regulator – removal and installation

Manually-operated regulator
1   Remove the door trim panel and water deflector (see Section 14).

2   Raise the window completely and secure it in this position with two rubber wedges inserted between the glass and the door panel **(see illustration 18.2).**
3   Unscrew and remove the regulator mounting bolts.
4   Disengage the regulator lift arm from the lower sash guide plate cam and withdraw the regulator through the access hole.

Electrically-operated regulator
Warning: *On gear driven sector-type electrically operated regulators the control arms are under pressure and can cause serious injury if the motor is removed without locking the sector gear as described in Chapter 12, Section 25.*
5   Remove the window glass as described in Steps 1 through 4.

21   Door – removal, installation and adjustment

1   Remove the door trim panel (see Section 14). Disconnect any wire harness connectors and push them through the door opening so they won't interfere with door removal.
2   Place a jack or jackstand under the door or have an assistant on hand to support it when the hinge bolts are removed. **Note:** *If a jack or jackstand is used, place a rag between it and the door to protect the door's painted surfaces.*
3   Scribe around the door hinges.
4   Remove the hinge-to-door bolts or drive out the pins and carefully lift off the door.
5   Installation is the reverse of removal.
6   Following installation of the door, check the alignment and adjust it, if necessary, as follows:
   a) Up-and-down and forward-and-backward adjustments are made by loosening the hinge-to-body bolts and moving the door as necessary.
   b) The door latch striker can also be adjusted both up-and-down and sideways to provide positive engagement with the latch mechanism. This is done by loosening the mounting bolts and moving the striker as necessary.

22   Automatic shoulder harnesses – general information

Many late model vehicles are equipped with automatic front seat shoulder harnesses. They are termed automatic because you don't have to buckle them – the shoulder harness automatically positions itself when the door is closed and the key is turned on. An emergency release lever allows the harness to be manually removed for exit in an emergency. **Warning:** *Be sure to fasten the manual seatbelt as well. The automatic shoulder harness will not work properly unless the seatbelt is fastened.*

Most systems have a warning light and buzzer that indicate the emergency release lever has been pulled up, releasing the shoulder harness. Make sure the release lever is down and the light/buzzer are off to ensure proper operation of the automatic shoulder harness. Also, if you disconnect any wires or remove any automatic shoulder harness components when performing repair procedures on other vehicle components, be sure to reinstall everything and check the harness for proper operation when the repairs are complete.

Since the automatic shoulder harness is operated by several electrical switches and is computer controlled, diagnosis and repair must be done by a dealer service department. Do not jeopardize the safety of front seat occupants – if the automatic shoulder harness malfunctions, or you have questions regarding the proper use or operation of the system, contact a dealer service department.

Chapter 12 Chassis electrical system

Contents

1 General information

The electrical system is a 12-volt, negative ground type. Power for the lights and all electrical accessories is supplied by a lead/acid-type battery which is charged by the alternator.

This Chapter covers repair and service procedures for the various electrical components not associated with the engine. Information on the battery, alternator, distributor and starter motor can be found in Chapter 5.

It should be noted that when portions of the electrical system are serviced, the negative battery cable should be disconnected from the battery to prevent electrical shorts and/or fires.

2 Electrical troubleshooting – general information

A typical electrical circuit consists of an electrical component, any switches, relays, motors, fuses, fusible links or circuit breakers related to that component and the wiring and connectors that link the component to both the battery and the chassis. To help you pinpoint an electrical circuit problem, wiring diagrams are included at the end of this book.

Before tackling any troublesome electrical circuit, first study the appropriate wiring diagrams to get a complete understanding of what makes up that individual circuit. Trouble spots, for instance, can often be narrowed down by noting if other components related to the circuit are operating properly. If several components or circuits fail at one time, chances are the problem is in a fuse or ground connection, because several circuits are often routed through the same fuse and ground connections.

Electrical problems usually stem from simple causes, such as loose or corroded connections, a blown fuse, a melted fusible link or a bad relay. Visually inspect the condition of all fuses, wires and connections in a problem circuit before troubleshooting it.

If testing instruments are going to be utilized, use the diagrams to plan ahead of time where you will make the necessary connections in order to accurately pinpoint the trouble spot.

The basic tools needed for electrical troubleshooting include a circuit tester or voltmeter (a 12-volt bulb with a set of test leads can also be used), a continuity tester, which includes a bulb, battery and set of test leads, and a jumper wire, preferably with a circuit breaker incorporated, which can be used to bypass electrical components. Before attempting to locate a problem with test instruments, use the wiring diagram(s) to decide where to make the connections.

Voltage checks

Voltage checks should be performed if a circuit is not functioning properly. Connect one lead of a circuit tester to either the negative battery terminal or a known good ground. Connect the other lead to a connector in the circuit being tested, preferably nearest to the battery or fuse. If the bulb of the tester lights, voltage is present, which means that the part of the circuit between the connector and the battery is problem free. Continue checking the rest of the circuit in the same fashion. When you reach a point at which no voltage is present, the problem lies between that point and the last test point with voltage. Most of the time the problem can be traced to a loose connection. **Note:** *Keep in mind that some circuits receive voltage only when the ignition key is in the Accessory or Run position.*

Finding a short

One method of finding shorts in a circuit is to remove the fuse and connect a test light or voltmeter in its place to the fuse terminals. There should be no voltage present in the circuit. Move the wiring harness from side to side while watching the test light. If the bulb goes on, there is a short to ground somewhere in that area, probably where the insulation has rubbed through. The same test can be performed on each component in the circuit, even a switch.

Ground check

Perform a ground test to check whether a component is properly grounded. Disconnect the battery and connect one lead of a self-powered test light, known as a continuity tester, to a known good ground. Connect the other lead to the wire or ground connection being tested. If the bulb goes on, the ground is good. If the bulb does not go on, the ground is not good.

Continuity check

A continuity check is done to determine if there are any breaks in a circuit – if it is passing electricity properly. With the circuit off (no power in the circuit), a self-powered continuity tester can be used to check the circuit. Connect the test leads to both ends of the circuit (or to the "power" end and a good ground), and if the test light comes on, the circuit is passing current properly. If the light doesn't come on, there is a break somewhere in the circuit. The same procedure can be used to test a switch, by connecting the continuity tester to the switch terminals. With the switch turned On, the test light should come on.

Finding an open circuit

When diagnosing for possible open circuits, it is often difficult to locate them by sight because oxidation or terminal misalignment are hidden by the connectors. Merely wiggling a connector on a sensor or in the wiring harness may correct the open circuit condition. Remember this when an open circuit is indicated when troubleshooting a circuit. Intermittent problems may also be caused by oxidized or loose connections.

Electrical troubleshooting is simple if you keep in mind that all electrical circuits are basically electricity running from the battery, through the wires, switches, relays, fuses and fusible links to each electrical component (light bulb, motor, etc.) and to ground, from which it is passed back to the battery. Any electrical problem is an interruption in the flow of electricity to and from the battery.

---

3   Fuses – general information

Refer to illustrations 3.1a, 3.1b and 3.4

The electrical circuits of the vehicle are protected by a combination of fuses, circuit breakers and fusible links. The fuse block on earlier models is located under the left side of the dashboard **(see illustration)**. On later models, the fuse block is at the lower left corner of the dash, under a cover **(see illustration)**.

Each of the fuses is designed to protect a specific circuit, and the various circuits are identified on the fuse panel itself.

A blown fuse on earlier models can be readily identified by inspecting the element inside the glass tube. If this metal element is broken, the fuse is inoperable and must be replaced with a new one.

On later models, miniaturized fuses are employed in the fuse block. These compact fuses, with blade terminal design, allow fingertip removal and replacement. If an electrical component fails, always check the fuse first. A blown fuse is easily identified through the clear plastic body. Visually inspect the element for evidence of damage **(see illustration)**. If a continuity check is called for, the blade terminal tips are exposed in the fuse body.

3.1a   On earlier models the fuse block is located under the dash to the left of the driver

3.1b   On later models, the fuse block is located at the lower left of the dash, under a cover

3.4   To test for a blown fuse on later models, pull it out and inspect it for an open circuit (1), then, with the circuit activated, use a test light across the terminals (2)

Be sure to replace blown fuses with the correct type. Fuses of different ratings are physically interchangeable, but only fuses of the proper rating should be used. Replacing a fuse with one of a higher or lower value than specified is not recommended. Each electrical circuit needs a specific amount of protection. The amperage value of each fuse is molded into the fuse body.

If the replacement fuse immediately fails, don't replace it again until the cause of the problem is isolated and corrected. In most cases, the cause will be a short circuit in the wiring caused by a broken or deteriorated wire.

4   Fusible links – general information

Some circuits are protected by fusible links. The links are used in circuits which are not ordinarily fused, such as the ignition circuit.

Although the fusible links appear to be of a heavier gauge than the wire they are protecting, the appearance is due to the thick insulation. All fusible links are four wire gauges smaller than the wire they are designed to protect.

Fusible links cannot be repaired, but a new link of the same size wire can be put in its place. The procedure is as follows:
a) Disconnect the negative cable from the battery.
b) Disconnect the fusible link from the wiring harness.
c) Cut the damaged fusible link out of the wiring just behind the connector.
d) Strip the insulation back approximately 1/2-inch.
e) Position the connector on the new fusible link and crimp it into place.
f) Use rosin core solder at each end of the new link to obtain a good solder joint.
g) Use plenty of electrical tape around the soldered joint. No wires should be exposed.
h) Connect the battery ground cable. Test the circuit for proper operation.

5   Circuit breakers – general information

Circuit breakers protect components such the power windows, power door locks and headlights. Some circuit breakers are located in the fuse box.

On some models the circuit breaker resets itself automatically, so an electrical overload in a circuit breaker protected system will cause the circuit to fail momentarily, then come back on. If the circuit does not come back on, check it immediately. Once the condition is corrected, the circuit breaker will resume its normal function. Some circuit breakers must be reset manually.

6   Relays – general information

Several electrical accessories in the vehicle use relays to transmit the electrical signal to the component. If the relay is defective, that component will not operate properly.

The various relays are grouped together in several locations. If a faulty relay is suspected, it can be removed and tested by a dealer service department or a repair shop. Defective relays must be replaced as a unit.

7   Turn signal and hazard flashers – check and replacement

Turn signal flasher
1   The turn signal flasher, a small canister-shaped unit located in the fuse block or on the underside of the steering column, flashes the turn signals.
2   When the flasher unit is functioning properly, an audible click can be heard during its operation. If the turn signals fail on one side or the other and the flasher unit does not make its characteristic clicking sound, a faulty turn signal bulb is indicated.

3   If both turn signals fail to blink, the problem may be due to a blown fuse, a faulty flasher unit, a broken switch or a loose or open connection. If a quick check of the fuse box indicates that the turn signal fuse has blown, check the wiring for a short before installing a new fuse.
4   To replace the flasher, simply pull it out of the fuse block or steering column mount.
5   Make sure that the replacement unit is identical to the original. Compare the old one to the new one before installing it.
6   Installation is the reverse of removal.

Hazard flasher
7   The hazard flasher, a small canister-shaped unit located in the fuse block or the wiring harness, flashes all four turn signals simultaneously when activated.
8   The hazard flasher is checked in a fashion similar to the turn signal flasher (see Steps 2 and 3).
9   To replace the hazard flasher, pull it from the back of fuse block.
10   Make sure the replacement unit is identical to the one it replaces. Compare the old one to the new one before installing it.
11   Installation is the reverse of removal.

8   Headlight – removal and installation

Refer to illustration 8.2
1   Whenever replacing a headlight, be careful not to turn the spring-loaded adjusting screws of the headlight, as this will alter the aim.
2   Remove the headlight bezel screws and remove the bezel **(see illustration)**.
3   Use a cotter pin removal tool or similar device to unhook the spring from the retaining ring.
4   Remove the two screws which secure the retaining ring and withdraw the ring. Support the light as this is done.
5   Pull the headlight out slightly and disconnect the electrical connector from the rear of the light. Remove the light from the vehicle.
6   Position the new unit close enough to connect the electrical connector. Make sure that the numbers molded into the lens are at the top.
7   Install the retaining ring with its mounting screws and spring.
8   Install the bezel and check for proper operation. If the adjusting screws were not altered, the new headlight will not need to have its aim adjusted.

8.2 Typical headlight installation details

1   Headlight bezel
2   Left side marker light housing
3   Front end panel
4   Left inner (high beam) headlight
5   Spring
6   Left side outer (low beam) headlight
7   Left side parking and turn signal housing

12

9   Headlights – adjustment

Refer to illustration 9.1

Warning: *The headlights must be aimed correctly. If adjusted incorrectly they could blind the driver of an oncoming vehicle and cause a serious accident or seriously reduce your ability to see the road. The headlights should be checked for proper aim every 12 months and any time a new headlight is installed or front end body work is performed. It should be emphasized that the following procedure is only an interim step which will provide temporary adjustment until the headlights can be adjusted by a properly equipped shop.*

1   Headlights have two spring-loaded adjusting screws, one on the top controlling vertical movement and one on the side controlling horizontal movement **(see illustration)**.

2   There are several methods of adjusting the headlights. The simplest method requires a blank wall 25 feet in front of the vehicle and a level floor.

3   Position masking tape vertically on the wall in reference to the vehicle centerline and the centerlines of both headlights.

4   Position a horizontal tape line in reference to the centerline of all the headlights. **Note:** *It may be easier to position the tape on the wall with the vehicle parked only a few inches away.*

5   Adjustment should be made with the vehicle sitting level, the gas tank half-full and no unusually heavy load in the vehicle.

6   Starting with the low beam adjustment, position the high intensity zone so it is two inches below the horizontal line and two inches to the right of the headlight vertical line. Adjustment is made by turning the top adjusting screw clockwise to raise the beam and counterclockwise to lower the beam. The adjusting screw on the side should be used in the same manner to move the beam left or right.

7   With the high beams on, the high intensity zone should be vertically centered with the exact center just below the horizontal line. **Note:** *It may not be possible to position the headlight aim exactly for both high and low beams. If a compromise must be made, keep in mind that the low beams are the most used and have the greatest effect on safety.*

8   Have the headlights adjusted by a dealer service department or service station at the earliest opportunity.

10   Bulb replacement

Refer to illustrations 10.1, 10.3a, 10.3b and 10.4

1   The lenses of many lights are held in place by screws, which makes it a simple procedure to gain access to the bulbs **(see illustration)**.

9.1   Typical headlight adjusting screw locations (round headlights shown, rectangular headlights similar)

10.1   The opera light bulb can be replaced after removing the lens assembly

10.3a   Tail light details

1	Wiring harness and bulb holder assembly	3	Bezel
2	Side marker	4	Tail light housing

10.3b   The reading light bulb can be pulled out after detaching the lens

2   On some lights the lenses are held in place by clips. The lenses can be removed either by unsnapping them or by using a small screwdriver to pry them off.

3   Several types of bulbs are used. Some are removed by pushing in and turning them counterclockwise (see illustration). Others can simply be unclipped from the terminals or pulled straight out of the socket (see illustration).

4   To gain access to the instrument panel lights, the instrument cluster will have to be removed first (see illustration).

10.4   The instrument cluster bulbs are accessible after removing the cluster from the instrument panel

11   Headlight switch – removal and installation

Earlier models

Refer to illustration 11.5

1   Disconnect the negative battery cable.

2   Remove the lower steering column cover.

3   Unplug the switch electrical connector and lower illumination bulb.

4   Pull the headlight control knob to the On position.

5   Reach up under the instrument panel and depress the switch rod retainer (see illustration). Remove the knob, escutcheon and rod assembly.

6   Remove the retaining screw, lower the switch, disconnect the upper bulb, then remove the switch. Installation is the reverse of removal.

Later models

Refer to illustration 11.10

7   Disconnect the negative battery cable.

8   Remove the left hand instrument panel insert and the three screws securing the switch to the instrument panel (some models).

9   On models so equipped, detach the cruise control and Guidematic potentiometer connector from the headlight switch. Slide the cruise control switch forward.

10   Unplug the headlight switch connector, reach up under instrument panel and depress the switch rod retainer (see illustration). Remove the knob, lever and rod assembly.

11   Remove the screws or unscrew the nut from the lens housing and remove the headlight switch.

12   Installation is the reverse of removal.

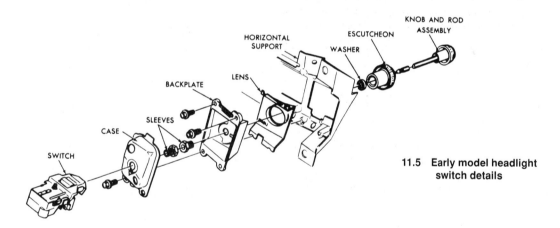

11.5   Early model headlight switch details

11.10   Later model headlight switch details

12

12   Windshield wiper/washer switch – removal and installation

1   Disconnect the negative battery cable.

Earlier models

2   If necessary, remove the left hand air outlet grille for access.
3   Remove the retaining screw so the switch can be withdrawn and unplugged. Installation is the reverse of removal.

Later models

4   Remove the left hand insert and applique from the instrument panel.
5   Remove the mounting screws and remove the switch.
6   Installation is the reverse of removal.

13   Turn signal switch – removal and installation

Refer to illustrations 13.3, 13.4, 13.5 and 13.8

1   Disconnect the negative battery cable and remove the steering wheel
(Chapter 10).
2   Remove the steering column trim cover located below the dashboard.
3   At the end of the steering column, late models have a plastic cover
plate which should be pried out of the column, using a screwdriver in the
slots provided **(see illustration)**.
4   The lockplate will now have to be removed from the steering column.
This is held in place with a snap-ring which fits into a groove in the steering
shaft. The lockplate must be depressed to relieve pressure on the snap-
ring. A special U-shaped tool which fits on the shaft should be used to depress the lockplate as the snap-ring is removed from its groove **(see
illustration)**.
5   Slide the canceling plate, upper bearing preload spring and thrust
washer off the end of the shaft **(see illustration)**.
6   Remove the turn signal lever attaching screw and withdraw the turn
signal lever from the side of the column.
7   Push in the hazard warning knob and unscrew the knob.
8   Remove the three turn signal assembly mounting screws **(see illustration)**.
9   Pull the switch connector out of the bracket on the steering column
jacket. Tape the connector terminals to prevent damage. Feed the wiring
connector up through the column support bracket and pull the switch, wiring harness and connectors out the top of the steering column.
10   Installation is the reverse of removal; however, make sure the wiring
harness is in the protector as it is pulled into position. Before installing the
thrust washer, upper bearing preload spring and canceling plate, make
sure the switch is in the neutral position and the warning knob is pulled out.
Always use a new snap-ring on the shaft for the lock plate.

13.3   Use a screwdriver to pry out the cover plate

**13.4   A special tool is required to depress the steering lockplate
so the snap-ring can be removed – the numbers shown are GM
tool numbers; equivalent tools are available through larger auto
parts stores and tool suppliers**

13.5   Lift off the cancelling plate and spring

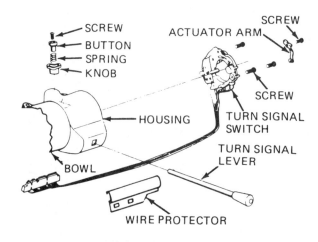

13.8   Turn signal switch details

14.3   On earlier models, the lock cylinder is retained by
a spring latch

---

14   Ignition lock cylinder – removal and installation

Earlier models

Refer to illustration 14.3

1   The lock cylinder is located on the upper right-hand side of the steering column. It should be removed only in the Run position, otherwise damage to the warning buzzer switch may occur.

2   Remove the steering wheel (Chapter 10) and turn signal switch (Section 13). **Note:** *The turn signal switch need not be fully removed provided that it is pushed to the rear far enough for it to be slipped over the end of the shaft. Do not pull the harness out of the column.*

3   Insert a thin blade screwdriver into the slot in the turn signal switch housing. Break the housing flash loose and at the same time depress the spring latch at the lower end of the lock cylinder. Holding the latch depressed, withdraw the lock cylinder from the housing **(see illustration)**.

4   To install the new lock cylinder/sleeve assembly, hold the sleeve and rotate the lock clockwise against the stop.

5   Insert the cylinder/sleeve assembly into the housing so the key on the cylinder sleeve is aligned with the housing keyway.

6   Insert a 1/16-inch diameter drill between the lock bezel and the housing and then rotate the cylinder counterclockwise, maintaining pressure on the cylinder until the drive section mates with the sector.

7   Press in the lock cylinder until the snap-ring engages in the grooves and secures the cylinder in the housing. Remove the drill and check the lock action.

8   Install the turn signal switch and the steering wheel.

Later models

Refer to illustration 14.12

9   The lock cylinder should be removed in the Run position only.

10   Remove the steering wheel (Chapter 10) and turn signal switch (Section 13). It is not necessary to completely remove the switch. Pull it up and over the end of the steering shaft. Do not pull the wiring harness out of the column.

11   Remove the ignition key warning switch.

12   Using a magnetized screwdriver, remove the lock retaining screw. Do not allow this screw to drop down into the column, as this will require a complete disassembly of the steering column to retrieve the screw **(see illustration)**.

13   Pull the lock cylinder out of the side of the steering column.

14   To install, rotate the lock cylinder set and align the cylinder key with the keyway in the steering column housing.

15   Push the lock all the way in and install the retaining screw.

16   Install the remaining components, referring to the appropriate Sections.

---

15   Speedometer cable – replacement

Refer to illustration 15.2

1   The instrument cluster must first be removed as described in Section 16.

14.12   On later models, the lock cylinder is held in place by a screw

12

15.2   Use pliers to pull the speedometer cable out of the housing

2   Once the end of the speedometer drive cable is exposed, grip the inner cable with pliers and draw it out of the housing **(see illustration)**.
3   Lubricate the entire new cable. Use special speedometer cable lubricant, not oil, for this purpose.

4   Insert the cable into the housing using a twisting movement until the lower end is felt to engage with the pinion gear at the transmission. The remainder of installation is the reverse of removal.

16   Instrument cluster – removal and installation

Refer to illustrations 16.4a, 16.4b and 16.4c
1   Disconnect the negative cable at the battery.
2   Remove the instrument cluster bezel and steering column cover.
3   Place the shift lever in Park and detach the indicator cable screw.
4   Remove the cluster retaining screws or nuts, pull the cluster out and disconnect the speedometer cable **(see illustrations)**.
5   Unplug any electrical connectors which would interfere with removal.
6   Detach the cluster from the instrument panel.
7   Installation is the reverse of removal.

17   Windshield wiper arm – removal and installation

Refer to illustration 17.3
1   Open the hood and make sure the wiper arms are in the self-parked position, the motor having been switched off in the low speed mode.
2   Note carefully the position of the wiper arm in relation to the windshield lower molding. Use tape on the windshield to mark the exact location of the wiper arm on the glass.

16.4a   Typical earlier model instrument cluster details

16.4b Later model instrument cluster (except Seville)

LOWER INSTRUMENT PANEL ASSEMBLY

SPEEDOMETER CLUSTER

VIEW A

SHIFT INDICATOR CABLE

WINDSHIELD WIPER SWITCH

HEADLAMP SWITCH

CRUISE CONTROL SWITCH

LOWER STEERING COLUMN COVER

STEERING COLUMN GASKET

LEFT INSTRUMENT PANEL INSERT (CLUSTER BEZEL)

SEAL

VIEW B

CLUSTER BEZEL

CLUSTER ASSEMBLY

REMOVE ONLY FOR SERVICE OF SPEEDOMETER CABLE

TO REMOVE CLUSTER ASSEMBLY REMOVE THIS SCREW, BOTH SIDES, PLUS UPPER ATTACHMENTS

VIEW A

LOWER STEERING COLUMN COVER

16.4c Seville instrument cluster details

12

3   Using a special tool (available at a dealer or auto parts store) or a small screwdriver, pull aside the small spring tang which holds the wiper arm to the splined transmission shaft and at the same time pull the arm from the shaft **(see illustration)**.

4   Installation is the reverse of removal, but do not push the arm fully onto the shaft until the alignment of the arm has been checked. If necessary, the arm can be pulled off again and turned through one or two serrations of the shaft to correct the alignment without the necessity of pulling aside the spring tang.

17.3   This tool (available at auto parts stores) or a small screwdriver can be used to detach the wiper arm

5   Finally, press the arm fully onto its shaft and then wet the windshield glass and operate the motor on low speed to ensure the arc of travel is correct.

---

18   Windshield wiper motor – removal and installation

Refer to illustration 18.5

1   Raise the hood and remove the cowl screen.

2   Reaching through the opening, loosen the drive link-to-crank arm nuts.

3   Remove the transmission drive link from the motor crank arm.

4   Disconnect the wiring and the washer hoses from the wiper motor.

5   Remove the three motor mounting screws and withdraw the motor, guiding the crank arm through the hole in the rear firewall **(see illustration)**.

6   Installation is the reverse of removal, but before connecting the drive link, check that the motor is in Park.

---

19   Radio and speakers – removal and installation

Radio

Refer to illustrations 19.3, 19.5a and 19.5b

1   Disconnect the negative cable at the battery.

2   On earlier models and Sevilles, remove the control knobs and bezel. Use a deep socket to remove the control shaft nuts and washers.

18.5   Typical windshield wiper motor installation details

3   On later models except Seville, remove the radio trim cover **(see illustration)**.

4   On all models except Seville, remove the mounting bolts and pull the radio from the instrument panel until the wiring can be reached and disconnected. Remove the radio.

5   On Sevilles, remove the Electronic Control Unit (ECU) **(see illustration)**. Remove the rear support rod nut and pivot the rod out of the way, then angle the rear of the radio down and for access and disconnect the wiring harness and antenna **(see illustration)**.

6   Lower the radio and remove it from under the instrument panel.

19.3   Typical radio installation details (except Seville)

19.5a   Seville radio installation details

19.5b   Seville ECU installation details

12

TOP COVER ASSEMBLY

TOP COVER ASSEMBLY

DIGITAL CLOCK

SENSOR SEAL

FUEL GAGE

TELLTALE HOUSING

CLIMATE CONTROL SENSOR

UPPER SHROUD PANEL REINFORCEMENT

TOP COVER

L.H. TELLTALE HOUSING EXTENSION

R.H. TELLTALE HOUSING EXTENSION

UPPER SHROUD PANEL

TOP COVER ASM

VIEW A   **VIEW B**

19.8a   Typical instrument panel top cover details (early models except Seville)

INSTRUMENT PANEL COVER ASSEMBLY

19.8b   Seville instrument panel top cover details

19.8c   Instrument panel top cover details (later models except Seville)

19.9   Typical front speaker details

7   Installation is the reverse of removal. Make sure all speaker leads, the antenna lead and any other connectors are plugged in before turning on the power to the radio.

Front speakers

Refer to illustrations 19.8a, 19.8b, 19.8c and 19.9

8   Remove the instrument panel top cover **(see illustrations)**.
9   Unplug the electrical connector, remove the nuts and detach the speaker **(see illustration)**.
10   Installation is the reverse of removal.

Rear speakers

Refer to illustration 19.12

11   Open the trunk, remove the retainers and detach the baffles for access to the rear speakers.

12

GRILLE ASSEMBLY

VIEW A   VIEW B

ROSE — BUD
ATTACHING CLIP

VIEW C   SPEAKER ASSEMBLY

SPEAKER ASSEMBLY RETAINER

BAFFLE RETAINER

SPRING HOOK   RIVET

VIEW D   VIEW E

19.12   Typical rear speaker details

12   Unplug the connectors and remove the retaining nuts or unhook the retaining clips and remove the speakers **(see illustration)**.
13   Installation is the reverse of removal.

20   Antenna mast and motor – replacement

Refer to illustrations 20.4a, 20.4b and 20.4c

1   Lower the antenna. Disconnect the negative cable at the battery.
2   Block the rear wheels, raise the front of the vehicle and support it securely on jackstands.
3   Remove the right front wheel (all models except Seville) or left front wheel (Seville). On some models it will be necessary to remove or detach the wheelhouse from the fender for access.
4   Remove the escutcheon or retaining nut securing the antenna to the fender **(see illustrations)**
5   On later models except Seville, attach a piece of thin wire or string, approximately four-feet long, to the antenna.
6   Disconnect the wires, remove the bolts and guide the antenna and motor assembly out through the fenderwell.
7   Installation is the reverse of removal. On later models, attach the string or wire to the new antenna mast, pull the assembly up into position and hold it before installing the bolts.

21   Electric grid-type rear defogger – testing and repair

Refer to illustrations 21.5a, 21.5b and 21.11

1   This option consists of a rear window with a number of horizontal elements that are baked into the glass surface during the glass forming operation.

2   Small breaks in the element system can be successfully repaired without removing the rear window.
3   To test the grids for proper operation, start the engine and turn on the system.
4   Ground one lead of a test light and lightly touch the other lead to each grid line.
5   The brilliance of the test light should increase as the probe is moved across the element from left to right **(see illustration)**. If the test light doesn't change exactly as described above, check for breaks in the element or a loose ground wire for the system **(see illustration)**. All of the grid lines should be checked in at least two places.

ESCUTCHEON   RIGHT FENDER

GASKET

ANTENNA   SCREW
ASSEMBLY

ELECTRICAL
CONNECTOR

LEAD-IN ASSEMBLY

SPLASH SHIELD

BRACKET   TO SPLITTER WITH CB RADIO
                                         TO ENTERTAINMENT RADIO
GROMMET   WITHOUT CB RADIO
                                         SCREW

SCREW

20.4a   Early model antenna installation details (except Seville)

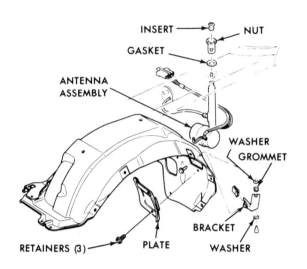

20.4b Later model antenna installation details (except Seville)

1	Antenna mast and motor assembly	3	Escutcheon
2	Gasket	4	Wiring harness
		5	Wires

20.4c Typical Seville antenna details

21.5a The test light should increase in brilliance as the probe is moved from left to right across the defogger element

21.5b The test light will respond as shown here if there are broken grid lines

21.11   Use a wood spatula to apply the repair material to the grid lines

6   To repair a break in a grid line it is recommended that a repair kit specifically for this purpose be purchased from a GM dealer. Included in the repair kit will be a decal, a container of silver plastic and hardener, a mixing stick and instructions.
7   To repair a break, first turn off the system and allow it to de-energize for a few minutes.
8   Lightly buff the grid line area with fine steel wool and then clean the area thoroughly with alcohol.
9   Use the decal supplied in the repair kit, or use electrician's tape above and below the area to be repaired. The space between the pieces of tape should be the same as existing grid lines. This can be checked from outside the car. Press the tape tightly against the glass to prevent seepage.
10   Mix the hardener and silver plastic thoroughly.
11   Using the wood spatula, apply the silver plastic mixture between the pieces of tape, overlapping the damaged area slightly on either end **(see illustration)**.
12   Carefully remove the decal or tape and apply a constant stream of hot air directly to the repaired area. A heat gun set at 500 to 700-degrees F is recommended. Hold the gun about one inch from the glass for one to two minutes.
13   If the new grid line appears off color, tincture of iodine can be used to clean the repair and bring it back to the proper color. This mixture should not remain on the repair for more than 30 seconds.
14   Although the defogger is now fully operational, the repaired area should not be disturbed for at least 24 hours.

22   Cruise control system – description and check

The cruise control system maintains vehicle speed with a vacuum actuated servo motor, located in the engine compartment, which is connected to the throttle linkage by a cable. The system consists of the servo motor, brake switch, control switches, a relay and associated vacuum hoses.
Because of the complexity of the cruise control system and the special tools and techniques required for diagnosis, repair should be left to a dealer service department or a repair shop. However, it is possible for the home mechanic to make simple checks of the wiring and vacuum connections for minor faults which can be easily repaired. These include:
   a) Inspecting the cruise control actuating switches for broken wires and loose connections.
   b) Checking the cruise control fuse.
   c) Checking the hoses in the engine compartment for tight connections, cracks and obvious vacuum leaks. The cruise control system is operated by vacuum, so it's critical that all vacuum switches, hoses and connections are secure.

23   Power door lock system – description and solenoid replacement

Refer to illustration 23.4
1   This optional system incorporates a solenoid actuator inside each door. The solenoid is electrically operated from a control switch on the instrument panel and operates the lock through a linkage. Each actuator has an internal circuit breaker which may require one to three minutes to reset.
2   To remove the solenoid, raise the door window and remove the door panel trim pad as described in Chapter 11.
3   After prying away the water deflector, the solenoid can be seen through the large access hole. The solenoid can be mounted to either the rear door lock pillar or the inner metal door panel.
4   Early models use attaching screws through the door panel and into the solenoid bracket **(see illustration)**. Later models use rivets to secure the solenoid to the pillar. These must be drilled out using a 1/4-inch drill bit.
5   Once the securing devices are removed, disconnect the wiring harness at the solenoid and the actuating link, held in place with a metal clip. Remove the solenoid from the door cavity.
6   To install, place the solenoid in position and connect the electrical connector and actuating link. If rivets were drilled out, new aluminum rivets (1/4 x 0.500-inch size) can be used upon reassembly. Optionally, 1/4 – 20 screws and U-nuts can be used.
7   Check the operation of the door locks before installing the water deflector and trim panel.

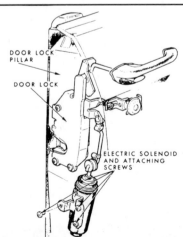

23.4   Typical power door lock solenoid installation details

24   Power window system – description and motor replacement

1   This system incorporates an electric motor and an independent control switch for each of the door windows. The driver's door has a master control switch permitting operation of all windows.

2   The electric motor which powers the window regulator is a reversible-direction motor and operates on 12 volts. It features an internal circuit breaker for protection. The motor is secured to the regulator with bolts.

3   The electric motor can be removed from the regulator with the remainder of the window system intact only if the door glass is intact and attached to the regulator. If the door glass is broken or removed from the door, the motor must be separated after the regulator is removed from inside the door.

Glass intact and attached

Refer to illustrations 24.7a, 24.7b and 24.7c

4   Raise the window and remove the door trim panel and water deflector as described in Chapter 11.

5   Reach inside the door access hole and disconnect the wiring harness at the motor.

6   It is imperative at this point that the window glass be taped or blocked in the up position. This will prevent the glass from falling into the door and possibly causing injury or damage.

7   Since the bolts used to secure the motor to the regulator are inaccessible, it is necessary to drill three large access holes in the metal door panel. The position of these holes is critical. Use the full-size templates as shown in the accompanying illustration for the models shown. All other models have locating dimples stamped into the inner door skin to eliminate the need for templates. The template should be positioned on the door with tape after properly aligning it with the regulator attaching rivets (late models) or bolts (early models).

8   Use a centerpunch to dimple the panel at the center of the template access holes and then cut the 3/4-inch holes with a hole saw.

9   Reach in through the access hole and support the motor as the attaching bolts are removed. Remove the motor through the access hole, being careful that the window glass is firmly supported in the up position.

10   Before installation, the motor drive gear and regulator sector teeth should be lubricated.

11   Upon positioning the motor, make sure the drive gear properly engages with the regulator sector teeth. Install the remaining components in the reverse order of removal. Waterproof tape can be used to seal the three access holes drilled in the metal inner panel.

24.7b   On 1976 through 1979 models, use this template for locating the front door power window motor bolts

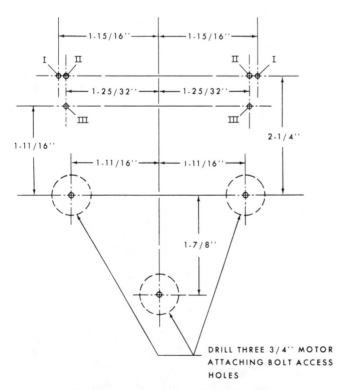

24.7a   On 1971 four-door models, use this template for locating the power window motor bolts

24.7c   On 1976 through 1979 models, use this template for locating the rear door power window motor bolts

24.14   The window regulator motor must be locked in position
before removal because the spring is under considerable tension

BLK 8905205

25.3   Trunk pull-down motor connecter terminals

Glass broken or not attached

Refer to illustration 24.14

12   Remove the window regulator as described in Chapter 11. Make sure
the wiring harness to the motor is disconnected first.

13   **Warning:** *It is imperative that the regulator sector gear be locked into
position before removing the motor from the regulator. The control arms
are under pressure and can cause serious injury if the motor is removed
without performing the following operation.*

14   Drill a hole through the regulator sector gear and backplate **(see illustration)**. Install a bolt and nut to lock the gear in position. Do not drill closer
than 1/2-inch to the edge of the sector gear or backplate.

15   Remove the three motor attaching bolts and remove the motor assembly from the regulator.

16   Prior to installation, the motor drive gear and regulator sector teeth
should be lubricated. The lubricant should be cold weather approved to at
least 20-degrees F. Lubriplate Spray Lube "A" is recommended by GM.

17   When installing the motor to the regulator, make sure the sector gear
teeth and drive gear teeth properly mesh.

18   Once the motor attaching bolts are tightened, the locking nut and bolt
can be removed. Install the regulator as described in Chapter 11. Don't forget to connect the motor wiring.

25   Trunk lid pull-down motor – check and replacement

1   On models so equipped, the trunk pull-down motor allows the trunk to
close smoothly and automatically when it is lowered near the closed post-
ition.

Check

Refer to illustration 25.3

2   If the trunk does not automatically close after the latch contacts the
striker, first check that all wiring connections are tight. Blow the horn to
make sure it operates, since the pull-down motor is on the same circuit; the
horn circuit breaker in the fuse block may have tripped. Check the GA-
TRANS fuse in the fuse block to make sure it hasn't blown.

3   Unplug the pull-down motor electrical connector and connect a test
lamp between the H terminal and a good ground **(see illustration)**. If the
lamp does not light, check the orange and black wire for damage and the
inline fuse for an open.

4   If the lamp lights, connect it between the H and J terminal. If it does not
light, check the black wire for an open. If it does light, replace the pull-down
motor.

5   If the Trunk Open light on the dash doesn't light up when the trunk is
open and the ignition switch is On, connect the test light between the K
terminal and ground. If the lamp does not light, check the dark green wire
for an open. Further checks should be left to a dealer service department
or other properly equipped shop.

25.7   **Remove the bolts and detach the cover assembly**

25.8   **Trunk pull-down motor details**

1	Motor	4	Switch trip lever
2	Electrical connector	5	Striker
3	Switch lever		

Replacement

Refer to illustrations 25.7 and 25.8

6   Disconnect the battery negative cable.
7   Remove the bolts and detach the pull-down unit cover assembly **(see illustration)**.
8   Unplug the electrical connector, remove the bolts and remove the pull-down motor and latch assembly **(see illustration)**.
9   Installation is the reverse of removal.

---

26   Wiring diagrams – general information

Refer to illustration 26.4

Since it isn't possible to include all wiring diagrams for every year covered by this manual, the following diagrams are those that are typical and most commonly needed.

Prior to troubleshooting any circuits, check the fuse and circuit breakers (if equipped) to make sure they're in good condition. Make sure the battery is properly charged and check the cable connections (Chapter 1).

When checking a circuit, make sure that all connectors are clean, with no broken or loose terminals. When unplugging a connector, do not pull on the wires. Pull only on the connector housings themselves.

Refer to the accompanying table for wire color codes applicable to your vehicle.

WIRING COLOR CODE

Example:

RED

Red

RED-GRN

Red   Green

Wire colors are indicated by an alphabetical code.

DRK or DK = Dark	GRY = Gray
LGT or LT = Light	ORN = Orange
STR = Stripe	PNK = Pink
DBL = Double	PPL = Purple
BLK = Black	RED = Red
BLU = Blue	TAN = Tan
BRN = Brown	WHT= White
GRN = Green	YEL = Yellow

26.4   This chart will help you identify wire colors from the diagrams that follow

12

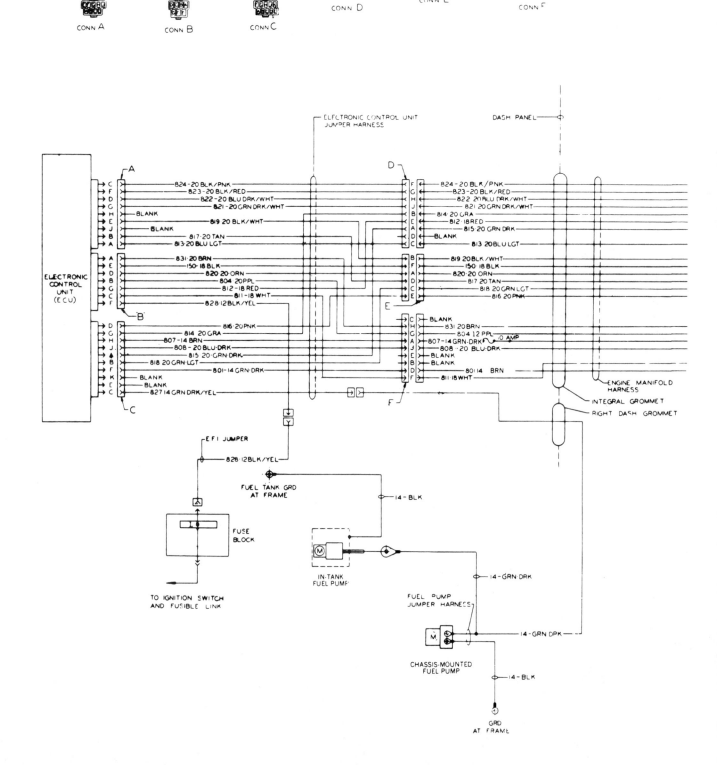

Early full-size model Electronic Fuel Injection (EFI) wiring diagram (1 of 5)

Early full-size model Electronic Fuel Injection (EFI) wiring diagram (2 of 5)

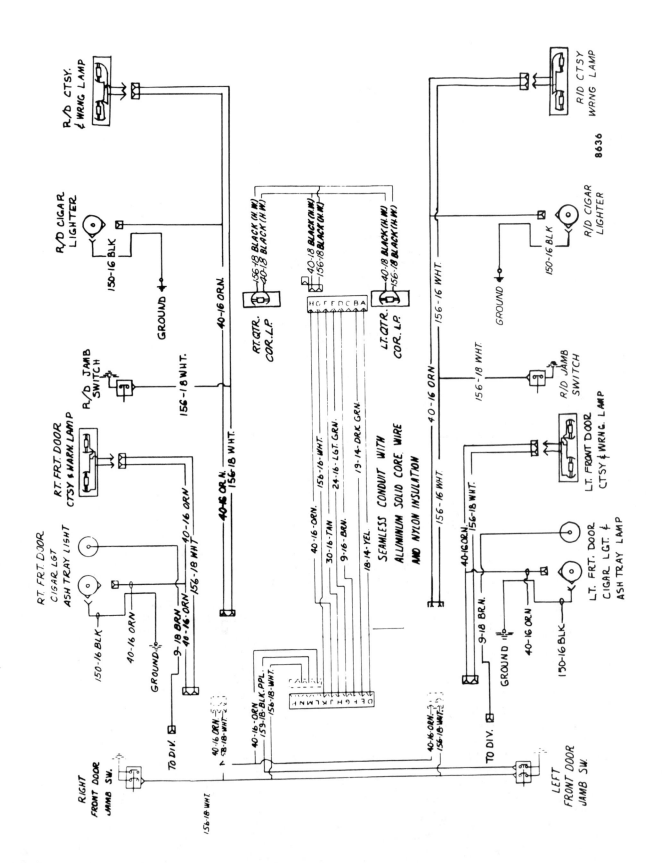

Early full-size model body wiring harness wiring diagram (3 of 5)

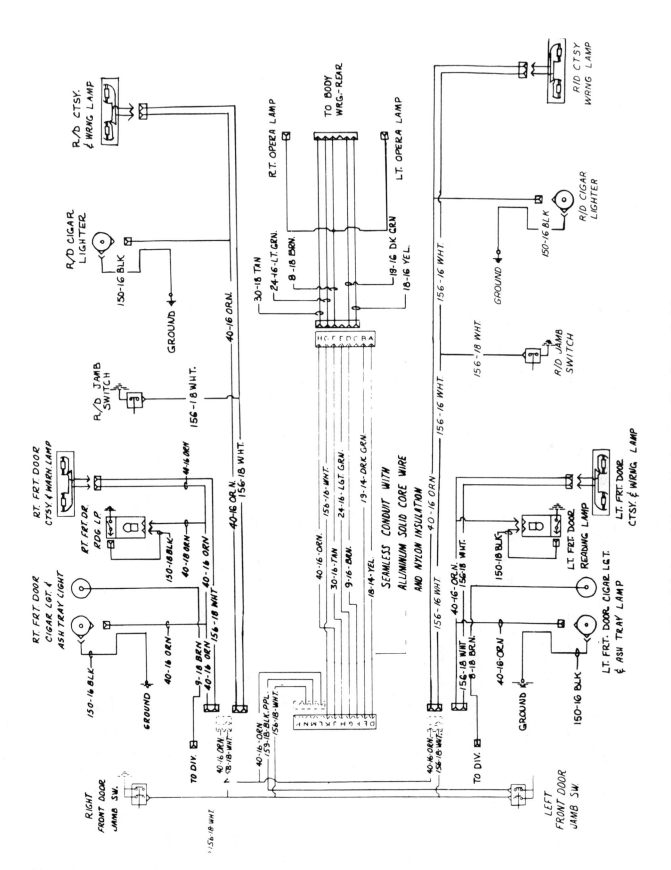

Early full-size model body wiring harness wiring diagram (4 of 5)

Early full-size model body wiring harness wiring diagram (5 of 5)

1976 through 1979 Seville Electronic Fuel Injection (EFI) wiring diagram (2 of 4)

1976 through 1979 Seville body wiring harness diagram (3 of 4)

Later full-size model starter and charging system wiring diagram (1 of 21)

Later full-size model Computer Command Control system diagram (2 of 21)

POWER INPUT AND VEHICLE SENSORS

Later full-size model Computer Command Control system diagram (3 of 21)

ENGINE DATA SENSORS AND EMISSION CONTROLS

Later full-size model Computer Command Control system diagram (4 of 21)

VEHICLE SENSORS AND TRANSMISSION CONVERTER CLUTCH

Later full-size model Computer Command Control system diagram (5 of 21)

Later full-size model power distribution system wiring diagram (6 of 21)

Later full-size model power distribution system wiring diagram (7 of 21)

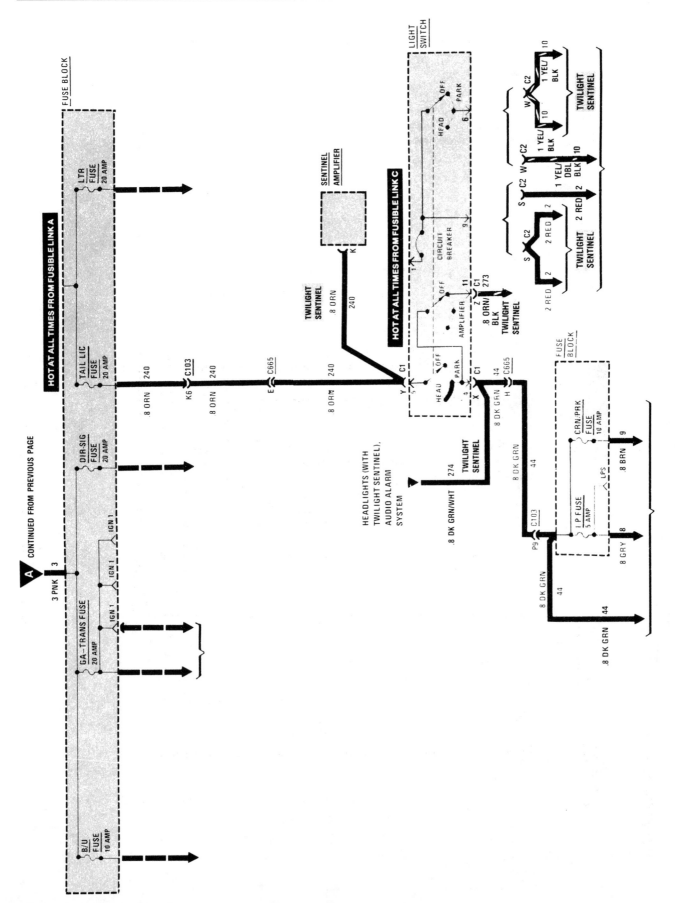

Later full-size model power distribution system wiring diagram (8 of 21)

Later full-size model ground distribution system wiring diagram (9 of 21)

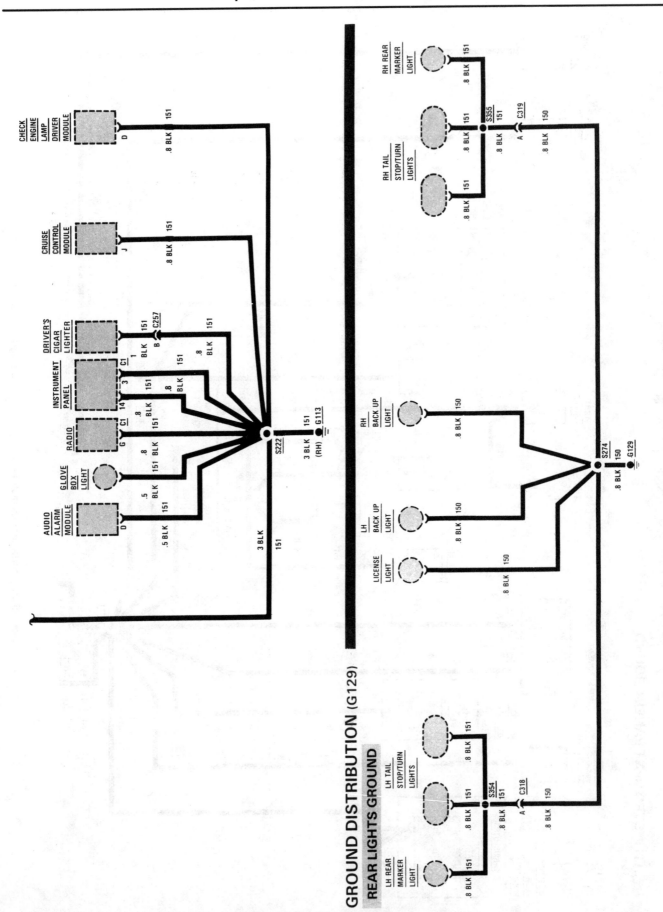

GROUND DISTRIBUTION (G129)

REAR LIGHTS GROUND

Later full-size model ground distribution system wiring diagram (10 of 21)

GROUND DISTRIBUTION (G243)
ELECTRONIC CLIMATE CONTROL GROUNDS

GROUND DISTRIBUTION (G111 AND G112)
FRONT LIGHTS GROUNDS

Later full-size model ground distribution system wiring diagram (11 of 21)

GROUND DISTRIBUTION (G250)
ECM & CRUISE CONTROL GROUND

GROUND DISTRIBUTION (G400)
OPERA LAMP & TRUNK LID PULL-DOWN GROUND

Later full-size model ground distribution system wiring diagram (12 of 21)

Later full-size model power antenna wiring diagram (13 of 21)

Later full-size model radio wiring diagram (14 of 21)

Later full-size model trunk pull-down system wiring diagram (15 of 21)

Later full-size model power door lock system wiring diagram (16 of 21)

Later full-size model power window system wiring diagram (17 of 21)

Later full-size model headlight wiring diagram (18 of 21)

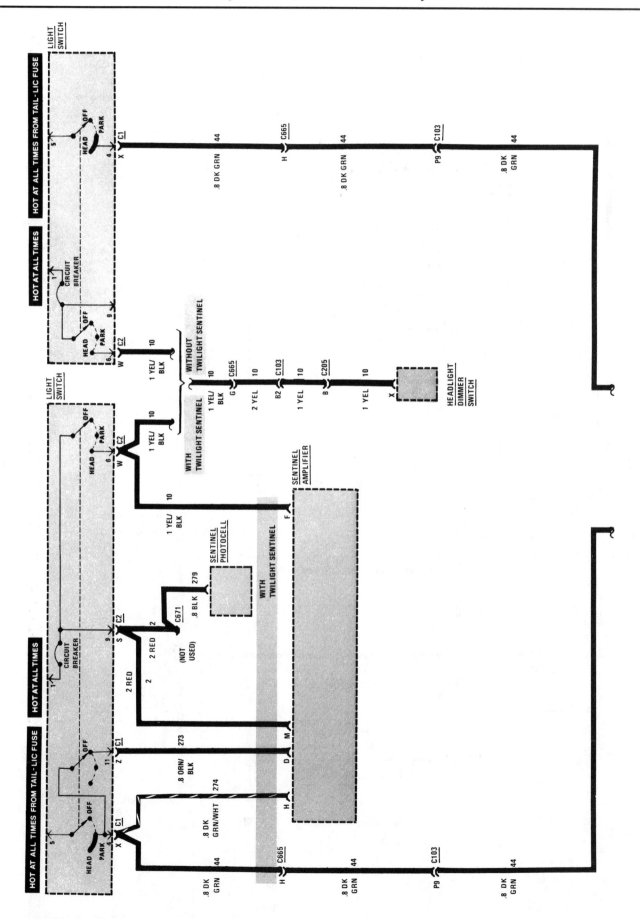

Later full-size model light switch wiring diagram (19 of 21)

Later full-size model light switch wiring diagram (20 of 21)

Later full-size model light switch wiring diagram (21 of 21)

Index

A